Trends in European Tourism Planning and Organisation

MIX
Paper from responsible sources
FSC® C014540
www.fsc.org

ASPECTS OF TOURISM

Series Editors: Chris Cooper, *Oxford Brookes University, UK*, C. Michael Hall, *University of Canterbury, New Zealand* and Dallen J. Timothy, *Arizona State University, USA.*

Aspects of Tourism is an innovative, multifaceted series, which comprises authoritative reference handbooks on global tourism regions, research volumes, texts and monographs. It is designed to provide readers with the latest thinking on tourism worldwide and push back the frontiers of tourism knowledge. The volumes are authoritative, readable and user-friendly, providing accessible sources for further research. Books in the series are commissioned to probe the relationship between tourism and cognate subject areas such as strategy, development, retailing, sport and environmental studies.

Full details of all our publications can be found on http://www.multilingual-matters.com, or by writing to Multilingual Matters, St Nicholas House, 31–34 High Street, Bristol BS1 2AW, UK.

Trends in European Tourism Planning and Organisation

Edited by
Carlos Costa, Emese Panyik and Dimitrios Buhalis

CHANNEL VIEW PUBLICATIONS
Bristol • Buffalo • Toronto

Library of Congress Cataloging in Publication Data
Trends in European Tourism Planning and Organisation/Edited by Carlos Costa,
Emese Panyik and Dimitrios Buhalis.
Aspects of Tourism: 60
Includes bibliographical references.
1. Tourism--Europe--Planning. 2. Tourism--Europe--Management. I. Costa, Carlos.
G155.E8T76 2013
338.4'7914–dc23 2013022565

British Library Cataloguing in Publication Data
A catalogue entry for this book is available from the British Library.

ISBN-13: 978-1-84541-411-5 (hbk)
ISBN-13: 978-1-84541-410-8 (pbk)

Channel View Publications
UK: St Nicholas House, 31–34 High Street, Bristol BS1 2AW, UK.
USA: UTP, 2250 Military Road, Tonawanda, NY 14150, USA.
Canada: UTP, 5201 Dufferin Street, North York, Ontario M3H 5T8, Canada.

The policy of Multilingual Matters/Channel View Publications is to use papers that are
natural, renewable and recyclable products, made from wood grown in sustainable forests. In the manufacturing process of our books, and to further support our policy, preference is given to printers that have FSC and PEFC Chain of Custody certification. The FSC
and/or PEFC logos will appear on those books where full certification has been granted
to the printer concerned.

Typeset by Techset Composition India (P) Ltd., Bangalore and Chennai, India.
Printed and bound in Great Britain by Short Run Press Ltd.

Contents

Figures

Tables

Acronyms

7FP	7th Framework Programme
ACF	Autocorrelation function
ADLM	Autoregressive distributed lag model
AR	Autoregressive
ARIMA	Autoregressive and moving average
ASEAN	Association of Southeast Asian Nations
ATB	Area Tourism Boards
B&B	Bed and breakfast
BITS	International Bureau of Social Tourism
BRIC	Brazil, Russia, India and China
BVAR	Bayesian vector-autoregressive model
CAP	Common Agricultural Policy
CEN	European Committee for Standardisation
CIP	Competitiveness and Innovation Framework Programme
CISET	Centro Internazionale di Studi sull'Economia Turistica
CPA	Cost per acquisition/action
CPC	Cost per click
CPL	Cost per lead
CPM	Cost per thousand impressions
CPS	Cost per sale
CRS	Computerised reservation systems
CTR	Click through rate
CVB	Convention and Visitor Bureau
DG ENTERPRISE	Directorate for Enterprise and Industry
DG TREN	Directorate for Energy and Transport
DGP	Data generating process
DMO	Destination management organisation
DMS	Destination management system
DOC	Denominazione *di origine controllata* (It.)/Controlled designation of origin (Eng.)

DOCG	*Denominazione di Origine Controllata e Garantita* (It.)/Controlled designation of origin guaranteed (Eng.)
DOP	*Denominazione di Origine Protetta* (It.)/Protected Designation of Origin (Eng.)
EAFG	European Agricultural Fund Guarantee
EAFRD	European Agricultural Fund for Rural Development
EC	European Commission
ECAA	European Common Aviation Area
EDEN	European Destinations of Excellence
EEA	European Economic Area
EG	Engle and Granger two-stage approach
EQF	European qualifications framework
ERDF	European Regional Development Fund
ESF	European Social Fund
ESPON	European Observation Network for Territorial Development and Cohesion
ETC	European Travel Commission
ETP	European transport policy
EU	European Union
EURODITE	*Regional Trajectories to the Knowledge Economy: A Dynamic Model* (6th EU Framework Programme)
FDI	Foreign direct investment
GDP	Gross domestic product
GDS	Global distribution systems
GHG	Greenhouse gas
GIT	General interest tourism
GPS	Global positioning system
HEGY	Hylleberg–Engle–Granger–Yoo
HLN	Harvey–Leybourne–Newbold
HOTREC	Confederation of National Associations of Hotels, Restaurants, Cafes and Similar Establishments in the European Union and the European Economic Area
HR	Human resources
ICT	Information and communications technology
ILO	International Labour Organization
IMF	International Monetary Fund
ISO	International Organization for Standardization
IT	Information technology
JML	Johansen-maximum-likelihood approach
KM	Knowledge management
LCC	Low cost companies
LL	Leisure landscapes

LSC	Large-scale businesses
MAPE	Mean absolute percentage error
MGN	Morgan–Granger–Newbold
MIT	Mixed interest tourism
NET	Network of European private entrepreneurs in the tourism sector
NFT	New forms of tourism
NGO	Non-governmental organisation
NSRF	National Strategic Reference Framework
NTA	National tourism administration
NTO	National tourism organisations
NUTS	Nomenclature of territorial units for statistics
OECD	Organisation for Economic Cooperation and Development
OP	Operational programme
PACF	Partial autocorrelation function
PDMFC	Percentage of directions of movement forecast correctly
PDO	Protected designations of origin
PGI	Protected geographical indications
PI	Performance indicators
PPP	Public private partnerships
RMF	Recommended methodological framework
RMSPE	Root mean square percentage error
RTB	Regional tourism boards
RTO	Regional tourism organisation
RTP	Regional tourism partnership
SAARC	South Asian Association for Regional Cooperation
SARIMA	Seasonal integrated autoregressive and moving average model
SEM	Search engine marketing
SEO	Search engine optimisation
SIP	Special interest products
SIT	Special interest tourism
SME	Small and medium-sized enterprises
SMTE	Small and medium-sized tourism enterprises
SNA	System of national accounts
STG	Sustainable tourism group
TGV	*Train a Grand Vitesse*
TIES	International Ecotourism Society
TOS	Tourist opportunity spectrum
TSA	Tourism Satellite Accounts
TSG	Traditional specialty guaranteed
TVP	Time-varying parameter

UGC	User-generated content
UN	United Nations
UNESCO	United Nations Educational, Scientific and Cultural Organization
UNWTO	United Nations World Tourism Organisation
VAR	Vector autoregressive
VAT	Value added tax
VECM	Vector error correction model
VFR	Visiting friends and relatives
WB	Wickens and Breusch one-stage approach
WEFA	Wharton Econometric Forecasting Associates
WHO	World Health Organization
WOM	Word-of-mouth
WTTC	World Travel and Tourism Council

Contributors

Constantia Anastasiadou is a lecturer in tourism and postgraduate programme leader in Tourism, Hospitality and Events at Edinburgh Napier University, Edinburgh, UK. Her main research interests lie in the impact of regionalisation on tourism development, tourism policy and stakeholder involvement in the policy process. She is the leading authority on tourism in the European Union and has published extensively on this topic. She is currently involved in funded research that examines regional cooperation in tourism in Southern Africa. She is Reviews Editor for the *Journal of Policy Research in Tourism, Leisure and Events.*

Rodolfo Baggio has a degree in physics and a PhD in tourism management. He is Professor at the Masters in Economics and Tourism and Research Fellow at the Dondena Centre for Research on Social Dynamics at Bocconi University, Milan, Italy. He actively researches on the use of information and communication technology in tourism and on the applications of quantitative complex network analysis methods to the study of tourism destinations.

Zélia Breda holds a PhD in Tourism, an MA in Chinese Studies (Business and International Relations) and a BSc in Tourism Management and Planning from the University of Aveiro, where she is an Invited Assistant Professor at the Department of Economics, Management and Industrial Engineering. She is a member of the Research Unit 'Governance, Competitiveness and Public Policies' of the University of Aveiro, and a founding member and Vice President of the Observatory of China and the Portuguese Institute of Sinology. She has authored and co-authored several national and international papers and communications on tourism development, networks, tourism in China and Goa (India), gender and tourism, and the internationalisation of the tourism economy.

Dimitrios Buhalis is Professor of eTourism and Director of eTourism Lab at Bournemouth University. His research focuses on strategic management and marketing, tourism marketing, technology and eTourism. He has written or co-edited a total of 18 books and published more than 100 articles in scholarly journals, books, conference proceedings and consultancy reports.

Maria João Carneiro is Assistant Professor of Tourism at the University of Aveiro (Portugal) and researcher at the 'Governance, Competitiveness and Public Policies' Research Unit at the same university. She has a *Licenciatura* (5 year degree) in Tourism Management and Planning from the University of Aveiro, an MBA from the New University of Lisbon (Portugal) and a Doctoral Degree in Tourism, also from the University of Aveiro. She is at present, at the University of Aveiro, the coordinator of the Degree programme in Tourism and member of the Executive Committee of the 'Department of Economics, Management and Industrial Engineering'. She published papers in international tourism journals and she has been involved in several research projects financed by the Portuguese Foundation for Science and Technology and by organizations of the tourism industry.

Magda Antonioli Corigliano is Professor of Tourism Economics and Director of the Master in Tourism and Economics at Bocconi University and at the SDA Bocconi School of Management. She is also a Special Counsellor for the EU Commissioner for tourism, and a visiting professor in many universities, as well as director of research for UNWTO, the EU, the Italian National Council for Research, Italian ministries, regions and private institutions. She is a member of various scientific committees on tourism, and a member of AIEST, ATLAS and the UNWTO. She is the author of publications on tourism, industrial and environmental economics and policy.

Jason Chen is lecturer in Tourism and Event Management in the School of Hospitality and Tourism Management, University of Surrey. His background is in economics with research interests in tourism forecasting and tourism satisfaction studies.

Alan Clarke works at the Tourism Department of the University of Pannonia. He has researched widely across Europe and the Pacific Rim, exploring cultural aspects of and in tourism development. His interest in partnerships comes from his early experiences in community development in Sheffield and reached tourism through the European funded DETOUR project – where he also met his co-author for the first time.

Chris Cooper has degrees in Geography from University College London. He is Pro Vice-Chancellor and Dean of the Business School at Oxford Brookes University, UK. He is joint editor of Channel View's Aspects of Tourism series and co-editor of *Current Issues in Tourism*. His research interests include knowledge management and innovation as well as tourism destination development and tourism education and training. He was awarded the UN World Tourism Organisation Ulysses prize for contributions to tourism policy and education in 2009.

Carlos Costa is Full Professor of Tourism at the University of Aveiro and Editor of the Journal of Tourism & Development (Revista de Turismo e Desenvolvimento). Carlos is the leader of the Tourism Research Unit and of the PhD Tourism Programme of the University of Aveiro. His main research interests are tourism planning and management, organisations, networks, gender in tourism and education.

John Crompton holds the rank of University Distinguished Professor and is both a Regents Professor and a Presidential Professor for Teaching Excellence at Texas A&M University. Dr Crompton's primary interests are in the areas of marketing and financing public leisure and tourism services. He is author or co-author of 18 books and a substantial number of articles which have been published in the recreation, tourism, sport and marketing fields. Dr Crompton has conducted many hundreds of workshops on Marketing and/or Financing Leisure Services.

Eduardo Anselmo de Castro is Associate Professor in the Department of Social, Political and Territorial Sciences, University of Aveiro, Portugal, where he lectures on courses of Regional Economics and Planning, and Social and Economic Analysis. He is a member of the Governance, Competitiveness and Public Policy Research Unit (GOVCOPP) and of the Department's Unit. Since 1992 he has coordinated research teams participating in several European and national projects.

Janet Dickinson is a lecturer in the field of leisure, tourism and events. Her research interests include sustainable tourism and transport, with a particular focus on adapting tourism for a lower carbon future. Her recent work has focused on the emerging concept of slow travel.

John Fletcher is Director of the International Centre for Tourism & Hospitality Research at Bournemouth University, UK. He is an economist who has developed an international reputation through his pioneering work in tourism impact and development research, author of numerous articles and book chapters on tourism's economic impact, co-author of the leading textbook, *Tourism Principles and Practice*, now in its 4th edition, and editor of the *International Journal of Tourism Research*.

Alan Fyall is Professor in Tourism and Deputy Dean Research & Enterprise in the School of Tourism, Bournemouth University, UK. Alan has published widely in his fields of expertise and is the author of over 100 articles, book chapters and conference papers as well as 11 books, including *Tourism Principles & Practice*, one of the leading international textbooks on the subject. Alan has organised a number of international conferences and workshops and sits on the editorial boards of *Annals of Tourism Research, Journal of Heritage*

Tourism, International Journal of Tourism Research and *Tourism Recreation Research*, while he is book review editor for *Anatolia*. His current research interests lie in destination management and emerging destination management structures and the impact of generational change on patterns of buying behaviour in the context of attractions and destinations.

Henrik Halkier is Professor of Regional and Tourism Studies in the department of Culture and Global Studies at Aalborg University, Denmark. His research experience is primarily related to the role of institutions and discourse in public policy, specifically in relation to tourism and regional development policies in Europe. His recent research projects focus on the politics of place branding, and on knowledge processes in tourism and regional development from a policy perspective.

Myriam Jansen-Verbeke is Professor Emeritus at the Catholic University of Leuven (Belgium), Member of the International Academy for the Study of Tourism, and Visiting Research Professor at the Chinese Academy of Sciences. Myriam's teaching, research and publications have mainly been focused on the 'territorial' study of tourism. Her ongoing search is for integrated planning models to 'use' cultural resources for a sustainable development in urban, industrial and rural areas.

Savvina Karyopouli is a PhD researcher, currently undertaking her PhD at the Business School of Bournemouth University, UK. Her research interests are in tourism sustainability, power relations, organisational behaviour and business ethics.

Christina Koutra lectures in Global Corporate Social Responsibility at the Business School of Bournemouth University, UK. Prior to her joining Bournemouth University, Christina undertook an ESRC postdoctoral fellowship at the University of Brighton. Her research interests are: corporate social responsibility and its application not only in corporations per se, but also to organisations and governmental institutions, mainly in developing countries; tourism development, policy and planning; poverty reduction; and neo-colonialism and its role in tourism development, among others. Her primary research has taken her to Ghana, Vietnam and Peru. Christina has published in the *Journal of Travel Research, European Journal of Travel Research, Journal of Global Research* and the *Journal of Sustainable Tourism*.

Adele Ladkin is Professor of Tourism Employment in the School of Tourism, Bournemouth University, UK. Educated at the University of Surrey, her research interests and publications are in the areas of labour migration, tourism employment, and labour issues in the tourism, hospitality and conference industries. This includes the role of education in developing human capital and human resource issues. She was joint Editor in Chief for the *International Journal of Tourism Research* from 2003 to 2009, and she serves on the Editorial Board for *ACTA Turistica*, the *Journal of Convention & Event Management* and the *International Journal of Event Management*.

Gang Li is reader in tourism economics in the School of Hospitality and Tourism Management, University of Surrey. His research interests are in the areas of tourism demand modelling and forecasting using econometric approaches with a particular focus on the almost idea demand system (AIDS) modelling method. His publications have appeared in *Annals of Tourism Research, Tourism Management, Journal of Travel Research* and *International Journal of Forecasting*.

Mara Manente is Director of CISET – Ca' Foscari University (Venice). She has over 20 years' experience in teaching and researching on the macroeconomics of tourism, the economic impact of tourism, tourism demand analysis and forecasting, transport and tourism and tourism statistics. She is a member of the UNWTO Steering Committee on Statistics, Macroeconomic Analysis of Tourism and Tourism Satellite Accounts and a consultant for many national and international institutions (Eurostat, European Commission, etc.).

Joanna Matloka is a new media strategist at 77Agency in London and specialises in Facebook marketing solutions. She is experienced in media buying, search engine marketing, performance and affiliate marketing. Joanna graduated from Bournemouth University, completing MSc Tourism Management and Marketing and focusing her studies on online marketing for tourism destinations. The research that she carried out together with Professor Dimitrios Buhalis on destination marketing through User Personalised Content was presented during the Enter 2010 Conference in Lugano.

Valeria Minghetti is Senior Researcher at CISET – Ca' Foscari University (Venice). She has over 15 years' experience in teaching, researching and writing on tourism subjects and has worked on a number of projects for national and international organisations (Eurostat, European Commission, UNWTO, etc.). Her main research interests include tourism demand analysis, the economic impact of tourism, the interconnections between tourism and transport and the diffusion of innovation technologies in the tourism industry.

Federica Montaguti is Researcher at CISET – Ca' Foscari University (Venice). In the past years, she has worked specifically on destination planning and management and on the analysis of destination competiveness and branding. She is also involved in the management and tutorship of the Masters Programme in Economics and Management of Tourism, and she teaches in other masters and undergraduate programmes.

Cristina Mottironi is a lecturer at Bocconi University. She teaches Local Development and coordinates the Destination Planning area at the Master in Tourism Economics and at the SDA Bocconi School of Management. Her current research interests are on the intersectoral links of tourism and on territorial competitiveness. She has participated in various strategic projects for tourism organisations and public authorities. She has an MSc in Tourism Economics from Bocconi University and a PhD in Tourism from the University of Surrey.

Luiz Moutinho is Foundation Chair of Marketing, University of Glasgow. He is the Founding Editor of the *Journal of Modelling in Management* (JM2). One of Professor Moutinho's primary areas of academic research is related to modelling processes of consumer behaviour. He has developed a number of conceptual models over the years in areas such as tourism destination decision processes, automated banking, supermarket patronage, among other areas. Other current areas of research interest are Neuroscience in Marketing, Marketing Futurecast, Futures Research and human-computer interface.

Emese Panyik is Assistant Professor of Tourism at the Catholic University of Portugal (UCP), Braga Regional Centre. Her research interests include strategic tourism planning and management, integrated rural tourism, EU tourism policy, rural governance, local policymaking and partnerships and host community impacts of tourism.

Andreas Papatheodorou is Associate Professor in Industrial Economics with Emphasis on Tourism at the School of Business Administration, University of the Aegean, Greece. He is also an external examiner at Cranfield University and the University of Hertfordshire. He gained an MPhil in Economics and a DPhil in Geography at the University of Oxford and commenced his academic career at the University of Surrey. He is a fellow of the UK Tourism Society and is a board member of the Hellenic Aviation Society. He is also a Partner at the Air Consulting Group, and Editor-in-Chief of the *Journal of Air Transport Studies*. In 2009 he was recognised as an Emerging Scholar of Distinction by the International Academy for the Study of Tourism. His principal research interest is tourism, focusing on issues related to competition, pricing and corporate strategy in air transport and travel distribution, mostly in the Mediterranean region.

Mike Peters is Associate Professor at Management Center Innsbruck, MCI Tourism, Innsbruck, Austria. He is the author and editor of several papers and books in the field of tourism research. He was appointed associate professor at the University of Innsbruck in 2005. In 2009 he was invited to work as a visiting associate professor at the School of Hotel and Tourism Management,

Hong Kong Polytechnic University. In 2011 he became part of the MCI tourism team, contributing to the field of research in 'entrepreneurship and innovation' in tourism and leisure. His research interests focus on the processes of entrepreneurship and associated problems, such as succession planning, product development and innovation.

Ágnes Raffay is a senior lecturer at the Tourism Department of the University of Pannonia. Her interest in tourism stakeholders and partnerships has been triggered by having worked in public sector tourism management as well as by her involvement with the tourism partnership of Veszprém. Her PhD focused on stakeholder involvement in tourism development and she has been researching tourism partnership development in Hungarian tourism destinations ever since.

Derek Robbins trained as a transport planner and has developed and taught transport courses to tourism students for 20 years. In his recent research he has explored tourism's contribution to greenhouse gas emissions and sustainable development strategies. He has published widely, and currently chairs the Leisure and Tourism programme committee at the European Transport Conference.

Jarkko Saarinen is Professor of Geography at the University of Oulu, Finland. He has published widely on many aspects of tourism geography and currently serves on the editorial boards of several international journals. He also currently serves as Chair of the International Geographical Union's Tourism, Leisure and Global Change group. Dr Saarinen's current tourism research interests include the transformation of destinations, globalisation processes, tourism and place identity, development and sustainability, and tourism impacts in peripheral regions.

Gonçalo Santinha is a lecturer in the Department of Social, Political and Territorial Sciences, University of Aveiro, Portugal, as well as a member of the Governance, Competitiveness and Public Policy Research Unit (GOVCOPP) and of the Department's Unit. His main research areas of interest are Spatial Planning Policies and Health Geography, participating both in the design of development strategies for local and regional levels and in several national and international research projects.

Christine Scherl is a PhD research student at Nottingham University Business School Having studied hospitality and tourism she went on to study for a Masters degree in tourism management and marketing. Christine is doing her research on inter-organisational knowledge transfer among SMEs in tourism and firms' absorptive capacity.

Noel Scott has extensive experience as a senior tourism manager and researcher and over 25 years' experience in industry research positions. He holds a doctorate in Tourism Management and Masters degrees in Marketing and Business Administration. He is Associate Professor at the University of Queensland, Brisbane, Australia.

Egon Smeral is an economist at the Austrian Institute of Economic Research (WIFO, Arsenal, Object 20, Vienna, Austria) and teaches at the University of Innsbruck and the MODUL University, Vienna, Austria. Areas of research are applied economic theory and politics (especially in the fields of tourism economics, leisure and service sector economics), tourism forecasting and modelling, impact analysis and tourism satellite accounts, and designing and evaluating tourism policy programmes as well as marketing strategies.

Stephen L.J. Smith is a Professor of Tourism at the University of Waterloo, Waterloo, Ontario. His research interests focus on visitor profiles, supply chains and trends in culinary tourism product development. He advises graduate students on research on various aspects of tourism statistics, methodology and policy. He also works with students on research topics in culinary tourism, including product trends, branding of culinary destinations, economic impacts and the role of food festivals in promoting local cuisine. In addition to his work in culinary tourism, Steve specialises in tourism economics, policy and destination marketing and management. His two most recent books (2010) are *Practical Tourism Research*, a research methods text, and *The Discovery of Tourism*, the biographies of the pioneers of tourism research from around the world.

Haiyan Song is Chair Professor of Tourism and Associate Dean of the School of Hotel and Tourism Management, the Hong Kong Polytechnic University. His main research interests include tourism demand modelling and forecasting, tourism impact assessment, tourism supply chain management and tourist satisfaction indexes. He has published widely in such journals as *Annuals of Tourism Research, Tourism Management, Journal of Travel Research* and *Tourism Economics*. Professor Song also received the International CHRIE John Willey and Son's Lifetime Achievement Award in Research in 2010.

Thanasis Spyriadis is Lecturer in the Department of Food and Tourism Management at Manchester Metropolitan University, UK. He has studied Tourism and Hospitality Mangement in Greece and was awarded an MSc in Tourism Mangement and Marketing at Bournemouth University. Thanasis has worked in various sectors of the visitor economy as well as in the FMCG sector. Curently, he is a PhD candidate at Bournemouth University and his research focuses on the performance management of sub-regional destination management organisations. His research interests include collaborations and partnerships, relationship marketing, strategic management and destination governance.

Theodoros A. Stavrinoudis is elected assistant professor in Management of Tourism Enterprises at the University of the Aegean and tutor at the Postgraduate Program in Management of Tourism Enterprises at the Hellenic Open University. Dr Stavrinoudis is co-author of several books, has contributed to many collective editions and has published papers in international scientific journals in the field of tourism. He has presented papers at international scientific conferences and has conducted extensive research in the field of tourism. His major research interests are management of tourism enterprises, strategic management in tourism, human resource management in tourism and special interest tourism.

Dallen J. Timothy is Professor of Community Resources and Development and Senior Sustainability Scientist at Arizona State University, USA. He is also Visiting Professor at the Universiti Teknologi Mara, Malaysia and Adjunct Professor of Geography at Indiana University. Dr Timothy is editor of the *Journal of Heritage Tourism* and is currently working on tourism research projects in Latin America, Asia and Europe, related to heritage, religion and spirituality, international borders and tourism iconography.

Paris Tsartas is the Rector of the University of the Aegean. He is Professor of Tourism Development in the Department of Business Administration, in which he served as a head during the periods 2001–2003 and 2007–2009. He is head of department of Tourism Economics and Management and also director of the Laboratory for Tourism Research and Study (ETEM) at the University of the Aegean. He was director of the Interdepartmental Program of Postgraduate Studies in Tourism Planning, Management and Policy (2002–2009). He was a member of senate of the University of the Aegean during the periods 2001–2003 and 2005–2009.

Geoffrey Wall is Professor in the Department of Geography and Environmental Management, University of Waterloo, Ontario, Canada. He also holds a Visiting Professorship with the Chinese Academy of Sciences. His research focuses on the consequences of tourism of different types for destinations with different characteristics, and the planning implications that follow on from them. He is particularly interested in tourism in Asia and is involved in research and consulting in China, including Taiwan, particularly on issues related to tourism and the environment, the involvement of ethnic minorities in tourism and the implications of heritage designation on people that live in and around the sites. He holds Honorary Professorships from Nanjing University and Dalian University of Technology, and is a member and past President of the International Academy for the Study of Tourism.

Stephen Wanhill is Professor of Tourism Economics at the University of Limerick and Emeritus Professor of Tourism Research, Bournemouth University. He is a Director of Global Tourism Solutions (UK) and the Editor of *Tourism Economics*. His principal research interests are in the field of tourism destination development, undertaking project studies from airports to attractions, both in the UK and worldwide, covering some 50 countries.

Esmat Zaidan worked as a lecturer in the Faculty of Environment at the University of Waterloo in Canada where she finished her Master of Applied Environmental Studies in Local Economic Development and a PhD in Geography and Environmental Management. She currently works as an Assistant Professor at Birzeit University in Palestine. She worked for nine years in many development projects of the World Bank including tourism development in her country, Palestine.

1 Towards a Conceptual Framework: An Introduction

Carlos Costa, Emese Panyik and Dimitrios Buhalis

Positioning Tourism in the Global World Economy

The world has changed dramatically over the last few decades. During the 1990s there was an emerging dialogue arguing that globalisation would change the face of the world's economy, and much was written about the benefits and shortcomings of globalisation. In the first quarter of the 21st century most of the rhetoric associated with this discussion materialised quickly and dramatically in many ways. The world has undoubtedly become borderless; competition at a global scale has come to stay. The emerging reality in the first decades of the 21st century is dominated by a world where people travel easily from one destination to another, where environmental problems created in one place impact on other parts of the world, and where information technology, particularly social networks, brings people together, turning the world effectively into a common village where citizens communicate with each other without any kind of barrier.

At the same time, globalisation has brought about a restructuring of the political space, challenging the traditional physical and administrative organisation of locations. Supranational and subnational formations are mushrooming around the world, which have become equally as or even more important than nation states in global negotiations (Ohmae, 1995). Paradoxically, globalisation has not only triggered this restructuring, but it has also reinforced it through processes of fragmentation, notably regionalisation and localisation. As Gamble *et al.* (1996: 3) put it:

A new stage in the development of the world economic and political system has commenced, a new kind of world order, which is characterised both by unprecedented unity and unprecedented fragmentation.

The shift of focus from the autonomous nation states towards the global market economy implies that the development of countries ultimately lies in their ability to adapt to rapidly changing global economic conditions. Consequently, contemporary geopolitical trends are intimately tied to the global economic architecture.

On top of this, the world's economy has not only become interlocked but also multipolar. Europe, America and China have become the leaders of the world economy, and the currencies of these regions have turned out to be the blood of the world's commercial transactions. Competition among these economic areas has become fierce, and the rationale supporting chaos theory has come to stay: whenever an economic crisis emerges within one of these blocks, the other regions – and the other countries in the world – feel the consequences.

The economic evolution of the world is sparking new but contrasting approaches. Far from the scenario of economic expansion of the post-World War II period, when governments acted as leaders and boosters of the economic expansion, there has been a shift towards the market as the guiding principle of government activity. Most nations are reducing their operations in order to release resources, to strengthen the private sector, to increase organisations' efficiency and effectiveness and to reduce public debt. The challenges faced by the welfare state in the early 1980s showed that all-round national welfare systems are untenable in the long run, even in advanced capitalist nations. Perhaps nowhere is this more evident than in Europe, where the diversity of cultures and the legacy of long histories and strong human rights policies have shaped the evolutionary path of planning and welfare systems. Today, the aging of populations is more advanced and the social welfare net is more extended in Europe than in most other parts of the world. As a result of this, the world is increasingly witnessing a retreat from welfare state activities and the market provision of formerly public goods and services (Larner, 2000).

While the bureaucratic structures of state intervention are being challenged, governments are also becoming aware that markets ought to be regulated properly. The problems created by, and within, the financial markets at the beginning of the 21st century have fuelled that need.

Considering the recent global economic highlights, the OECD's global outlook on the world economy suggests that cracks are forming in the conglomerate of Western world economies as Europe and the United States drift apart. While the United States stays on the track of economic recovery, European budget cuts depress demand in the region, contributing to a prolonged recession (Parussini & Hannon, 2012). The OECD has urged the European Union's (EU's) leading authorities to introduce measures aimed at boosting the bloc's competitiveness, particularly that of the service sector. This directs the spotlight onto tourism, which has proved capable of growth despite the restraining conditions.

The Challenges of European Tourism

In an era characterised by stalled global economic recovery, tourism upholds a remarkable upward trend. International tourist arrivals grew by over 4% in 2011 to reach 980 million. According to the estimation of the United Nations World Tourism Organization (UNWTO), international tourist arrivals are on track to reach the 1 billion milestone by the end of 2012. As UNWTO Secretary-General, Taleb Rifai, said:

> For a sector directly responsible for 5% of the world's GDP, 6% of total exports and employing one out of every 12 people in advanced and emerging economies alike, these results are encouraging, coming as they do at a time in which we urgently need levers to stimulate growth and job creation. (UNWTO, 2012)

Europe in particular, with the greatest diversity and density of tourist attractions among the continents, is the most visited tourist destination in the world. It accounts for 51% of international tourist arrivals and 44% of international tourist receipts (UNWTO, 2011, 2012). Europe is also one of the main tourism-generating markets in the world, although European tourism is largely domestic. Approximately 90% of European outbound tourism was recorded in the EU (EC, 2010). Despite persistent economic uncertainty, international tourist arrivals in Europe surpassed the half-billion mark in 2011 (503 million: UNWTO, 2012), and, long-term forecasts suggest that the old continent is likely to retain its leading position.

Tourism is also a cross-cutting sector and an essential economic activity in the EU, representing the third largest socio-economic activity after the trade and distribution and construction sectors. It generates over 5% of EU GDP, employing approximately 5.2% of the total workforce (EC, 2010). During recent decades, the tourism policy of many European countries has gone through structural change and innovation, showing a continuous concern for improving its management by way of adapting structures, investing in new product development and reinforcing public–private partnerships (WTO, 2003). Particular attention was given to the role that the EU could play in tourism development and the leverage it could provide to the member states and the Community as a whole. The 1995 Green Paper on Tourism was the first EC communication dedicated entirely to the role of the EU in assisting tourism, with the aim of stimulating thoughts on deepening its future involvement. Indeed, the potential of tourism in job creation has been recognised, due to the fact that the annual growth rate of people employed in the HORECA (Hotels, Restaurants and Cafes) sector in the EU has almost always been above the growth rate of total employment (EC, 2006). Hence, as an area of mutual interest for politics and business, employment generation has attracted growing attention. Notably, the 'Tourism and Employment' process launched in 1997 has been themed around strategic areas, including information technology, training, quality development, environmental protection and sustainability.

New Perspectives in Light of the Lisbon Treaty

Until very recently, there has been no success in exploiting the potential of a coherent EU tourism policy, due to the lack of a direct legal base for Community measures on tourism. Decision making was hampered by restrictive conditions, in that any act of the Council of Ministers needed unanimity among all member states. The failure to adopt the first multiannual programme, 'Philoxenia', to assist European tourism in 1996 was one example of such a procedural obstacle.

Two decades ago, Johnson and Thomas (1992) envisioned that the EU had developed a rudimentary but nevertheless evolutionary tourism policy that was capable of expansion into an effective and timely action programme. The inclusion of tourism in the areas of the EU's supporting competence by the Lisbon Treaty in 2009 may lend support to this claim. As laid down by Article 195, the EU can promote the competitiveness of undertakings in this sector, encourage cooperation between the member states in the area and develop an integrated approach to tourism.

In order for European tourism to evolve in the face of the current economic recession, change is required at all levels. This may provide the EU with a historic opportunity for active involvement by means of supranational coordination. The new action framework put forward by the Commission set out 'sustainable competitiveness' as the main goal of European tourism policy, which calls for a new approach to tourism planning and organisation at the European level.

Towards a New Conceptual Framework

The existing research with a supply-side focus on European tourism is fairly limited and mostly outdated (Bramham et al., 1993; Davidson, 1998; Hall et al., 2006; Pompl & Lavery, 1993; Williams & Shaw, 1998), lacking a systematic analysis of mainstream European planning and organisation trends through the key underlying concepts. Planners often tend to undervalue the importance of the administrative component of planning and focus rather on the procedural component, although in fact both are equally important for the improvement of the efficiency and effectiveness of the planning activity. Furthermore, the links between territory and actors in the planning process are often neglected. Bearing this in mind, the present textbook aims to fill the gaps mentioned above and offers a new, holistic perspective on European tourism planning.

New linkages between development and governance: A procedural approach

The planning and organisation of the tourism sector have evolved significantly over the past decades (Costa, 2001). At the beginning of the 20th century, planning was undertaken under the sphere of influence of urban and regional planning, and was mainly oriented towards the physical organisation of the territory (the classic planning paradigm). At that time, most of the problems in tourism were concerned with the location and quality of the infrastructure and equipment of emerging hotels and small facilities, which were solved within town planning. 'Tourism planning' was then viewed as a minor activity, without its own body of knowledge.

As the classic planning paradigm faded out and the rational planning paradigm emerged, physical planning and the organisation of tourism systems began to be approached in a broader way, encompassing variables related to demographic trends, mathematical models and cybernics. The importance of the social sciences also increased, as the Chicago School developed and brought into practice a new generation of ideas and models. During this phase, planning was seen as a technocratic, rational and scientific approach, because it was believed that it had the capacity to create scientific and 'right' decisions for the communities.

Since the late 1970s profound changes have started to emerge worldwide. First, most of the physical problems related with the (previously) poor quality of the infrastructure and equipment were solved. Secondly, market-led orientations and neoliberalism began to emerge. Moreover, the world's population became increasingly better educated and willing to participate in decision-making processes. In addition, governments had to diminish their capacity in to intervene in society, because many public organisations had become too bureaucratic, inefficient, ineffective and poorly regarded.

A call for new planning and organisational approaches has recently started to emerge (Costa, 2001). In the first quarter of the 21st century it is believed that the evolution of successful planning and organisation in the tourism sector should take account of the development of the territory and its governance (Figure 1.1). The development of tourism systems should be founded on an efficient and effective economy, linked to an interconnected local economic basis that orients its production towards the export of their products and services, because, as a result of this, they will gain competitive advantages in relation to other destinations. Due to increasing worldwide competition and easier delocalisation of investment, destinations should also look for local investment in addition to international sources of funding in order to ensure forms of sustained economic development.

The new economics of tourism destinations should also be viewed with very close ties to the actors and to the territory. Human capital is becoming the cornerstone of successful destinations. The emphasis on human resources

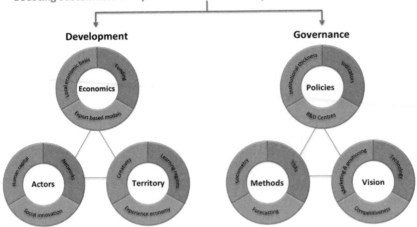

Figure 1.1 New linkages between development and governance: A procedural approach

has to be seen through the creation of modern and effective public participation which leads destinations towards social innovation. Networks play a critical role in achieving this, because they are among the most effective ways of linking together local stakeholders. In the new economy the territory gains even more importance not only because it is critical for the establishment of the price of products and services, but also because people choose destinations that offer them quality of life. The need to develop creative regions capable of providing new experiences and also to create destinations that learn how to achieve competitive advantages has come to the top of the planners' agenda.

The success of tourism destinations depends increasingly not only on the way they succeed/perform from an economic point of view but also on the way they are governed. Beside this, economic efficiency and effectiveness depend on how destinations create organisational structures capable of managing and leading them into the future.

In accordance with this, the call for the introduction of effective tourism policies will return as a matter of priority to the planners' agenda. In a modern vision, policies have to be designed through the direct involvement of all stakeholders, because they are designed for them and also because they may make them knowledgeable. Since most of the tourism organisations are small and do not have an agenda for innovation, policies ought to be designed in close association with research centres. Also, they should be supported with clear management indicators, so they can be scrutinised and so that the public will better understand and support them.

While it is no longer possible to design policies under the principles of the technocratic rational paradigm, it is also increasingly believed that how public resources are spent must be supported by evidence. Therefore, policies should be justified by clear forecasting methods, by how they will benefit a networked society, and by how the economy will benefit from them (TSAs). Besides, policies must be set up by clearly defining the targets they will reach and how they will introduce more competitiveness into the systems. The need for a better vision for tourism destinations also includes the development of modern information technology systems capable of connecting destinations.

New synergies between territory and actors: A structural approach

On the basis of this conceptualisation, the underlying tenet applied in this book is that planning and organisation systems form at the interface of the physical and social dimensions of the global world economy. Territory constitutes the physical dimension, whereas actors and their structures form the social dimension. As presented in Figure 1.2, planning and organisation systems evolve through links between territory and actors, which are shaped by the competing trends of globalisation.

First considering the physical dimension, globalisation has fundamentally changed the traditional understanding of locality. Due to the emergence of virtual space, the concept of location is no longer defined merely in terms of geographical distance, but also in terms of accessibility. The co-existence

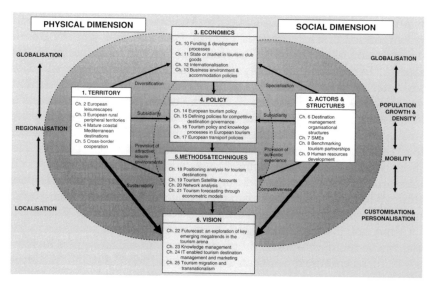

Figure 1.2 Key elements linking the physical and social dimensions of European tourism planning and organisation systems

of concentration and de-concentration has led to a differentiation of the physical space in which the location of an entity is defined not only by its geographical position but also by its virtual position in the relational network. This has transformed the formerly hierarchical role of different spatial levels, and globalisation, regionalisation and localisation have created patterns of multipolarity in the blurring of physical and virtual space. In Part 1 of this book, dedicated to territory, we address the challenges and opportunities that the diverse and distinctive European destinations – including urban and cultural, rural, coastal and cross-border areas – face in view of this spatial transformation.

In the social dimension of planning and organisation systems, the differentiation process manifests itself in the increasing trends of mobility, customisation and personalisation in a rapidly growing world population. According to the United Nations *State of the World 2011* report, the world's population reached 7 billion in October 2011, and by the end of this century it will be likely to reach 10 billion. Although great disparities exist, some of the major trends are evident; the aging of the population is accelerating and people are living longer, healthier lives. The interconnectedness of the world economy has forced the different sectors of society – citizens, companies and organisations alike – to focus on transport. While mobility is a plausible consequence of globalisation, this also highlights the vulnerability of the globalised world. For example, in illustrating how easily swine flu could spread through air travel, the World Health Organization (WHO) estimated that up to 500,000 people are on planes at any one time (Woolls, 2009).

Unprecedented population growth coupled with world-wide utilisation of information and communication technologies has induced increasing personalisation of consumption, which in turn has generated the growing customisation of production. The shift towards the consumer as the ultimate link in demand and supply chains highlights that the 'globalisation–localisation' dichotomy in the physical dimension is reflected in the 'globalisation–personalisation' dichotomy of the social dimension. This trend is evident in the prevailing focus on the critical role of local organisations in the provision of tourism worldwide. For a long time it has been recognised that tourism occurs in the local community, since the local communities are the destination of most travellers (Blank, 1989). Indeed, the EU argues in its tourism sustainability guidelines that consumption behaviour is formed individually and tourism takes place locally; thus, policies targeting them need to be devised and implemented at this level (EC, 2003a). Part 2 of this book discusses this trend in the context of the actors and structures of the highly fragmented European tourism industry, in which over 99% of firms employ fewer than 250 individuals (EC, 2003b). In addition to the small and medium-sized enterprises, destination management organisations, tourism partnerships and human resources management are the focus of analysis.

The amalgamation of territorial and human resources forms the link between the two dimensions of planning and organisation systems and delivers economics, policy, methods and techniques and, ultimately, vision, as key phases of the planning process. Economics provides the fundamental basis for planning. In the EU the principal sources of funding and development in tourism are the main financial instruments, notably the Structural and the Cohesion Funds. These instruments support social and economic restructuring and altogether account for over one-third of the EU budget in the 2007–2013 financial period. In Part 3 of this book, which concentrates on economics, these funding processes will be addressed first.

As can be seen in Figure 1.2, the territorial dimension is linked to economics through the diversification of activities and businesses on the basis of the territorial resources of tourism. In turn, the actors and structures of tourism supply in the social dimension are going through extensive specialisation. One potential product discussed in this context is developed by public partnerships through the transformation of public goods into club goods, which are collectively financed by the members of the joint venture. Here, the underlying tenet is that tourism operators in fact sell goods which they do not possess or control: the attractiveness of hotels, restaurants and services depends on external factors such as the surrounding environment. In addition, the influence of EU regulations and directives on the external operational environment of the European accommodation sector will be explored. Lastly, one potential strategy to overcome the disadvantages arising from an overly fragmented structure and to increase the competitiveness of European businesses is internationalisation. Considering the worldwide expansion of Foreign Direct Investment flows, a chapter is devoted to examining what drives European companies to engage in international markets, how they establish international presence and what challenges and opportunities they face throughout this process.

The economic base established through territorial and human resources determines the policies aimed at its development. Within both spheres of planning, the principle of subsidiarity has become the guiding tenet of intervention in the EU since the Maastricht Treaty of 1992. Accordingly, decisions should be taken as closely as possible to the citizens, and powers should partly be delegated to mixed private and public entities at the local level. In this regard, Part 4, on policy, will first review the critical planning issues emerging throughout the evolution of the EU's approach in tourism, and discusses the potential implications of the new tourism competence. Next, it will move on to explore the role of the EU in distributing competences and responsibilities among different stakeholders at various levels. By identifying the directions and target of strategic change sought by public policy, the outcomes of public intervention will be discussed in terms of knowledge processes. The section will close by illustrating how negotiations on the integration of strategies in tourism take place between different administrative departments in the EU, through the case of transport policy.

Policies use a range of tools to attain specific development goals. In order to establish sustainable competitiveness, the sustainability of assets within the territorial dimension and the competitiveness of organisations and businesses in the social dimension should be balanced within the scope of the general goal to provide attractive leisure environments and authentic experiences. To this end, Part 5, dedicated to methods and techniques, explores the role of positioning analysis, statistical data collection through Tourism Satellite Accounts, network analysis and forecasting methods, as advanced tools used at the forefront of improving the efficiency and effectiveness of tourism planning.

The previously defined elements culminate in a vision of future developments regarding planning and organisation systems. Understanding the key trends in the turbulent environment of the increasingly dynamic and complex European tourism market is essential for a successful planning and management strategy. The final part of this book therefore highlights the emerging megatrends in the tourism arena, and further analyses key operational issues of knowledge management, new mobility patterns emerging from the relationships of tourism and migration and the far-reaching implications of information and communication technology in destination management and marketing.

References

Blank, U. (1989) *The Community Tourism Industry Imperative: The Necessity, The Opportunities, Its Potential.* State College, PA: Venture Publishing.

Bramham, P., Henry, I., Mommaas, H. and Van Der Poel, H. (eds) (1993) *Leisure Policies in Europe.* Wallingford: CAB International.

Costa, C. (2001) An emerging tourism planning paradigm? A comparative analysis between town and tourism planning. *International Journal of Tourism Research* 3 (6), 425–441.

Davidson, R. (1998) *Travel and Tourism in Europe* (2nd edn). New York: Addison Wesley Longman.

EC (2003a) *Basic Orientations for the Sustainability of European Tourism.* COM(2003) 716 final. Brussels: European Commission.

EC (2003b) *Structure, Performance and Competitiveness of European Tourism and its Enterprises.* Luxemburg: Office for Official Publications of the European Communities.

EC (2006) *A Renewed EU Tourism Policy: Towards a Stronger Partnership for European Tourism.* COM(2006) 134 final. Brussels: European Commission.

EC (2010) *Europe, the World's No 1 Tourist Destination – A New Political Framework for Tourism in Europe.* COM(2010) 352 final. Brussels: European Commission.

Gamble, A., Payne, A., Hoogevelt, A., Dietrich, M. and Kenny, M. (1996) Editorial: New political economy. *New Political Economy* 1 (1), 5–11.

Hall, D.R., Smith, M.K. and Marciszewska, B. (eds) (2006) *Tourism in the New Europe: The Challenges and Opportunities of EU Enlargement.* Wallingford: CABI.

Johnson P. and Thomas, B. (eds) (1992) Perspectives on Tourism Policy. London: Mansell Publishing.

Larner, W. (2000) Neo-liberalism: Policy, ideology, governmentality. *Studies in Political Economy* 63, 5–25.

Ohmae, K. (1995) *The End of the Nation-State: The Rise of Regional Economies*. New York: Simon & Schuster.

Parussini, G. and Hannon, P. (2012) OECD sees Europe, U.S. drifting apart. *The Wall Street Journal*, accessed 29 March 2012. http://online.wsj.com/article/SB100014240527023 03816504577311043529851790.html?mod = WSJ_hp_us_mostpop_read.

Pompl, W. and Lavery, P. (ed.) (1993) *Tourism in Europe: Structures and Developments*. East Lansing, MI: CABI.

UNWTO (2011) *World Tourism Barometer*, September. Madrid: United Nations World Tourism Organization.

UNWTO (2012) *World Tourism Barometer*, January. Madrid: United Nations World Tourism Organization.

Williams, A.M. and Shaw, G. (1998) *Tourism and Economic Development: European Experience* (3rd edn). Chichester: Wiley.

Woolls, D. (2009) Swine flu prompts EU warning on travel to US. AP Foreign, *The Guardian*, 28 April, accessed November 2011. http://www.guardian.co.uk/world/feedarticle/8477508.

WTO (2003) *Tourism Market Trends: Europe*. Madrid: World Tourism Organization.

Part 1

Territory

2 The Mutation of Cultural Landscapes: The 'Unplanned' Tourism Map of Europe

Myriam Jansen-Verbeke

Introduction

Tourism is one of the many vectors in the mutation process of cultural landscapes, in some places clearly manifest, in others less obvious. The current challenge for spatial planners, regional authorities and tourism agents is to analyse landscape changes in their different expressions and in various socio-economic and geographical contexts. This implies the mapping and labelling of cultural landscapes and the identification of relevant factors of change in the perspective of emerging 'new' types of leisure landscape (LL). Such an approach can lead to a better understanding of the differential values of landscapes for tourism and on the multidimensional parameters of *tourismification*, that is, inducing irreversible mutations.

The endless diversity of landscapes, in terms of natural setting and cultural characteristics, on the one hand, and the hybrid nature of tourism, on the other, has inspired numerous writings, mostly descriptive and rarely analytical. The fact that the study of landscape changes can be approached from various disciplinary angles might be one explanation for the lack of a coherent conceptual framework in the analysis of territorial dynamics. Certainly, disciplinary structures in policy making and research design became inadequate to understand such universal and dynamic changes. This implies a resetting of thinking in terms of theories, models, frameworks and concepts, methods and techniques (Ateljevic *et al.*, 2007).

Landscapes are constantly in transition and are hence mirrors of social and economic evolution. This can be observed throughout Europe, albeit with variable intensity, scale, focus and format. The transformation of European landscapes started with mechanisation, up-scaling and rationalisation, all leading to agribusiness-branded landscapes with an increased risk of creating greater uniformity (e.g. the man-made polder landscapes). Yet in the European context many cultural landscapes managed to keep their historical roots and identity in terms of territorial cohesion between space use patterns. In addition, valuable new landscapes have been created (Dietvorst, 1998; Sijmons, 2008). Most landscape changes can be characterised as a gradual transition from a production to a consumption function, from agriculture to various forms of agri-tourism or rural tourism, from industrial landscapes to settings for theme parks and entertainment, from fishing harbours to marinas. The social perception of landscapes has changed: from hiking through farmland to farming in a LL (Buys et al., 2006). Although this process tends to be global, its impact differs from one region to another, as the result of local or national struggles for power and the space claims of various stakeholders (Aitchison et al., 2001; Hazendonk et al., 2008). Each landscape is unique with respect to its morphology, history and habitat and, as a consequence, also in terms of cultural resources.

A new debate has been launched about the sustainability of traditional cultural landscapes in the process of becoming spaces for leisure and tourism. The awareness about threats is growing, in particular in mixed cultural landscapes listed by UNESCO as world heritage sites. Tourism is invading valuable cultural landscapes, such as the wine-growing region of Wachau, a stretch of the Danube Valley in Austria between Melk and Krems. These landscapes have a high visual quality and a rich heritage (monasteries, castles, ruins, towns and villages) in addition to the cultivation of vines. Another example is the Tokay wine region in Hungary, often referred to as one of the best managed cultural landscapes, which has evolved organically and harmoniously over time and has survived intact up to the present. The question is whether or not the growing success of wine tourism will eventually unbalance these historical habitats. Moreover, awareness of tourism potential is growing, even in peripheral regions (off the beaten tourist tracks) or in post-industrial landscapes with less aesthetic attractions. The key issue for policy makers is to implement models of economic reconversion by using leisure settings and tourism potential in a strategic and sustainable way.

Although there are many similarities in the way LLs are created and designed, the resources tend to be site-specific, as are the potentials and constraints. Above all, guidelines and planning practices depend highly on national policies. In fact, many leisure and tourism landscapes have emerged in Europe without actually being planned in terms of location, scale or activities. This is one of the many challenging outcomes of an explorative European project. The contributions from 31 institutions, embracing 20 countries in Europe, resulted in a series of maps and various interesting interpretations of the genesis of leisurescapes. The map – 'European Leisurescapes', 2008 – illustrates well the complexity of landscape typologies and, even better, the lack of a coherent view on relevant parameters and comparable data (Hazendonk et al., 2008).

The focus of this chapter is on spatial transformations induced by leisure, recreation and tourism and their role in the conservation and/or mutation of landscapes (de Haan & van der Duim, 2008; Dietvorst, 1998). Tourism is generally considered to be a strong mutagen. The paradox is that an increasing tourist attraction threatens to downgrade the traditional structural role of farming and farmers. In addition, local trade networks are being replaced by new commercial networks, often with the ambition of benefitting *'hic et nunc'* from the current opportunities.

The identification of commonalities in the tourismification of landscapes is useful from the perspective of space management and an actual planning for the development of *leisurescapes* and *tourismscapes* (Jansen-Verbeke *et al.*, 2008). Even more important is the identification of the uniqueness of the territory, a prime condition for sustaining or re-creating regional identities. The critical issues should be taken into account when planning and analysing the map of 'European Leisurescapes'.

Mapping and Labelling Landscapes

Reflections on the mutagenesis of landscapes start with a methodological question concerning valid parameters of landscape changes. Which indicators are relevant to assess the intensity and direction of the mutagenesis, in a quantitative and/or qualitative way? Throughout the history of cultural landscapes, the mapping of territories and the labelling of their characteristics have been a mirror of social and economic values, technological evolution and types of space use. Moreover, mapping and labelling specific territories has become a political tool, used differently by distinct stakeholders. Until today, the way territories are mapped and marked plays a crucial role in the shaping and branding of leisure and tourism landscapes. The renewed interest in territorial anchors for regional development planning also affects the geography of tourism spaces (Jansen-Verbeke, 2009). The mapping of coherent territorial units – including their cultural resources – and the labelling of 'typical' space uses is now a challenging trans-disciplinary research track, dealing with multi-functionality and the mobility patterns of users, a 'volatile reality' (Haldrup & Larsen, 2010).

A scientific data-based study on space use and the fluid categories of uses is required to understand and eventually manage the ongoing territorial mutations. This is a relevant exercise when discussing both historical landscapes and newly created landscapes. Constructing yet another classification system, with even more overlapping typologies, does not serve the purpose of policy makers and planners. However, the building of a framework for spatial analysis of landscape dynamics has high priority nowadays. This can only be a realistic mission once consensus has been reached about selected crucial concepts. Apparently, even the origin of the word 'landscape', as referred to in the literature, varies and new meanings and values have been ascribed recently. Obviously it is frequently used as a descriptive concept in regional geography and spatial planning, but also increasingly in tourism literature and place marketing (Terkenli, 2002). According to some, the word 'landscape' is derived from the Middle Dutch concept *'lant-scap'* – *'lant'* meaning region or territory and the people living there, and *'scap'* referring to the process of shaping or creating. Throughout the history of civilisation 'landscape' has been associated with a territory characterised by peoples' interaction, thus becoming, by definition, a cultural landscape. In fact the idea of distinct cultural landscapes has been strongly promoted by the French scientist Vidal de la Blache (1845–1918) in his regional geographical work. He emphasised the interconnectivity of natural landscapes and their physical characteristics with the people and their way of life (de la Blache, 1911). *'Habitats'* were unique, and some survived through a sustainable symbiosis between man and his territory. Territorial cohesion was reflected in, and supported by, the lifestyle – *'genre de vie'*. This aspect marks, to a large extent, the regional differences in habitat and *'habitudes'*: settlement patterns, agricultural production systems, tools and skills, traditional transport systems, all considered to be important dimensions of the social organisation of communities. A recent comeback of regional studies in geography and tourism, together with the trendy branding of regions (the French concept of *'Pays'*) in the context of economic and political globalisation is no surprise (Jansen-Verbeke, 2009). Global tourist flows and tourism development need local anchors and 'typical' images. In fact, the association of landscape with *'picturesque'* (a scene to paint, to take pictures of, to evoke images) and natural scenery had already been introduced in late 16th-century Dutch and Flemish landscape painting. The connotation with scenery and scenic images and views has been emphasised even more in the drive to promote 'landmarks' and the iconic attributes of a particular area.

The ambiguity of the term 'landscape' also arises from the connotation with region or territory and view or panorama. According to some scholars, a 'landscape' cannot be quantified or mapped, because it is a cultural concept, a way of identifying an area, and therefore open to various interpretations. Clearly there is now a need to agree upon an adequate definition that expresses the multidimensional character of landscapes. The European Landscape Convention, 'Living Landscape – The European Landscape Convention in research perspective' (18–19 October 2010, Florence) redefined landscape as an area as perceived by people, whose character is the result of the action and interaction of natural and/or human factors. This definition emphasises that landscape is a mental construct based on memory and association, understanding and interpretation. The multiple attempts to mark landscapes as a set of 'resources' – tangible and intangible – for the cultural economy makes the discussion even more diffuse. The ascription of new values to the concept of landscape is the result of a renewed cultural interest in territorial differentiation and of the current hype for creative 'region branding'. The often-cited statement that 'landscapes have no borders' causes major problems on the worktable for spatial planners; there is an urgent need to define 'landscape' in terms of scale, borders, attributes, content and cohesion (ESPON, 2006). The mismatch between spatial categories (spatial planning units such as NUTS 3) and their functional labels, as a rule based on well-defined and measurable uses and users of space (production and consumption), require alternative paradigms. The traditional practice in spatial planning to define spaces from a mono-functional (read dominant) viewpoint fitted well into the traditional hierarchical approach in planning (a heritage from Christaller, Von Thünen and colleagues). The present hybrid reality of multifunctional space claims and the emergence of clusters of activities and values impose new labels for these mixed categories. Landscapes were usually *labelled* according to their traditional historic space use (for example, traditional agricultural areas such as vineyards, rice fields, cornfields), not taking into account the recent mixed development of leisure-oriented uses and activities such as cycling, golf, fishing, horse riding, or newly built infrastructure such as second homes, beauty farms, theme parks, shopping clusters, race circuits, etc. The capacity to map, not only the tourism infrastructure, but also the actual tourist's space use is the dream of many planners. New methods are explored and the applications of innovative tracking systems as a planning tool in managing space use patterns are now being discovered. This also requires ways to take into account the time dimension, the synchronic and diachronic uses of space, and the patterns of seasonal and temporal space use that are typical for many tourist spaces.

Matching spatial labels with territorially structured policies is still a considerable problem in spatial planning, in particular in the design and branding of leisure and tourismscapes. This is well illustrated in the 'European Leisurescapes' map, where landscapes are presented as fixed territorial units – a restricted piece of land – with distinct localised characteristics. The legend of this map clearly exposes the deficiencies of conventional monofunctional labelling when trying to map LLs in terms of intensity of use and type of infrastructure, such as campsite beds for rural tourism, hotel beds for urban tourism, protected landscapes for leisure experiences. The NUTS 3 scale was chosen for the presentation of basic data indicating leisure/tourism intensity, with the objective of mapping territorial differentiation on the basis of leisure potential and tourism activities (mainly from the supply side). The exercise constitutes an attempt to meet the needs of planners, but obviously it still lacks the tools to visualise a multifunctional and often volatile reality. However, the great merit of this explorative map is that it clearly demonstrates the deficiencies of present labelling and the existence of incomplete territorial databases. The search goes on for new and innovative typologies capable of capturing the diversity of the activities and the intensive interaction between functions, transcending the simplistic dichotomy of production and consumption, of work and leisure, of urban and rural.

Mutation of Cultural Landscapes: Vectors of Change

A basic assumption in the territorial approach to landscapes is that the symbiosis and conservation of cultural and natural resources is a key factor in the strengthening of regional identities. However, landscapes and their interaction of natural and cultural systems change over time; it is the task of researchers to identify the vectors of change. Industrialisation and urbanisation were the primary agents of change in the 19th and 20th centuries, but nowadays the search for attractive leisure environments is one of the agents driving factors in landscape mutation. More than any other factor, population growth, population density and mobility can be identified as the main driving forces in the mutation process of landscapes.

The flows between densely populated urban regions and some coastal zones on the one hand and rural inland areas with lower density areas on the other form the basic matrix of tourism mobility in Europe (Williams & Hall, 2000). Landscape transformations are highly dependent on both demographic evolution and distance to urban concentration areas. The demand for leisure and recreation is particularly high in urban and suburban areas, whereas claims for tourism space affect a wide spectrum of landscapes ranging from urban to rural. Obviously, this implies different dynamics and space use patterns. The analysis of landscape transformation processes might require alternative approaches. Among the many vectors of landscape change, tourism is only one mutagen, never as an independent agent, but always in conjunction with exogenous factors, such as specific trends in the global leisure and tourism markets, as well as socio-economic and political mega forces (Lew et al., 2004). Tourism, unlike other activities, can cause irreversible social and spatial mutations in functions, uses and users (Terkenli, 2002; Wlodarczyk, 2009). Some changes are intentionally planned, such as in tourism development projects, in the protection of valuable landscapes (natural or historical complexes), the conservation of heritage sites, the revitalisation of post-industrial landscapes and urban renovation. Urbanisation, revitalisation and gentrification are intertwined with the emergence of a new cultural economy, in which tourism can be an important driving force. Nevertheless, multiple forms of tourism uses and space claims that have arisen were neither planned, anticipated nor expected, and nor was their irreversible impact.

A systematic scanning of landscape changes induced by leisure and tourism, including unintentional (unplanned) impact of space use, has become a major concern of policy makers and researchers. This is particularly problematic in areas where tourism is a secondary agent, with seasonal users (e.g. second home owners) or occasional users (e.g. event participants) taking no responsibility for continuity or long-term impacts. The re-creation of cultural landscapes can indeed play a significant role in attracting new and diversified tourism markets.

This perspective has become a strong incentive for local and regional authorities, for destination managers and local entrepreneurs, to further explore and develop the tourism potentials of a place or region. The main points of interest in the development of a new leisure economy are the relationship between cultural resources and the territory, and between the conservation of traditional and the injection of innovative economic activities. Introducing new functions in the various landscapes also leads to a change in symbolic values, both for locals and tourists. The tendency to ascribe new cultural values to traditional landscapes in Europe – both in urban and rural settings – has not yet been studied as a dynamic factor of change, with the exception of some case studies (ESPON, 2006; Jansen-Verbeke *et al.*, 2008). Cultural resources are often seen as tourism products. This is an excessively simplistic view of the transformation from resources to product. The use of cultural resources for the development of a new leisure economy, which includes cultural tourism, requires a systematic interpretation of assets and comparative advantages and, above all, skills and strategies to turn these into competitive advantages for the local economy. In this perspective, an analytical approach to the mutation process was proposed (Table 2.1; Jansen-Verbeke, 2010a).

Table 2.1 The mutation process of cultural landscapes

Cultural resources *Assets for a new leisure economy*	*Tourism landscapes* *Strategies for a new leisure economy*
HISTORY, HABITAT, HERITAGE	Integrated policies Managing the *ORGWARE*
TANGIBLE HERITAGE	Conservation of the *HARDWARE* Landmarks Clustering of tourism-supporting amenities and activities
Historical elements: sites, monuments, historical complexes, museums, archaeological sites	Inscribing new infrastructure New uses and new values, flagship museums, tourist trails, integration in the *TOS*
Landscape morphology	Perception of historic (authentic?) setting Tourist map
INTANGIBLE HERITAGE	Creative development of *SOFTWARE* Icons, image building, branding spots Narratives of the past Experiences
CULTURAL HERITAGE Catalyst for creativity Identity Competitive innovation	*SHAREWARE* Linking tangible and intangible heritage, local products and grass-roots events with global markets Arts, crafts and souvenirs
New cohesion **IN THE CULTURAL LANDSCAPES**	**New dynamics** **IN THE TOURISMSCAPES**

Source: Based on Jansen-Verbeke (2010a)

The assumption is that the comparative advantages of a tourism land-scape are directly linked to the presence of cultural resources, the history, the habitat and the heritage of the territory. This refers in the first place to tangible heritage assets, which can be strategically integrated in the tourism space. Spatial planning policies can be implemented, geared at clustering and zoning with a vision for conservation and an optimal integration of the tourist opportunity spectrum (TOS) around the landmarks. Investment in image building and communication of narratives, legends, stories and icons, creating and matching expectations and experiences has become a critical success factor in the competition between tourism destinations. In this respect it is the creative use of intangible heritage and innovative experience-scaping that often makes the difference. In fact, comparative advantages in terms of the hardware – the built environment: historical landmarks and modern icons – can only be reaped, making a destination truly competitive, with the support of a coherent marketing strategy – *'the software'*. The eventual result depends on the organisational capacities in the region and community, the support of public–private partnerships and the actual involvement of different stakeholders. In fact, the strength and efficiency of *'the orgware'* has proved to be the most crucial success factor in the development of sustainable tourismscapes. And so, it happens all over that cultural landscapes defined as physical and territorial units are gradually transformed into 'tourismscapes'. This concept is based on a sociological actor network interpretation of the process of tourismification (de Haan & van der Duim, 2008; Jansen-Verbeke, 2010a).

The sustainability of cultural landscapes for leisure and tourism is strongly connected to the capacity to strengthen the cohesion between various cultural resources, maintaining the links with habitat and history in tangible and intangible expressions. Certainly, cohesion has become a key

Table 2.2 Analysis of territorial cohesion in cultural landscapes

Territorial expressions		*Cultural resources*		
Networks		*Tourism assets*		
Physical connections	*Hardware*	Location of elements Infrastructure Landmarks		
Functional links	*Software*	Positioning marketing profile/icons/images/uses		
Knowledge networks	*Orgware*	Organisational capacity Partnership		
		Level		
Global European	Intraregional	Regional		Local

Source: Based on Jansen-Verbeke (2007)

concept in the planning of leisure and tourism landscapes. The study of territorial cohesion and network development can benefit from an analytical approach by distinguishing the three dimensions: hardware, software and orgware. The importance of networks in each aspect is included in this conceptual model (Table 2.2). The territorial expressions and networks involved can be studied at a local, regional, national and international scale.

Typologies of Cultural Landscapes

The sustainable development of the tourism/leisure environment requires new and innovative typologies that capture multi-use and shared use of space and flow – and user-based dynamics of the use. In addition, new typologies need to take into account the land use needs of/for specific tourist-related infrastructure and amenities. Typologies are more than labels; they can be instrumental in classification systems that eventually support more in-depth research of specific transformation processes. The rich diversity of European cultural landscapes have been, and still are, a source of inspiration for many, all looking at the heritage and territories in different ways. The objective of the ESPON Project 1.3.3. was to study the role and spatial effects of cultural heritage and identity (2004–2006). Inspired by a series of case studies that were carried out internationally in the context of this EU project, it was made possible to define some key factors in regional differentiation. As an experiment, two key factors were selected for further analysis: the degree of urbanisation (population density), and the presence of tangible heritage assets (Figure 2.1). As suggested in this tentative model, each of the four types of LL deals with a typical range of problems and therefore requires a specific focus in spatial management plans and adapted strategies. Case studies for each of these types of LL can be considered stepping-stones to more targeted spatial management policies. This framework needs further tuning to be useful in different geographical and economic situations. The various types of LL have a different spectrum of territorial attractiveness and hence require specific management models.

LL.I Historic cities with a rich heritage

Historic cities – world heritage cities in particular – have a long tradition in balancing urban tourism with conservation policies (Figure 2.2). The competition in this market of cultural tourists is fierce, a situation that leads to diversification policies with an increasing number of events and even more commoditisation of tangible and intangible heritage. They have in common the problems of carrying capacity, the 'museification' of the historic city, tourism clustering in hot spots and the harmony between past and present in a living city. The trend to add modern architectural icons and flagship museums implies new planning visions on the integration of old

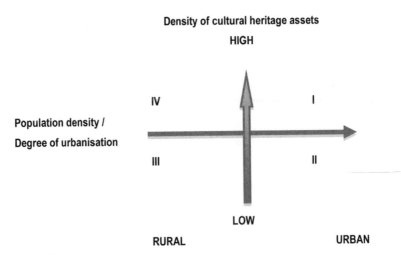

(I)   Historic urban landscapes, heritage complexes in an urban setting – *tourism clusters*
(II) 'Manmade' leisure landscapes in a semi-urban setting – *recreation based*
(III) Rural landscapes with dispersed heritage assets – *tourist routes – villages*
(IV) Heritage tourism – top destinations (e.g. archaeological sites) – *tourism zoning*
       Industrial heritage in peripheral locations – create *experiences – site development*

Figure 2.1 Typology of cultural landscapes for leisure (LL): Assessing tourism potential and key policy issues
Source: Based on ESPON (2006) and Jansen-Verbeke *et al.* (2008: 128)

and new and on the competitive advantages of such investments. Urban clusters of hotels, shops and street markets in a historic setting are highly dependent on the leisure economy, but they cannot to be labelled as exclusive tourism landscapes, given their imbedding in the multifunctional pattern of a living city.

LL.II Leisure landscapes in a suburban setting

The creation of new leisure resorts is booming worldwide: marinas, golf courses, ski slopes and other leisure facilities (Figure 2.3). Most of these designed urbanised LLs have no historic roots. In general, cultural resources are scarce, but these can gradually be imported when second homes become permanent residences for third-age or retired population groups. The large-scale designed resorts, hotels and second homes, mostly in a standard 'holiday' style, sometimes with a touch of vernacular architecture, are typical in many Mediterranean coastal areas. The emphasis lies on local recreation and exclusive sports facilities, implying limited integration with local communities. Making these 'exclusive' and seasonal leisure facilities more accessible for the local communities is just one example of the social issues on the policy agenda.

Figure 2.2 Leisure landscapes I. (a) heritage cityscape and tourism (Royal Crescent, Bath, UK: World Heritage site); (b) historic icons in the cityscape: flower event on the main market square (Brussels); (c) historic setting for mixed urban recreation (Marseille). All photographs by the author

LL.III Rural landscapes with dispersed heritage assets

Sometimes strategies are designed to boost tourist potential in rural areas, whereas some places have to be protected from the agglomeration of too many tourists and day visitors coinciding at any one time. The latter applies to natural parks, protected areas, and mountain villages with highly seasonal frequentation patterns (Figure 2.4). Capacities and policies for visitor management are a high priority in these tourist hotspots. Some rural and

Figure 2.3 Leisure landscapes II. (a) mountain resort – LL based on mountain setting (skying, sport and wellness, shopping); (b) LL in the mountains – seasonal intensive recreation use (Fiss–Ladis, Austria; photograph by the author); (c) golf resorts all over 'leisure' Europe – natural landscapes manicured for recreation activities (Donnagata, Sicily; photograph by the author)

scenic landscapes that are long-standing natural attractions are now facing the challenge of maintaining the perception of authenticity while embracing tourism as a welcome alternative for the loss of traditional jobs. Several wine-growing areas in Europe are among the best positioned territories to take advantage of new opportunities in this leisure market. Nowadays, many

Figure 2.4 Leisure landscapes III. (a) agricultural heritage system – traditional wine landscape, tourism opportunities (Beaujolais, France); (b) rural heritage settlements = tourist magnets (traps) (Alberobelo World Heritage site, Puglia, Italy); (c) war heritage – reimaging the past, connecting the battlefields in Europe (near Sedan, France). All photographs by the author

rural and peripheral regions – off the beaten track – are developing strategies to connect with mainstream tourism flows. Supported by the EU Cultural Route Program, some of them manage to penetrate into the tourists' mental map. Linking aspects of their intangible heritage with the territory can do the trick in creating 'unique experiences'; this is even more so when the staging of attractive 'grass-roots' events catches the attention of the tourism media. Mapping intangible heritage can indeed bridge the gap between the virtual past and the experienced present (Jansen-Verbeke, 2010b).

LL.IV Post-industrial heritage and archaeological sites in peripheral locations

There are now several examples of the successful transformation of industrial landscapes into post-industrial leisure areas (Figure 2.5). However, when it comes to 'creating' and designing LLs, the challenges in the brown coal-mining areas of Germany clearly differ from those encountered in the Arcadian Tuscan hills. Since the closing of the mines in many European regions, the high concentration of industrial heritage sites has been waiting for a new destiny. Various reconversion models have been experimented with, but in all of the plans elements of culture and entertainment, leisure and sports, tourism and trade have been incorporated, albeit in diverse forms and at different scales and levels of ambition. The mutation in the Ruhrgebiet, from a black territory to a green LL for cycling and other sports, with exciting places for arts, music, fashion and entertainment, is spectacular. Their location within the wider context of a densely populated and multicultural

Figure 2.5 Leisure landscapes IV. Post-industrial LL (Docklands, South Bank, London). Photograph by the author

area explains the success of a range of events in 'unique techno locations'. Certainly, the *orgware* in such post-industrial regions seems to be well established, if one can judge by the agenda of Cultural Capital of Europe, 2010.

The conditions for creating new LLs might be less favourable in many other post-industrial areas in Europe; for example, images of derelict harbour areas can be found in many places. There are, however, no blueprints for a reconversion through tourism in these territories. The creativity of local communities or external incentives can slowly open up new perspectives, as is the case of Puglia. With Alberobello as the icon, a revival of local traditions, architecture, the reconversion of traditional 'Masseria' into B&Bs, together with a new awareness of a regional rich heritage, are inspiring a revival.

However efficient spatial management in Europe might be in its planning and creation of sustainable, attractive, functional and aesthetic leisurescapes, it is hard to predict possible shifts in the perception of what are regarded as being desirable landscapes. Tourist preferences are socially constructed and subject to diversity and change. A tourist's place of origin and everyday environment, together with the society that surrounds them, all play an increasingly important role in preferences and behaviour patterns (Haldrup & Larsen, 2010).

The Unplanned Tourism Map of Europe

European leisure and tourism maps tend to have a short lifecycle; the preferences of tourists change, tour operators look for new destinations in order to stay competitive and, above all, many cultural landscapes are revalorised or even redesigned to facilitate leisure experiences. European LLs are dynamic, looking for local anchors and meeting global trends. New values are introduced and much has changed since the early days of tourism and travel (in the mid-18th century) when there was an overwhelming preference for romantic and picturesque scenery. Travel, transport and tourism facilities developed later (since the 19th century) and pioneers discovered the sublime nature landscapes of 'wildernesses in the mountains' and along 'rugged and hostile' coastlines. Images (paintings and photos) circulated everywhere and the interest in mountaineering and in visits to the Alps exploded. Ever since, the Alps and Alpine landscapes have been at the core of tourism development. Attractive mountain areas, valleys and 'typical villages and their habitat' were discovered and made accessible. The wave of seaside and, later on, beach tourism followed (from the beginning of the 20th century) and soon took on tsunami proportions all along the European coasts. This was the start of what after World War II became a seasonal mass migration, mainly from the north to the south of Europe.

The process of tourismification has spread ever since, as has awareness about the possible negative impacts of tourism not only on vulnerable landscapes and ecosystems, but on precious sites appreciated as cultural heritage. The movement to protect landscapes was supported by a European centralised landscape policy. The awareness of the public authorities has led to a system for the protection of quality in specific landscapes, including the conservation of particular heritage values. As a result of this 'protected landscapes', national parks seem to be the most clearly defined category of landscapes and have been systematically mapped.

'Protected' landscapes and 'cultural' landscapes were approached differently and the organisations involved followed distinctly different paths, definitions and policies, despite the fact that they share common ground (Mitchell & Buggey, 2000). The recent convergence in conservation strategies in spite of their divergent traditions and disciplinary background will hopefully lead to more integrated policies. It was in this spirit that the European LLs were mapped. Regardless of the mismatch or overlap of criteria, the map opens new perspectives. The experiment of mapping LLs at a European level was indeed the most ambitious, but nevertheless a most inspiring one.

Conclusions

The reflections above about an interdisciplinary and explorative field of research, about the mutation of landscapes and the genesis of leisure and tourismscapes in Europe, have no pretention at all towards presenting the state of the art or criticising the attempts made so far. The objective of this chapter has been to introduce a conceptual approach that contributes to the accumulation of knowledge and provides insights acquired from case studies in a structured way. The following perception on knowledge lacunae should be regarded as a constructive input for a future research agenda.

(1) The *meaning* and values of landscapes as leisure settings or as tourist pull factors change. In addition, too little is known about the attractiveness of territories. The perception of landscapes as leisure settings in everyday life or as tourism destinations when escaping from daily life and looking for new experiences needs to be studied, and not only from a marketing point of view.

(2) Rediscovering *territoriality* as a planning concept and model implies (re)defining landscapes as territorial units. This facilitates the monitoring of the processes of change using a quantitative databased and comparative methodology when relevant data are available and the marketing of landscapes and their icons in a more transparent and efficient way.

(3) Landscape *mutations* are an issue of (political) concern, with respect to the management of this process; a shared vision on wanted and unwanted impacts is necessary. According to some, leisure and tourism act as parasites, consuming life, space and meaning without regard. There is no

doubt about the fact that in the sheer volume of its geographical flows and presence impact, tourism represents a highly effective factor of change in the landscape. The pre-existing landscape is either greatly modified (as in heritage planning in urban areas) or totally obliterated (as in the building of Disney-like theme parks) (Terkenli, 2002: 227).

(4) Concerning the *tourism destiny* of cultural landscapes, the question arises about the long-term impact of tourismification on all types of cultural landscapes. Is there an alternative for rural regions that are suffering the exodus of the younger generations? Emigration flows due to increasing unemployment and an accelerated restructuring of production systems have marked several regions, not only in Portugal, Spain and Greece, but also in Finland and Ireland. In many cases the development of tourism (e.g. agri-tourism, rural tourism, heritage tourism) is seen as the best option, if not the only one. The other side of the coin is the possible negative impact of tourism through resulting changes in scenic landscapes. The more these landscapes are physically adjusted to leisure purposes, the less 'wild' and authentic they become. Depending on the context, scale and type of leisure activities, impacts can be positive or negative. There are examples of cultural landscapes that, supported by clever regional branding in the media, manage to create an attractive image. The objective of such public and private promotion campaigns is, of course, the expected economic impulses.

An increasing number of tourism spots in Europe project the image of overcrowded places, uncontrollable tourism pressure and environmental degradation (increased traffic and litter problems, water shortage, visual and noise pollution, etc.). The physical, social and cultural carrying capacity of local communities risks being overstretched and this can induce a downward trend in visitation. Product differentiation and re-imaging seems to be the remedy, although the effect of such marketing efforts can take time. The re-imaging of the 'upgraded' Balearic Islands is one such experiment. By introducing selected examples of explorative work in this field, and reflections on some tentative results and experimental maps, we hope to strengthen conceptual thinking in future studies on leisure, recreation and tourism as key agents in landscape mutations – for better or for worse!

References

Aitchison, C., Macleod, N.E. and Shaw, S.J. (2001) *Leisure and Tourism Landscapes: Social and Cultural Geographies*. London: Routledge.

Ateljevic, I., Morgan, N. and Pritchard, A. (eds) (2007) *The Critical Turn in Tourism Studies: Innovative Research Methodologies*. Oxford: Elsevier.

Buys, A.E., Pedroli, B., and Luginbühl, Y. (2006) From hiking through farmland to farming in a leisure landscape: Changing social perceptions of the European landscape. *Landscape Ecology* 21 (3), 375–389.

de Haan, H. and van der Duim, R. (eds) (2008) *Landscape, Leisure and Tourism*. Delft : Eburon.

de la Blache, V. (1911) Les genres de vie dans la géographie humaine. *Annales de Géographie* 20, 193–212; 289–304.

Dietvorst, A. (1998) Tourist landscapes: Accelerating transformations. In S. Scraton (ed.) *Leisure, Time and Space: Meanings and Values in People's Lives* (pp. 13–24). LSA Publication No. 57. Brighton: Leisure Studies Association.

ESPON (2006) *ESPON 1.3.3: The Role and Spatial Effects of Cultural Heritage and Identity*. Luxembourg: Eurostat.

Haldrup, M. and Larsen, J. (2010) *Tourism, Performance and the Everyday*. London: Routledge.

Hazendonk, N., Hendriks, M. and Venema, H. (eds) (2008) *Greetings from Europe, Landscape & Leisure*. Rotterdam: OIO Publishers.

Jansen-Verbeke, M. (2007) Cultural resources and tourismification of territories. *Acta Turistica Nova* 1, 34.

Jansen-Verbeke, M. (2009) The territoriality paradigm in cultural tourism. *Turyzm/ Tourism* 19 (1/2), 27–33.

Jansen-Verbeke, M. (2010a) Transformation from historic cityscapes to urban tourismscapes – a discussion note. *Revista di Szience del Turismo* 1 (2), 31–49.

Jansen-Verbeke, M. (2010b) Mapping intangible heritage. In S. Lira and R. Amoeda (eds) *Constructing Intangible Heritage* (pp. 57–70). Barcelos: Green Lines Institute.

Jansen-Verbeke, M., Priestley, G. and Russo A.P. (eds) (2008), *Cultural Resources for Tourism; Patterns, Processes, Policies*. New York: Nova Science Publishers.

Lew, A.M., Hall, M. and Williams, A.M. (eds) (2004) *A Companion to Tourism*. Oxford: Blackwell Publishing.

Mitchell, N. and Buggey, S. (2000) Landscape stewardship: New directions in conservation of nature and culture. *The George Wright Forum* 17 (1), 35–46.

Sijmons, D. (2008) A European holiday plan. In N. Hazendonk, M. Hendriks and H. Venema (eds) *Greetings from Europe: Landscape & Leisure* (pp.10–19). Rotterdam: OIO Publishers.

Terkenli, T.S. (2002) Landscapes of tourism: Towards a global cultural economy of space? *Tourism Geographies* 4 (3), 227–254.

Williams, A. And Hall, C.M. (2000) Tourism and migration: New relationships between production and consumption. *Tourism Geographies* 2 (3), 5–27.

Wlodarzyk, B. (2009) The landscapes of tourism space. *Tourism/Turyzm* 19 (1–2), 83–89.

3　Planning and Management of European Rural Peripheral Territories Through Multifunctionality: The Case of Gastronomy Routes

Magda Antonioli Corigliano and Cristina Mottironi

Introduction

Many people may imagine Europe as characterised by metropolises, business cities and industrial sites. Rural areas represent, however, a large part of the European territories, covering nearly 90% of the European Union (EU). More than half of its total population live in these regions which generate 43% of the gross value added and 55% of the employment of the EU, mainly in sectors related to agriculture. The importance of agriculture is then quite obvious; this may be clearly expressed by the fact that Europe is the biggest producer worldwide of foods and beverages, with a value estimated as €675 billion per year, and the second largest exporter of agricultural products (EU, 2009). Moreover, the contribution of agriculture is relevant to rural areas and to Europe itself at a social, cultural and environmental level. This chapter mainly concerns so-called *multifunctionality* in agriculture. Through this concept the EU acknowledges the environmental and social functions of agriculture besides its productive functions, making it more than an economic activity.

Over the centuries, farming has contributed to the shaping of the European natural landscape and the generation and maintenance of a variety of semi-natural habitats which have become a particular feature of the specific regions and are now part of their heritage. At the same time, the production methods and associated culinary traditions, which have developed over time, generated a culture for cookery and quality productions which are now part of the European identity. Therefore, multifunctionality contributes to the overall livability of rural areas because it implies a set of functions pertaining to the preservation and improvement of the landscape, the protection of the natural environment – against calamities as well – and the preservation of their cultural values and social balance. It is evident that this feature of European agriculture may also represent an advantage in terms of its effects on the secondary sector, mainly with regard to high-quality production in the food industry, and on the service sector, particularly in terms of tourism opportunities.

Nonetheless, agriculture and rural territories also face problems related to lower competitiveness and labour productivity when compared to urban areas and their economies, often coupled with a lack of infrastructure and services for the local communities, making them peripheral or less favoured regions both in geographic terms and with regard to their economic and social development.

For these reasons, the EU has developed reforms and policies over time to support the catch-up of rural areas and, at the same time, to guarantee that they will fulfil their important role. Agriculture represents the main objective of these initiatives; however, they have moved over time towards a broader approach to rurality. In particular, the Common Agricultural Policy (CAP) was established in the 1950s and has evolved over the decades, reflecting changes in the needs of agriculture and in society as a whole. In the beginning, the CAP was introduced to boost agricultural productivity, in order to assure at the same time a stable supply of affordable food for citizens and a secure and lasting source of income for farmers in a society devastated by years of war. However, since the 1980s, the focus of the CAP has changed and shifted toward a wider concern for rural development and the environmental sustainability of agriculture (see Figure 3.1).

On this premise, the current Rural Development Policy (2007–2013) of the EU is based on three main themes: increasing the competitiveness of the agricultural sector; maintaining and improving the environment and countryside, through support for land management; and, finally, enhancing the quality of life in rural areas and promoting the diversification of economic activities.[1] With the aims of supporting the economic development of rural areas and of improving the quality of life of its inhabitants, it endorses diversification into non-agricultural activities, among which tourism is considered one of the key opportunities for rural territories.[2] Notably, this chapter will discuss how the relationship between agriculture and tourism is tight and favourable for both sectors, generating mutual benefits and sustaining rural development overall. In this process the rural habitat, or as we say the *terroir*, represents the vital link between the two sectors.

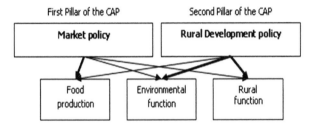

Figure 3.1 The EU Common Agricultural Policy
Source: European Commission (2006)

Terroir of Production, *Terroir* of Experience

The 'couple' of tourism–agriculture has always played a relevant role, underlined by the fact that food and catering necessarily represent a complementary part of any type of tourism experience. During recent years, however, the explicit searching out and consumption of local gastronomy has rapidly asserted itself in tourism consumption behaviours, creating a growing demand for the supply of local ingredients (Richards, 2002). Local gastronomy and foodstuffs tend to be considered by new consumers (foodies) as a guarantee of authenticity and genuineness, as well as a way to experience the culture of a place.

The basis of both aspects is the territory, in its broad sense of *terroir*, as a set of local resources and distinctive environmental and traditional signs that mark the places of production. If linked to a *terroir*, agricultural products are not just local but more importantly they become typical. The word 'typical' defines everything that is characterised by precise historical, cultural and material traits that are deeply rooted in the territory of origin; local means, instead, everything that is produced in a certain area, without necessarily being tied to its traditions and to the geophysical peculiarities of its natural environment. In this approach, the rural habitat thus emerges not only as the place of origin of typical wines and foods, but also as a possible place of consumption of new types of goods and services which sink their roots in the increasingly perceived need to regain possession of a material culture.

Terroir and typical agricultural products

Re-rooting agricultural products in their places of origin emerges as a reaction to the process of delocalisation of the food system in industrialised countries, meaning the cutting of economic and cultural bonds between foodstuffs and their territory and between the production and the consumption phases. At the base of this delocalisation lies, on the one side, the revolution in transportation systems and the global improvement of the distribution chain. On the other side, there is the development of technologies for processing and preserving food and agricultural products. This leads to an increasing uniformity of food models, which show a higher degree of homogeneity, risking being undervalued through the elimination of any specificity, differentiation or distinctive features.

A significant consequence is an increasing lack of awareness of food that is consumed, which can be seen precisely in the separation between the production and the consumption phases. It is getting more difficult to figure out the origin of products, as much as the market supply gets wider and more varied, in contrast to what happened in the past, when the attribution of the products to their territory was taken for granted and, in a sense, was unavoidable.

When the direct relationship between the territory and the product disappears, this is frequently replaced by a relationship mediated by images of nature in places committed to traditional and genuine production. In particular, an increased attention to aspects of quality emerges, with implications for a growing search for quality certification, designation of origin, organic farming and the traceability of products and raw materials. As regards buying and consumption choices, product quality, the authenticity of the ingredients, their national origin and the existence of guarantees and protections seem to be increasingly relevant factors.

This trend corresponds, in the EU's policy interventions, to the valorisation of the products' quality through a guarantee of the relationship between the territory of origin and the products themselves. This line of direction is gradually replacing or accompanying the quantitative approach aimed at the definition of production quotas that prevalently characterised the CAP of the last decades. One of the most relevant aspects of the European model of agricultural development is, to be precise, the preservation – beside large-scale and high-tech production processes – of a wide range of local productions, mostly handcrafts and handmade ones, whose processes are inseparably linked to the geographical and historical identity of the territory. These are products that surely do not possess the competitive advantages of large production scales, where price plays a predominant role, but which maintain a strong competitive position as regards product quality. The EU sets, among its goals, an increase in the number and volume of these quality and typical productions endowed with protected designations of origin. The quality and typicality of agricultural products usually refers to those tangible and intangible characteristics that make a product unique and immediately distinguishable. The elements of quality and typicality that are most frequently recognised, by the EU legislation as well, are the geographical origin of raw materials, the localisation of production and processing activities and the fact that the product maintains aspects of local traditions and culture.

Protected geographical indications and designations are recognised at the European level in order to be legally acknowledged as well outside the national boundaries of the country where the registration is made. As is well known, with the specific purpose of avoiding controversy and unequal treatment, the EU has introduced uniform discipline in the matter of the geographical origin of agricultural products, assuring a homogeneous protection of Protected Designations of Origin (PDO), Protected Geographical Indications (PGI), and Traditional Specialty Guaranteed (TSG). This has occurred thanks to EU Regulation no. 2081/92, which allowed the registration of several national PDOs, GPIs and TSGs for many agricultural products, mainly wines, olive oils and cheeses, which now enjoy complete legal protection within member countries.[3] Moreover, the EU is currently committed to preserving PDOs, PGIs and TSGs against falsification attempts. The number and type of food designations registered at the present by the EU for single member countries (excluding wines) is summarised in Table 3.1.

Table 3.1 EU-registered quality designations

State	PDO	PGI	TSG	Total
Italy	130	78	2	210
France	82	93	–	175
Spain	73	59	3	135
Portugal	58	58	–	116
Greece	63	23	–	86
Germany	30	39	–	69
United Kingdom	16	18	1	35
Czech Republic	6	17	–	23
Poland	4	5	6	15
Austria	8	5	–	13
Belgium	3	5	5	13
Netherlands	5	1	1	7
Finland	2	1	3	6
Hungary	3	1	–	4
Ireland	1	3	–	4
Luxemburg	2	2	–	4
Slovakia	–	4	–	4
Slovenia	1	–	3	4
Sweden	–	2	2	4
Denmark	–	3	–	3
Cyprus	–	1	–	1
Lithuania	–	–	1	1
Total	487	418	27	932

Source: EU (2009)

Finally, it is worth mentioning the Slow Food Movement's initiative as a different example of the valorisation of quality and typical production enacted within the private sector. Slow Food is an Italian not-for-profit association that has gained international recognition. It applies to very small scale but valuable productions (e.g. Carmagnola Ox-Horn pepper, Mountain Castelmagno cheese, Modenese White cow) which, because of their small quantities, could not apply for EU registration. Through its year-round projects (Ark of Taste, Presidia project, Slow Food Foundation for Biodiversity and Terra Madre), this association is mainly committed to the protection of the food supply's biodiversity from the prevalence of convenience food, industrial agribusiness and standardisation of taste. In order to save traditional products that are disappearing, Slow Food is engaged in promotional and educational activities (Salone del Gusto, Cheese, Slow Fish, Aux Origine du Goût, A Taste of Slow). Such a philosophy, in order to protect products, promotes food and opens up new markets, including through events and tourism, making the work of small-scale producers economically rewarding, as has been proved by the increase in employment, quantities and prices generated by the initiative (Antonioli Corigliano et al., 2002).

The enhancement of the *terroir* through authentic tourism experiences

As has been seen, the use of the term 'typical' can be legitimately applied to the agricultural products of a particular geographic area, due to the sense of belonging to the territory and to local traditions that they embody. This represents a new paradigm of production, where resources are no longer factors to be exploited but, rather, to be valorised. Moreover, from the demand point of view, the *'terroir* factor' is increasingly a market value that also inspires gastronomic tourism experiences linked to the authentic local cultures.

These tourism experiences play an important role in enhancing food and rural identity, because – besides legislative and policy actions – this also depends on the knowledge and attitudes developed by customers for typical agricultural products. It is then also a matter of communication and education, where a key aspect is to create in the customers' minds a recognition of the inseparable link between the territory and its typical fine foods and wines. It is quite clear that tourism has great potential in promoting and inducing this link in a persuasive way, because tourists can have a living experience of the productive environment (see, for example, Antonioli Corigliano, 1996, 1999; Hjialager & Richards, 2002). In addition, tourism can be a valuable tool for the sustainable development of rural peripheral areas because, if properly managed, it leads to a better maintenance of the rural environment, to the protection and renovation of cultural and social traditions and to a diversification of the agricultural economy (Antonioli Corigliano & Viganò, 2005; Scarpato, 1999, 2002).

To be effective, this requires the understanding of this segment, its main benefits and the most appropriate tools with which to develop it.

The Wine and Food Tourism Segment

The importance of the wine and food tourism segment has grown noticeably in the last few years, in terms of tourist numbers and consequently revenues, occupancy and territorial development. According to some researchers, this industry is becoming one of the most promising segments of the tourism sector (Bruwer, 2003; Hashimoto & Telfer, 2003). Wine tourism is predominant, even though it is generally coupled with the discovery of the local gastronomy and with attention to the overall typical agricultural products (olive oil, cheese, truffles and so on) of rural destinations. The phenomenon interests the old wine regions of Europe as much as the new wine regions of Australia, South Africa and the Americas. Moreover, the rediscovery of typical products and the rural lifestyle turns rural tourism into a high-standard segment in terms of price/spending patterns and the quality of services delivered. Notably, this happens mainly when it is developed in areas recognised for the quality of their wine and culinary products (Antonioli Corigliano, 1999; Getz & Brown, 2006).

As for many tourism segments, the conceptualisation of wine and food tourism has not resulted in a uniform view. However, travellers' motivations and experiences are mentioned in most definitions of wine tourism, among which the following contains key aspects: 'visitation to vineyards, wineries, wine festivals and wine shows for which grape wine tasting and/ or experiencing the attributes of a grape wine region are the prime motivating factor for visitors' (Hall et al., 2003: 161). In reality, as in any tourism segment, there are different degrees of interest for wine and culinary resources. Wine and food as prime factors for travelling interest a niche segment – 'gourmet' or 'gastronomic' tourism – but they are increasingly important as secondary or subsidiary factors, sustained by a moderate or low interest (Hall et al., 2003). The reference here is, however, to a type of tourist (the 'foodie'), who travels to discover the wine and food world, even though this has different levels of relevance. Since this is mainly linked with the desire to experience the *terroir* of production and its environment and material culture, wine and food tourism can be considered as an important cultural embodiment (Hjalager & Antonioli Corigliano, 2000) and, as such, as a significant feature of national identity. As a consequence, wine and food tourism can be considered simultaneously both as a form of consumer behaviour, a strategy by which destinations develop and market wine-related attractions and imagery, and as a marketing opportunity for wineries to educate consumers and to sell their products directly to them (Getz & Brown, 2006).

The Relevance of Wine and Fine Food Tourism for the Agricultural Industry and for Peripheral Rural Territories

The wine and food tourism industry's growth attracts the interest of policy makers and of academia: in the last few years several studies have been dedicated to wine regions, wine routes, wine festivals and events and wine tourism strategies. That may be explained because it is a relatively emergent phenomenon and expression of new lifestyles, and also because of the advantages and benefits that it brings to farms and territories.

For wineries, farmers and the agri-industry these advantages are plentiful and quite clear: increasing consumer exposure to products, brand awareness and loyalty, increasing margins, providing additional sales outlets, developing marketing intelligence about products and consumers (Hall *et al.*, 2003) and heightening consumer awareness and understanding of wine and food products. Moreover, wine and food tourism also provides a wide range of returns at a territorial level, such as the creation of full- and part-time jobs, the generation of secondary economic activities, and tourism and corporate investments (O'Neill & Charters, 2000), thus contributing to the sustenance of the economic and social bases of rural regions. Food and wine tourism also provides horizontal and vertical linkages within the rural tourism and agricultural environment; in many cases activities for this segment are explicitly created in order to strengthen these back-linkages (Hashimoto & Telfer, 2003). In addition, wine and food tourism is an effective tool to promote regional image. According to Peters (1997), when viticulture is successful, it can transform the local landscape into something more – a combination of agriculture, industry and tourism. Hall and colleagues (2003) argue that the wine, fine food and tourism industries support regional brands as critical sources of differentiation and value for rural regions.

All this considered, the interrelations between tourism and food/beverages are relevant for policy makers and planners engaged in regional economic development since they 'can represent the shifting emphasis in the way in which governance for rural development is being reconceived from a sectorally-based approach, to a territorially-based one' (Boyne *et al.*, 2003: 143). Besides the economic aspects, tourism can benefit rural areas in various ways while sustaining the production of typical and quality wines and foods, as is synthesised in Figure 3.2.

Wine and Food Routes as a Tool to Develop Tourism in Rural Areas

As has been seen, tourism is a significant means of territorial enhancement, image transfer, consumer education, revitalisation and preservation of

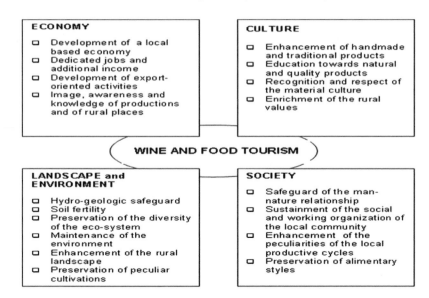

ECONOMY

- Development of a local based economy
- Dedicated jobs and additional income
- Development of export-oriented activities
- Image, awareness and knowledge of productions and of rural places

CULTURE

- Enhancement of handmade and traditional products
- Education towards natural and quality products
- Recognition and respect of the material culture
- Enrichment of the rural values

WINE AND FOOD TOURISM

LANDSCAPE and ENVIRONMENT

- Hydro-geologic safeguard
- Soil fertility
- Preservation of the diversity of the eco-system
- Maintenance of the environment
- Enhancement of the rural landscape
- Preservation of peculiar cultivations

SOCIETY

- Safeguard of the man-nature relationship
- Sustainment of the social and working organization of the local community
- Enhancement of the peculiarities of the local productive cycles
- Preservation of alimentary styles

Figure 3.2 Benefits from the interdisciplinarity of wine and food tourism

rural areas. However, this is not straightforward and largely depends on the strategies adopted: since wine and food tourism is growing globally and competition is fierce, the success of rural/agricultural territories in promoting themselves as tourist destinations is not guaranteed. Moreover, the sustainability of rural areas can be threatened by an uncontrolled and uneducated tourism growth.

Among different possible strategies and initiatives, wine routes – 'usually a designed itinerary through the wine region' (Hall *et al.*, 2003) 'involving an interaction between different material and immaterial components, facilities, services, environment and local communities' (Antonioli Corigliano, 1999) – provide an important contribution to the governance of this process. Most wine routes, in fact, bounded in 'an officially demarcated wine region or geographical indication (GI) that has an identity in the form of a branded descriptive name, such as Champagne (France) or Stellenbosch (South Africa)' (Bruwer, 2003), express the regional attributes of a place, such as environmental, cultural and social features, thus giving the region a distinctive trademark or brand identity. As such, wine and food roots are a significant tourist attraction in the main wine-producing countries such as France, Italy, Spain and the USA, which bring into the market about the 61% of total world wine production and the 46% of its consumption – but also in countries that produce smaller quantities, like Portugal, Canada and Australia (Jaffe & Pasternak, 2004).

Most importantly, wine and food routes are an example of a 'co-operative tourism product' that can support the enhancement of the overall tourism value chain of a rural destination and the development of inter-sectoral links between tourism and agriculture. A wine and food route is a complex tourist product, involving an interaction between different tangible and intangible components: producers, accommodation, facilities, complementary services and events, but also environment, culture and local communities. Therefore, different typologies of stakeholders are involved, such as local authorities, tourism and agricultural enterprises, investors and even residents. A wine route is first of all a formal network among the several operators that are connected to fine wine and food tourism. This network can achieve different levels of complexity: there are wine routes where only the producers are involved and others where various public and private operators are members of the route. A possible sophisticated value chain that a wine and fine food route can create through the networking of different typologies of agricultural and tourism operators is proposed in Figure 3.3.

The number and typologies of stakeholders involved are a function of the characteristics of the area. In rural destinations lacking other possible forms of destination organisation and management, a large involvement is recommended. Another discriminating factor is the long-term goal of the wine and food route, which can be focused either on the promotion of the producers or on the overall development of the territory. If the primary focus is on the latter objective, it is clear how several public and private operators play a relevant role. On the other hand, a large number of stakeholders require increased managerial and organisational efforts.

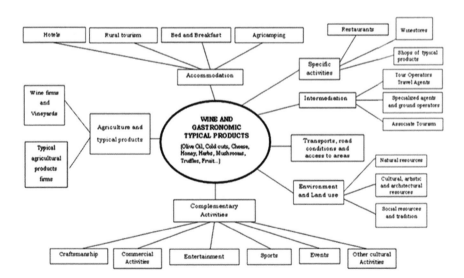

Figure 3.3 Stakeholders of a wine and food route

The case of an integrated wine route: *Strada del Vino Franciacorta*

The Italian context is rich in fine wine and food resources that are considered an integral part of the national cultural heritage: over 500 varieties of cheese, 300 different types of hams and salami, over 2000 varieties of wines and the largest number of EU designations. Moreover, initiatives to promote wine and food tourism have been encouraged since the 1980s.[4] Nowadays, Italian wine and food routes number around 140 and include 15% of the Italian municipalities. In total, 7.5 million tourists are driven by motivations strictly related to wine and food, while 20 million have included some oeno-gastronomic experience in their vacations (Censis, 2009). On average, the value of the economic multiplier is five: each euro spent in the wineries generates an expenditure of €5 on the territory. It is also estimated that Italian wineries are now re-investing 5–10% of their annual income in improving hospitality.

The Franciacorta wine route (*Strada del vino Franciacorta*) is an interesting example of the virtuous relationship among quality wines and tourism. The route is an 80 kilometre itinerary within the Franciacorta territory. Franciacorta is located in Lombardy, northern Italy, and includes 19 rural municipalities. The area produces DOP cheeses and DOC red and white wines. However, the most famous product is the sparkling 'Franciacorta' which received the DOCG classification in 1995 and, at the moment, boasts an eminent place among the most prestigious international wines.

After a period of spontaneous tourism growth sustained by the increasing national and international fame of its wine, the Franciacorta wine route was established in 2000 by a few wineries to act as the local Destination Management Organization (DMO). Ten years later, the partners have increased to 90, including different typologies of stakeholders ranging from wineries to restaurants, hotels and other accommodations, historic houses, wine bars, incoming travel agents, golf clubs and sports associations. The public sector is involved as well, since the municipalities are partners of the wine route together with trade and agricultural associations. This indicates the ability of the wine route to consolidate cooperation in the area over the years, at the same time involving and representing different interests within the same initiative. Nonetheless, the management of the route recognises how real cooperation is still a critical issue and requires constant attention in order to balance the different interests of the partners and to reduce possible conflicts.

The type of tourism promoted in the territory is characterised by small but qualified flows and the partners of the route agree on a formal commitment to reach specific quality standards, controlled by the route management. The accommodation stock consists overall of 67 small-scale structures, 22 of which are represented by hotels (in particular, half are four- and five-star properties, thus denoting their attention to quality hospitality), while 17 are rural farmhouses and the other 17 are bed and breakfasts, thus representing micro and family entrepreneurship. The tourism economy has been sustained by a growth of 84% in tourist flows, 34% of which are international, distributed throughout the year thanks to various activities and events organised locally, and despite the area not having a mild climate. Besides the wine and food supply, congress venues, golf courts, spas and wine museums have been created to diversify tourism opportunities. In addition to the typical marketing activities of a DMO, the Franciacorta wine route is investing in three strategic fields, as synthesised in Table 3.2: training programs for its local partners; the improvement of the tourist experience through ICTs and quality

Table 3.2 Main strategic goals and activities of the Franciacorta Wine Route

Goals	Current activities	Examples
To enhance competences in the territory and to create a coherent image of Franciacorta. To improve the overall quality of the tourist experience.	Courses for the wine route's partners	Main contents: Geology of Franciacorta land; Technical aspects of wine production; How to talk about Franciacorta with tourists; How to welcome visitors.
To offer a new tourism service welcoming tourists in Franciacorta. To network all the information. To distribute tourist flows on the territory.	Use of ICT	*METAFACILE* is a virtual tourist guide (palmtop) of Franciacorta and it is Franciacorta Wine Route's trademark.
To know and communicate local history, culture and traditions to tourists. To guarantee a high level of skills. To improve service quality.	Implementation of a set of mandatory quality standards for all the partners	*Being Franciacorta Award*: based on customer satisfaction indexes related to the quality standards, it is awarded to the best partners for any typology of companies.
To help visitors to discover hidden places (treasures). To push cooperation among local operators. To increase tourism flows in the back season.	High-scale events	*The Franciacorta Festival* (target: wine lovers). *The Treasure Hunt* (target: cycle and walking tourism).

standards; and large-scale events to increase the first-class image of the destination. It clearly emerges that to be innovative, customer-oriented and committed to pushing cooperation and networking are the key drivers of the DMO's activity. Moreover, the wine route is committed to sustaining the local culture and promoting environmental standards since both aspects are acknowledged as key assets for long-term development.

Conclusions

Wine and food tourism has high potential but its growth challenges rural areas: competition is increasing, thus requiring entrepreneurship, quality commitment and market orientation. At the same time, because this form of tourism is fashionable, there is a risk of a short-term view and commodification of rural areas.

Some future guidelines are therefore recommended for those involved in rural development at different levels. First of all, creating, diffusing and safeguarding a specific culture around traditional quality products among consumers and economic operators remain a key issue because their preservation and enhancement are unlikely without proper knowledge. It is then not just a matter of communication but, more deeply, of education. On the other side, there is a need to develop a homogeneous tourism culture among operators who often belong to other sectors than accommodation. This means qualifying human resources in the sector and providing professional training for specific professional roles. Action is also needed to create a 'destination product', in order to be commercialised, promoted and segmented according to the needs of tourist demand and the local economy, and to undergo changes in marketing determined by the diffusion of new technologies. In this process, it is paramount to recognise the specificity, significance and relevant features of initiatives as wine routes and to reach cooperation agreement on tourism projects involving operators, public authorities, agricultural and tourist bodies on the basis of the issues discussed above. In developing tourism, however, the real challenge for long-term development is to preserve and improve the environment, through impact control and the adoption of environmental standards.

Notes

(1) The financing of the CAP, which represents 40% of the EU's budget, is delegated to two funds: the European Agricultural Fund for Guarantee (EAFG) and the European Agricultural Fund for Rural Development (EAFRD).
(2) Funds are granted for the realisation of small-scale infrastructures and recreational structures, as well as for the conservation and upgrading of rural heritage and the marketing of the territory as a tourist destination. Moreover, training and support for skills acquisition and the stimulation of rural areas are provided to

the local population. Female and youth employment are key factors within this framework.

(3) The EU Regulation no. 479/08 standardises in a common classification wine and other agricultural products. The proceedings pass from national identification to European official recognition. The time required is quite long and the final cost of the initiative is high.

(4) The first law dedicated to farm tourism (Law no. 730) was promulgated in 1985 in order to help farmers remain in rural areas while improving their living conditions and fostering the development and balance of the agricultural regions through tourism. Law no. 268 on wine routes followed in 1999 in order to incentivise the creation of this type of tourism product and to aid networks for tourism growth. In such a context, the role played by culture heritage, local attractiveness, events and so on, and by related services such as guides, ICT devices for information, sports facilities, etc., is very relevant for the development of the initiatives.

References

Antonioli Corigliano, M. (1996) *Enoturismo. Caratteristiche della domanda, strategie di offerta e aspetti territoriali e ambientali*. Milan: Franco Angeli.

Antonioli Corigliano, M. (1999) *Strade del Vino ed enoturismo. Distretti turistici e vie di comunicazione*. Milan: Franco Angeli.

Antonioli Corigliano, M. and Viganò, G. (eds) (2004) *Turisti per gusto. Enogastronomia, territorio, sostenibilità*. Novara: DeAgostini.

Antonioli Corigliano, M. *et al.* (2002) *I Presidi Slow Food: da Iniziativa Culturale ad Attività Imprenditoriale*. Milan: Il Sole24Ore.

Boyne, S., Hall, D. and Williams, F. (2003) Policy, support and promotion for food-related tourism initiatives: A marketing approach to regional development. *Journal of Travel & Tourism Marketing* 14 (3/4), 131–154.

Bruwer, J. (2003) South African wine routes: Some perspectives on the wine tourism industry's structural dimensions and wine tourism product. *Tourism Management* 24, 423–435.

Censis (2009) VIII Osservatorio sul turismo del vino. *Censis – Città del vino*. http://www. cittadelvino.it/node/50.

EU (2009) *Rural Development in the European Union: Statistical and Economic Information*. Brussels: Directorate General for Agriculture and Rural Development.

Getz, D. and Brown, G. (2006) Critical success factors for wine tourism regions: A demand analysis. *Tourism Management* 27, 146–158.

Hall, C.M., Sharples, L., Mitchell, R., Macionis, N. and Cambourne, B. (eds) (2003) *Wine Tourism Around the World: Development, Management, and the Markets*. Amsterdam: Butterworth Heinenmann.

Hashimoto, A. and Telfer, D.J. (2003) Positioning an emerging wine route in the Niagara region: Understanding the wine tourism market and its implications for marketing. In C.M. Hall (ed.) *Wine, Food and Tourism Marketing* (pp. 61–76). New York: Haworth Press.

Hjalager, A. and Antonioli Corigliano, M. (2000) Food for tourist-determinants of an image. *International Journal of Tourism Research* 2, 281–293.

Hjalager, A. and Richards, G. (eds) (2002) *Tourism and Gastronomy*. London: Routledge-ATLAS.

Jaffe, E. and Pasternak, H. (2004) Developing wine trails as a tourist attraction in Israel. *International Journal of Tourism Research* 6, 237–249.

O'Neill, M. and Charters, S. (2000) Service quality at the cellar door: Implications for Western Australia's developing wine tourism industry. *Managing Service Quality* 10 (2), 112–122.

Peters, G.L. (1997) *American Winescapes*. Boulder, CO: Westview Press.

Richards, G. (2002) Gastronomy: An essential ingredient in tourism production and consumption? In A.M. Hjalager and G. Richards (eds) *Tourism and Gastronomy* (pp. 3–20). London: Routledge.

Scarpato, R. (1999) Food globalisation, new global cuisine and the quest for a definition. In R. Dare (ed.) *Cuisines: Regional, National or Global*. Adelaide: Research Centre for the History of Food and Drink.

Scarpato, R. (2002) Gastronomy as a tourist product: The perspective of gastronomy studies. In A.M. Hjalager and G. Richards (eds) *Tourism and Gastronomy* (pp. 51–70). London: Routledge.

4   Mature Coastal Mediterranean Destinations: Mitigating Seasonality

Savvina Karyopouli and
Christina Koutra

Introduction

Tourism, as one of the first commercial activities, has now developed into the world's biggest and fastest growing economic industry (UNWTO, 2011a). Increasing choice in tour packages, cruises, exploration experiences and independent agendas has increased the appeal of travelling to consumers (Goeldner & Ritchie, 2009). In 2010 the United Nations World Tourism Organisation (UNWTO) reported 940 million international tourists, generating €693 billion, and forecast that international tourists would reach 1.6 billion by 2020 (UNWTO, 2011a). Tourism is believed to be a successful medium for development, with the potential for socio-economic advancement through job creation, infrastructure development, income generation and the ability to attract foreign exchange and promote sustainable development (Oreja Rodríguez et al., 2008; Sharpley, 2004; UNWTO, 2011a).

The capability of the tourism industry to aid in the economic development of an area where not many alternative sources exist for economic diversification has been recognised by a number of governments. Consequently, tourism has been acknowledged as a key part of many development and regeneration strategies within the sustainability context, that is, the smooth integration of economy, society and environment (Andriotis & Vaughan, 2004).

Furthermore, the direct[1] and indirect[2] ties of tourism to a number of sectors within the economy further increase its importance to governments (Andriotis & Vaughan, 2004; EC, 2010). For instance, the tourism industry is the third biggest socio-economic activity in the European Union (EU); more than 5% of the EU gross national product (GDP) is generated by the

European tourism industry, and around 1.8 million businesses provide work for approximately 5.2% of the total workforce – about 9.7 million jobs (EC, 2010). Even more important is when the indirect contribution of the tourism industry to related sectors is considered, where the estimated input to GDP is more than 10% of the EU GDP and it employs around 12% of the workforce (EC, 2010). In November 2011 the UNWTO affirmed that despite the current volatile international environment, EU countries had received the highest number of international tourist arrivals, receiving most of the economic benefits (UNWTO, 2011b). The UNWTO Secretary-General, Taleb Rifai, emphasises, 'UNWTO encourages European governments to support tourism and consider the sector as one that can back economic recovery given its capacity to distribute wealth and create jobs across the region' (UNWTO, 2011b).

Indeed, many coastal areas and islands depend on the tourism industry for economic development, such as Malta, Spain and Cyprus (Andriotis, 2006; Chapman & Speake, 2011; Claver-Cortés et al., 2007). The core tourism product for the coastal areas is based on their climatic conditions and beaches – to be exact, the sun, sea and sand, also identified as the 3Ss (Spilanis & Vayianni, 2004). The blend of these three products is still attractive to the largest segment of the market, since coastal areas can attract tourists who are stimulated by 'passive recreation', such as lounging in a deckchair and watching the sea, as well as tourists seeking 'more active pastimes' such as swimming and water sports (Holloway, 2006: 189).

The Mediterranean basin in the southern part of Europe is an example of a coastal region which, by exploiting its core coastal product of the 3Ss, has managed to boost its economic and social development and become one of the world's main tourist destinations (Apostolopoulos et al., 2001; Ioannides et al., 2001; UNWTO, 2011a). The Mediterranean area is comprised of a number of European member states, including Greece, Spain, France, Portugal, Italy, Slovenia and Croatia, as well as two island states, Cyprus and Malta. This region has been described as the 'pleasure periphery' of Europe (McElroy, 2003: 231). This is not surprising, since it is the most visited area in Europe, with 169.7 million international arrivals, holding an 18.1% market share of the 50% that Europe had as a whole in 2010 (UNWTO, 2011a).

Europe is the number one destination in the world; however, its member states face a number of issues that need to be resolved, in order for Europe's tourism industry to become more sustainable in a holistic way. In particular, sun-and-sea destinations in the Mediterranean basin are currently facing a number of tourism challenges that threaten their economic viability, with one being the seasonal nature of tourism (EC, 2010). For instance, destinations focusing on the sun-and-sea product face extreme seasonality which creates many economic, sociocultural and environmental issues such as low profitability during the low season, seasonal employment and the overstretching of natural and built resources, among others (Andriotis, 2005; Koening-Lewis & Bischoff, 2010).

This chapter discusses the major challenges and opportunities that coastal mature tourism destinations in the Mediterranean region face, due to their seasonal fluctuations of demand. In addition, the chapter examines current market trends and how, through tourism, these Mediterranean destinations can address their challenges, promote economic and social development and become more sustainable. This is an issue which supports one of the EU's aims from the Treaty of Lisbon, that is, that all policies should seek to create a better life, by boosting employment and social care as well as making Europe a more competitive destination (Europa, 2009).

The European Union and the Tourism Industry

Tourism in Europe is a vital economic activity for many of its member states, and for the EU as a whole, due to its contribution to the socio-economic development of the EU's member states. Especially in the Mediterranean area, tourism plays a crucial role in the everyday life of its citizens. For instance, in 2011 the total contribution of travel and tourism to GDP was 25.4% in Malta; tourism's contribution to employment was 26.1% of total employment and export profits were estimated at 17.4% of total exports (WTTC, 2011a). Additionally, for Spain in 2011 the contribution of travel and tourism to GDP was 14.4% and it accounted for 12.7% of the total workforce and approximately 15.5% of total export profits (WTTC, 2011b).

In order to understand the successful development of tourism in the Mediterranean, it is important to present the characteristics that make this area appealing to tourists, since all these features need to be utilised in order to continue the upward trend. Four main characteristics have aided this explosive growth: (a) the diversity and wealth of the historical, cultural, natural and scenic heritage; (b) the favourable climate and coast; (c) the cultural and physical closeness to the European market; and (d) the fact that it is considered as a traditional tourist destination (UNEP, 2005). Nevertheless, the adoption of mass sun-and-sea tourism, with its numerous contradictory environmental, economic and sociocultural dimensions, has jeopardised the resources that made these areas appealing in the first place (Chapman & Speake, 2011; Falzon, 2012).

Several threats are recognised for the economic strength of these destinations, including old infrastructure, the disintegration of the natural environment, changes in tourists' expectations, the conventional image focusing on the sun, coast and landscapes, and rising competition from new destinations around the world (Bramwell, 2004; Chapman & Speake, 2011). In particular, destinations such as Spain, Malta and Cyprus face intense competition from less crowded, more natural and exotic new destinations, such as southeast

Asia and the Indian and Pacific Oceans (Falzon, 2012). These issues have produced many challenges for the Mediterranean destinations with one being the short tourism season, owing to their narrow and seasonal sun-and-sea tourism product and their 'could be anywhere' sun-and-sea image that is extremely substitutable (Ioannides, 2002: 80; Kozak & Martin, 2012; Valle et al., 2011).

This seasonality has created a number of economic, sociocultural and environmental problems, causing many Mediterranean destinations to demonstrate characteristics of having reached the consolidation or even stagnation stage in their lifecycle (Chapman & Speake, 2011; Ioannides, 2002). However, if these destinations decline, this will have damaging effects on the economies and the lives of their citizens, given that the Mediterranean receives most of Europe's international arrivals and significantly contributes to the GDP and employment rate of the EU. The impact of seasonality on the Mediterranean member states of the EU is discussed in more detail below.

The Seasonal Nature of Tourism and its Impact on Member States

Seasonality is described by Butler (1994, cited in Koenig-Lewis & Bischoff, 2005: 202) as:

> (...) a temporal imbalance in the phenomenon of tourism [which] may be expressed in terms of dimensions of such elements as numbers of visitors, expenditure of visitors, traffic on highways and other forms of transportation, employment and admissions to attractions.

In particular, seasonality denotes the concentration of tourist flow in fairly short periods that reoccur relatively in the same period, but can change over time. This concentration of tourist flow can be expressed by measuring the number of tourist arrivals, the money that tourists spend, the employment rate, and the tourists visiting attractions (Koenig-Lewis & Bischoff, 2005).

In Europe, tourism demand is strongly focused on the months of July and August, and this seasonal characteristic is especially common in the Mediterranean basin (EC, 2010; Garau-Vadell & de Borja-Solé, 2008). In Cyprus in 2010, for instance, 54% of annual arrivals were between the months of June and September (CTO, 2010). Given that tourism is an important economic driver for most Mediterranean regions, seasonality has a tremendous impact on the economic, social and environmental aspects of a destination.

The causal factors of seasonality are natural and institutional (Cuccia & Rizzo, 2011). The natural causes are the climatic conditions that make some destinations unappealing, while the institutional concerns are cultural, ethnic and social aspects and any other general issues that affect consumers' decision making (Cuccia & Rizzo, 2011). For example, the social factors can be affected and linked with public, company or school holidays (Andriotis, 2005).

By the same token, social pressure or fashion, sporting calendars and inertia or tradition have been distinguished as additional contributing factors to seasonality (Cuccia & Rizzo, 2011; Koenig-Lewis & Bischoff, 2005). Sporting activities may encompass skiing or football, whereas tradition and inertia include the fact that 'many people take holidays at peak seasons because they have always done so' (Butler, 1994, cited in Koening-Lewis & Bischoff, 2005: 205). In other words, people holiday at certain times due to their need to attend a specific event in a particular destination at a certain time because it has become a habit.

Moreover, Andriotis (2005) argues that from the supply side constraints could exist with no links to the human decision factor, such as the inability of the government to persuade owners of enterprises to remain open during the off-peak season, the lack of a labour force, and the unwillingness of tour operators and air carriers to continue their flights during the low season. Especially in the sun-and-sea Mediterranean destinations such as Cyprus, Malta and Spain, tour operators have enormous influence on tourist flows and prices (Aguiló et al., 2005; Falzon, 2012; Sharpley, 2004).

One of the implications of the seasonal nature of tourism is the huge quantity of resources that are required to fulfil the demand during the high season for food, water, electricity and so on. Therefore, the Mediterranean has become a region that regularly suffers short periods of over-demand and over-use of resources. Malta and Cyprus, for example, are confronted with many problems due to the lack of water. Moreover, there is an extreme pressure on the environment that could prove unsustainable in the long run if the carrying capacity of the destination is exceeded (Cuccia & Rizzo, 2011). Additionally, individual tourism enterprises are negatively affected, specifically the micro, and small and medium-sized enterprises (SMEs) such as hotels and restaurants, that have low occupancy rates during the low season and hence really low profitability (Kastenholz & Lopes de Almeida, 2008; Cuccia & Rizzo, 2011). Therefore, due to the under-use of infrastructure, micro enterprises and SMEs are either forced to close or to reduce their staff during the low season. In turn, this creates an instability in the levels of employment that negatively affects tourism staff and businesses (Andriotis, 2004a). Tourism workers are usually forced to find alternative employment or stay unemployed during the low season (Andriotis & Vaughan, 2004). In 2009, for instance, 21% of the total unemployment rate during the off-peak season in Cyprus was attributed to the tourism workforce, forcing the government to pay more unemployment benefits during this period (Adamou, 2009). The micro enterprises and SMEs find it extremely difficult to hire and retain qualified staff, a factor that decreases the quality of service offered (Kastenholz & Lopes de Almeida, 2008).

Additionally, tourism's seasonal nature, low pay and excessive working hours have resulted in a high staff turnover, and tourism businesses do not have the opportunity to offer the necessary training to new staff (Andriotis, 2004b; Lacher & Oh, 2012). This prevents the owners/managers from building knowledgeable and innovative businesses (Andriotis, 2004b).

However, seasonality can also have a positive impact on destinations, since it provides an opportunity for businesses to undertake maintenance work on infrastructure and amenities (Kastenholz & Lopes de Almeida, 2008). Furthermore, it can contribute towards social and environmental benefits, since it gives time to a destination to recuperate from any pressure caused during the high-peak season (Andriotis, 2005; Cuccia & Rizzo, 2011). In addition, seasonality could also provide the opportunity to create sustainable seasonal tourism, if the destination were able to integrate other forms of tourism production (Kastenholz & Lopes de Almeida, 2008). To be more precise, developing other forms of tourism for the low season, such as fishing and bird watching, can help to support the hinterland areas by spreading the economic benefits of tourism.

Despite some positive impacts of seasonality, it is still a major problem for many destinations, especially those which depend on the one-dimensional sun-and-sea product. Therefore, as Garau-Vadell and de Borja-Sole (2008) and Valle et al. (2011) argue, it is crucial that these sun-and-sea destinations diversify their product to attract low-season tourists, thus aiding the extension of their tourism season. This could be done by creating new products targeting tourists with special interests, such as maritime and sport events or short holiday weekends (Kastenholz & Lopes de Almeida, 2008).

Thus, seasonality creates a number of problems for these holiday locations which inevitably affect the EU as a whole. Therefore, year-round tourism is not only one of the more significant goals of EU tourism destinations but also for the European Commission (EC) (Blažević & Alkier Radnić, 2006; EC, 2010). Current EU initiatives, as well as suggestions on how these initiatives could be adapted to member states, are explored below.

Changing the Product Mix: A Proposed Action Framework for the European Union

In their 2010 communication, the EC states that the main target of European tourism policy is to encourage competitiveness in the tourism sector, while taking into account that in the long term competitiveness relates to the sustainable manner in which tourism is developed (EC, 2010). This goal is also in line with the Lisbon Treaty, where economic development and job creation must come with social and environmental aims (Juganaru et al., 2008). In 2010, after an informal ministerial meeting that took place in Madrid, the EC, along with tourism ministers from member states, established a number of recommendations and actions to support sustainable competitiveness in the tourism sector (EC, 2010). One of the aims is the need to 'stimulate competitiveness in the European tourism sector', which will essentially reinforce the dynamic and sustainable growth of this industry (EC, 2010: 7). In order to accomplish this aim, two of the actions proposed were 'promoting diversification of the supply of tourist services' and 'encouraging an extension of the tourist season' (EC, 2010: 7).

The importance of diversifying the product and addressing seasonality has been highlighted throughout this chapter and it is apparent these issues are not only crucial for the sun-and-sea Mediterranean destinations but also for the EU as a whole, due to the social, economic and environmental impact that they have. Therefore, it is essential to recognise those actions which have been taken elsewhere and which could be adapted to other sun-and-sea destinations of the EU as well. It is necessary to identify the issues that need to be considered for successful implementation of these actions.

Consumption Trends

Post-war affluence, increased leisure time and the considerably lower cost of travel have resulted in an explosive growth in people travelling abroad (Apostolopoulos & Gayle, 2002). In addition, the arrival of the jet aircraft and the confluence of airlines, hotel groups, tour operators and travel agents, in combination with gov ernments, have formed a huge worldwide network of holiday opportunities (Apostolopoulos & Gayle, 2002; Falzon, 2012). These agents have contributed to the formation of the existing trends of demand in the international tourism market.

The current tourism trends of demand indicate that tourists are now more experienced and demand flexibility; they travel more during the year and there is evidence of an increase in independent travelling (Claver-Cortés et al., 2007). As the travelling experiences of people are growing and becoming richer, a desire is created to travel even more and thus to become 'career travellers' (ETC, 2006: 5). Therefore, due to their increasing travel experience, tourists are now more demanding; they look for 'an endless flow of new experiences' and seek meaningful experiences from the places that they visit (ETC, 2006: 5; Kozak & Martin, 2012). Furthermore, tourists now seek a range of new leisure activities away from conventional tourism forms such as mass sun-and-sea. A rise in demand for active and cultural tourism is evident where authenticity is more appealing, such as excursions to the countryside or cultural sites (ETC, 2006; Kozak & Martin, 2012).

Additionally, tourists should be segmented and targeted according to their motivations, by developing more niche products that cater for the specific markets with special interests such as the health and wellbeing and adventure markets (Boo & Jones, 2009; ETC, 2006). The Mediterranean destinations that depend on their narrow and highly seasonal sun-and-sea product could be easily replaced by other destinations that offer a more diverse mix of products (Kozak & Martin, 2012).

These new trends in the tourism market demonstrate a change from conventional tourism to new forms of tourism (NFT). Conventional tourism – that is, the 3Ss and mountain (winter) forms of tourism – stresses the significance of the market, the effect it has on the destination's prices and resources and the dismissal of any impact on the society, culture and environment (Spilanis & Vayianni, 2004). NFT, however are alternative forms of tourism which include ecotourism and nature among others, and special interest tourism (SIT), examples of which are sport, education, business and so on (Spilanis & Vayianni, 2004). Alternative tourism refers to the method by which the trip is arranged – the travellers' degree of autonomy – and the tourists' motivation to learn about the destination and to use environmentally friendly products (Spilanis & Vayianni, 2004), while SIT forms of tourism describe the specific motives that instigate travelling.

In view of current tourism trends, NFT are thought to be key to fulfilling present demands and overcoming the challenges, as they promote the feel of the host area and an appreciation of its uniqueness (Bramwell, 2004). Mature destinations should expand their target markets and improve the quality of their present conventional product while looking at new processes for discovering NFT. This approach would address seasonality and dependency on a one-dimensional tourism product (Cuccia & Rizzo, 2011; Kozak & Martin, 2012; Rebollo, 2001). Destinations should focus on increasing their range of products, while concentrating on creating products that are appealing throughout the year (Andriotis, 2004b). Hence, from a strategic point of view, diversifying the product should improve the seasonal fluctuations of demand, which will essentially aid in improving the life of the locals at these Mediterranean destinations.

However, it is important to note that although NFT are thought to be more sustainable than the conventional mass form of tourism, this is not always the case. It is difficult to compare these forms of tourism due to the extensive mix of tourism forms that they embody. The need to fulfil tourism demands has forced destinations to diversify their mass tourism product (Bramwell, 2004; Chapman & Speake, 2011). For instance, the marketing strategy adopted in Malta focused on attracting 'quality tourists' and updating their product (Chapman & Speake, 2011). Attracting quality tourists required the extensive building of golf courses, marinas and other luxury infrastructure, and these actions had an impact on the residents, who were unhappy about the environmental damage that such development would cause. As Bramwell (2004) argues, amenities such as these can create many problems; golf courses, for instance, need a huge amount of water to be maintained, and can create issues of 'social exclusion'. On the other hand, the strategy for product diversification in the islands of Lesvos, Santorini and Samos in Greece was successful because the resultant small-scale conference centres have assisted tourism development (Spilanis & Vayianni, 2004). The plans were based on the restoration of old buildings, which has helped to retain the host community's traditional architecture (Spilanis & Vayianni, 2004).

It should be noted that NFT can be extremely diverse and can bring problems of their own. For example, cultural tourism in the city of Mdina in Malta has resulted in pressure on the community due to the number of visitors (Salanniemi, 2001). From this case it is apparent that cultural tourism might have more elements from conventional mass tourism in terms of its impact, rather than NFT which are thought more sustainable. The impact of tourism is determined by several factors, which include the number of tourists and the type of the travellers' encounters, in terms of the type of activities pursued and who manages them, such as tour operators, individual businesses and so on (Ayres, 2002). Therefore, sustainability has to be taken into account for all forms of tourism, and cultural or other types of tourism should not always be perceived as ethical, green and small scale (Ayres, 2002; Farsari et al., 2007).

Culture and eco-tourists, for instance, may demand luxury, specialised facilities and accommodation which are often situated near large resorts (Bramwell, 2004). The combination of tourism types is vast and includes small-scale NFT, mixed mass tourism and small-scale NFT, environmentally improved mass tourism, and so forth. Moreover, in many locations they may be blended still further, as the mixture or the individual use of the two types is based on the context of the area (Bramwell, 2004).

Mediterranean destinations should mix an appropriate combination of nature, sea, landscape, history and myth, thus enhancing their tourism products, services and overall tourism experience in order to improve their competitive position (Kozak et al., 2010; Rebollo, 2001). This blend will meet the current tourism demand for new cultural experiences and will provide the authenticity that visitors are looking for. An issue that still has to be considered is the matching of different products to the appropriate market segments, while taking into account the impact on sustainability that can arise from the new product mix (Bramwell, 2004; Farsari et al., 2007). Through its policies and regulations, the EU influences tourism activity in Europe, focusing on both economic and social development (Halkier, 2010). Therefore, the EU should be aware of the impact that these tourism forms could have on the destinations and should promote policies that encourage products which have been developed, taking into account all the factors that could influence their sustainability. Moreover, products that have an all-year-round appeal, as discussed below, should be promoted, thus addressing the seasonal nature of tourism and supporting the Lisbon strategy.

Special Interest Tourism: Key to Addressing Seasonality

SIT has been identified as key to overcoming the seasonal fluctuations of demand in sun-and-sea destinations, as special motives stimulate travel (Andriotis, 2005; Spilannis & Vayiannis, 2004). In other words, SIT is the hub around which the entire trip experience is arranged and developed (McKercher & Chan, 2005). To be specific, the principal reason for the trip is the special interest that a traveller has in a certain activity. This special interest is essentially what motivates the traveller to visit a specific destination, and all the activities that she or he will take part in will be linked with that special interest. For instance, Kim and Ritchie (2012), in their study on golfers' motivations when choosing a destination, found that accessibility and availability of the golf course as well as the facilities and services offered at the golf resort and course were the key factors; other tourist attractions, amenities, nightlife, cost and accessibility were the least considered. It is believed that special interest tourists seek rewarding, adventurous, enriching, learning experiences, as well as a sense of belonging (Douglas *et al.*, 2001; Hall & Weiller, 1992). In order to comprehend the tourist's behaviour and successfully target these niche markets, it is essential to identify the decision-making process of tourists within the SIT context (Spencer, 2010).

After an extensive review of leisure and tourism literature, Brotherton and Himmetoglou (1997, cited in Trauer, 2006: 187) proposed a 'tourism interest continuum' concept in order to better understand the decision-making processes of tourists. They suggest that the traveller will go through three phases: first, general interest tourism (GIT); second, mixed interest tourism (MIT); and third, special interest tourism (SIT). All these phases correspond to a question that the traveller will raise during the decision-making process. GIT refers to 'where would I like to go?'; during this phase the tourist does not essentially have particular requirements from the destination. MIT refers to 'where do I want to go and what activities can I pursue there?' – a phase where the activities are still not a principal aim for the trip, but rather a complimentary factor, as the tourist does have some demands regarding the pursuits that the place has to offer. Lastly, SIT asks 'what interest/activity do I want to pursue, and where can I do it?'. During this phase the activity becomes the principal purpose of the trip and the tourist has precise demands of the destination. Ultimately, the choice of destination will be determined on the pursuits provided and whether they will satisfy the demands of the tourist. Still, vacation choice is a multi-motivational decision-making process; therefore, MIT and SIT are interrelated (Trauer, 2006). Furthermore, Trauer (2006) suggests that in all three phases – GIT, MIT and SIT – a number of pursuits within the SIT, for example, sports, business and health, may occur.

From the above examination it is apparent that the diversification of the product mix through SIT could help to expand the tourism season (Andriotis, 2005; Garau-Vadell & Borja-Sole, 2008). This is also supported by Kastenholz and Lopes de Almeida (2008) who found that tourists visiting during the low season in Portugal are attracted to the nature of the area, along with the peace and quiet that exists, and the somewhat isolated and picturesque environment of the destination as well as the cultural aspects offered. In contrast, the summer tourists are more interested in the sun and nightlife, and mostly favour the coastal areas (Kastenholz & Lopes de Almeida, 2008). Hence, it could be suggested that low-season tourists prefer to explore a destination and look for unique experiences. Diversifying the narrow sun-and-sea product of the Mediterranean destinations and promoting special interest products (SIP) could entice tourists to visit during the off-peak season (Bartolome *et al.*, 2009).

Moreover, new demographic trends indicate an increase in mature travellers, in particular the over-65 market which has both purchasing power and leisure time (EC, 2010). Due to their increased leisure time and fewer commitments, mature travellers stay longer at destinations and have the ability to travel at any time of the year. Additionally, mature tourists prefer to engage in special interest activities, such as hiking, sports, and cultural entertainments including sampling local food and visiting museums (Littrell *et al.*, 2004). This population group offers a great opportunity for Mediterranean destinations to extend their season.

However, due to the diversity of the off-peak season market, in order to be successful, attention should be focused on attracting and serving particular segments of the market suitable to the destination, rather than on off-peak tourists in general (Spencer & Holecek, 2007). As Kozak and Martin (2012) point out, a destination must understand the needs and wants of its specific customers, and bespoke policies and strategies have to be developed. SIP are the focal point of the travel experience; therefore, provided that the product offered is directed at a suitable market, then tourists can be attracted to a destination throughout the year.

Conclusions

Tourism is an important sector within the EU, a sector that provides a number of economic opportunities and encourages job creation. However, the seasonal nature of tourism presents a challenge for the member states of Europe as well as the EU as a whole. The seasonal fluctuations in demand create a number of problems such as environmental damage, loss of profit during the off-peak season, and seasonal employment, among others.

This chapter explores the current trends in the tourism market, with a special focus on the Mediterranean region, where the tourism industry plays a vital part in the sustainability of the destination as a whole. Following the EU's initiatives to improve the life of its citizens through tourism by promoting diversification of tourist services and tackling its seasonal nature, it offers suggestions on how these two initiatives could be applied in the Mediterranean region where seasonality is extremely common.

This seasonality is mainly the result of dependency on the seasonal and narrow product that these sun-and-sea destinations have been promoting for many years. Although this product is a great advantage and assisted the destinations to develop economically, the extreme reliance on this sun-and-sea product is now detrimental to their sustainability. This is mainly due to both changing trends in the market and to the intense competition that they face from new and exotic destinations such as the Caribbean.

Following the current tourism trends, travellers are now more demanding, seeking new and unique products that will be more meaningful and will enhance their travel experiences. In particular, a shift has been observed of movement away from conventional forms of tourism towards NFT, where attention is paid to promoting the feel of the area and the uniqueness of the destination – in short, a trip that will give the tourist a new and distinct experience that no other destination will be able to provide. Moreover, fulfilling the special interest motives of tourists has been identified as essential to extending the tourism season. This is because SIP will attract the tourist at any time of the year, since the activity offered is the primary driver and the time of year and place are secondary. Nevertheless, due to the diversity of the low-season market, it is important to promote the right product to the appropriate market in order to be successful.

Additionally, due to the diversity of forms of tourism, tourism management organisations should be aware of the sustainability of their destinations when creating a new product mix. Misinterpretation and lack of knowledge regarding the sustainability concept could result in the flawed implementation of sustainable development plans, as seen in the cultural tourism development in Malta.

By creating a new product mix, focusing on SIP that could attract tourists with special motives, the tourism season in the Mediterranean could be extended and its products customised to fit current tourism trends. The new demographic trends that show an increase in the number of travelling over-65s also offer a great opportunity for these destinations to address seasonality in a sustainable way. By developing SIP, the EU could support its strategy for developing a more competitive and sustainable European tourism sector. Consequently, encouraging its member states through financial initiatives for SIP, offering resources to improve the knowledge of tourism organisations with regard to new tourism trends, and increasing their awareness of sustainable development could be valuable to address seasonality. Improving seasonal fluctuations of demand is thought to be vital to economic growth and increased employment opportunities in the destinations as well as in the EU as a whole.

Notes

(1) In particular, travel agencies, hotels, car rentals, catering businesses, tourist attractions, and so on.
(2) Specifically construction, transport businesses, retailing, services, and so on.

References

Adamou, A. (2009) Δεδομένη η μείωση των αδειών για ξένους εργάτες [Significant decline in working licences for foreign workers]. Politis 31 March, 15.
Aguiló, E., Alegre, J. and Sard, M. (2005) The persistence of the sun and sand tourism model. *Tourism Management* 26 (2), 219–231.
Andriotis, K. (2004a) Problems of island tourism development: The Greek insular regions. In B. Bramwell (ed.) *Coastal Mass Tourism: Diversification and Sustainable Development in Southern Europe* (pp. 114–132). Clevedon: Channel View Publications.
Andriotis, K. (2004b) European Union influence over tourism employment. *Tourism – An International Interdisciplinary Journal* 52 (3), 277–284.
Andriotis, K. (2005) Seasonality in Crete: Problem or way of life? *Tourism Economics* 11 (2), 207–224.
Andriotis, K. (2006) Researching the development gap between the hinterland and the coast – evidence from the island of Crete. *Tourism Management* 27 (4), 629–639.
Andriotis, K. and Vaughan, D.R. (2004) The tourism workforce and policy: Exploring the assumptions using Crete as the case study. *Current Issues in Tourism* 7 (1), 66–87.
Apostolopoulos, Y. and Gayle, D.J. (eds) (2002) *Island Tourism and Sustainable Development: Caribbean, Pacific and Mediterranean Experiences*. Westport, CT: Praeger Publishers.
Apostolopoulos, Y., Loukissas, P. and Leontidou, L. (2001) Tourism development, and change in the Mediterranean. In Y. Apostolopoulos, P. Loukissas and L. Leontidou (eds) *Mediterranean Tourism: Facets of Socioeconomic and Cultural Change* (pp. 3–13). London and New York: Routledge.
Ayres, R. (2002) Cultural tourism in small-island states: Contradictions and ambiguities. In Y. Apostolopoulos and D.J. Gayle (eds) *Island Tourism and Sustainable Development: Caribbean, Pacific and Mediterranean Experiences* (pp. 145–160). Westport, CT: Praeger Publishers.
Bartolome, A., Ramos, V. and Rey-Maquieira, J. (2009) Residents' attitude towards diversification sports tourism in the Balearics. *Tourism Recreation Research* 34 (1), 55–65.
Blažević, B. and Alkier Radnić, R (2006) EU tourism trends and the outlook for Croatia. *Tourism and Hospitality Management* 12 (2), 83–92.
Boo, S. and Jones, D.L. (2009) Using a validation process to develop market segmentation based on travel motivation for major metropolitan areas. *Journal of Travel and Tourism Marketing* 26 (1), 60–79.

Bramwell, B. (2004) Mass tourism, diversification and sustainability in southern Europe's coastal regions. In B. Bramwell (ed.) *Coastal Mass Tourism: Diversification and Sustainable Development in Southern Europe* (pp. 1–31). Clevedon: Channel View Publications.

Chapman, A. and Speake, J. (2011) Regeneration in a mass-tourism resort: The changing fortunes of Bugibba, Malta. *Tourism Management* 32 (3), 482–491.

Claver-Cortés, E., Molina-Azorín, J.F. and Pereira-Moliner, J. (2007) Competitiveness in mass tourism. *Annals of Tourism Research* 34 (3), 727–745.

Cuccia, T. and Rizzo, I. (2011) Tourism seasonality in cultural destinations: Empirical evidence from Sicily. *Tourism Management* 32 (2), 589–595.

CTO (2010) *Tourist Arrivals 2010.* Lefkosia: Cyprus Tourism Organisation, accessed 12 February 2012. http://www.visitcyprus.biz.

Douglas, N., Douglas, N. and Derret, R. (2001) *Special Interest Tourism.* Milton: John Wiley & Sons Australia.

EC (2010) *Commission Communication 2010: Europe, the World's No 1 Tourist Destination – A New Political Framework for Tourism in Europe.* Brussels: European Commission, accessed 10 February 2012. http://ec.europa.eu/enterprise/sectors/tourism/files/communications/communication2010_en.pdf.

ETC (2006) *Tourism Trends for Europe.* Brussels: European Travel Commission, accessed 20 February 2012. http://www.etc-corporate.org/images/library/ETC_Tourism_ Trends_for_Europe_09-2006_ENG.pdf.

Europa (2009) *Treaty of Lisbon: Policies for a Better Life.* Brussels: European Union, accessed 12 February 2012. http://europa.eu/lisbon_treaty/glance/better_life/index_en. htm.

Falzon, J. (2012) The price competitive position of Mediterranean countries in tourism: Evidence from the Thomson brochure. *Tourism Management* 33 (5), 1080–1092.

Farsari, Y., Butler, R. and Prastacos, P. (2007) Sustainable tourism policy for Mediterranean destinations: Issues and interrelationships. *International Journal of Tourism Policy* 1 (1), 58–78.

Garau-Vadell, J.B. and de Borja-Solé, L. (2008) Golf in mass tourism destinations facing seasonality: A longitudinal study. *Tourism Review* 63 (2), 16–24.

Goeldner, C.R. and Ritchie, J.R.B. (2009) *Tourism: Principles, Practices, Philosophies* (11th edn). Hoboken, NJ: John Wiley & Sons.

Halkier, H. (2010) EU and tourism development: Bark or bite? *Scandinavian Journal of Hospitality Management and Tourism* 10 (2), 92–106.

Hall, C.M. and Weiler, B. (1992) What's special about special interest tourism? In B. Weiler and C.M. Hall (eds) *Special Interest Tourism* (pp. 1–14). London: Belhaven Press.

Holloway, J.C. (2006) *The Business of Tourism* (7th edn). Harlow: Pearson Education.

Ioannides, D. (2002) Tourism development in Mediterranean islands: Opportunities and constraints. In Y. Apostolopoulos and D.J. Gayle (eds) *Island Tourism and Sustainable Development: Caribbean, Pacific and Mediterranean Experiences* (pp. 67–89). Westport, CT: Praeger Publishers.

Ioannides, D., Apostolopoulos, Y. and Sonmez, G. (2001) Searching for sustainable tourism development in the insular Mediterranean. In D. Ioannides, Y. Apostolopoulos and G. Sonmez (eds) *Mediterranean Islands and Sustainable Development: Practices, Management and Policies* (pp. 3–22). London: Continuum.

Juganaru, M., Juganaru, I. and Anghel, A. (2008) European institutions initiatives regarding the development of sustainable tourism. *International Business and European Integration* I (V), 356–360.

Kastenholz, E. and Lopes de Almeida, A. (2008) Seasonality in rural tourism – the case of North Portugal. *Tourism Review* 63 (2), 5–15.

Kim, J.H. and Ritchie, B.W. (2012) Motivation-based typology: An empirical study of golf tourists. *Journal of Hospitality and Tourism Research* 36 (2), 251–280.

Koenig-Lewis, N. and Bischoff, E.E. (2005) Seasonality research: The state of art. *International Journal of Tourism Research* 7 (4/5), 201–219.

Koenig-Lewis, N. and Bischoff, E.E. (2010) Developing effective strategies for tackling seasonality in the tourism industry. *Tourism and Hospitality Planning & Development* 7 (4), 395–413.

Kozak, M. and Martin, D. (2012) Tourism lifecycle and sustainability analysis: Profit-focused strategies for mature destinations. *Tourism Management* 33 (1), 188–194.

Kozak, M., Baloğlu, S. and Bahar, O. (2010) Measuring destination competitiveness: Multiple destinations versus multiple nationalities. *Journal of Hospitality Marketing and Management* 19 (1), 56–71.

Lacher, R.G. and Oh, C.O. (2012) Is tourism a low-income industry? Evidence from three coastal regions. *Journal of Travel Research* 51 (4), 464–472.

Littrell, M., Paige, R.C. and Song, K. (2004) Senior travellers: Tourism activities and shopping behaviours. *Journal of Vacation Marketing* 10 (4), 348–362.

McElroy, J.L. (2003) Tourism development in small islands across the world. *Geografiska Annaler Series B: Human Geography* 85 (4), 231–242.

McKercher, B. and Chan, A. (2005) How special is special interest tourism? *Journal of Travel Research* 44 (1), 21–31.

Oreja Rodríguez, J.R., Parra-López, E. and Yanes-Estévez, V. (2008) The sustainability of island destinations: Tourism area life cycle and teleological perspectives. The case of Tenerife. *Tourism Management* 29 (1), 53–65.

Rebollo, J.V. (2001) Increasing the value of natural and cultural resources: Towards sustainable tourism management. In D. Ioannides, Y. Apostolopoulos and G. Sonmez (eds) *Mediterranean Islands and Sustainable Development: Practices, Management and Policies* (pp. 47–68). London: Continuum.

Salanniemi, T. (2001) Trapped by image: The implications of cultural tourism in the insular Mediterranean. In D. Ioannides, Y. Apostolopoulos and G. Sonmez (eds) *Mediterranean Islands and Sustainable Development: Practices, Management and Policies* (pp. 108–123). London: Continuum.

Sharpley, R. (2004) Tourism, modernisation and development on the island of Cyprus: Challenges and policy responses. In B. Bramwell (ed.) *Coastal Mass Tourism: Diversification and Sustainable Development in Southern Europe* (pp. 321–340). Clevedon: Channel View Publications.

Spencer, D.M. (2010) Segmenting special interest visitors to a destination region based on the volume of their expenditures: An application to rail-trail users. *Journal of Vacation Marketing* 16 (2), 83–95.

Spencer, D.M. and Holecek, D.F. (2007) Basic characteristics of the fall tourism market. *Tourism Management* 28 (2), 491–504.

Spilanis, I. and Vayanni, H. (2004) Sustainable tourism: Utopia or necessity? The role of new forms of tourism in the Aegean islands. In B. Bramwell (ed.) *Coastal Mass Tourism: Diversification and Sustainable Development in Southern Europe* (pp. 269–291). Clevedon: Channel View Publications.

Trauer, B. (2006) Conceptualizing special interest tourism-frameworks for analysis. *Tourism Management* 27 (2), 183–200.

UNEP (2005) *Dossier on Tourism and Sustainable Development in the Mediterranean.* Athens: United Nations Environment Programme.

UNWTO (2011a) *UNWTO Tourism Highlights.* Madrid: World Tourism Organisation, accessed 10 February 2012). http://mkt.unwto.org/sites/all/files/docpdf/unwtohighlights11enhr_1.pdf.

UNWTO (2011b) *European Tourism Grows Above Expectations*. Madrid: World Tourism Organisation, accessed 17 February 2012. http://media.unwto.org/en/press-release/2011-11-08/european-tourism-grows-above-expectations.

Valle, P, Guerreiro, M., Mendes, J. and Silva, J.A. (2011) The cultural offer as a tourist product in coastal destinations: The case of Algarve, Portugal. *Tourism and Hospitality Research* 11 (4), 233–247.

WTTC (2011a) *Travel and Tourism Economic Impact: Malta*. London: World Travel and Tourism Council, accessed 17 February 2012. http://www.wttc.org/site_media/uploads/downloads/malta.pdf.

WTTC (2011b) *Travel and Tourism Economic Impact: Spain*. London: World Travel and Tourism Council, accessed 17 February 2012. http://www.wttc.org/site_media/uploads/downloads/spain.pdf.

5 Cross-border Cooperation and Tourism in Europe

Dallen J. Timothy and Jarkko Saarinen

Introduction

One of the most widespread manifestations of globalisation today is supranationalism, or regional cross-border cooperation and the transfer of some powers by member states to multinational alliances, primarily in the area of economic development. Most countries today belong to some sort of supranational coalition, which includes trading blocs, free trade areas, customs unions and economic alliances. Dozens of these alliances exist in all parts of the world and take on many forms, some being more politically integrated than others. Among the most incorporated are the European Union (EU), the South Asian Association for Regional Co-operation (SAARC) and the Association of Southeast Asian Nations (ASEAN). While all of these associations have underlying political and social aims, their primary purpose is economic development and cross-border trade.

Most of these intergovernmental organisations are authorised by member states to enact policies that affect the entire alliance. Many regional strategies affect tourism directly or indirectly, most notably in the areas of environmental protection, cross-border trade in goods and services, cross-border movement of tourists and human resources, common currencies and passports, reductions in tariffs and duties, supranational funding for development, and the establishment of planning principles (Blatter, 2004; Church & Reid, 1999; Turnock, 2002).

This chapter examines the notion of supranational and cross-border cooperation in the context of tourism. It approaches cross-border initiatives in the EU, the structural funds and programmes that promote tourism growth and development, and emphasises the importance of scale in how cross-border collaborative efforts play out in tourism.

Cross-border Cooperation

For most of modern history, international frontiers have not only demarcated lines of sovereign territory, but have also functioned to limit contact and cooperation between states and peoples. Their role as barriers to trade and human movement has been a hallmark of post-medieval territoriality and one of the most simultaneously intriguing and frustrating elements of international travel (Prokkola, 2010; Timothy, 2001). To protect domestic production and in many cases reduce contact with the outside world, borders were used as filters or impediments to commerce, trade and travel. Most countries tried to be as self-sufficient as possible, producing as much as they could for domestic consumption.

The devastation wreaked by World War II began to change the views of many nations, however. In the face of significant socio-economic destruction and need for deeper political cooperation and stability, several countries of Europe began to consider the idea that partnering with their neighbours might be fruitful. Post-war, anti-isolationist perspectives suggested that the production and consumption of goods and services could be expanded, and thereby economies healed, by opening their borders to increased trade. The primary notion behind this relates to economies of scale, where the cost of merchandise is reduced by increasing production. In small countries, it made little economic sense to try to produce all that was needed for domestic consumption. Cross-border partnerships were thus seen as a way of expanding supply and demand, as each collaborating country could specialise in what it produced most efficiently and abundantly.

Belgium and Luxembourg were the forerunners of this idea, with their 1921 Belgium–Luxembourg Economic Union, which lifted many economic barriers and aligned their two currencies on a par. After World War II, Belgium, Luxembourg and The Netherlands signed the Benelux Agreement in 1944, establishing a customs union, which abolished customs duties within the coalition and instituted common external import tariffs. As word spread, Italy, France and West Germany joined in the early 1950s to form the European Coal and Steel Community. From this grew the European Economic Community, which eventually became the European Union in 1993. Following Europe's example, many supranationalist coalitions have been formed all over the world, but none of them has advanced as far as the EU in their degree of political and economic integration.

Scale is crucial in understanding cross-border cooperation, especially in Europe. There are at least four different scales of trans-frontier collaboration: global organisations, regional alliances, bilateral networks and inter-local cooperation (Timothy & Teye, 2004). At the largest scale are organisations that have a multiplicity of member countries throughout the world. Good examples of this include the United Nations (UN), the World Trade Organisation and the Organisation for Economic Cooperation and Development.

The EU is an illustration of the second scale – regional alliances. These are usually more geographically bounded and cohesive, and typically involve three or more countries. They are variously known as trade alliances, customs unions, economic communities or free trade areas, although the mandates of many go beyond economics to include political and social dimensions. The Council of Europe is another example at a slightly larger scale (47 member states) than the EU (28 members).

The third level of cross-border cooperation includes bilateral arrangements, such as the Belgium–Luxembourg Economic Union mentioned earlier. Some of Europe's smallest countries (e.g. San Marino, Vatican City, Liechtenstein and Monaco) have important customs and trade treaties with their largest neighbours. Italy takes care of many international trade arrangements on behalf of San Marino and the Vatican City (Holy See), just as France does for Monaco and Switzerland for Liechtenstein.

Inter-local cooperation refers to small regions or areas of countries reaching across political frontiers to work with adjacent areas or communities on the other side. Euroregions are probably the best example of this. These are relatively small, trans-frontier regions where public agencies and private associations work together to address common social, economic and technical issues in borderlands. They began to appear in the 1950s but have gained momentum during the 1990s and 2000s as more cross-border areas realise they have common socio-economic and environmental concerns that can be addressed more holistically via collaboration from both sides of the boundary. At an even smaller scale are urban areas or natural zones divided by international borders which could function as intact entities if they were permitted to do so without the presence of a border. There are many examples of bisected towns working together to promote a shared socio-economic space within the limitations of national sovereignty. Tornio and Haparanda on the border of Finland and Sweden function as a cohesive community, as do Geneva, Switzerland, and its suburbs in France.

Cross-border Cooperation: Implications for European Tourism

Each one of these scales of trans-boundary networks has salient implications for tourism. The sections that follow elaborate in more depth on some of the most salient manifestations of cross-border collaboration at varying scales.

Global alliances

At the grandest scale, almost every country in Europe belongs to the UN. The only exception is Vatican City (Holy See). Kosovo, which is only recognised as an independent nation by 103 countries, is also not a member. While the UN itself does relatively little directly in terms of tourism, it is the parent organisation of the World Tourism Organisation and UNESCO. Aside from Liechtenstein, every country in Europe has ratified the UNESCO World Heritage Convention, and most countries, except Monaco and Liechtenstein, have heritage properties inscribed on the World Heritage List. While World Heritage status does not automatically translate into increased tourist arrivals, it has been shown to be an important global marketing and branding mechanism for heritage sites around Europe.

The notion of cross-border cooperation is particularly relevant for World Heritage Sites in Europe. Sixteen UNESCO sites straddle international boundaries in Europe. Some are relatively small, although others include large areas that are linked across frontiers by their shared cultural features or ecosystems. The historic belfries of northern France and southern Belgium are an example of a common cultural feature recognised by UNESCO that sits astride an international boundary. Monte San Giorgio, which is bisected by the Switzerland–Italy border is home to some of the best marine fossils from the Triassic Period.

Regional supranationalism

At the regional level, the EU and the Council of Europe are important organisations for tourism. The Council of Europe's main objectives include cultural cooperation, heritage development, enhancing human rights, and democratic development. One particularly interesting Council project is the Europe Cultural Routes programme. This began in 1987 to illustrate how the varied heritages of European countries can be linked together to form a common pan-European cultural heritage. In 1998, the Council established the European Institute of Cultural Routes to oversee the programme, and today there are 29 long-distance cultural routes traversing many European countries, based on common themes. The Viking Routes, the Jewish Heritage Routes and the Santiago de Compostela Pilgrim Routes are three illustrative examples. The aim of the Cultural Routes undertaking is to:

- raise awareness of a European cultural identity rooted in shared values by means of cultural routes that link developments, which have moulded European cultures and identities;
- encourage intercultural dialogue through a better understanding of European history;
- protect the cultural and natural past as a way of improving quality of life and socio-cultural and economic development;
- provide opportunities for the development of heritage tourism and enhance tourism's role in sustainable development (European Institute of Cultural Routes, 2010).

Equivalent to the Cultural Routes programme is the European Commission's programme on the European City of Culture. It was initiated in 1985 (and revised in 2005) by the Resolution of the European Cultural Ministers (EUR-Lex, 2010). The City of Culture programme aims to:

- highlight the richness and diversity of European cultures;
- celebrate the cultural ties that link Europeans together;
- bring people from different European countries into contact with each other's culture and promote mutual understanding;
- foster a feeling of European citizenship (EC, 2010).

The role of tourism is clearly emphasised in the programme outcomes. According to the Commission, the programme regenerates participant cities, vitalises their cultural life and raises the international profile and boosts tourism in 'the cities of culture' (EC, 2010).

The EU is a major supporter of tourism, and many of its policies have been influential in the development of tourism projects in the most peripheral areas of Europe. The EU's Structural Funds are monies set aside to help some of the alliance's poorest regions by reducing regional economic disparities and enhancing economic development and employment opportunities. Through its European Regional Development Fund (RDF), the EU encourages inter-regional cooperation and cross-boundary economic and social development initiatives (Faby, 2006). Financed through the RDF, one of the most celebrated initiatives is the Interreg programme, which motivates collaboration between EU member states. One of its primary goals is to bring down the real and perceived borders between member states and to put neighbouring economies on a more even playing field (Interreg, 2010). Much of Interreg's focus in recent years has been on transnational cooperation in peripheral regions that share borders with the EU. Tourism has played a prominent role in the programme's directives and grants to encourage entrepreneurialism, coastal development, labour market skills building, cultural development and human capital growth.

There are many other ways in which regionalism in Europe has a bearing on tourism. The EU's Economic and Monetary Union is a coalition of member states that have elected to adopt the euro as their national currency. Not all EU members have adopted the euro (e.g. Denmark, Sweden, United Kingdom), although some of the newer members, such as Estonia, will join the Monetary Union in the near future. Tourists can now travel through 16 of the EU's 28 members without having to exchange currencies, and tour operators can essentially do all their accounting in a single currency.

The various treaties associated with the intra-EU customs union have eliminated essentially all trade tariffs and other economic barriers between member countries, with the exception of some alcohol-related regulations still in place. With the demise of inner-EU customs duties, most goods now circulate across borders freely, and there are fewer structural barriers to other forms of commerce, including most services.

The EU also deals with the movement of Europeans and non-Europeans across intra-regional borders. A common passport is used by all EU member states, with each country issuing its own documents with similar characteristics; citizens of member states are also citizens of the union, which grants many rights for EU citizens to work, reside and study, unfettered by work permits and student visas.

The 1985 Schengen Agreement brought down the borders of most EU member states; Ireland and the United Kingdom have opted not to ratify the Schengen treaty, and a few of the newest EU members (i.e. Romania, Bulgaria and Cyprus) are not yet part of the Schengen area. Additionally, Iceland, Norway and Switzerland, while not members of the EU, have joined the Schengen Accord and have therefore eliminated passport and immigration regulations for people traveling to and from other Schengen states. Liechtenstein is currently considering its options but is expected to join Schengen in the near future. The Schengen Area issues a single visa, which any signatory state can distribute through its embassies abroad; it is valid throughout the entire Schengen area. In short, most travel within the EU and between the EU and members of the European Free Trade Association (Norway, Iceland, Switzerland and Liechtenstein) is unhindered by border checkpoints and passport controls, thereby creating a freer flow of people, goods and services across national boundaries.

Bilateral scale

There are numerous examples in Europe of bilateral, and sometimes trilateral, collaboration in various aspects of tourism. The most common cross-national linkages, however, are in the area of tourism marketing (Ioannides et al., 2006; Tosun et al., 2005). As suggested earlier, the European microstates are inevitably connected socially, economically and politically to some degree to their larger neighbours through bilateral agreements. Diplomacy and national security are good examples, as in most cases the smallest microstates are unable to station diplomats abroad. While Liechtenstein has an embassy in the United States (since 2002), it does not have diplomatic representation in most other countries; usually the Swiss embassies care for the principality's wellbeing. Although San Marino has an embassy in Italy, and Monaco has one in Argentina, it is uncommon. Italy almost always represents San Marino's consular affairs abroad, as does France for Monaco.

In the area of tourism specifically, each microstate has its own national tourism organisation, but they rely a great deal on the economies of scale that their larger neighbours have to disseminate tourist information. Likewise, many online booking services do not distinguish between the small countries and their larger neighbours. In the case of Monaco, most travel websites consider it to be simply an appendage of France. As for visas and entry formalities, only Andorra has its own customs and immigration services; the other small countries' border regulations are enforced in combination with those of their partner states.

Ireland and Northern Ireland (UK) provide another example of binational collaboration. While Northern Ireland and Ireland are separated by an international boundary, it has become quite invisible in the landscape compared to how it used to be during the island's political 'troubles'. Today, not only is the line almost invisible, but both Irish entities work closely together to market the entire island as a single destination (Greer, 2002). Joint promotional materials are printed, including borderless road maps, and both polities attend international travel trade shows as destination Ireland.

Inter-local scale

Inter-local cooperation across international boundaries is now commonplace in Europe. This is especially true in areas where cultural and natural resources lie adjacent to, or overlap, political borders. While municipalities and regions have no control over matters of sovereignty and cannot officially enter into binding international agreements, there are many ways of approaching this sensitive issue in an informal manner. Cities, towns, villages and rural areas intersected by borders have been creative in their efforts to work at the grassroots level. In most cases, these low-level cooperative efforts result in jointly sponsored events, festivals or specific attractions.

The twin towns of Valga, Estonia and Valka, Latvia, which comprise one village in two countries, have worked out in considerable detail local agreements on fire services, health care and infrastructure development. Likewise, residents of both towns can use sports facilities and libraries on either side. There is currently a cross-border bus line, and plans are under way to work together to develop a joint Valka–Valga tourist office/visitor centre, and to restore some old military foxholes as a war heritage attraction to benefit both communities.

Another example is the Haparanda–Tornio (Sweden–Finland) area, which is part of the Tornio Valley Euroregion. As already noted, these twin towns have been functioning as one city in two countries for many years. Haparanda (Sweden) has long been an important shopping destination for Finns who live near the border. While the major economic differences between the countries have disappeared, the shopping has transformed towards a leisure and pleasure-oriented activity rather than essential shopping for staple foodstuffs (Prokkola, 2007). Today the two towns have reciprocal agreements for school attendance, fire brigades and various public services, for example. They share a joint tourist information office (on the Finland side of the boundary), and there are grand plans to develop a large recreational facility directly on the borderline (over a branch of the Tornio

River) with shops and other leisure services. The master plan is supposed to be implemented incrementally over the next several years. The first phase has already been completed with a large IKEA store having been built in 2006 just 200 metres inside Sweden, and a large shopping centre just 30 metres inside Finland by the name of *Rajalla-På Gränsen* ('on the border' in Finnish and Swedish). In addition, extra pedestrian and traffic lanes have been constructed over the small border inlet of the Tornio River. The master plan calls for the eventual connection of IKEA and *Rajalla-På Gränsen* by constructing the recreation and shopping complex over the border between them. Besides the joint tourism office and the current phase of the border development project, the communities' truly international border attraction is the binational golf course, the Green Zone, which lies astride the border. The boundary line zigzags between holes and greens, requiring players to cross the international border and a time zone several times in the course of a single game.

Euroregions have evolved to help improve stagnating economies in peripheral areas, to provide opportunities for public officials and grassroots populations on both sides of a border to cooperate in areas that will mutually benefit both sides and improve the standard of living (Yoder, 2003; Zimmermann, 2001). There is no single authority that designates or maintains Euroregions. Rather, they are voluntary relationships created by local or regional initiatives and therefore have no political power or legislative authority, although the Association of European Border Regions acts as a point of contact for each of the regions and helps set pan-European standards for Euroregion development. At present there are 74 Euroregions, and the Council of Europe is working to establish more in areas where natural and cultural resources in island and coastal areas need to be managed more holistically (Ioannides, 2006). Many of the EU's borderlands are included in some type of Euroregion. Some of these cross-border areas involve several countries rather than just two; nonetheless, they are an example of grassroots efforts to try to solve common problems locally by the stakeholders most impacted by them.

Euroregions have been quite successful in their funding efforts through Interreg and other EU programmes, as well as support from the Council of Europe. Tourism is a major player in these cross-border regional efforts for several reasons. First, borderlands are almost always viewed as marginal spaces with little social or economic value to state machines. Therefore, many national governments have traditionally ignored peripheral border areas in favour of national cores and large population centres. Tourism is now seen as a tool for diversifying the overlooked economies of peripheral regions. Second, because of their peripherality, borderlands are often physically underdeveloped and therefore have considerable potential for tourism as their natural and cultural resources are more pristine than those located elsewhere in the country. Third, many state borders divide peoples of the same cultural background or ethnicity. Cultural groups working together in contiguous regions are able to provide a broader heritage tourism foundation, and can also help each other preserve their traditions and cultural patrimony in more integrated ways.

One final perspective on inter-local efforts is the establishment of trans-frontier nature preserves and parks. Peace parks, trans-boundary nature preserves and international parks refer to conservation areas, or in some cases purposefully planned and developed parklands or botanical gardens, which overlap national boundaries. The primary concept behind international parks and nature preserves is that nature does not respect human-imposed boundaries, and ecosystems should be managed holistically without the disruption of political barriers (Timothy, 1999). Purpose-built peace parks are developed on a much more local level and usually commemorate peaceful relations between neighbours. Europe is home to many trans-frontier parks and protected areas (Timothy, 2000; Turnock, 2001).

The European Monument, a very small park (approximately 6000 square metre) near Ouren, Belgium, was created bestride the Luxembourg–Belgium border and very near the tripoint with Germany, to commemorate European integration. It is a popular walking and picnicking venue for local recreationists, and tourists stop by in conjunction with visits to the tripoint and areas nearby in Germany, Belgium and Luxembourg.

The Tatra Mountains are protected as an international park comprised of Tatrzanski National Park (Poland) and Tatranský National Park (Slovakia). An important natural area astride the Finnish–Russian border is Oulanka National Park (Finland) and Paanajärvi National Park (Russia), and the body of water where Albania, Greece and Macedonia meet is known as Prespa Lake National Park, Prespes National Park and Galicica National Park, respectively. A host of other countries in Europe share natural ecosystems and protect them via adjoining national parks and nature preserves, where efforts are made to coordinate conservation and visitor management.

Conclusions

Because many countries of Europe have devolved some of their sovereignty in favour of supranationalist organisations and alliances, such as the EU and the Council of Europe, legal mechanisms have been created by which various levels of cross-border cooperation have been able to thrive. Transfrontier collaboration occurs at many levels, from global alliances to village-to-village links in planning special events or protecting features of a natural environment. Each scale of international network is crucial in the success of tourism and in the sustainable use of natural and cultural resources.

Today cross-border cooperation is one of the main ideas in EU regional policies. In spite of its potential benefits, however, cross-border cooperation is not without challenges. Despite borders being torn down literally and figuratively, boundaries still exist in the minds of many politicians, community members and other stakeholders. The utilisation and practices of the EU Structural Funds, for example, are affected by the EU's internal borders and also by the internal administrative borders of individual member states. And because sovereignty still rests with each individual nation state, true deep integration has not yet become a reality anywhere in Europe from a tourism perspective. Similarly, national laws and policies still slow the progress of many binational, multinational or inter-local endeavours. International parks that encompass a single ecosystem but are managed differently on opposite sides of a frontier because of varying environmental regulatory frameworks are a good example. Besides a lack of political will and legal limitations, there are many financial constraints, not least of which is the current global economic crisis (2007–2013), which prevent many programmes and projects from being conceived and implemented. Many observers see these and other cultural, social, political and economic constraints as being formidable barriers to the goals and practices of trans-boundary collaboration. As long as people realise the benefits of working across state boundaries to create common solutions to common problems, however, they will find creative ways to overcome the challenges before them.

References

Blatter, J. (2004) 'From spaces of place' to 'Spaces of flows'? Territorial and functional governance in cross-border regions in Europe and North America. *International Journal of Urban and Regional Research* 28 (3), 530–548.

Church, A. and Reid, P. (1999) Cross-border co-operation, institutionalization and political space across the English Channel. *Regional Studies* 33 (7), 643–655.

EC (2010) *European Capitals of Culture*. Brussels: European Commission, Culture, accessed 13 August 2010. http://ec.europa.eu/culture/our-programmes-and-actions/capitals/european-capitals-of-culture_en.htm.

EUR-Lex (2010) *Resolution of the Ministers Responsible for Cultural Affairs, Meeting Within the Council of 13 June 1985 Concerning the Annual Event 'European City of Culture'* (85/C 153/02). Luxembourg: EUR-Lex, accessed 13 August 2010. http://eur-lex.europa.eu/en/index.htm.

European Institute of Cultural Routes (2010) *Cultural Routes and Landscapes, a Common Heritage of Europe*. Luxembourg: Program of Cultural Routes of the Council of Europe, accessed 1 August 2010. http://www.culture-routes.lu/php/fo_index.php?lng=en.

Faby, H. (2006) Tourism policy tools applied by the European Union to support cross-border tourism. In H. Wachowiak (ed.) *Tourism and Borders: Contemporary Issues, Policies and International Research* (pp. 19–30). Aldershot: Ashgate.

Greer, J. (2002) Developing trans-jurisdictional tourism partnerships – insights from the island of Ireland. *Tourism Management* 23 (4), 355–366.

Interreg (2010) *Interreg IVC*, accessed 20 July 2010. http://www.interreg4c.eu/.

Ioannides, D. (2006) Interregional co-operation between Europe's island regions: A case study of the GEDERI Project. In H. Wachowiak (ed.) *Tourism and Borders: Contemporary Issues, Policies and International Research* (pp. 31–45). Aldershot: Ashgate.

Ioannides, D., Nielsen, P. and Billing, P. (2006) Transboundary collaboration in tourism: The case of the Bothian Arc. *Tourism Geographies* 8 (2), 122–142.

Prokkola, E.-K. (2007) Cross-border regionalization and tourism development at the Swedish–Finnish border: 'Destination Arctic Circle'. *Scandinavian Journal of Hospitality and Tourism* 7 (2), 120–138.

Prokkola, E.-K. (2010) Borders in tourism: The transformation of the Swedish–Finnish border landscape. *Current Issues in Tourism* 13 (3), 223–238.

Timothy, D.J. (1999) Cross-border partnership in tourism resource management: International parks along the US–Canada border. *Journal of Sustainable Tourism* 7 (3/4), 182–205.

Timothy, D.J. (2000) Tourism and international parks. In R.W. Butler and S.W. Boyd (eds) *Tourism and National Parks: Issues and Implications* (pp. 263–282). Chichester: Wiley.

Timothy, D.J. (2001) *Tourism and Political Boundaries*. London: Routledge.

Timothy, D.J. and Teye, V.B. (2004) Political boundaries and regional cooperation in tourism. In A.A. Lew, C.M. Hall and A.M. Williams (eds) *A Companion to Tourism* (pp. 584–595). London: Blackwell.

Tosun, C., Timothy, D.J., Parpairis, A. and McDonald, D. (2005) Cross-border cooperation in tourism marketing growth strategies. *Journal of Travel and Tourism Marketing* 18 (1), 5–23.

Turnock, D. (2001) Cross-border conservation in East Central Europe: The Danube-Carpathian complex and the contribution of the World Wide Fund for Nature. *GeoJournal* 55, 655–681.

Turnock, D. (2002) Cross-border cooperation: A major element in regional policy in East Central Europe. *Scottish Geographical Journal* 118 (1), 19–40.

Yoder, J.A. (2003) Bridging the European Union and Eastern Europe: Cross-border cooperation and the Euroregions. *Regional and Federal Studies* 13 (3), 90–106.

Zimmermann, F.M. (2001) European Union cross-border cooperation: A new tourism dimension. In V.L. Smith and M. Brent (eds) *Hosts and Guests Revisited: Tourism Issues of the 21st Century* (pp. 323–330). New York: Cognizant.

Part 2

Actors and Structures

6 Destination Management Organisational Structures

Thanasis Spyriadis, John Fletcher and Alan Fyall

Introduction

Destinations are widely regarded as complex phenomena to manage (Howie, 2003). Therefore, it is essential that, in the fiercely competitive environment of tourism, a destination excels in its ability to maintain all dimensions of sustainability (environmental, economic, social, cultural and political) if it is to successfully develop and preserve its competitiveness in the marketplace. Moreover, satisfying (or even better exceeding) visitor expectations by providing quality products and services can improve the profitability of the local tourism businesses, which are fundamentally the lifeblood of any destination's visitor economy. With this in mind, the role of destination management organisations (DMOs) is critical as they are organisations from both the public and the private sectors, which have vested interests in all aspects of society affecting and being affected by tourism (Carter & Fabricius, 2006; Michael, 2007). The purpose of this chapter is to explore the rationale for and key strategic objectives of DMOs. In so doing it will explore the different levels of destinations, structural organisational types and the extent to which the focus is on the management or marketing of destinations and the roles, tasks and responsibilities of those responsible for the future competitiveness of destinations.

Managing Destinations

Defining destinations

Defining a destination seems to necessitate a multifaceted approach. A destination can be argued to be a 'purpose built area' at which visitors temporally base themselves to participate in 'tourism related activities' (Pike, 2004). The United Nations World Tourism Organization (UNWTO) (2002, cited in Lew & McKercher, 2006: 405) meanwhile provide a more explicit and detailed definition that describes a destination as:

> a physical space that includes tourism products such as support services and attractions, and tourism resources. It has physical and administrative boundaries defining its management, and images and perceptions defining its market competitiveness. Local destinations incorporate various stakeholders, often including a host community, and can nest and network to form larger destinations. They are the focal point in the delivery of tourism products and the implementation of tourism policy.

The notion of destination can relate to various spatial or geographical levels, which means that the term destination may relate to: a whole country (i.e. Greece or Spain); a region (i.e. the Lake District or the Alps); an island (i.e. Crete or Bali); a village, town or city; or even a self-contained centre (i.e. a cruise ship or Disneyland) (WTO, 2007). For the purpose of this chapter, it is useful to highlight the fact that destinations are places with a unique composition of their tourism products that attract visitors. These products encompass a diversity of component features that are tangible, intangible and symbolic, which stem from an amalgam of resources (natural, built, socio-cultural) and services (transport, hospitality, support). As the characteristics of the tourism product and the combination of the resources and services varies from one destination to another, each destination is deemed to have its individual character and uniqueness (Seaton & Bennett, 1996). It is important to note, however, that this portfolio is dynamic as it changes and evolves over time, being to some extent dependent on the changes in demand and preferences of the targeted tourist markets (Davidson & Maitland, 1997; Middleton, 2001).

The management of destinations

Destination management is widely viewed to be a destination (micro-) level activity whereby several resident and industry stakeholders perform their individual and organisational responsibilities on a daily basis in an endeavour to integrate and adapt the national or regional (macro-)level vision contained in policy, planning and development. As such, destination management focuses on the activities which implement the broader policy and planning frameworks. These activities enhance the appeal of the core resources and attractions, strengthen the quality and the effectiveness of the competences and resources, and adapt best to any constraints or opportunities. They also embody the greatest capacity for managing a destination's competitiveness and contain programmes, structures, systems and processes that are highly actionable and manageable by individuals and organisations through collective action (Ritchie & Crouch, 2003).

In view of the complexities of managing destinations, DMOs need to embrace and engage all bodies (public and private) who are concerned with actions that encourage the industry to develop and improve supply. The bewildering range of stakeholders involved in destination management includes additional players: the host communities (local residents); the local tourism businesses (industry); public sector organisations; companies that are based outside the physical boundaries of the destination; the tourists, and elected representatives (Carter & Fabricius, 2006; Swarbrooke, 1999). For the purpose of this chapter, tourism destination stakeholders can be defined as any entity that is influenced by, or that can influence, the accomplishment of the destination management activities as performed by the DMO (Presenza *et al.*, 2005). Importantly, a [destination] stakeholder has a legitimate interest in some or all aspects of the organisation's [DMO's] activities, and has either the power to affect its performance and/or has a stake in its performance (Sautter & Leisen, 1999). Consequently, the identification of DMO objectives and activities is important for the purposes of this study, and will be explored later in this chapter.

The role of DMOs is multifaceted, as repeatedly 'DMOs provide leadership in policy and planning, marketing, product development, industry advocacy and coordination, and increasing professionalism in tourism through education and training'. However, one of the strongest difficulties DMOs face in their attempts to influence, facilitate and coordinate stems from the fact that the independent tourism operators govern, direct and control their own business, internal environment and product (Ritchie & Crouch, 2005). For instance, DMOs usually do not have direct control over the products they promote and represent, or even the packaged offerings of the intermediaries such as airlines, tour operators and travel agents. Similarly, a DMO often represents a great assortment of destination features that include natural characteristics, commercial and not-for-profit facilities and amenities, and the local population. Promoting such multi-attributed destinations in heterogeneous and dynamic markets involves enhanced challenges that need to be dealt with by sophisticated marketing that bares both the demand and the supply-side perspectives (Pike, 2004). Such a dynamic and complex environment needs effective governance mechanisms and collaborative arrangements that promote mutual benefits and methods of doing business (Palmer, 1998). Palmer finds governance style and internal compatibility among members to be significant determinants of the success of local tourism marketing arrangements. He concludes that 'tight governance' is argued have a positive relationship, and the level of compatibility among the members a negative relationship to effectiveness. As a consequence, identifying and analysing the destination stakeholders is highly significant for the DMO.

From a political economy standpoint, tourism is potentially an exploitative force where residents of a destination have relatively limited influence on the development process, whereas it often occurs that planning decisions are imposed on the local population from outside groups or planning bodies (Sautter & Leisen, 1999). On the other hand, from a functional perspective, tourism is often seen as a proactive force. The catalyst is argued to be a development approach that promotes the interests of the local community and maximises overall growth. A strong challenge towards realising this practice is that of 'collective management' of the tourism system, which actively involves all stakeholders in a process of joint decision making, planning and/or managing the destination. In parallel, effective destination marketing necessitates a 'participative management' approach that involves every destination stakeholder (Prideaux & Cooper, 2002). To address this challenge, Sautter and Leisen (1999) employ a stakeholder theory approach. They find that this theory can be used as a 'normative tourism planning tool' to address the multiple stakeholder interests and roles in the processes of tourism development and planning. The authors highlight that the stakeholder theory can provide a robust conceptual framework in which the interests of all stakeholders can be proactively incorporated in the destination management challenge. Tourism planners should consider the particular 'stakes', values, interests, and/or 'perspectives of the different stakeholder groups as defined by the roles which they serve with regard to the particular development initiative' (Sautter & Leisen, 1999: 316). Destination stakeholders exert their influence from a diversity of bases, such as economic, political and formal voting power. Moreover, stakeholder management gains significance as the reliance of the visitor economy on information technologies (IT) increases. Information synergies seek to encourage brand loyalty and repetitive customers, while end users seek for wider variety of tourism experiences (Sautter & Leisen, 1999).

In such socio-economic environments, where multiple agents and stakeholders are involved, the search for co-governance is critical. This is attributed to the different power bases of the stakeholders, which affects their collaborative capacity and results in strategic imbalances. To overcome such intricacies, management and governance theories, and their understandings of power relationships in inter-organisational and cross-sartorial settings could be incorporated (Sullivan et al., 2006). Moreover, the notion of partnership is more realistically approached when seen as co-opetition, rather than cooperation. Critically, DMOs lack any direct control over the actual delivery of the brand promise by the local tourism community. Without buy-in from these stakeholders the strategy bears high failure risks. A number of authors support that some form of intervention of public agencies (like local authorities) is to the benefit of each destination in establishing a new destination, creating demand, minimising the adverse impacts of increased tourism demand (Davidson & Maitland, 1997; Prideaux & Cooper, 2002).

Despite the fact that DMOs function at various levels (national, regional, sub-regional, state, provincial, urban, municipal, city-state) certain commonalities exist across these levels, as the fundamental roles of a DMO are generally similar. Significant variations tend to occur in the type of structure that is incorporated, their size, as well as their approaches to funding. In terms of governance, these DMOs present higher levels of consistency at a national level. At a regional, sub-regional or local level the consistency in governance is much lower and more private sector involvement is evident. DMO management structures include a government department, or a division of a government department, a quasi-governmental organisation (e.g. crown/government corporation), some form of public–private partnership, a non-profit membership-based organisation and private organisations. The nature of funding often reflects the structure of the DMO, and it may be derived from public funds, specific tourism taxes and levies, hotel taxes, user fees, membership fees payable by tourism organisations, sponsorship or advertising in destination promotional activities or commissions for bookings and sales (Presenza *et al.*, 2005; WTO, 2004). Clearly, the source of funding may bring with it implications for the structure and operation of DMOs.

Destination levels

As introduced in the preceding section, destinations exist and function at various levels. At the national level national tourism administrations (NTAs) represent central government bodies with administrative responsibility for tourism at the highest level (Jeffries, 2001). It is a relatively new concept of tourism management at national level and it is adopted by a plethora of countries which are moving away from the conventional system where the national tourist organisation (NTO) is essentially a central publicity body, to the newer concept of a NTA, which sees promotion and marketing as one of many other functions (Pike, 2004). NTOs 'are the primary instruments – and often producers – of their sponsoring government's tourism policies' (Pike, 2004: 140). Most of the NTOs are operating as a government agency with the aim of developing tourism. These organisations may be incorporated within a higher body or may be autonomous, and may also include central organisations legally or financially linked to the NTA (Jeffries, 2001). Although their activities differ greatly from country to country, these are basically focused on the provision of services which the private sector itself is least likely to undertake on a national scale: international and domestic marketing of the country as a whole; the provision of tourist information; and the collection and analysis of tourism statistics. There are two main tendencies within the EU that differentiate between the levels at which the NTO is undertaking tourism functions and is actively involved in the management of the visitor economy. At one side of the spectrum sit the northern European countries where NTOs are involved in only a few and basic functions incorporating a more 'liberal market-driven ethos'; while at the other end there are the Mediterranean countries where the NTO adopts a more interventionist and regulating approach. With regard to the UK's approach, it is seen to lie somewhere between the two groups (Davidson & Maitland, 1997). Moreover, NTAs and NTOs have some common functions, as is illustrated in Table 6.1 (Jeffries, 2001).

Regional tourism organisations (RTOs), meanwhile, are official organisations with similar roles to those of the NTAs, but focused at a regional level and concerned with specific regions, sub-regions and localities. With the primary objective being to attract visitors from outside their regional boundaries, these organisations are responsible for the promotion and marketing of a concentrated tourism area (such as cities, towns, villages, coastal resort areas, islands and rural areas) as a tourism destination. There is a great variety of RTO names in both the policy-making and operational arms that exist across different regions and countries. For instance, they are named convention and visitor bureaus (CVBs) in the USA, regional tourism boards (RTBs) or regional tourism partnerships (RTPs) in England, and area tourism boards (ATBs) in Scotland (Jeffries, 2001; Pike, 2004). At a regional level, dual structures are also present, where regional or local government departments constitute the senior policy-making element with subsidiary bodies to take charge of operations, which in the majority of cases is external marketing. As seen earlier, there is a myriad of organisations, either from public or private sectors, which have a vested interest in tourism. However, a regional DMO is the entity that has such an active and holistic interest (at the regional level) in the quality of the traveller experience, the host community's sense of place and the profitability of tourism businesses (Pike, 2004). Irrespective of the level of the DMO, be it public or private sector driven, its foundation

Table 6.1 Common functions of NTAs/NTOs

Operation of services **regulating** the most obvious producers of the basic product such as hotels and incoming tour operators

Education and **training** of the workforce with, again, emphasis on the providers of the basic product

Research, statistics, forecasting

Preparation of **strategic plans** – often **advisory** documents rather than true plans

Marketing

Development, with an emphasis on the pioneering of new products (the R&D function)

Advising policy makers on the likely effects on tourism of upcoming legislation or proposed government action

Source: Jeffries (2001)

necessitates certain key characteristics. For example, Ritchie and Crouch (2003: 175) suggest that:

- It must be clearly identifiable as the organisation responsible for coordinating and directing the efforts of the many parts of the diverse and complex tourism system;
- It must command the support of all important sectors and all major actors in the tourism system;
- It must be capable of influencing the decisions and actions of the many public sector agencies/departments and private firms that directly determine the nature and quality of the tourism experience provided to visitors;
- It must possess the tools necessary to stimulate and encourage the type and amount of supply development that is required by the overall tourism mega-policy;
- It must be sufficiently independent and flexible to develop innovative strategies that can be implemented in a timely manner in response to rapidly evolving market and environmental conditions.

Organisational structure of the DMO: An industrial versus internal perspective

The structure of a DMO determines the nature of the challenges that destination management faces. Moreover, the pattern of DMO reporting is a principal issue. The DMO management may report to a publicly elected official, to a board of directors elected by industry members, to a corporate/agency board of directors, or to a partnership involving a joint public/private sector board of directors. The structure of the DMO management modifies both the manner and practices that dominate. In cases where the DMO management reports to a public-oriented board emphasis is given to public service and community development. In contrast, when the DMO management reports to a private sector-oriented board, the DMO is viewed as a business where cost controls and accountability manipulate the DMO management functions (Ritchie & Crouch, 2003). The nature of the destination and the level of funding that is required, or that can be made available, are notably two of the many factors that determine the industrial structure of a DMO. However, what is paramount is that the DMO is functional from both a strategic as well as an operational perspective. Although DMOs traditionally have to perform leadership and coordination roles, what is becoming common practice is their effective performance in various tactical roles that often demand close daily attention in order to maintain the competitiveness of the destination. On the other hand, the internal structure, the roles and the means of funding of a DMO are decided on the basis of its organisational policy. In some cases, the internal structure of a

DMO reflects its true identity as a department of the government (Ritchie & Crouch, 2003).

For destinations in countries where tourism is an important economic factor, the most effective organisational form of a DMO is that of an independent organisation (e.g. Ministry of Tourism, or convention and visitor bureau), which raises the significant issue of fund acquisition to support expenditures. Alternatively, a DMO's structure is based on individual membership or even structured as a partnership of supporting organisations (e.g. chambers of commerce or hotel/restaurant associations). Contemporary practice in a few countries is that the forms of organisational structure are a mixture of the public and the private models (Carter, 2006; Ritchie & Crouch, 2003). By definition, national and state/provincial (local, regional) administrations have similar structures and modes of functioning. Essentially, different organisational structures are identified at the urban/municipal/ city-state level. There are cases where a type of DMO falls into both the private and the public sector framework. For instance, the city tourism department is equivalent to the national/provincial (local, regional) tourism department, whereas 'The City Convention Bureau regularly claims to be a private sector organisation (despite the fact that it often draws heavily on public funds)' (Ritchie & Crouch, 2003: 185).

DMOs: Management versus marketing?

Before entering the discussion about the roles and responsibilities of DMOs, it is worth noting that throughout the destination management literature there is an evident ambiguity in the use of the acronym 'DMO'. When discussing DMOs, some scholars use the term *marketing* while others prefer the term *management*; namely they refer to DMOs as 'destination marketing organisations' and 'destination management organisations', respectively. Organisations have been discussed generally as 'formal entities in which a complex interaction of people, materials and money is used for the creation and distribution of goods and services' (Inkson & Kolb, 1998: 6, cited in Pike, 2004: 13). However, in the specific context of destination development and management, tourism organisations can be purposefully regarded as those 'whose aim is to market and monitor the quality and development of the tourist region' (Manson, 2003: 10).

Pike (2004) sees a destination marketing organisation as 'any organisation, at any level which is responsible for the marketing of an identifiable destination. This therefore excludes separate government departments that are responsible for planning and policy' (Pike, 2004: 14), as these organisations 'are concerned with the selling of places' (Pike, 2004: 1). Thus, Pike generally identifies (at a country level) three distinctive types of tourism organisations with interests in destination development: the government ministry, providing policy advice to government; the destination marketing organisation, 'responsible for promotion'; and the private sector umbrella (industry association) that defends the interests of member organisations (Pike, 2004). One may argue that this is a rather simplistic and narrow approach to DMOs. However, Kotler *et al.* (2006) argue that the concept of marketing, as applied traditionally in destination management, tends to focus on the promotion and selling of the destination. Nevertheless, they note that there is an organisation function in destination management, where contemporary wisdom emphasises total management practice, rather than simply applying the principles of marketing. Moreover, they find that a successful destination is the one that principally focuses on sustainability and competitiveness, rather than employing destination marketing as merely a means of designing a destination to satisfy the needs of its target markets. Success of the destination marketing function is also determined by the level to which local citizens and businesses are satisfied with their communities, in addition to the level to which the expectations of visitors and investors are met. Thus, there is a high significance in promoting public–private collaboration and involving all stakeholders in shaping the destination's future (Kotler *et al.*, 2006).

Destinations differ in terms of history, culture, politics, leadership and ways of managing public–private relationships. This variety brings strong divergence in their strategies, use of resources and definition of products, as well as in the implementation of plans. This is why strategic destination marketing is advocated as 'the most adaptive and productive approach to the problems of places' (Kotler *et al.*, 1993: 20). Strategic destination marketing of destinations involves various levels. However, Blumberg (2005) acknowledges both a promotional and a facilitation aspect in strategic destination marketing, where the former focuses on traditional marketing functions (promotion, advertising, creation of awareness), while the latter concentrates on the initiation and coordination of cooperative arrangements (between the DMO and individual tourism operators), which aim to join recourses in order to achieve the shared goals of destination marketing.

DMOs are increasingly attaining a more proactive role in advancing, fostering and managing the benefits of tourism development; hence, they are seen as catalysts and facilitators for the realisation of destination development (Ritchie & Crouch, 2003; Sautter & Leisen, 1999). Clearly, although the marketing function of the DMO is still acknowledged and valued as highly important (Blumberg, 2005; Dore & Crouch, 2003; Kozak, 2004; Prideaux & Cooper, 2002), a competitive and sustainable perspective of a tourism destination calls for a DMO that extends this function and includes additional functions: strategy formulation, representation of the interests of stakeholders, marketing of the (overall) destination, and coordination of planning and development activities (Blain *et al.*, 2005; Presenza *et al.*, 2005). Increased complexity, incorporated by the diversity and heterogeneity of both tourism supply and demand, multiplies challenges to destination development and management. Further to the above, a more holistic approach would suggest as more appropriate the use of *management* instead of *marketing* in the acronym 'DMO' (Presenza *et al.*, 2005; WTO, 2004).

Roles, tasks and responsibilities

Morrison *et al.* (1998: 5) argue that the DMO roles can be described through five primary functions:

- an 'economic driver' generating new income, employment, and taxes contributing to a more diversified local economy;
- a 'community marketer' communicating the most appropriate destination image, attractions and facilities to selected visitor markets;
- an 'industry coordinator' providing a clear focus and encouraging less industry fragmentation so as to share in the growing benefits of tourism;
- a 'quasi-public representative' adding legitimacy for the industry and protection to individual and group visitors;
- a 'builder of community pride' by enhancing quality of life and acting as the chief 'flag carrier' for residents and visitors alike.

DMOs function as economic drivers, preserving or generating a new image for the destination. Thus, DMOs undertake tasks that include coordinating the constituent diverse and independent elements (of the tourism destination supply) with the aim of developing and sustaining a homogeneous and desirable destination image (Gartell, 1988); destination branding (Blain *et al.*, 2005; Gnoth, 2002; Pike, 2007); and destination promotion (advertising, direct marketing, sales promotion, personal selling, publicity and public relations) (Buhalis, 2000; Dore & Crouch, 2003). Additionally, DMOs are seen to be involved in product development and enhancing perceptions for destination image and service quality (Getz *et al.*, 1998; Presenza *et al.*, 2005). Having said that, the determinants of consumer (visitor/tourist) destination decision making need to be incorporated into a systematic planning process, which will aid strategic management of such information and better enable the implementation of strategies and enhance destination competitiveness (Hanlan *et al.*, 2006).

Quality image and branding

Tourism product/service quality is seen to reflect the attributes of a product or service, which are controlled by the tourism supplier. Customer satisfaction is seen to be a relevant concept as to the quality of the product/service, as it refers to the emotional state after a tourist's/visitor's exposure to it (or to the 'experience'). Thus, the evaluation efforts of the DMO should include both concepts, as improvement in both performance quality and satisfaction is expected to result in the retention or expansion of tourist numbers, more enthusiastic and active tourism support, and ultimately enhanced profitability and political support for the sector. Paradoxically, perceived quality is seen to be more influential than actual satisfaction (Baker, 2000). However, quality must reflect the image of the destination, so as to secure the long-term profit maximisation of tourism activities (Moutinho, 2000). The systematic approach to quality management for the whole subregional destination requires the identification of quality indicators for the destination. Such an approach evolves in various phases: supply and demand analysis, quality system design and quality system implementation. Primarily, the DMO needs to understand the overall scope of quality. Assessing the current situation is important when identifying quality gaps in terms of the nature of the tourist targeted, the local stakeholders or outside entities (global players and tour operators: DMCs), as well as identifying improvement priorities by sector of activity (cross-sector factors). Cross-sector quality factors that need to be managed relate to:

(1) technical skills;
(2) languages;
(3) attitude;
(4) personal appearance;
(5) security;
(6) environment;
(7) maintenance;
(8) cleanliness;
(9) information;
(10) price–quality relationship;
(11) product variety;
(12) additional services;
(13) service speed/efficiency;
(14) opening hours;
(15) signposting system.

Defining the core business as a tourism destination (urban, cultural, coastal, nature, etc.) can assist in developing performance indicators (PIs), while the use of international references as a benchmark can help to establish the destination's own list of standards. Despite the existence of over 100 public or private certification labels, the utilisation of quality management systems in DMOs is still the exception rather than the rule. Overall, there is an identified need for the DMO to act as a management body for quality at the destination. Its role will be to generate awareness of quality issues among public or private organisations and the local population; to define quality values, criteria and indicators encompassing all of the value chain; to build up consensus among local stakeholders regarding quality issues, priorities and action plans; to monitor quality improvement programmes and PIs; and to instigate an overall quality improvement process at the destination. Designing and implementing a quality system for the destination demands that the DMO managers decide on the technical issues of the system, the kind of auditing undertaken, certification and accreditation, the collaborative arrangements between public and private sectors, internal (among organisations of the destination) and external (tourists, intermediaries, sponsors) promotion, and funding issues (Carter & Fabricius, 2006; de Bruyn, 2006).

DMOs have the challenging role of 'catalysts' for action on behalf of the area's visitor economy by engaging in sophisticated planning which is focused on economic development. Thus, successful tourism destination development necessitates the development, implementation and evaluation of comprehensive strategic business plans that optimise fit between resources and opportunities, and link the destination's goals with the destination's general and task (operational) environment (e.g. demand and competitors) (Carter & Fabricius, 2006). The variety of the ideas and needs of the diverse amalgam of industry partners and stakeholders means that there are significant levels of complexity in determining the goals of the destination development. As the market interests of the diverse group of stakeholders are heterogeneous, DMOs are faced with challenges such as attracting a wide range of market segments and matching them with the range of the destination's products/services, as well as making sensitive decisions about capacity (and volume) levels, and the distribution of the products and services of the destination. Moreover, it is highly significant that the strategic business plans of DMOs address the various determinants of the quality of the tourism product. Such determinants of destination tourism product quality relate to overcrowding, environmental problems and concerns, visitor safety and security, seasonality issues, and sensitivity to local culture (Evans *et al.*, 1995; Pike, 2005).

Performance

As mentioned previously, destination performance is assessed over the long term, and depends on the implementation of the tourism strategy which results in a set of actual achievements that can be compared with the (pre-) established goals. Thus, a destination is regarded as successful when strategies are successfully implemented. Successful implementation of strategies calls for identifying timelines and assigning responsibilities, while the market and the competition need to be monitored continuously so that plans can be adjusted in real time. The latter, in particular, allows for contingencies to be implemented in a timely manner when required. It is the DMO that takes on the challenging task of tourism destination strategy implementation, as it is seen to have the function of a focal organisation that is able to see events from a wider and holistic perspective. The DMO endeavours to assist and facilitate the achievement of multiple goals, and to involve all stakeholders in the development of the destination in terms of policy formulation, planning and product delivery (Morrison *et al.*, 1998; Pike, 2004). Thus, the DMO has the critical and vital role of providing leadership and coordination for the many destination stakeholders that must contribute and work together. Clearly, DMOs aim to ensure that the expectations of (internal and external) stakeholders are satisfied to the greatest extent possible. In order to assess the destination's performance, a wide range of information needs to be gathered by the DMO, while the use of PIs is important in measuring the outcomes of strategy implementation efforts. Moreover, DMOs have the responsibility of disseminating timely key market and performance information to their members in order to ensure destination productivity and effectiveness (Middleton, 2001; Ritchie & Crouch, 2003).

Conclusions

Although this chapter merely scratches the surface of the issues and challenges confronting destinations, it does introduce the complexity and dynamics of destinations and the need for all stakeholders and vested interests to understand the rationale and consequences of the structures put in place to both manage and market them in what are increasingly competitive marketplaces across the world. In Europe, as elsewhere, the current financial and economic crisis across the continent serves as a warning and potential catalyst for change, because the consequent squeeze on the public purse will force all those involved with maintaining and enhancing destination competitiveness to rethink existing structures and seek more cost-effective, more sustainable and more flexible structures to accommodate the challenges that lie ahead.

References

Baker, D.A. (2000) Quality, satisfaction and behavioral intentions. *Annals of Tourism Research* 27 (3), 785–804.

Blain, C., Levy, S.E. and Ritchie, J.R.B. (2005) Destination branding: Insights and practices from destination management organizations. *Journal of Travel Research* 42, 328–338.

Blumberg, K. (2005) Tourism destination marketing – a tool for destination management? A case study from Nelson/Tasman region, New Zealand. *Asia Pacific Journal of Tourism Research* 10 (1), 45–57.

Buhalis, D. (2000) Marketing the competitive destination of the future. *Tourism Management* 21, 97–116.

Carter, R. (2006) Destination management and governance: A framework paper for discussion. UNWTO Ulysses Conference, June.

Carter, R. and Fabricius, M. (2006) *Introduction to Destination Management*. World Tourism Organization Seminar, March, Addis Ababa.

Davidson, R. and Maitland, R. (1997) *Tourism Destinations*. Bath: Bath Press.

de Bruyn, C. (2006) *Managing Quality in Tourism Destinations*. 22nd Philoxenia: International Tourism Exhibition, Thessaloniki, Greece.

Dore, L. and Crouch, G.I. (2003) Promoting destinations: An exploratory study of publicity programmes used by national tourism organisations. *Journal of Vacation Marketing* 9 (2), 137–151.

Evans, M.R., Fox, J.B. and Johnson, R.B. (1995) Identifying competitive strategies for successful tourism destination development. *Journal of Hospitality and Leisure Marketing* 3 (1), 37–45.

Gartell, R.B. (1988) *Destination Marketing for Convention and Visitor Bureaus.* Dubuque, IA: Kendall Hunt Publishing.

Getz, D., Anderson, D. and Sheehan, L. (1998) Roles, issues, and strategies for convention and visitors' bureaux in destination planning and product development: A survey of Canadian bureaux. *Tourism Management* 19 (4), 331–340.

Gnoth, J. (2002) Leveraging export brands through a tourism destination brand. *Brand Management* 9 (4–5), 262–280.

Hanlan, J., Fuller, D. and Wilde, S. (2006) Destination decision making: The need for a strategic planning and management approach. *Tourism and Hospitality Planning and Development* 3 (3), 209–221.

Howie, F. (2003) *Managing the Tourist Destination: A Practical Interactive Guide.* Oxford: Cengage Learning EMEA Tourism.

Jeffries, D. (2001) *Governments and Tourism.* Oxford: Butterworth-Heinemann.

Kotler, P., Heider, D.H. and Rein, I. (1993) *Marketing Places: Attracting Investment, Industry, and Tourism to Cities, States, and Nations.* Oxford: Free Press.

Kotler, P., Bowen, J. and Makens, J. (2006) *Marketing for Hospitality and Tourism* (4th edn). Upper Saddle River, NJ: Pearson Prentice-Hall.

Kozak, M. (2004) *Destination Benchmarking: Concepts, Practices and Operations.* Wallingford: CABI Publishing.

Lew, A. and McKercher, B. (2006) Modeling tourist movements: A local destination analysis. *Annals of Tourism Research* 33 (2), 403–423.

Manson, P. (2003) *Tourism Impacts, Planning and Management.* Oxford: Butterworth-Heinemann.

Michael, E. (2007) *Micro-clusters and Networks: The Growth of Tourism.* Advances in Tourism Research Series. Amsterdam: Elsevier.

Middleton, V.T. (2001) *Marketing in Travel and Tourism* (3rd edn). Oxford: Butterworth-Heinemann.

Morrison, A.M., Bruen, S.M. and Anderson, D.J. (1998) Convention and visitor bureaus in the USA: A profile of bureaus, bureau executives, and budgets. *Journal of Travel and Tourism Marketing* 7 (1), 1–19.

Moutinho, L. (2000) *Strategic Management in Tourism.* Wallingford: CABI Publishing.

Palmer, A. (1998) Evaluating the governance style of marketing groups. *Annals of Tourism Research* 25 (1), 185–201.

Pike, S. (2004) *Destination Marketing Organisations.* Advances in Tourism Research Series. Oxford: Taylor & Francis.

Pike, S. (2005) Tourism destination branding complexity. *Journal of Product & Brand Management* 14 (4), 258–259.

Pike, S. (2007) Consumer-based brand equity for destinations: Practical DMO performance measures. *Journal of Travel & Tourism Marketing* 22 (1), 51–61.

Presenza, A., Sheehan, L. and Ritchie, J.R.B. (2005) Towards a model of the roles and activities of destination management organizations. *Journal of Hospitality, Tourism and Leisure Science* 3, 1–16.

Prideaux, B. and Cooper, C. (2002) Marketing and destination growth: A symbiotic relationship or simple coincidence? *Journal of Vacation Marketing* 9 (1), 35–51.

Ritchie, J.R.B. and Crouch, G.I. (2003) *The Competitive Destination: A Sustainable Tourism Perspective.* Wallingford: CABI Publishing.

Sautter, E.T. and Leisen, B. (1999) Managing stakeholders: A tourism planning model. *Annals of Tourism Research* 26 (2), 312–328.

Seaton, A.V. and Bennett, M.M. (1996) *Marketing Tourism Products: Concepts, Issues, Cases.* London: Thomson Learning.

Sullivan, H., Barnes, M. and Matka, E. (2006) Collaborative capacity and strategies in area-based initiatives. *Public Administration* 84 (2), 289–310.

Swarbrooke, J. (1999) *Sustainable Tourism Management.* Wallingford: CABI Publishing.

WTO (2007) *A Practical Guide to Tourism Destination Management.* Madrid: World Tourism Organization.

WTO (2004) *Survey of Destination Management Organisations.* Madrid: World Tourism Organization.

7 SMEs in Tourism Destinations

Mike Peters and Dimitrios Buhalis

Introduction

European tourism is a 'fragmented industry', as it consists of many small and medium-sized enterprises (SMEs) producing and selling undifferentiated products or services in a highly competitive marketplace. Fragmentation is far stronger in leisure tourism as compared to business tourism. It is also less of an issue in underdeveloped economies where tourism arrived late and with the helping hand of multinational enterprises. Small businesses can be treated as a 'distinct analytical category' (Thomas, 2000: 351), because they show significant differences when comparing them with large-scale businesses (LSC).

In a free market economy, the role of the government is to provide an institutional framework for economic activity. Direct intervention is not justified since it distorts competition (Socher, 2001). This is, however, necessary in developing economies where there is a lack of entrepreneurial skills and resource constraints. The role of the government and aid agencies is then crucial in strengthening small and medium-sized tourism enterprises (SMTEs) to perform better. In developed economies is it also reasonable to support the growth of small businesses.

This chapter discusses the importance of SMEs in the tourism industry and presents their strategic strengths and challenges while exploring strategies for their future evolution. The aim of this chapter is to highlight the characteristics of these actors in the context of tourism destinations and regional development. Beside the discussion of SME characteristics, the main stakeholders in the tourism destination value chain are highlighted and destination governance implications are derived. The final section of this chapter highlights initiatives of the European Communities to foster SME development.

The Economic Contribution of Small and Medium-sized Tourism Enterprises

The European Commission (EC) defines as SMEs all organisations with fewer than 250 employees, less than €50 m turnover or a total balance sheet of less than €43 m (Table 7.1). However, until today there existed various definitions of small and medium-sized firms in tourism; for example, while Morrison (1998) defined small tourism businesses as directly managed and financed by an individual or smaller group of individuals, Halcro et al. (1998) define small hotels as those with fewer than 15 rooms, and Rowson and Lucas (1998) define them as having fewer than 25 employees. Thomas (2000) discusses these conceptual issues and important premises for tourism research and concludes that we need to recognise the heterogeneity of small tourism businesses.

Based on theories of economic development in general and those of tourism development in particular, some of the main contributions of SMEs include: absorbing people who were unemployed but capable of working; saving hard currency that could have been expended on the acquisition of high-technology goods; fulfilling local consumption needs; the growth of local entrepreneurs and mid-level qualifications; and the promotion of equitable income distribution (Atomsa et al., 2003). This holds true for SMTEs in many European countries, where tourism has emerged through local small businesses with owner-managers who in many cases were farmers or who are still part-time farmers.

Especially in less developed countries, the role of SMEs is significant as there is a shortage of capital but abundant labour. As stated by Todaro (1985: 112), the less developed countries' 'development of low-cost, efficient, labor-intensive (capital saving) techniques of production is one of the essential ingredients in any long-run employment-oriented development strategy'. Above all, the development of tourism SMEs can help in stimulating agriculture and other sectors of the economy through linkages and multiplier effects. That is, the role of SMTEs is vital in transforming the economic structure through the participation of diverse segments of the population.

The importance of SMEs is evident from the following facts: Section 2 of the Annual Report on EU Small and Medium-Sized Enterprises (2010/2011)

Table 7.1 EU definition of SMEs

Enterprise category	Personnel headcount	Turnover	or	Balance sheet total
Medium-sized	<250	≤€50 million		≤€43 million
Small	<50	≤€10 million		≤€10 million
Micro	<10	≤€2 million		≤€2 million

Source: EC (2013)

demonstrated that 99.8% of all enterprises have fewer than 10 employees (Table 7.2). As can be seen from the table, there were almost 21 million enterprises in the European Union (EU-27) in 2010. Only about 43,000 of these were large-scale enterprises (LSEs), i.e. 0.2% of all enterprises. Hence, the very vast majority of enterprises in EU-27 are indeed SMEs. About two-thirds of total employment in the private sector is found in SMEs. Micro firms (who have on average two employees) employ 30% of the total private labour force. There are 20.5 million enterprises in the European Economic Area (EEA) and Switzerland, providing employment for 130 million people. On average, an enterprise provides work and income for six persons. This measure of enterprise size varies between only two in micro enterprises and over 1000 in LSEs. Employment differs between European countries, and the United States and Japan. When considering Iceland, Switzerland and Norway, their SMEs have an employment share of approximately 70%, which is comparable to the EU average employment share. In Japan, SMEs account for an identical share of employment to that of the EU, whereas the average enterprise size is significantly higher, namely more than eight people. This shows that there are differences in the average number of employed people by an enterprise. The average European enterprise employs six people (Eurostat, 2010).

Some 93% of all enterprises are micro (0–9 employees), 6% are small (10–49), less than 1% are medium-sized (50–249) and only 0.2% are large enterprises (250+). Two-thirds of all jobs are in SMEs. Employment differs between countries, as the share of micro enterprises in total employment is 48% in Italy and 57% in Greece, while large enterprises account for over 45% in Iceland and the UK. The average European enterprise employs six people. This also varies between countries as on average an enterprise employs two persons in Greece and three in Italy and Liechtenstein, against 10 in Ireland, Luxembourg and The Netherlands. The average age of new entrepreneurs is about 35 years and more than 29% are women. The decision to found one's own business is frequently taken some years after completing education and acquiring some specific know-how as an employee and/or manager (Buhalis & Peters, 2005).

Table 7.2 Basic facts about SMEs and large enterprises in Europe, 2010 (estimates)

	SME		Large		Total	
Number of enterprises	20,796,192	99.8%	43,034	0.2%	20,839,226	100%
Employment	87,460,792	66.9%	43,257,098	33.1%	130,717,890	100%
Occupied people per enterprise	4.21	—	1005.18	—	—	—
Gross value added (million€)	3,492,979	58.4%	2,485,457	41.6%	5,978,436	100%

Source: Wymenga et al. (2011)

SMTEs' potential can be evident through increased linkages and multiplier effects, fewer income leakages, balanced regional development and further economic growth (Buhalis & Peters, 2005). SMTEs contribute to individual countries' GDP: more than 5% of the EU-27's GDP is generated by SMTE (EC, 2013). A similar experience can be observed worldwide.

Especially in countries facing high unemployment, SMTEs can play an important role in employment creation and income generation. Small enterprises are very important even in developed economies. Moreover, SMEs still dominate the tourism industry in Europe and it is estimated that more than 90% of all accommodation providers are family-managed SMTEs (Bastakis *et al.*, 2004).

About 95% of the accommodation and food sector is classified as small businesses employing nine employees or fewer. This is prevalent in the hospitality industry: in Europe, SMEs employ more than 80% of all hospitality workers, while across all industries SMEs provide employment for around 70% of the labour force. The average size of hotels was 48 beds in 2001 and 59 beds in 2008 (Eurostat, 2010). The trend towards hotels with higher bed capacities and towards higher levels of concentration is confirmed in the hospitality industry all over Europe (Table 7.3).

Table 7.3 Indicators for hotels and similar enterprises in selected countries, 2008

Country	Number of hotels (and similar enterprises) (000s)	Number of beds (000s)	Average number of beds per hotel (and similar enterprises)
Austria	13.8	580.0	42.0
Belgium	2.0	125.0	62.5
Denmark	0.5	73.0	146.0
Finland	0.9	121.0	134.4
France	18.0	1256.0	69.8
Germany	35.9	1677.0	46.7
Greece	9.4	716.0	76.2
Ireland	3.9	169.0	43.3
Italy	34.2	2202.0	64.4
Luxemburg	0.3	14.0	46.7
The Netherlands	3.2	199.0	62.2
Portugal	2.0	274.0	137.0
Spain	18.0	1685.0	93.6
Sweden	1.9	218.0	114.7
United Kingdom	39.0	1176.0	30.2

Source: Eurostat (2010)

Competitive Challenges for SMTEs in Tourism Destinations

Simultaneity of production and consumption, as in most service production processes, implies non-storability of production and the necessity for an accurate fine-tuning between tourists' demand requirements and firms' production capabilities. Unlike industrial production, where faulty products can either be reworked or scrapped, services have to be produced right the first time and, unlike manufacturing where demand fluctuations can be smoothed by changes in the level of inventories, tourism and hospitality, like most other service industries, cannot store unsold hotel space, non-rented vehicles or unsold airline tickets.

Tourism, and even more so hospitality, has traditionally depended on a variety of stakeholders along its value chain (Bieger, 2008; Porter, 1990). The great advantage of the tourism value chain is the fact that while 'manufacturing' or 'staging' a tourism product which is holistically perceived and consumed by the tourist, it helps to analyse in detail the various steps of a tourism product, including all service providers. Beside these typical tourism service providers the tourism 'product' involves passive stakeholders, such as destinations' locals who play an important role in the provision of an authentic tourism destination experience.

When analysing tourism destinations one invariably recognises further differences: in some places a few pioneering entrepreneurs have become involved in getting tourism started early and on a relatively large scale, while in other places farmer/part-time/more risk-averse tourism entrepreneurs have survived (examples include Ischgl, Galtuer in the Austrian Alps) (Weiermair *et al.*, 2007). The fact that many of these SMTEs should provide a holistic valuable holiday product and service bundle forces them to create cooperation and to form clusters with formalised and informal links. Recent research focuses on the development and evolution of tourism clusters in destinations and attempts to explain the governance patterns of various stakeholders. In these networks, SMTEs usually follow those LSCs who have a strong reputation in the destination (Strobl & Peters, 2013).

A number of advantages and disadvantages affect the SMTEs' competitiveness, growth and profitability in tourism destinations. Advantages often relate to the small size and independence that allows entrepreneurs the flexibility that larger organisations lack. Advantages include:

- Entrepreneurial sacrifices: entrepreneurial motivation is usually quite high in small businesses, as entrepreneurs perceive their businesses as income opportunities but also as their lifework. In tourism destinations with many small businesses we might also find innovative entrepreneurs who hold the key to differentiating and strengthening the region (Page *et al.*, 1999).

- Dominance of family businesses: many family businesses have created informal but strong ties to other players in the tourism destination. These personal relationships might enable competitors to conquer the tourism destination (McCann *et al.*, 2001; Shaw & Williams, 1994).
- Small businesses in tourism destinations often create unique and non-standardised tourism products, where transaction costs might occur for the consumer, but individuality is guaranteed.
- Small business owners are usually in close contact with their customers as they are involved in operational issues. This might create strong linkages to customers, create tailor-made products and improve service processes in the service encounter stage.

Globalisation and the concentration of power in a few corporations will jeopardise the SMTEs' future. Many of the disadvantages of SMTEs occur due to their lack of economies of scale and scope, resulting in high fixed costs and relatively high costs per unit. SMTEs find it difficult to achieve overall cost leadership, which requires facilities on an efficient scale and tight control on costs and overheads. Economies of scope can be generated by internalising and sharing services and products which cannot be produced by the market at the same price or quality level. SMTEs can raise their economies of scope when they are willing and able to cooperate with other tourism industry partners. Beside these basic size disadvantages, small businesses also face a number of typical problems or growth hurdles in the tourism destination:

- Unwillingness to cooperate: several studies support the fact that small tourism business owners seldom work together in developing or delivering sustainable destination products. Underlying reasons are the fear of competition in the destination or a lack of professionalism in creating strategic alliances or clusters (Peters & Buhalis, 2004; Weiermair & Kronenberg, 2004).
- Lack of economies of scope: SMTEs can only offer multi-option services and product bundles when they cooperate with one another. However, to stimulate motivation, destinations with large proportions of small businesses need to communicate best practices from different regions (Buhalis & Peters, 2005; Weiermair, 2001).
- Role accumulation: in tourism destinations, governance structures often mean that a few stakeholders accumulate various roles in different stakeholder groups, e.g. entrepreneurs being majors or members of non-profit associations. As all stakeholders in destinations contribute to the overall tourism product, many development decisions are dominated by lobbyism and informal relationships. This especially holds true for the so-called community-oriented tourism destinations (Flagestad & Hope, 2001).

- Barriers to clustering: many tourism destinations lack the critical mass of firms or of strategic infrastructure (e.g. financial or professional human infrastructure) needed for cluster development or growth. In addition, some lifestyle businesses do not want to grow and do not even view themselves as part of the destinations tourism industry (Braun, 2005; Buhalis & Cooper, 1998).

The EU and SMTEs: Policies and Measures

The above-mentioned fragmentation of the industry might be an argument for financial assistance from public funds. Wanhill (1999) points out that potential market failure, where market mechanisms do not create optimal solutions, calls for public financial support. Therefore, many EU member states and the EU itself offer programmes that support SMTEs. The question remains if and how public supra-national or international institutions should financially support the development of SMTEs.

The EU initiated the European Charter for Small Enterprises which can be interpreted as a self-commitment from member states to support their SMEs in creating the ideal business environment. The charter was approved in June 2000 and focuses on the following 10 key policy areas (EC, 2008b):

(1) education and training for entrepreneurship;
(2) cheaper and faster start-up;
(3) better legislation and regulation;
(4) availability of skills;
(5) improving online access;
(6) getting more out of the single market;
(7) taxation and financial matters;
(8) strengthening the technological capacity of small enterprises;
(9) making use of successful e-business models and developing top-class small business support;
(10) developing stronger, more effective representation of small enterprises' interests at Union and national level.

Since then the charter has published the SME good practice selection, an annual report that fosters learning processes between and among SMEs. Many of the best practice cases were influenced by former reports of best practices and by new cooperations between SMEs in Europe (EC, 2008b).

In addition, in June 2008 the EU adopted the Small Business Act (SBA) of 2007 for Europe. This initiative symbolises the political will of the EC to highlight the importance of SMEs in the EU economy and creates not only a policy framework for the EU but also for the member states. Again, in this document the EC formulates 10 principles to 'guide the conception and implementation of policies both at EU and Member State level' (EC, 2008a: 4):

(1) Create an environment in which entrepreneurs and family businesses can thrive and entrepreneurship is rewarded.
(2) Ensure that honest entrepreneurs who have faced bankruptcy quickly get a second chance.
(3) Design rules according to the 'Think Small First' principle.
(4) Make public administrations responsive to SMEs' needs.
(5) Adapt public policy tools to SME needs: facilitate SMEs' participation in public procurement and better use State Aid possibilities for SMEs.
(6) Facilitate SMEs' access to finance and develop a legal and business environment supportive to timely payments in commercial transactions.
(7) Help SMEs to benefit more from the opportunities offered by the Single Market.
(8) Promote the upgrading of skills in SMEs and all forms of innovation.
(9) Enable SMEs to turn environmental challenges into opportunities.
(10) Encourage and support SMEs to benefit from the growth of markets.

The EC is attempting to become more concrete in formulating principles to put these goals into action. They highlight that the 2010 *Flash Eurobarometer* on entrepreneurial mindsets (Gallup Organization, 2010) shows that only 45% of Europeans would prefer to become self-employed – compared to 55% in the United States. Therefore, many of the challenges for the Commission and for the member states focus on the improvement of entrepreneurial culture as well as on the stimulation of innovative and entrepreneurial mindsets. The Commission and the member states are invited to support actions which help to achieve these goals. The EC attempts to govern the SBA as follows: National Reform programmes should focus on these goals and member states are provided with good practice cases all over Europe. The EU wants to stimulate governments to include the SBA into their national frameworks. The Commission assesses the progress made in implementing the SBA and reports annually in the framework of the Growth and Jobs Strategy.

The Future of SMTEs in Europe

SMTEs are relevant for economic growth. Several studies support that the start-up of new firms is positively related to the economic growth rate of nations (Audretsch & Keilbach, 2007). Other authors support that those regions with a higher rate of business ownership tend to exhibit lower levels of unemployment, and more start-ups result in higher rates of economic growth (Audretsch & Thurik, 2002; Thurik & Carree, 2008). Despite the fact that there is no empirical evidence for tourism-dominated destinations, we might expect that these relationships also hold true for tourism.

Thus, the EC is focusing on the right needs and small business gaps. It attempts to avoid spreading funds for small business growth, forcing industries to orientate towards best practice examples in various countries of the EU. However, member states need to take up the basic principles of the SBA and transform them into concrete measures. At the national level, governments should translate those EU principles into funding programmes.

Several examples of national measures to implement the SBA are reported in the database of good practice. However, initiatives in the tourism sector are quite scarce. Nevertheless, some initiatives indirectly support the product development initiatives of tourism and tourism-related enterprises, such as the summer university programme for entrepreneurship in the Tyrolean tourism destination Kitzbühel in Tyrol, Austria. Hitherto, there has been a severe lack of SBA measures in the member states of the EU. Therefore, national institutions such as chambers or hotel associations should take advantage of the SBA and consider increasing pressure on their governments to develop concrete funded initiatives to support SMTEs.

References

Atomsa, T., Peters, M. and Weiermair, K. (2003) Tourism development through SMEs in Africa: Prospects and problems. *Second International ATLAS Conference: Community Tourism – Options for the Future, Arusha/Tansania, February.*

Audretsch, D.B. and Keilbach, M. (2007) The theory of knowledge spill-over entrepreneurship. *Journal of Management Studies* 44 (7), 1242–1254.

Audretsch, D.B. and Thurik, R. (2002) Linking entrepreneurship to growth. STI Working Paper No. 2081/2. Paris: OECD.

Bastakis, C., Buhalis, D. and Butler, R. (2004) The perception of small and medium sized tourism accommodation providers on the impacts of the tour operator's power in Eastern Mediterranean. *Tourism Management* 25 (2), 151–170.

Bieger, T. (2008) *Management von Destinationen.* München: Oldenbourg.

Braun, P. (2005) *Creating Value to Tourism Products Through Tourism Networks and Clusters: Uncovering Destination Value Chains.* Paper presented at the 2005 OECD & Korea Conference on Global Tourism Growth: A Challenge for SMEs.

Buhalis, D. and Cooper, C. (1998) Competition or co-operation: Small and medium sized tourism enterprises at the destination. In E. Laws, B. Faulkner and G. Moscardo (eds) *Embracing and Managing Change in Tourism* (pp. 324–346). London: Routledge.

Buhalis, D. and Peters, M. (2005) SMEs in tourism. In D. Buhalis and C. Costa (eds) *Tourism Dynamics, Challenges and Tools: Present and Future Issues* (pp. 116–129). Oxford: Butterworth-Heinemann.

EC (2008a) *Communication from the Commission to the Council, the European Parliament, The European Economic and Social Committee and the Committee of the Regions.* Brussels: European Commission.

EC (2008b) *European Charter for Small Enterprises. 2008 Good Practice Selection.* Brussels: European Commission.

EC (2010) *Enterprise and Industry – Small and Medium-Sized Enterprises (SMEs).* Brussels: European Commission, accessed 30 June 2010. http://ec.europa.eu/enterprise/policies/sme/best-practices/charter/index_en.htm.

EC (2013) *Eurostat Tourism Trends*, accessed 22 May 2013. http://epp.eurostat.ec.europa.eu/statistics_explained/index.php/Tourism_trends retrieved 22 May 2013.

Eurostat (2010) Eurostat, Luxembourg, accessed 1 July 2010. http://epp.eurostat.ec.europa.eu/tgm/table.do?tab=table&init=1&language=de&pcode=tin00041&plugin=1.

Flagestad, A. and Hope, A.C. (2001) Strategic success in wintersports destinations: A sustainable value creation perspective. *Tourism Management* 22 (1), 445–461.

Gallup Organization (2010) *Entrepreneurship in the EU and Beyond: A Survey in the EU, EFTA Countries, Croatia, Turkey, the US, Japan, South Korea and China*. Brussels: European Commission.

Halrco, K., Buick, I. and Lynch, P. (1998) *A Preliminary Investigation into Small Scottish Hotels*. Paper presented at the CHME Research Conference, Glasgow.

McCann, J.E., Leon-Guerrero, A.Y. and Haley, J.D. (2001) Strategic goals and practices of innovative family businesses. *Journal of Small Business Management* 39 (1), 50–59.

Morrison, A. (1998) Small firm co-operative marketing in a peripheral tourism region. *International Journal of Contemporary Hospitality Management* 10 (5), 191–197.

Page, S.C., Forer, P. and Lawton, G.R. (1999) Small business development and tourism: Terra incognita? *Tourism Management* 20, 435–459.

Peters, M. and Buhalis, D. (2004) Family hotel businesses: Strategic planning and the need for education and training. *Education and Training* 46 (8/9), 406–415.

Porter, M.E. (1990) The competitive advantage of nations. *Harvard Business Review* 68 (2), 73–93.

Rowson, W. and Lucas, R. (1998) *The Role of Pay Structures and Labour Costs in Business Success and Failure with Particular Reference to Small Hotels*. Paper presented at the CHME Research Conference, Glasgow.

Shaw, G. and Williams, A. (1994) *Critical Issues in Tourism: A Geographical Perspective*. Oxford: Blackwell.

Socher, K. (2001) Tasks of the state providing the framework for tourism. *Tourism Review* 56 (1/2), 57–60.

Strobl, A. and Peters, M. (2013) Entrepreneurial reputation in destination networks. *Annals of Tourism Research* 40 (1), 59–82.

Thomas, R. (2000) Small firms in the tourism industry: Some conceptual issues. *International Journal of Tourism Research* 2 (5), 345–353.

Thurik, R.A. and Carree, M.A. (2008) Does self-employment reduce unemployment? *Journal of Business Venturing* 23 (6), 673–686.

Todaro, M.P. (1985) *Economic Development in the Third World*. New York: Longman.

Wanhill, S. (1999) Small and medium tourism enterprises. *Annals of Tourism* 27 (1), 132–147.

Weiermair, K. (2001) The growth of tourism enterprises. *Tourism Review* 56 (3/4), 17–25.

Weiermair, K. and Kronenberg, C. (2004) Stuck in the middle: Strategies for improving the market position of SMEs in tourism. *Poznan University Economics Review* 4 (1), 103–112.

Weiermair, K., Peters, M. and Schuckert, M. (2007) Destination development and the tourist life cycle: Implications for entrepreneurship in Alpine tourism. *Tourism Recreation Research* 32 (1), 83–93.

Wymenga, P., Spanikova, V., Derbyshire, J. and Barker, A. (2011) Are EU SMEs recovering? *Annual Report on EU SMEs 2010/2011*. Rotterdam and Cambridge: European Commission, DG-Enterprises.

8 Benchmarking Tourism Partnerships

Alan Clarke and Ágnes Raffay

Introduction

This chapter seeks to develop a critical understanding of the formation and development of tourism partnerships, which have emerged as an important way of working within tourism, recognising the complexities of tourism as a multi-sector, multi-core, multi-agency operation with a clear sense of interdependency among the key players. This sense of interdependency has also been seen in the financing of tourism development becoming increasingly focused on public–private partnerships and external funders seeing partnerships as the essential context of delivery mechanisms. These factors have seen a rapid growth in the number of partnerships working within tourism, from single project partnerships to destination management partnerships.

Within the European Union (EU), it has become almost impossible to think of tourism policy without invoking the spirit of partnership. When Brussels issued 'A Renewed EU Tourism Policy' in 2006, it carried the defining subtitle, 'Towards a stronger partnership for European Tourism'. The policy stated:

> Partnerships amongst all involved stakeholders are also necessary at every level of the decision-making process related to tourism. Partnerships must be a central component of action at all levels (European, national, regional and local; public and private). (EC, 2006: 4)

The document concluded by asserting the core reason for this commitment:

> The complexity of tourism and the broad diversity of involved actors require the collaboration of all stakeholders in the planning and implementation of related European policies and measures. Community institutions, national administrations, professional organisations, employers

and employees, NGOs and researchers, should build up partnerships at all levels to improve the competitiveness and demonstrate the importance of European tourism. The development of the collaboration and partnerships in the framework of the renewed policy can be reviewed regularly during the European Tourism Forums. (EC, 2006: 10)

The evidence so far collected suggests that there are common characteristics underpinning the development of partnerships which transcend the specific developmental context which may have inspired the original idea. This chapter will explore the lessons to be drawn from the examinations of current partnership developments through a benchmarking approach to those activities. The chapter therefore consists of three parts.

The first part is a benchmarking study of the benchmarking literature and best practice analysis. This critical review unpacks the literature from quality management and the work specifically undertaken in hospitality and tourism to develop a framework approach to benchmarking. It is particularly important to recognise the processual accounts in these works as the study of partnership development has to be able to capture the changing, evolving and emerging nature of the partnerships and their members. Static notions of best practice are less helpful as the dynamics and complexities of tourism development cannot be adequately or appropriately mapped in this way. The framework attempts to provide a context for the effective study of partnerships by highlighting the critical points in partnership formation, development, operation and evaluation.

The second part of the argument reviews the work which has already been undertaken on partnerships and particularly the work on tourism partnerships. There have been many individual case studies presented on partnership formation and operation which provide interesting if idiosyncratic views about the life and times of the tourism partnership. More recently we have seen attempts to produce overviews of partnership development from Europe, South Africa and Australia that have attempted to identify the critical success factors for partnerships (Laing et al., 2009). The section will conclude with an outline of the critical success factors for tourism partnerships which again captures the dynamic relations within and around the partnership development.

The final part of the chapter will present a study of partnership development in terms of the key success factors our research has identified and the trends we have observed in the field.

Benchmarking

Benchmarking is the process, drawn from management and quality research (Kozak, 2002), used to understand and evaluate how an organisation operates and should operate. This entails analysing the current operation and using the 'best practices' to establish a competitive position and way forward (Ritchie & Crouch, 2003). Originally such practices were located in the study of production and functions within the sector, but increasingly benchmarking has included international and process-based best practices (Wober, 2002). The EU's 2001 'White Paper on European Governance' (EC, 2001) refers to 'benchmarking' as one of the main tools for improving governance in Europe and a major contributor to the relevant national policies in the member states. Benchmarking was seen as one of the key mechanisms of cooperation, learning and innovation in Europe's future. Earlier, in 1997, when the European Commission (EC) issued its Strategic Communication (EC, 1997), benchmarking was promoted as the 'utilisation of a reference to best practice as a tool to identify necessary changes and to encourage social and economic initiatives and actors in order to progress in that direction'. Since then, benchmarking has been largely referred as to an 'important tool to improve competitiveness', available to both economic actors and public authorities in European policies and practice, of which tourism has emerged as a significant domain.

The literature highlights that benchmarking needs to be a continuous process, an integral part of the commitment to continuous improvement, which informs the direction and processes throughout the organisation (Wober, 2002). Although much of the literature has produced comparative studies, benchmarking has to go beyond comparisons with competitors to unpack the practices that lie behind the identified performance and process gaps. There are many benefits of benchmarking, including:

- providing realistic and achievable targets;
- preventing companies from being industry led;
- challenging operational complacency;
- creating a belief that there is a need for change;
- helping to identify weak areas and indicating what needs to be done to improve.

Studies used to be focused on product or output comparisons but we see the significance of benchmarking in analysing the processes behind the production of the outcome. Benchmarking examines how others achieve their performance levels by exploring the processes they use, thus identifying the processes behind excellent performance. There have been several initiatives in different European countries which have attempted to introduce benchmarking into tourism, including the UK 'Best Value' programme (assessing local authorities' performance in delivering tourism services and 'value for money' appraisal; the Austrian 'TourMIS' project (provision of online tourism data and evaluation programme to transform data into management information); the Marca de Calidad Turistica Española initiative in Spain

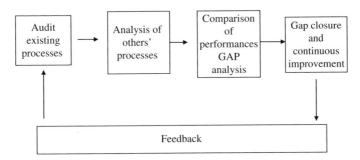

Figure 8.1 The benchmarking process (authors' own diagram)

(management model based on key criteria for six tourism sectors); the Q1000 of the Travel Development Centre in Finland (common quality criteria and instruments for SME tourism businesses); and Destination 21 in Denmark (a labelling scheme for tourist destinations with sustainable development) (Burhin *et al.*, 2003). These were different applications but shared similar core approaches and it is these similarities which we draw out in the next part of our analysis.

Benchmarking should not be considered a one-off exercise; it should be a continuous process designed to inform continuous improvement (see Figure 8.1).

Types of benchmarking

We will summarise a number of different types of benchmarking (outlined in Figure 8.2), which utilise different analytical foci, and review their strengths and weaknesses.

- *Internal benchmarking* operates within the same organisation, reviewing functions, departments, projects and businesses in the same company or

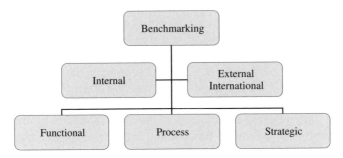

Figure 8.2 Types of benchmarking (authors' own design)

group at the same or another location to stimulate continuous improvement. The aim is to improve competitiveness and economic efficiency. This is the simplest form of benchmarking, as access to sensitive data is relatively straightforward. There should be similarity of language, culture, mechanisms and systems, meaning that standardised data is often readily available. There should be fewer barriers to implementation as practices should transfer easily within the same organisation. Relatively quick returns should be possible. The drawbacks are that real innovation may be lacking and best-in-class performance is more likely to be found through external benchmarking. An internal focus might inhibit the use of external examples and could foster complacency.

- *External benchmarking* analyses other organisations that are known to be the best in class. These can include international examples of best practices analysed from throughout the world. Globalisation and advances in information technology are increasing opportunities. This may take more time and resources to set up and the results need careful analysis due to national differences, but there is the possibility that this could provide opportunities for learning from the 'cutting edge'. There are possibilities of breakthroughs with the broadening of the corporate perspective. This approach stimulates challenge and changes may be greater. It is relatively difficult to access data, needing significant time and resources to ensure the comparability and the credibility of the findings and the development of sound proposals. It can be less sensitive to ethical and political reservations.

- *Competitive benchmarking* operates where examples are drawn from within the same sector, considering their positions in relation to performance characteristics of key products and services. This type of analysis is often undertaken through trade associations or third parties to protect confidentiality. Data is often protected.

- *Functional benchmarking* uses examples drawn from different business sectors or areas to find ways of improving similar functions. This allows the investigation of core business functions. Such an approach can lead to innovation and dramatic improvements. It does not need to focus on direct competition but the benchmark examples may need to be in a similar sector for useful comparisons to be made.

- *Process benchmarking* seeks examples from best practice organisations that perform similar work or deliver similar services. The focus is on improving specific critical processes, involving producing process maps to undertake the analysis. This type of benchmarking often results in short-term benefits.

- *Strategic benchmarking* examines the long-term strategies to improve overall performance and what has enabled high performers to succeed. This involves considering high-level aspects such as core competencies, new products and services development and improving capabilities for dealing with changes in the external environment. Changes resulting from this type of benchmarking may be difficult to implement and the benefits can take a long time to materialise.

These summaries and the analytical separation of the different types of benchmarking are useful but, in practice, we would argue that observation of actual practice testifies to the way that organisations have created hybrids of these types to fit them to the immediate needs of the organisation. For example, an examination of the VisitScotland report (2002) reveals that the benchmarking reported included functional, process, strategic and international elements. The data was drawn from eight destinations, including Scotland – the other investigations explored the tourism operations of Ireland, Norway, New Zealand, Germany, Costa Rica, South Africa and British Columbia.

We have critically explored the literature on benchmarking to demonstrate that what is at the heart of the benchmarking project should be seen as a continuous ongoing programme of review and reflection. The benchmarking process must be specified as precisely as possible in terms of level and range. This will also influence the selection of comparators and the determination of the criteria for the evaluation of the processes. The crucial decisions for the organisation are centred on the choice of the most relevant and significant comparators. It is possible to identify key components of the operations involved, highlighting core functions, looking at capacities and competences, weighed against local and/or international organisations involved in similar tasks or ones utilising similar processes.

EDEN is the acronym for European Destinations of Excellence, a project promoting sustainable tourism development models across the EU. The project is based on national competitions that take place every year and result in the selection of a tourist 'destination of excellence' for each participating country. We have outlined the benchmarking of the Hungarian EDEN destinations elsewhere (Lőrincz et al., 2007). However, we have found that the processes of the competition have been given greater significance with the EU through the Sustainable Tourism Group (TSG) in 2011, using the EDEN initiative as the basis for working towards the development of a single system of performance measures for sustainable tourism development. They are using the review of the EDEN projects undertaken by the Universtat Autònoma de Barcelona (2010) to model the system. This work established a 20-point set of indicators which can be seen as the basis for benchmarking. However, although these 20 indicators do provide a way of reviewing sustainable tourism development, only factor 17 actually directly monitors the significant elements of partnership processes. This demonstrates the importance of determining the focus of the benchmarking. It is not sufficient to assume that other evaluations will address the issues identified as the focus for the benchmarking.

Collaboration and Partnerships

Issues of collaboration and partnerships have become key areas in the tourism literature in the past two decades (Getz & Timur, 2005; Moisey & McCool, 2001; Ritchie & Crouch, 2003), linked to sustainable tourism (Selin, 1999) and to integration and participation (Mitchell & Reid, 2001; Tosun, 2000). The recognition of numerous problems arising in tourism development due to the lack of coordination and cohesion among the vast number of players in the tourism industry has brought with it the need for finding ways of bringing the 'interested parties' together (Imperial, 2005). The tourism industry is characterised by a plethora of actors with different interests and values. It is, therefore, an enormous challenge to try and persuade these individuals and organisations to sit down together and work towards a mutually accepted solution. Tourism development at local and regional levels aims to widen the range of the interested actors and make as wide a range as possible of the affected parties interested in tourism.

Our approach to benchmarking partnerships focuses on process rather than product and is influenced by Gray (1989) who differentiates between cooperation, coordination and collaboration, all of which describe some form of working on a common problem. 'Coordination means formal institution-alized relationships among existing networks of organisations' (Gray, 1989: 15). Cooperation is characterised by 'informal trade-offs' (Gray, 1989: 15), where no set rules are involved. Gray suggests that both cooperation and coordination are often part of the collaboration process 'in which those parties with a stake in the problem actively seek a mutually determined solution. They join forces, pool information, knock heads, construct alternative solutions, and forge an agreement' (Gray, 1989: xviii). Recognising that this does not capture the possible differences in interest and values of those collaborating, she elaborates the definition so that it allows for the participants having differing views and stakes: 'Collaboration is a process through which parties who see different aspects of a problem can constructively explore their differences and search for solutions that go beyond their own limited vision of what is possible' (Gray, 1989: 5).

Benchmarking partnerships in practice

Our application of international strategic benchmarking identified the following factors as having been instrumental in developing partnerships which endure and achieve. The review is based on our interviews with the emerging tourism partnerships in four countries and key stakeholders throughout Europe over the period from 2005 to 2010. These semi-structured interviews were conducted in an open way and recorded for subsequent analysis. Our research has included the opportunity to review the tourism partnerships in Hungary as part of the conference organised by the

West Balaton Tourism Destination Management Organisation (Nyugat Balatoni Turisztikai Iroda Non-Profit Kft), where the partnerships were asked to share their successes and failures within a forum of partnership builders (http://www.helikonportal.net/hir/partneri-kapcsolat-keszthely-balatonfured-siofok-kozott). We have also conducted participant observation in Veszprém and focus groups with the Hungarian Tourism Destination Management Organisations in 2010 and 2011. Our review has sought to model the process elements and key success factors. We present them here in Table 8.1, within a framework of continua where the desirable realities are on the left of the page.

These continua do not exist in isolation but should rather be seen as a processual, working together in reinforcing or hindering the development of tourism partnerships. They interconnect and work across the individual elements. We therefore propose a model that runs the elements together both simultaneously and dynamically, despite the visual representation suggesting that there is a linear sense to the processes (Figure 8.3).

Sustainable Partnerships

The focus groups we have conducted demonstrated that the benchmark criteria elaborated earlier are necessary but not sufficient factors for the growth of partnerships. We believe that the trend toward benchmarking will continue as both funders and participants seek to make sense of a messy world (Lachapelle *et al.*, 2003), but we acknowledge that it will also be necessary to reflect on the success factors that can be identified from the research. It will be important that these benchmarking exercises are not simple comparisons but actually seek to integrate the examination of best practices into a drive for continuous improvement within the partnerships. From our analysis of these discussions, we would highlight four significant trends that we believe underpin the sustainable success of partnerships:

- mission cultures,
- trust,
- identifying a champion,
- achievement.

Mission cultures

This refers to the need to establish the context of the partnership in a way that does not become identified with any single set of identifiable interests. The mission must be focused at the level of the destination and not the sectoral interests within the destination. The emphasis therefore becomes centred on the process cultures of how the partnership can begin and continue to work positively. This means that short-term output cultures are

Table 8.1 Partnership benchmarks

Continua of best and worst practices

Equity	Discrimination

This requires a full recognition of all the strategic stakeholders who have a legitimate interest with an appropriate approach to include the more marginalised stakeholders. Levelling the playing field between stakeholder groups whose 'traditional' lobbying activities largely depend on their resources and are often imbalanced; applying principles of gender and regional balance; providing equitable access to information.

Inclusiveness	Exclusiveness

Appropriate participatory methods for elaborating needs and possibilities, dialogue, prioritisation, forming partnerships, resolving conflicts and reaching conclusions. Agreed principles for widening participation and engagement should support and challenge stakeholders to be actively involved, including the promotion of diversity, equity, representation, transparency, learning, time to consult and inclusiveness to overcome stereotypical perceptions and prejudice.

Effectiveness	Ineffectiveness

Structures and mechanisms that enable and track stakeholders' participation, monitor and evaluate the progress of engagement and effectiveness. Providing tools for addressing urgent issues, promoting better decisions by means of wider input and thereby generating recommendations that have broad support. Creating commitment through participants identifying with the outcome, thus increasing the chances of successful implementation.

Transparency	Opacity

Bringing all relevant stakeholders together in one forum, within an agreed process, with honest, open and equitable participation. Accountability through agreed, transparent, democratic mechanisms of engagement, position finding and decision making.

Empowering	Disenfranchising

Building on and strengthening capacity and empowerment to ensure all stakeholders can participate meaningfully, with adequate resources, skills and time. This is about voices, not votes, as it is essential to give a real voice to all stakeholders and ensure that they are effectively heard with their views carefully considered. Ownership promoted through people-centred processes, allowing ownership for decisions.

Learning environments	Status quo

Taking a learning approach throughout, requiring participants to learn from each other with a phased approach beginning modestly, building on existing participation systems, then focusing further participation during each subsequent stage of the processes. Flexibility – policies and institutions that encourage, manage and reward participation in the partnership and allow the stakeholders to test approaches will support this.

Achievement	Failure

Specific acts and events focus participation. Demonstrable results and benefits, especially in the early phases support the long-term vision, convincing stakeholders that their investments of time and other resources will have an impact and a measurable return.

Table 8.1 (*Continued*)

Continua of best and worst practices

Legitimacy	Doubt
Creating trust, allowing all views to be represented and respected increases the legitimacy and credibility of the processes, building on democratic, transparent, accountable, equitable processes.	

Good governance	Poor governance
Cooperative management with developed partnerships and strengthened networks of stakeholders addressing conflicts; integrating diverse viewpoints; creating mutual benefits (win–win rather than win–lose situations). Clarity of roles and responsibilities based on clear norms and standards, entailing accountability and commitment of all stakeholders to the process and responsibility for the decisions, successes and failures. Developing shared power and responsibilities, strengthening the understanding of their contributions to the success of participation. Strengthening of (inter)governmental institutions: developing mechanisms of transparent, equitable and legitimate stakeholder participation. Organisations create feedback loops (local, national and international) and incorporating participants' views into the decision-making process.	

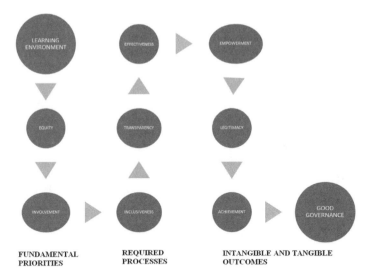

Figure 8.3 A processual view of best practice elements

displaced. Funders and participants are moving to a long-term view of achievement. The recent funding of tourism partnerships in Hungary is committed to the vision of the long-term project and will monitor the partnerships for five years after the funding has ceased in order to establish the longevity of the partnerships. The processes of partnership building must therefore be about embedding a mission which is shared and recognised as destination-wide with a series of actions connected to that vision. No one specific accomplishment could satisfy that target and therefore the partnership is built upon an ongoing and enduring search for a better future with a recognition that the processes are vital to arriving at this. This is important as all stakeholders then commit because of the overall mission and not only for their own vested interest. It is a question of putting overall mission interest above short-term considerations of personal interest.

Trust

If the partnerships are to be sustainable, it is essential that stakeholders recognise and respect each other. There will be multiple and diverse contributions but these must be acknowledged openly within the partnership. Trust has to be earned and secured in the ongoing play of relationships which develop within and around the partnership (Clarke & Raffay, 2010). Sources of trust come initially from the existing standing, status and expertise of the partners, but subsequently they are secured by relational values within the partnership – we identify patterns of who can be trusted and what with as we experience how people behave within the partnership. Openness and honesty are important elements and contribute greatly to the sense of trust within the working of the partnerships. The trend here is to legislate for such multi-sectoral collaboration, by making funding dependent upon having participants from the public, private and civil organisations actively involved in the developments.

Champion

Looking at the partnerships that have become successful, we can note that they have someone or a group who have taken on the challenge of fronting the partnership publicly. They have become the voice of the partnership. This is not necessarily the same thing as being the organiser or the leader of the partnership, as other people may well be 'feeding' the champion their lines. However, it is important that there is someone who is seen to raise the issues of the partnership to a wider audience and 'champion' the issues that define the partnership for the destination. We see this as a challenge to the traditional concepts of leadership and control, as the champion may exercise neither in that formal sense and yet becomes the 'voice' of the partnership and offers an effective leadership in terms of the public perceptions of the partnership.

Achievement

Although we have stressed the need for a mission culture for partnerships rather than an output culture, this does not mean that it is not important for partnerships to do anything. In fact it is vital that partnerships have something(s) to declare to their members and to a wider audience. The partnership must be seen as more than a 'talking shop'; otherwise motivation and commitment will fade away. The comment that most clearly marks out successful partnerships from unsuccessful ones is the ability of members to be able to claim that 'we are better off now than we were a year ago', or however long ago the partnership was established. The achievement should not be thought of in terms of the whole – whatever the partnership was established to achieve – as this would return us to a task focus. The process commitment to continuous improvement is only achievable through long-term and enduring commitment, but it does not mean that significant achievements cannot be recorded and celebrated along the way.

Conclusions

The dynamics of development are impossible for any one person, group or agency to control. The touristic offers that destinations will need to promote necessitate bringing together a wide range of stakeholders. This in turn focuses the challenge on partnership building, capacity building and the embedding of the partnership in the local civil society.

There will be an identifiable formal organisation (with clearly identifiable roles and responsibilities, a constitution and a budget). However there will also be an informal organisation that underpins the formal organisation and which makes it possible for the formal organisation to perform. It will be here that the sense of shared responsibility (and possibly even the sense of collective ownership) will emerge. The partnership will have established the basis for recognising that the shared benefits from the promotion of cultures and heritages within the tourism offer are a valuable and valued part of the destination's image and offer.

Partnerships will become increasingly important in the development of European tourism, both as a result of the top-down pressures from the EU to adopt this as a model of working across sectors and regions and because destinations have also recognised the benefits of partnership working within the destination. Benchmarking will inform the adoption of partnership working but it will be important that the rhetorical importance is supported and informed by rigorous research on partnerships. Moreover, we would stress that this research and monitoring leads to evaluation based not just on the tangible outcomes of the partnership but also probing the processes which underpin this performance. The intangible aspects are vital in capturing the ability of partnerships to develop successfully in terms of the capacities and capabilities within the partners and the destination.

The implications of benchmarking for the development of tourism partnerships become evident in the review of the processes which demonstrate the differences between partnerships that prosper and those which do not. If the partnerships identify the benchmarks specifically and accurately, the best practices will be highlighted and available to share among other emerging partnerships. Moreover, effective development will be supported by partnerships which have the capacity to cope with the dynamics of tourism development, which are not apparent in some of the earlier benchmarking studies that focused on capturing the static account of the current situation. We believe that the four key success factors that have emerged from our research will help to direct benchmarking attention to the intangible, human and dynamic aspects of partnership working by reinforcing the importance of processes as well as outcomes. The commitment to the continuous processes involved in benchmarking should reinforce the effectiveness of the partnerships, especially in the continuous improvement of capacity and competence levels.

References

Burhin, F., Paskaleva-Shapira, K. and Santamaria, S. (2003) European governance for sustainable urban tourism: Benchmarking report. SUTGovernance Project deliverable. http://sut.itas.fzk.de.

Clarke, A. and Raffay, Á. (2010) Trust. In T. Ratz and A. Irimiás (eds) *Creativity and Innovation in Managing Uncertainty and Risk* in *Tourism – Theory and Practice*. Szekesfehervar: Kodolanyi Press.

EC (1997) *Benchmarking: Strategic Communication*. COM/97/0153. Brussels: European Commission.

EC (2001) *Enhancing Democracy: A White Paper on Governance in the European Union*. Brussels: European Commission, accessed 24 May 2013. http://eur-lex.europa.eu/LexUriServ/site/en/com/2001/com2001_0428en01.pdf

EC (2006) *A Renewed EU Tourism Policy: Towards a Stronger Partnership for European Tourism*. COM(2006) 134. Brussels: European Commission. http://eur-lex.europa.eu/LexUriServ/LexUriServ.do?uri=COM:2006:0134:FIN:en:PDF.

Getz, D. and Timur, S. (2005) Stakeholder involvement in sustainable tourism: Balancing the voices. In W.F. Theobald (ed.) *Global Tourism* (3rd edn) (pp. 230–247). London: Elsevier.

Gray, B. (1989) *Collaborating: Finding Common Grounds for Multiparty Problems*. San Francisco, CA and London: Jossey-Bass.

Imperial, M.T. (2005) Using collaboration as a governance strategy: Lessons from six watershed management programs. *Administration and Society* 37 (3), 281–320.

Kozak, M. (2002) *Destination Benchmarking: Concepts, Practices and Operations*. Wallingford: CABI.

Lachapelle, P.R., McCool, S.F. and Patterson, M.E. (2003) Barriers to effective natural resource planning in a 'messy' world. *Society and Natural Resources* 16, 473–490.

Laing, J.H., Leeb, D., Moore, S.A., Wegner, A. and Weiler, B. (2009) Advancing conceptual understanding of partnerships between protected area agencies and the tourism industry: A postdisciplinary and multi-theoretical approach. *Journal of Sustainable Tourism* 17 (2), 207–229.

Lőrincz, K., Raffay, Á. and Clarke, A. (2007) Best practice in rural destination management – exploring Hungarian excellence. In P. Long (ed.) *Researching Destination Management, Policy and Planning: Linking Culture, Heritage and Tourism*. Leeds: Leeds Metropolitan University Press.

Mitchell, R. and Reid, D. (2001) Community integration: Island tourism in Peru. *Annals of Tourism Research* 28 (1), 113–139.

Moisey, R.N. and McCool, S.F. (2001) Sustainable tourism in the 21st century: Lessons from the past, challenges to address. In S.F. McCool and R.N. Moisey (eds) *Tourism, Recreation and Sustainability: Linking Culture and the Environment*. Wallingford: CABI.

Ritchie, B. and Crouch, G. (2003) *The Competitive Destination*. Wallingford: CABI.

Selin, S. (1999) Developing a typology of sustainable tourism partnerships. *Journal of Sustainable Tourism* 7, 260–273.

Tosun,C. (2000). Limits to community participation in the tourism development process in developing countries. *Tourism Management* 21 (6), 613–633.

Universtat Autònoma de Barcelona (2010) *Test to Implement Tourist Indicators in EDEN Destinations: An Evaluation*. Brussels: European Commission, DG Enterprise and Industry/Tourism Unit.

VisitScotland Report (2002) http://www.scotland.gov.uk/Publications/2005/11/18110937/09382.

Wober, K.W. (2002) *Benchmarking in Tourism and Hospitality Industries*. Wallingford: CABI.

9 Tourism Human Resources

Adele Ladkin

Introduction

There is little doubt that tourism activity is an important generator of jobs (Ladkin, 2011). The global tourism industry directly provides around 3% of global employment, or 192 million jobs, the equivalent to one in every 12 formal sector jobs. The International Labour Organization (ILO) predicts this is likely to rise to 251.6 million jobs by 2012, one in every 11 formal sector jobs (Ferguson, 2007). Taking the 27 European Union (EU) member states and five non-EU countries, in 2007 more than 9 million people were employed in the EU hotel, restaurants and catering sector, which was the equivalent of 4.2% of all people employed (Eurostat, 2008). While these broad statistics mask the large variations by country in the numbers of people employed in tourism, they provide an indication of the significance of tourism as a means of employment.

The capacity of tourism activities to generate jobs indicates that the tourism industry is highly dependent on human resources. While the many elements of physical infrastructure development are a visible and vital component of tourism, it is human labour that delivers the many products and services that comprise the tourism industry. Indeed, often in today's highly globalised travel and tourism industry, the quality of service is what differentiates products. Despite these merits, human resources are often overlooked in tourism planning and development activities and there is an assumption that there is a ready supply of labour to fulfil the requirements of an expanding industry. While this may be the case for the unskilled or low-skilled jobs, the industry also requires skilled professionals in a range of different sectors.

Despite a possible surplus of labour, there are many human resource challenges for the coming decades, including issues such as competition for skilled human resources, aging populations, labour shortages, skill gaps, lack of defined career opportunities and the poor image of the sector. Human resources are a key component of the tourism product and there is a need to plan and manage human assets for the sustainable growth of the tourism industry.

This chapter explores current European tourism human resource issues. Although the focus is on Europe, in fact many of the human resource issues are global in nature and not confined to particular geographical boundaries. However, where there is particular significance for Europe this is made explicit. The chapter is organised in the following way. First, it describes two international agencies that currently influence tourism employment and human resources, followed by a discussion of the influence of the EU on employment activities. This provides the wider context within which human resources issues are situated. Second, tourism migration in Europe is discussed to further provide the context of labour mobility evident in Europe and the implications of this for European tourism. Third, specific current tourism human resource issues facing Europe are discussed.

International Agencies

A discussion of tourism human resources cannot be considered in isolation from the wider labour market context and employment policy implications. Employment conditions, wage rates, labour policies, and so on all have a bearing on the characteristics and structure of employment opportunities. A detailed discussion of the many different structures and agencies that either directly or indirectly affect the nature of tourism employment within each European country is beyond the scope of this chapter; therefore, three organisations are singled out for discussion. These have been selected because their activities have a direct influence on global tourism employment and subsequent human resource development.

The International Labour Organization

The ILO was founded in 1919 to pursue a vision based on the premise that universal, lasting peace can be established only if it is based upon the decent treatment of working people. It became the first specialised agency of the UN in 1946. The organisation is devoted to advancing opportunities for women and men to obtain decent work in conditions of freedom, equity, security and human dignity. Enhancing social protection, encouraging decent employment opportunities, promoting rights at work and strengthening dialogue in handling work-related issues are some of its main aims. The ILO represents the interests of all types of employment, of which tourism employment plays a part. The significance of the ILO is in its activities to improve working lives, and as such it recognises human resources as a valuable asset. Set against this background, the ILO provides the overarching philosophy behind human resource development in general terms and, in particular, highlighting the value of human resources and the need to provide equitable, humane and sound employment conditions and opportunities.

This has particular significance for tourism as often jobs in the tourism sector fall into the category of low-paid, temporary employment where working conditions may be less than desirable. They often exist outside the formal economy and attract some of the most vulnerable workers, for example, migrants, ethnic minorities and women. Within the European context, as in the wider global context, many of the jobs are occupied by vulnerable worker groups. The efforts of the ILO therefore have a particular relevance for tourism workers.

The World Tourism Organization

The World Tourism Organization (UNWTO) is a specialised agency of the UN and is the leading international organisation in the field of tourism, serving as a global forum for tourism policy issues and practical knowledge. Crucially, the UNWTO has a role to play in human resource education and training for tourism and through the THEMIS foundation leads the way in tourism human resource development initiatives. The significance of the UNWTO is that it brings human resource development, education and training to the forefront of tourism policy-making agendas and supports initiatives that develop and recognise the importance of education and training for a skilled tourism workforce. The UNWTO has a significant role to play in raising an awareness of the value of human resources in the tourism industry, and it offers specific programmes tailored to assist countries who are developing their human resource capabilities. Eastern European countries who currently fall into this category are able to benefit from various educational programmes and workshops organised and facilitated by the UNWTO that aim to provide assistance in human resource development. National tourist organisations can seek assistance in terms of policy-making initiatives, and the education sector, through the THEMIS foundation, can develop appropriate educational programmes for training and developing the tourism workforce. The human resource development work of the UNWTO continues to grow, with more countries exploring the policy-making and training opportunities provided.

The two organisations described above have a working relationship that has developed specifically in relation to tourism human resources. Due to the importance of this partnership, the nature of this collaboration is outlined below.

ILO and UNWTO collaboration

Specifically for tourism employment and labour, the ILO and the UNWTO are collaborating in two areas: the measurement of employment and decent work in tourism. This collaboration has been formalised as the ILO/UNWTO Joint Project on Employment in the Tourism Industries. Both of these collaborative areas represent key issues that are central to the development of human resources for tourism.

In the first of these, the formal collaboration to improve the national methods of data collection for employment in the tourism industries has resulted in the joint publication of *Sources and Methods: Labour Statistics – Employment in the Tourism Industries, Special Edition* (ILO/UNWTO, 2008). The publication consolidates descriptions of the methods used by countries in the production of statistics on employment, wages and hours of work in the tourism industries. The aim is to provide users with a comprehensive description of the latest sources and methods used in countries throughout the world. This highlights the differences between countries and is also used to facilitate understanding of methods behind countries' tourism satellite accounts. The significance of this is that it represents an attempt to understand and measure labour markets, wage rates and working conditions, which is a step forward towards recognising the value of human resources.

In the second area, the decent work agenda provides a unified framework for the major areas of ILO work, specifically highlighting its four strategic objectives. These are: fundamental principles and rights at work and international labour standards; employment and income opportunities; social protection and social security; and social dialogue and tripartism. As previously stated, it is often vulnerable groups who are employed in the lower paid tourism occupations and these areas are of particular importance for them. Advancing the principles of decent work in the tourism sector will have a significant impact on a large number of employees, both in domestic tourism areas and major international tourism destinations (Chernyshev, 2009). Through the principles of decent work, employers experience improved working conditions and employers gain staff who are better motivated, and can provide better service and increased productivity. Decent work covers the following dimensions:

- employment opportunities;
- adequate earnings and productive work;
- decent hours;
- combining work, family and personal life;
- work that should be abolished;
- stability and security of work;
- equal opportunities and treatment in employment;
- safe work environment;
- social security;
- social dialogue, workers' and employers' representation.

Many of these principles of decent work represent challenges for the tourism sector. For example, adequate earnings raise the issue of low pay. While some countries have a minimum wage, others do not. In terms of decent hours, many tourism jobs include shift work where hours can be long and sometimes unpredictable, as is the case where staff are asked to work additional shifts or stay at work longer when there is demand. Combining work, family and personal life raises the issue of a work–life balance. It is a widely known fact that long hours and demanding work, particularly in the hospitality sector, present challenges for workers who spend increasing amounts of time at work rather than at home. Finally, workers' and employers' representation can also be an issue for the tourism industry, as while certain occupations have formal structures and agreements for representation, for example the airline industry, others do not. Again this comes back to the theme of vulnerable and marginalised groups occupying jobs in the informal economy, which can be the case in certain types of tourism employment.

Clearly, the tourism industry has many challenges with regard to the principles of decent work. However, few would argue against the idea that adherence to the concept of decent work combined with a better understanding of the dynamics and complexity of tourism employment will have a positive impact on those who seek tourism employment as a means to make a living. For this reason, this collaborative work between the ILO and the UNWTO has significant and long-term implications for tourism employment.

The European Union

The EU member states adhere to the many different EU policies, principles and guidelines developed by the EU. One of the key policy areas addressing human resources is the Employment and Social Affairs policy area. The main objective of this policy area is to ensure that Europe keeps up with the pace of change to remain competitive against new emerging economies. Europe must create the jobs needed by a dynamic knowledge-based society, requiring investment in education, science and employment policies that are mutually supportive. Five main areas are covered by this policy area:

- creating growth and jobs;
- preserving workers' rights and social protection;
- equal opportunities;
- investing in people;
- the right to mobility.

These five policy areas apply to all kinds of employment and are not specific to tourism. However, when considered in relation to tourism employment these areas have a clear significance. To begin with creating growth and jobs, it was stated earlier that tourism employment continues to grow. In countries dependent on tourism and where there is an opportunity for tourism development, the human resource element and potential for increased employment opportunities should not be ignored. Second, work-ers' rights and social protection are needed in order to ensure that vulnerable groups and those in unskilled and manual work receive adequate employ-ment protection. Included in this protection are equal opportunities, the third policy area. The fourth area, investing in people, again has particular significance for the tourism industry. It is an often-heard criticism that tour-ism occupations offer few long-term career development opportunities. Rather, many jobs are seen as temporary, a means to an end, before a more rewarding occupation is taken up. Part of this criticism reflects the lack of training and development opportunities within some tourism occupations, combined with low skill specificity where new skills are not required. Investing in people puts the emphasis firmly on the training and develop-ment of human capital and may result in improved attempts to retain and develop the best people for the industry. Finally, the right to mobility provides clear opportunities for the tourism industry in the form of labour migration.

As with other sectors, European tourism has to remain competitive against emerging destinations. The Employment and Social Affairs policy area pro-vides a focus on tourism employment issues that need to be considered to ensure a competitive tourism product.

The ILO, the UNWTO and the EU provide the overarching context of current agendas that have a direct relevance for tourism employment and subsequent human resource development. The common theme to arise from these different but compatible agendas is that in the longer term tourism employment opportunities will be strengthened and tourism employment conditions will be improved. Set in this context, the future for human resource development in tourism is positive, as issues are discussed and pos-sible solutions to any existing difficulties for tourism workers explored.

European Labour Migration

Europe has a long and sustained history of labour migration. In recent years, policy changes in European countries have created more opportunities for labour mobility. Problems of labour shortages and a mismatch of supply and demand have been behind many of these policy changes. Today, each of the European states are net immigration countries. For the more estab-lished host countries such as France, Germany, the UK, Austria, Switzerland, Sweden and Denmark, this has been the case since at least the 1960s and most have experienced high levels of immigration since the 1990s (Boswell, 2005). Due to growing economic prosperity, additional European countries became net receiving countries in the 1980s, such as Ireland, Spain, Portugal, Greece and Finland. Furthermore, more recently some central and eastern European countries have become host countries. After 1989, former socialist countries on the EU's eastern borders became important transit countries for migrants attempting to enter more prosperous western European countries. In terms of the countries that recently joined the EU, economic growth and political stability have meant that they too are now experiencing positive net migration, such as Cyprus, Hungary, the Czech Republic, Slovakia and Slovenia (Boswell, 2005). The majority of the labour migration to and within Europe is legal. However, some is illegal and takes place within the informal economy. For example, the EU suggested a figure of 500,000 irregular migrants entering EU states annually. Estimates of numbers of irregular migrants in European countries put the number in Italy at 800,000, Germany 500,000, France 300,000 and the UK 200,000 (Boswell, 2005).

The tourism industry represents one of the main areas of employment for migrant workers, particularly those who are newly arrived in a country. The hospitality industry in Europe has historically relied on migrant workers (Baum, 2007). The industry is easy to access due to the low-skilled nature of many of the jobs, and many migrants are drawn to lower paid, informal or casual employment, often in the hospitality sector. Spain, Germany, the UK and Ireland have all received many migrants in recent years, particularity from the new A8 accession countries. The more permeable national labour market boundaries within Europe have led to a transient, ethnically diverse workforce. However, migrants are often vulnerable workers and are subjected to some of the worst employment conditions. The hospitality workforce is characterised by a reliance on particular types of workers who are associated with being marginalised within secondary labour markets, specifically women, students, ethnic minorities, young people and migrants (Lucas & Mansfield, 2008). The groups are often marginalised by language and also a lack of understanding of the formal entitlements and regulations of host countries. Set within the context of an increasing freedom of movement for labour within the EU to meet shortages across a range of jobs, the reality is that migrant workers are more likely to work in lower paid jobs for which they are overqualified (MacKenzie & Forde, 2009).

Labour mobility is a feature of European labour markets which supply the tourism industry with a continuous supply of workers. This raises a number of issues for discussion. First, as previously described, migrant workers are often vulnerable to illegal employment practices. It is often difficult for migrant workers to escape such conditions due to a lack of language skills, a lack of understanding of the formal entitlements and regulations of host countries and no access to support networks. In such instances, migrant workers may be more at risk than others in terms of receiving equal pay, benefits and working conditions. Within this context, MacKenzie and Forde (2009) argue that this situation often suits employers; therefore the role of employers, labour market institutions and broader regulatory constraints cannot be ignored when considering how tourism employment conditions can be improved.

Second, migrant workers, as evidenced by their different nationalities from the local population, are highly visible within the tourism sector. This raises questions concerning the 'authenticity' of tourism services. The notion of authentic tourism products and experiences has a long history of debate. Within this area, there is an emerging area of discussion concerning the role of human resources in the authentic experience. For example, in the UK international visitors to certain tourist destination have remarked that they never meet a 'local' as all the service encounters are with migrant workers of different nationalities. In some destinations, migrant workers are changing the face of the tourist encounter which may have both positive and negative effects. This may have longer term implications that have not yet become realised.

Thirdly, migrant labour is usually by nature temporary. This has implications for the attraction and retention of key workers and raises questions of to what extent employers engage in employee training and education. If both sides view tourism as providing only temporary employment opportunities, there is less incentive for either party to develop human capital. Related to education and training, a final issue for discussion relates to the need for standardisation or harmonisation of European qualifications. If mobility increases as predicted and as mobility is encouraged through active EU policies, a mutual understanding of each country's tourism qualifications may be beneficial. Comparable qualifications may help employers to recruit those with appropriate skills and educational attainment. It may also have the effect of raising the profile and credibility of vocational tourism education if qualifications are transferable within the European community. The debates raised above are likely to continue. These issues notwithstanding, certainly migrant workers form a significant proportion of the tourism labour force. This presents its own set of challenges in terms of requirements for education, training and human resource development.

Human Resource Development Issues

Human resource development consists of three main areas: education, training and development. Garavan *et al.* (2000) outline the acquisition of skills, knowledge, attitudes and values in order to meet the needs of the business environment. The tourism industry has the potential to generate employment opportunities on a large scale, and with the increase in demand for domestic and international tourism across the globe, the supply of jobs looks set to continue. The freedom of movement for workers within the EU has created cross-boundary opportunities for employment and has created a European labour market for tourism employment. The European labour market, as with national, regional and local labour markets, is subject to issues such as supply and demand and labour economics. Taking both the employers' and employees' perspective, employers have the opportunity to attract labour from a wide geographical area, and employees can select from a wide labour market.

Set within the macro context of a desire to sustainably grow the number of tourism jobs, human resource development becomes increasingly important. There are a number of key issues that each have an impact on the ability of the tourism industry to attract, retain and develop human capital which is vital for the sustainability of the industry. Many are features of the sector in general and go beyond the European geographical region.

A gender-biased workforce

ILO estimates dating from 1983 suggest that one-third of the global workforce in tourism was made up of women (ILO, 2001). Current estimates are that this has risen to 46%, and in reference to catering and accommodation, a staggering 90%. While a gender-segregated workforce presents no issue in itself, the high number of women employed in the sector is symptomatic of many of the less favourable traits of the work, e.g. low-status and unskilled jobs, subcontracted, temporary, casual or part-time work, low wage rates and few career development opportunities. Although the gender bias is more pronounced in developing countries and to a lesser extent within Europe, the dominance of females in the workplace is marked. Despite the importance of female workers to the tourism industry, access to higher levels of corporate structures continues to be problematic and there is a gender-based income disparity across the sector. The glass ceiling in the hospitality sector is well documented elsewhere (for example, Knutson & Schmidgall, 1999). Essentially, despite European and national government regulatory frameworks and policies aimed at reducing gender-based discrimination, inequality remains a problem in the sector. Further attempts to address this issue, along with ensuring minimum wage regulation and decent employment conditions, would assist in assuring tourism is a viable employment opportunity for all. This also applies to the employment of other vulnerable groups, such as the young, child workers, migrant labour and undeclared labour. The gender issue is significant in relation to human resource development as access to education and training requirements have to be matched to the needs of the workforce. This requires not one blanket agenda and policy for all, but sensitivity in deciding the best approach to take and how to reach marginalised groups.

Seasonality

Due to fluctuations of demand in the tourism industry, it is inevitable that much of the employment is seasonal. Tourist destinations that rely heavily on one type of consumer or product experience fluctuations in demand with subsequent effects on employment. This is a feature of many European destinations that are largely summer sun, sand and sea product based. Seasonal employment may be well suited to those who are only seeking temporary work, as is the case of students who may travel abroad to earn money and take a holiday at the same time. Seasonality is not necessarily a negative factor in tourism employment but it may discourage those looking for a longer term or permanent occupation from pursuing this sector. Organisations can offer some assistance, such as job rotation or offering training opportunities in the low season. However, the reality is often that fewer workers are needed outside the high season. The seasonality of tourism inevitably means that for many it cannot offer a stable, reliable occupation. Fluctuating unemployment rates and seasonal migration are realities for many European destinations, and there is little incentive for employers to offer any training or development opportunities beyond the basic requirements to do a job, due to cost constraints.

The need for tourism education and training

Across Europe there is increasing recognition for dedicated tourism education and training to develop the skills and knowledge of the tourism workforce. Traditionally, employers, many of them small and medium-sized enterprises (SMEs), have argued that they cannot afford to provide training for employees; neither can they afford wage rates that will be demanded by employees with formal training and recognised qualifications. Furthermore, high levels of mobility mean that the return on investment for training is minimal. While these are all valid arguments, on the other hand it could be argued that training will increase productivity, and will alleviate some of the problems associated with staff recruitment and retention. Both are legitimate claims. Although the ability and need to provide training for employees vary considerably, few would doubt the value of skilled labour. The rapid and continued growth in formal tourism education programmes across Europe supports this argument, with many courses attempting to train future employees to meet industry needs. Continuous training is also important for human resource development, and should not be viewed as a once-only opportunity.

Given the high levels of mobility in European tourism labour markets, what many employers complain about is a lack of standardised qualifications by which they can compare different educational achievements. The European Qualifications Framework (EQF) goes some way to addressing this. While the EQF is not designed to replace national qualifications, it aims to facilitate cooperation between the member states. A greater understanding and recognition of qualifications will facilitate tourism labour mobility within Europe.

Image and job status

The tourism industry has long been plagued by poor images of working in the sector. These include long and antisocial working hours, seasonal employment, low status jobs, demanding physical work and low rates of pay. Conversely, certain elements of the sector also receive positive perceptions associated with the thrill and excitement of travel or the glamour of luxurious surroundings that exist in certain working environments. Ultimately, the image of the sector affects its ability to attract and retain human resources.

The recruitment and retention of high-quality staff is essential for the continued success of the European tourism industry. The ability of organisations and particular industry sectors to recruit staff is linked to a whole range of labour market conditions including pay, competition for resources, access, mobility, etc. All other things being equal, the perception of the industry becomes crucial. Once employees are recruited, job conditions, terms of employment and career development opportunities become significant in determining staff retention. There are two areas for reflection in relation to attracting and retaining staff.

The first of these is the role of the internet in recruitment. Dedicated online recruitment and employers' websites have made searching for a job easier than ever before, particularly in the case of European mobility. Increasingly, social networking sites provide an informal source of information on job opportunities, and employees' experiences – both good and bad – are discussed on internet forums. This has both positive and negative opportunities for employers.

Second, there is an emerging area of research concerning the employment aspirations and expectations of the younger generation, Generation Y (for example, Barron et al., 2007). Early indications are that generation Y employees have different expectations and are discerning when it comes to their choice of occupation. Career expectations are different from previous generations, with Generation Yers placing a high importance on the individualist aspects of a job (Ng et al., 2010). This has implications for the way in which jobs are organised, and management methods that include more autonomy may be appropriate. Ensuring that tourism occupations remain attractive to Generation Y is an issue for the tourism industry to address.

Career development opportunities

The tourism industry has few structured career opportunities. Often occupations are seen as transitory, with many people working in the sector for short periods of time and with the notion that it will only be temporary. For those who intend to remain in the sector, often they become frustrated by the lack of career opportunities and decide to leave. Therefore, the loss of talented individuals is a significant problem for the industry. There are of course exceptions to the rule, and those who find themselves working for international companies may experience greater opportunities within their companies either in their home country or overseas. International tour operators, travel agencies, finance providers and hotel companies provide career development opportunities for employees not only within Europe, but globally. In Europe, given that many young people are introduced to the world of work through tourism employment, there is an opportunity to develop this human capital. However, this is not easy as training is often limited to large hotel chains, and there is a shift within Europe away from specific skills towards more generic skills (ILO, 2001). Many European tourism companies are SMEs, and opportunities for formal training are limited, with 'on the job' training being undertaken where and when necessary. Investment in education, training and career development is limited by cost and opportunity, and this becomes a significant barrier for many employees hoping to develop a career in the industry. To meet the ever-increasing demand for high levels of customer-oriented service, human capital development opportunities are vital, both for employers and employees.

Information technology

Across Europe, information and communications technology (ICT) will have an increased impact on human resource skill requirements. The complexity of integrated internet, customer relationship management and supply chain management IT systems demands essential IT competencies. Although systems are designed to be as user friendly as possible, the technology changes so rapidly that there is a need for continuous training. Increasingly, an IT-literate workforce is a standard requirement for the successful operation of tourism businesses, and this is the area where training demands are likely to be the highest. IT-literate employees will be vital for all businesses and human resource development will have to embrace this challenge and ensure IT literacy is a fundamental part of training.

Conclusions

The need to attract, develop and retain labour for tourism has never been greater. Human resource development has become a significant factor in maintaining national or destination competitiveness, and it could be argued that tourism employees do more than create the product – they *are* the product. Certainly, travel and tourism companies are defined by the quality of their workforce. With increased competition and globalisation, developing tourism human resources is critical for sustained competitive advantage. Within European labour markets the tourism industry competes with other sectors for high-quality skilled labour; as such, the role of education, training, career development and improved employment conditions should not be overlooked. Significant challenges remain throughout Europe, but an improved understanding of labour needs and training requirements combined with a commitment to improving tourism employment conditions where necessary is a starting point for the effective development of human resources for tourism.

References

Barron, P., Maxwell, G., Broadbridge, A. and Ogden, S. (2007) Careers in hospitality management: Generation Y's experiences and perceptions. *Journal of Hospitality and Tourism Management* 14 (2), 119–128.

Baum, T. (2007) Human resources in tourism: Still waiting for change. *Tourism Management* 28, 1383–1399.

Boswell, C. (2005) *Migration in Europe*. Paper prepared for the Policy Analysis and Research Programme of the Global Commission on International Migration. Hamburg: Migration Research Group, Hamburg Institute of International Economics.

Chernyshev, I. (2009) Keynote session iii. *Employment in the Tourism Industries: Measurement Issues and Case Studies*. Fifth UNWTO International Conference on Tourism Statistics – Tourism: An Engine for Employment Creation, 30 March–2 April, Bali, Indonesia.

Eurostat (2008) Eurostat statistics, Luxembourg. http://epp.eurostat.ec.europa.eu/portal/page/portal/tourism/introduction

Ferguson, L. (2007) Global monitor – United Nations World Tourism Organization. *New Political Economy* 12 (4), 557–568.

Garavan, N.T., Gunnigle, P. and Morely, M. (2000) Contemporary HRD research: A triarchy of theoretical perspectives and their prescriptions for HRD. *Journal of European Industrial Training* 24 (2), 65–93.

ILO (2001) Human resources development, employment and globalization in the hotel, catering and tourism sector. Report No. TMHCT/2001. International Labour Organization, Geneva.

ILO/UNWTO (2008) *Sources and Methods: Labour Statistics. Employment in the Tourism Industries, Special Edition*. Madrid: World Tourism Organization.

Knutson, B.J. and Schmidgall, R.S. (1999) Dimensions of the glass ceiling in the hospitality industry. *Cornell Hotel & Restaurant Administration Quarterly* 40 (6), 64–75.

Ladkin, A. (2011) Exploring tourism labor. *Annals of Tourism Research* 38 (3), 1135–1155.

Lucas, R. and Mansfield, S. (2008) *Staff Shortages and Immigration in the Hospitality Sector*. London: Migration Advisory Committee. http://www.ukba.homeoffice.gov.uk/mac.

MacKenzie, R. and Forde, C. (2009) The rhetoric of the 'good worker' versus the realities of employers' use and the experiences of migrant workers. *Work, Employment and Society* 23, 142–159.

Ng, E.S.W., Schweitzer, L. and Lyons, S.T. (2010) New generation, great expectations: A field study of the Millennial generation. *Journal of Business Psychology* 25, 281–292.

Part 3
Economics

10 Funding and Development Processes

Stephen Wanhill

Introduction

At any one time the European Union (EU) has a tourism programme containing a series of actionable measures which it sees as improving the quality and competitiveness of tourism services among member states (EC, 2007), which are reviewed from time to time in annual documents on strategic policy. Tourism is estimated to employ directly some 9 million people in Europe, accounting for 5.5% of European GDP. As such, it is seen as having great potential in terms of contributing to the achievement of several major EU objectives, such as sustainable development, economic growth, employment, notably in peripheral areas (Wanhill, 1997), as well as economic and social cohesion as defined in Article 130a of the Treaty of the European Union (Maastricht Treaty), 1992.

However, it is generally accepted that the most important impact of the EU on tourism arises not from specific tourism-related policies, but rather from mainstream policies and measures targeted at business in general. These include areas such as airline liberalisation, environmental measures, competition policy, social legislation, consumer protection, unification of taxes and regional policy. It is the latter aspect, through intervention by means of the Structural Funds, which is the responsibility of the Directorate General for Regional Policy (EC, 2004), that are probably the most significant direct contribution that the EU offers, since many regional programmes have strands specifically devoted to the development of tourist-related infrastructure or projects, protection of heritage and similar actions. It is the objective of this chapter to convey the economic aspects governing the Structural Funds, which have helped make possible so many projects within the EU, such as the expansion of the Palma de Majorca air terminal in the Balearic Islands (Spain), the start-up of businesses in the creative industries in Rock City Hultsfred (Sweden), the Thayatal National Park visitors' centre (Austria) and the Dráva River Basin ecotourism development (Hungary).

On the purely commercial side, the European Investment Bank and the European Investment Fund also have lending and investment programmes that can benefit small businesses in a number of ways (Wanhill, 2005). These programmes can be accessed via financial institutions in the member states, and are expected to be coordinated with the National Strategic Reference Framework (NSRF), which comprises the description of the strategy of the state in question and its proposed list of operational programmes (OPs) that it hopes to implement with support of the Structural Funds.

Structural Funds

Before 1988 there was no coherent system for the disbursement of the Structural Funds, which resulted in the dissipation of funds over many areas, thus reducing their effectiveness. Therefore, in 1988 a multi-annual programming approach for expenditure planning was adopted for the first planning period 1989–1993 to assure member states of the stability and predictability of EU support (EC, 1991). Each subsequent planning period had its own dynamic in respect of the number of development themes adopted and their nature, so as to match the needs of member states and Europe in general (EC, 2006). The objectives of the Funds for the current period (2007–2013) are shown in Table 10.1.

EU assistance is currently given under three general funds and one that is specific to agriculture:

(1) the European Regional Development Fund (ERDF), which is focused mainly on productive investment, infrastructure and local business development in less favoured regions, and is the principal vehicle for regional support;
(2) the European Social Fund (ESF), which has the task of promoting jobs through investing in educational systems, vocational training and employment assistance;
(3) the Cohesion Fund to promote growth-enhancing conditions and factors leading to real convergence for the least-developed member states and regions, such as transport and environmental infrastructure;
(4) The European Agricultural Fund for Rural Development (EAFRD), which is targeted at improving agricultural competitiveness, managing the environment, improving the quality of rural life and diversifying the rural economy.

The objectives shown in Table 10.1 are used to identify regions and allocate funds. Thus, convergence is supported by ERDF, ESF and the Cohesion

Table 10.1 Structural funds' objectives, 2007–2013

Objective	Aim
Convergence	To promote growth-enhancing conditions and factors leading to real convergence for the least developed member states and regions (those whose GDP per capita is 75% or less than the EU average).
Regional competitiveness and employment	To strengthen the competitiveness, employment and attractiveness of regions other than those which are the most disadvantaged, by anticipating economic and social changes, and promoting innovation, business spirit, protection of the environment, accessibility, adaptability and the development of inclusive labour markets.
Territorial cooperation	To strengthen cross-border, trans-national and inter-regional cooperation through promoting common solutions for neighbouring authorities in the fields of urban, rural and coastal development, the development of economic relations and the creation of networks of small and medium-sized enterprises (SMEs).

Source: Commission of the European Communities

Fund, regional competitiveness and employment by ERDF and ESF, while ERDF is the sole fund for territorial cooperation. The ERDF is the principal instrument for regional intervention and the sums available dwarf the other structural funds.

Economics of Structural Assistance

The case for EU intervention in tourism rests on concepts of market failure, namely:

(1) developing tourism as a common good that collectively benefits (pecuniary externalities) many businesses, with the regional tourist authority acting as a broker between suppliers and potential visitors;
(2) infant industry development as part of regional policy, where commercial viability requires public sector support through the provision of essential infrastructure and financial incentives;
(3) improving the tourism product, via the implementation of measures such as training programmes for tourism workers.

Although Structural Fund moneys are ultimately limited by overall budget allocations, their impact at the bidding level of a regional authority is one of a conditional matching grant with an open-ended commitment. An analysis of this situation is shown in Figure 10.1, where in the initial situation the authority has a budget constraint

$$T_1 + O_1 = I_1 \tag{1}$$

where T_1 is expenditure on tourism, O_1 expenditure on other public services and I_1 the level of the authority's income. The regional authority is now invited to bid for funds for tourism development. How much assistance is given depends on the projects put forward by the authority and the agreement reached concerning the programme. The effect of EU funding is to rotate the authority's income line from I_1I_1 to I_1I_3, so that if there is no eligible tourist spending there will be no grant, as occurs at point I_1 on the axis for 'Other expenditure'. Suppose that agreement is reached to settle at point E. At this point expenditure on tourism is T_2 and other public services, O_2. The amount of grant payable will depend on the appropriate rate (g) for tourism in the NSRF and the amount of eligible expenditure within T_2, say eT_2, where e is the fraction that is eligible. The limit rate of grant is normally 50% of all public expenditure on the project put forward, but has been raised to 85% in the case of projects in the outermost regions. The majority of projects no longer receive support at the limit rate. For tourism investment,

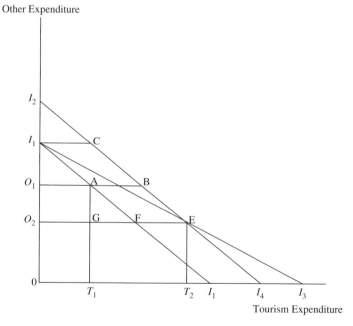

Figure 10.1   Economics of structural funds

grants are unlikely to be in excess of 45% of the investment cost and may usually be less.

From the above, the budget is now:

$$T_2 + O_2 = I_1 + geT_2$$
$$(1 - ge)T_2 + O_2 = I_1 \qquad (2)$$

where the first term on the left-hand side of Equation (2) is the amount the regional authority has to devote to tourist expenditure to gain the required grants. Subtracting Equation (1) from Equation (2) gives:

$$(1 - ge)T_2 - T_1 = -(O_2 - O_1) \qquad (3)$$

Thus any increase in regional authority spending on tourism to earn EU grants is matched by a reduction in spending on other public services. This is shown in Figure 10.1. By increasing expenditure to T_2 the authority receives a grant of EF and spends an extra FG of its own resources on tourism by diverting $O_1 - O$ from 'Other expenditure'. The ability of the authority to do this depends on the amount of discretionary spending it has in comparison to its statutory requirements.

The extent to which the application of EU rules constrains local development policies may be examined by considering alternative grant mechanisms. A lump-sum grant, without any conditions as to its use, that is equivalent to EF, will give the authority a budget line I_2I_4. A conditional grant (that it should be spent on tourism projects) but non-matching will present the authority with a budget line I_1CI_4. The EC's grant criterion constrains the authority to a budget line I_1EI_4, once the programme has been agreed. Consequently, any points on the line I_2E are unobtainable to the regional authority under this mechanism.

Consider the case of an unconditional grant: the authority's desired policy may be to position its expenditure at point C, using part of the grant to maintain tourism spending as before and switching the rest, plus own resources, to increase expenditure on other public services. Hence E is suboptimal and the EU mechanism is distorting planned expenditure. Experience has shown that this situation is unlikely because receiving authorities are normally quite willing to spend some of their own resources on grant-aided sectors. In fact, the availability of grant-in-aid often stimulates a change in political preferences enabling regional government officers to rally support and obtain political commitment to bring forward or maintain tourism spending programmes.

The more likely situation is the case of the conditional lump-sum grant represented by the budget line, I_1CI_4. Under this regime the authority may position itself anywhere along the line CI_4 of which CE is unobtainable under EU rules. It is not very probable that the authority will position itself at C for the reasons given above, but B is the critical point, for beyond B the authority has to switch expenditure from other public services to meet its EU commitments. Since E cannot be reached under the European system without regional authorities raising additional funds from elsewhere, then clearly a conditional non-matching grant system would be preferable from the perspective of the authority in terms of freedom of action, but not necessarily from the perspective of the EC, which is specifically trying to lever in a certain percentage of other funds to match its own contribution to the tourism projects in question.

Prior to 1992, when the additionality principle was adopted, some member states were using EU grants as a substitute for their own contribution. On the diagram, this practice had the effect of moving the I_1EI_4 to the left so that points E and F coincide, leaving the regional authority no better off in terms of income, but with reorganised expenditure. This was against the spirit of support from the Structural Funds and from 1993 onwards it was agreed that European moneys would be truly additional. However, in times when member states have been trying to limit public expenditure, as in the case of the current 'credit crunch' stemming from the financial failures of 2008, many authorities have complained that they have not been able to take full advantage of EU support because they have been unable to switch commitments from elsewhere. The fact that grant payments are retrospective and 5% is held back until the project is physically and financially complete also means that regional authorities have to earmark total project costs in their budget allocations.

Project Evaluation

The principles governing the bidding process for ERDF grants for productive investment are that:

(1) An indication of the market outlook in the sector concerned should be given.
(2) The effects on employment should be examined.
(3) An analysis of the expected profitability of the project should be undertaken.

In practice, local income and employment generation are the most significant factors affecting project acceptability, since the primary use of Structural Funds is to correct for regional imbalances. In terms of profitability, project feasibility is the main consideration, namely that the scheme has the capacity to generate revenues above operating costs so that it can support its own running arrangements. Project viability which relates to the return on capital employed is not so significant, because the objective of ERDF is to make up for shortfalls in finance to ensure that the investment will go ahead and has the means to service the cost of debt out of its operating surplus. Tourism and hospitality projects are normally well suited to this type of funding because they usually have a high operating leverage, that is, a relatively low level of operating costs and a high level of fixed costs caused by prior capital spending. Once the financing of the capital has been adequately taken care of, the project usually runs into surplus after three years and can maintain itself thereafter.

It is clear that a project cannot stand alone: its wider relevance and impact within an OP must be demonstrated, as well as ensuring that it meets one or more of the overall regional objectives laid down by the European Community (EC). As noted earlier, tourism projects in this category tend to be public-sector led and the principal aspects that should be addressed are:

(1) The use of the project should be 50% non-local.
(2) The project should result in an increase in overnight stays.
(3) The project should result in an increase in employment opportunities.
(4) The economic position of the project within the local area should be examined.
(5) The project should form part of a tourism strategy for the local area.
(6) National/regional tourist authority support will give weight to the application.

The important aspects to consider in respect of applications for ERDF support are the impacts of on-site and off-site tourist expenditure generated by the project. To derive the appropriate methodology, suppose there exists a tourist destination with a hotel and a seaside. It is proposed that an attraction should be established, with the use of public funds, to develop the destination. Visitors are surveyed at the hotel and on the beach to ascertain what motivated them to come to the area and the potential drawing power of an attraction.

Total spending at the destination (T), including the hotel, is expected to be made up of expenditure at the attraction (T_a) plus expenditure at the hotel (T_h) and all remaining expenditure (T_r). The pull factor (reason for visit) for the hotel is y; that for the attraction is estimated at x, leaving $1 - x - y$ as the significance of the seaside. It follows, therefore, that the attributable tourist expenditure by drawing power is:

$$\text{Attraction} = xT_a + xT_h + xT_r$$
$$\text{Hotel} = yT_a + yT_h + yT_r$$
$$\text{Seaside} = (1 - x - y)(T_a + T_h + T_r)$$
$$T = T_a + T_h + T_r$$

The benefits (B) of developing the attraction are the difference between with (T) and without (T_w) the project. The without situation is:

$$
\begin{aligned}
\text{Attraction} &= 0 \\
\text{Hotel} &= yT_h + yT_r \\
\text{Seaside} &= (1 - x - y)(T_h + T_r) \\
T_w &= (1 - x)(T_h + T_r)
\end{aligned}
$$

Hence,

$$
\begin{aligned}
B &= T - T_w \\
&= T_a + x(T_h + T_r)
\end{aligned}
\tag{4}
$$

The benefits are in two parts: the first term on the right-hand side of Equation (4) is the amount of on-site expenditure and the second, the off-site expenditure. The amount of off-site expenditure attributable to the attraction depends on its ability to generate additional visitors. Hence, this may be termed the 'visitor additionality factor'. The application of employment multipliers per unit of tourist spending to Equation (4), either on a full-time equivalent (FTE) or an employment headcount basis, will give the gross employment (E) generated by the project. These multipliers are calculated so as to encompass the direct employment effects of the project, the indirect effects arising out of intermediate purchases made by the project, and the induced effects on the local economy as a result of the re-spending of local incomes derived from the project, and similarly for off-site expenditure. Thus:

$$
E = T_a e_a + xOe_o
\tag{5}
$$

where e_a is the employment multiplier appropriate to the attraction, O is the sum of off-site expenditure ($T_h + T_r$), and (e_o) is the required job multiplier. However, Equation (5) ignores any demand diversion from elsewhere in the area. This is termed 'displacement', which in turn depends upon the boundary agreed for the project. The greater the area, the more likely is it that the project will displace business from elsewhere.

From the EC's standpoint, the boundary is the limit defined by the OP. Thus, if the project draws visitors in part from the local OP area or an alternative assisted region, then their spending is counted as displacement for evaluation purposes. The ideal development is one that brings in tourists from the richer parts of the country that are not eligible for regional assistance or from abroad. This is a rather strong ruling with regard to displacement, for some local demand generated by the project may be additional. More generally, if d is the proportion of locally diverted demand (or demand diverted from other assisted projects) in Equation (4), then from Equation (5) net employment is:

$$N = E - dE$$
$$= (l - d)(T_a e_a + xOe_o) \qquad (6)$$

Equation (6) forms the core of the basic evaluation model that can be used to judge in employment terms the return to capital invested. In EU terms, Equation (6) may be used to evaluate the worthiness of the project for grant support and, therefore, inclusion within an OP.

In Table 10.2 we present a numerical example that has been drawn from case study material on attractions, to show how the employment effects of a tourism project may be measured. The workings of Table 10.2 are along the following lines: using visitor expenditure surveys, the total expected on-site and off-site spending arising from the project is estimated at €28,000,000. It is at this point that the concept of visitor additionality is invoked: clearly, on-site expenditure by visitors is attributable absolutely to the attraction as the customers have demonstrated their preferences through their willingness to pay, but this is not the case with off-site spending.

Table 10.2 Assessing the impact of a tourist attraction

Item	On-site expenditure	Off-site expenditure
Visitor markets		
Stay	€3,000,000	€15,000,000
Day	€2,500,000	€2,000,000
Local residents	€4,000,000	€1,500,000
Total	€9,500,000	€18,500,000
Visitor additionality		
Stay	Not applicable	15%
Day	Not applicable	85%
Local residents	Not applicable	100%
Displacement		
Stay	0%	0%
Day	50%	50%
Local residents	100%	100%
FTE multipliers per €10,000		
Direct	0.075	0.060
Indirect	0.045	0.040
Indirect	0.006	0.006
Total	0.126	0.106

Source: Author

The extent to which off-site spending may be attributed to the attraction depends on the importance of the attraction in the customer's decision to visit the location. This can only be ascertained by surveying visitors and asking about their motivations for coming to the destination. It is expected that a much higher percentage will be recorded for day visitors and local residents, because they normally make a specific decision to go to a place, an event or an attraction. Using the visitor additionality factors in Table 10.2 to account for attributable off-site expenditure, the gross expenditure benefits (B) from the attraction are:

$$B = €9,500,000 + (0.15 \times €15,000,000) + (0.85 \times €2,000,000)$$
$$+ (1.0 \times €1,500,000)$$
$$= €14,950,000 \tag{7}$$

It is anticipated that the attraction will create 50.0 FTE jobs directly on site, and so the required additions to this number will be the expected indirect and induced employment generated from on-site spending. The direct multiplier is not used here as it refers to the average attraction, so it is better to use the direct estimate of employment in these circumstances. Using the appropriate FTE multipliers shown in Table 10.2 and calculated as a decimal fraction of a given amount of tourist expenditure, this figure comes to $(0.045 + 0.006) \times €9,500,000/€10,000 = 48.4$ FTE jobs. Off-site jobs amount to $0.106 \times €5,450,000/€10,000 = 57.8$ FTE jobs, where €5,450,000 is the total of attributable off-site benefits. Hence, the gross employment generated (E), in terms of FTEs, is expected to be:

$$E = 50.0 \text{ FTEs} + 48.4 \text{ FTEs} + 57.8 \text{ FTEs} = 156.2 \text{ FTEs} \tag{8}$$

So far the analysis has only measured gross FTEs likely to be generated by the attraction. The net figures have to account for what is termed displacement, which is factored into Table 10.2. Displacement has to do with the extent to which an attraction may capture tourist spending from competitors in the local area. It is estimated that 0% of staying visitors will be taken from competitors; the attraction is providing more to 'see and do' at the destination and the tourists' budgets have a sufficient margin of flexibility. For day visitors, it is probable that 50% will be displaced from other attractions, while for local residents a conservative assumption is made that all expenditure will be displaced from elsewhere in the local economy. The latter assumption is overly pessimistic in practice, for household budgets are more flexible than this.

Weighting the displacement factors in Table 10.2 by the different categories of visitor spending gives an overall displacement expenditure of €7,600,000, allowing for 100% displacement of local resident expenditure. Hence the value of d is €7,600,000/€14,950,000, which is equal to 50.8%.

Thus, the net employment (N) that can be expected to result from the attraction is:

$$N = 156.2 - 0.508 \times 156.2 = 76.8 \text{ FTEs} \tag{9}$$

It is this number of FTEs that should be used to evaluate the project's worth in public policy decision making when applications for European support or comparisons with alternative projects are being made.

Conclusions

It is not difficult to appreciate that, as leisure time increases and more people cross the income threshold for international travel, together with increased segmentation of the market, tourism projects will achieve greater importance in the EU through meeting:

(1)   the regional objectives of the Structural Funds;
(2)   developments originating from the Cohesion Fund, given the continued dominance of southern European sun, sand and sea destinations;
(3)   priorities set by EC initiatives in terms of structural adjustment, such as SME development, helping rural and remote areas, employment creation and the fostering of cross-border networks.

As a consequence it is expected that tourism will not only substantially increase the amount of regional aid it receives over succeeding planning phases, but will also increase its share of moneys coming from the various regional funds. Many of the newly eligible states included in the EU expansion programme either have an established tourism sector or the potential for developing tourism. Nevertheless, it should not be thought that new developments will be confined to the poorer regions, for tourism is known to thrive in rundown urban areas, such as redundant docks, old industrial complexes and obsolete market halls, where tourism may also act as a catalyst by attracting other investment. Nor is it possible for tourism to prosper in every locality, given the likely costs of generating sufficient volumes to sustain tourism businesses. Project support, with particular emphasis on job creation, has to be mindful of the clear intention of the EC to move forward with tourism developments in a sustainable manner, in order to guarantee that the activity continues on a regular basis.

The division of intervention in the tourist industry between Members States and the EU is always likely to remain contentious, but given the diversity of the tourist product, the EC has to work in close partnership with national and regional authorities. At the political level, this issue has been technically put to one side by Article 3b of the Maastricht Treaty which lays down the principle of 'subsidiarity'. The latter requires EC action to be taken only if and in so far as the objectives of the proposed action cannot be sufficiently achieved by the member states, and can therefore, by reason of the scale or effects of the proposed action, be better achieved by the Community.

References

EC (1991) *Guide to the Reform of the Community's Structural Funds.* Luxembourg: Office for Official Publications of the European Communities.

EC (2004) *Working for the Regions.* Directorate-General for Regional Policy. Luxembourg: Office for Official Publications of the European Communities.

EC (2006) *Regions for Economic Change.* COM(2006) 675 final. Brussels: Office for Official Publications of the European Communities.

EC (2007) *Agenda for a Sustainable and Competitive European Tourism.* Belgium: Office for Official Publications of the European Communities.

Wanhill, S. (1997) Peripheral area tourism: A European perspective. *Progress in Tourism and Hospitality Research* 3 (1), 47–70.

Wanhill, S. (2005) Investment support for tourism SMEs: A review of theory and practice. In E. Jones and C. Haven (eds) *Tourism SMEs, Service Quality and Destination Competitiveness* (pp. 227–254). Wallingford: CABI.

11 State or Market in Tourism: Why Not Something Else? ... Club Goods

Eduardo Anselmo de Castro and
Gonçalo Santinha

Introduction

Tourism is increasingly recognised as a major area in government, industry, academic and public concern. It is an important economic activity with a broadly positive impact, not only on economic growth and employment (with an overwhelming contribution to GDP and, in many countries such as Portugal, with a significant positive contribution to the balance of payments), but also on people's lives and the places in which they live. Not surprisingly, interest in tourism studies and tourism economics has grown swiftly both to contribute to a better understanding of this activity and to guide public policy, which in turn must be resilient enough to foster the development of services in a rapidly changing world (Edgell *et al.*, 2007; Hall, 2008; Mak, 2004; Veal, 2002). In this regard, a good example can be found in the recent efforts invested by the European Commission (EC) to strengthen the foundations for a European tourism policy (for more details, see Chapter 14).

Still, an additional fact that renders tourism particularly interesting is that tourism operators sell goods which they do not possess and control: the attractive capacity of restaurants, hotels and several other activities related to tourism depends on the characteristics of the surrounding environment. In other words, externalities, both positive and negative, have a pervasive effect on the tourism industry (Candela *et al.*, 2008; Schubert, 2010), well established in the literature, specifically in the *Asset Theory of Tourism* (Gray, 1982).

The emphasis of this chapter is placed on the analysis of tourism under the economic theory of externalities and on the discussion of the consequences of externalities to the definition of spatial development policies to promote tourism. The subject is addressed in four closely integrated sections. The first section sets some of the context within which externalities occur in tourism from a theoretical viewpoint. The argument is mainly based on the famous theorem of Coase (1960) in which it is implied that, under certain circumstances, negotiation leads to an agreement. The second section provides a brief example of different distribution rights in order to question the idea of the internalisation of externalities by the simple functioning of market mechanisms. This argument becomes even more evident in the third section, once an often-neglected issue is added: the existence of transaction costs. Here, we clarify why, in the presence of strong externalities like those related to tourism, markets break down. However, at the same time we also explain why the state has limited capacity to correct the situation. Drawing upon the core themes discussed in these three sections, the chapter concludes with a discussion of a possible way forward, by bringing in the idea of Club Goods.

Externalities and Internalisation in Tourism: Underlying Concepts

Externalities arise when specific third parties are affected (positively or negatively) by transactions between producers and consumers, hence sometimes referred to as *neighbourhood effects* or *third-party effects* (Veal, 2002). Negative externalities occur when a certain action by an individual or a group produces harmful effects on others. On the other hand, positive externalities take place when an action confers benefits on others.

In the tourism area, it can be easily noticed that some externalities arise from natural endowments or historic heritage, such as sun and beaches, places like Rome, Athens or Toledo, or even big economic centres attracting large numbers of business tourists with a high purchasing power. In these cases, externalities tend to be internalised by market mechanisms: the extra income which tourism operators get from their location in such privileged places is compensated by the much higher land rents they have to pay (Rodrigues, 2000) and, to a lesser extent, by higher costs of inputs such as labour. However, most externalities can only be maintained by incurring high maintenance and operation costs and by avoiding the expansion of activities which harm the environment. For example, a traditional neighbourhood with quiet traditional hotels, restaurants and residences will be negatively affected if a leisure centre with a Hard Rock Cafe, noisy dancing and several pubs are opened nearby. What will happen then?

For the sake of simplicity, we will give the generic name of *stakeholders* to the set of owners of hotels, restaurants, shops and residences as well as to the local authority which owns public infrastructure and utilities; in the same line of argument, we will designate as *investors* those entrepreneurs who are willing to open the leisure centre. The *Coase theorem*, based on the seminal paper *The Problem of Social Cost* (Coase, 1960), is well known in the literature. According to this theorem, if all the assets relevant to the neighbourhood are attached to clearly defined property rights, if all agents have rational behaviour and if there is a form of creating and exploiting the leisure centre which is an optimum trade-off between all the interests under scrutiny and represents a Pareto improvement for the area, such a solution will be reached by negotiation among investors and stakeholders. In this case, the leisure centre is a Pareto improvement if it generates enough income to exceed its own investment and operation costs plus the compensation of all the welfare net losses incurred by the neighbourhood stakeholders. Under these circumstances, such a trade-off will imply some restrictions to the investors in terms of acoustic isolation of the leisure centre, opening hours and a contract with the local police which will ensure, in a friendly way, that people leaving the centre late at night will not disturb the quiet environment by their noisy behaviour and other nuisances. However, it will also imply some inconveniences to stakeholders in terms of noise and some disturbance of the quiet image of the neighbourhood, although partially compensated by increased business for restaurants and shops. Depending on the initial distribution of property rights and the shrewdness of the different negotiators, costs and benefits will be distributed differently, but the optimum trade-off will be reached in any case. This is actually the key argument pointed out by those whose think that the internalisation of externalities can be reached by the simple functioning of market mechanisms.

Figure 11.1 (a and b) illustrates schematically the relevant elements of the trade-off. The first graphic (a) shows stylised curves of marginal costs (the additional costs arising from an elementary change in the situation) which affect the decisions of stakeholders and investors. For our purposes, the marginal cost curves are assumed to be linear, not only for the sake of simplicity, but also because a more sophisticated shape would not change the conclusions to be taken. If CI are the costs incurred by investors in relation to their optimal solution, the marginal cost curve $MCI = -CI/-L$ as a zero value when investors build and operate the leisure centre without any restriction (L_{max}) and a maximum when restrictions are such that the functioning of the leisure centre does not harm the stakeholders at all (L_0). If CS are the costs incurred by stakeholders, the marginal cost curve has a zero value for L_0 and a maximum for L_{max}. Between L_{max} and L^* $MCS > MCI$, hence as we move from L_{max} to the left, the additional costs incurred by investors are smaller than the gains obtained by the stakeholders. To the left of L^* the opposite occurs, which means that L^* corresponds to the optimum trade-off. As for graphic (b), it shows the corresponding curve of the net benefits arising from the opening of the leisure centre. For L_0, the amount of the restrictions is such that the leisure centre is no longer profitable. For L_{max}, the harm to the stakeholders is greater than the expected net benefit generated by the centre. Between L_1 and L_2, the functioning of the leisure centre will generate positive

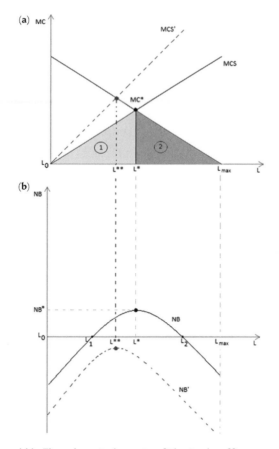

Figure 11.1 (a and b): The relevant elements of the trade-off

net benefits, which will be maximum for L* (NB*). It could be the case that points L_1 and L_2 do not exist and NB* < 0, which means that the optimal solution is not to build the leisure centre.

In this sense, if Coase's theorem implies that negotiation will lead to an agreement corresponding to L*, how do different distributions of property rights affect the outcome? In the next section we will discuss this issue by examining in detail the example discussed above.

Different Distribution of Property Rights: Exploring an Example

Imagine that the investors are legally enforced to compensate the stakeholders for the damage caused. In this case, the neighbours will be compensated by an amount which equates to marginal net losses either in their welfare or in their businesses. Such an amount corresponds to *area 1* (Triangle $L_0 - L^* - MC^*$). Compensation will be different for each stakeholder and it is possible that in some cases (restaurants, shops) the benefits created by the leisure centre are greater than the costs. So far, we have admitted that, in such cases, the winning stakeholders will agree to help the investors with the compensation given to those who lose out. Imagine now that there are no legal enforcements and the investors can do exactly what they like. In such a case, the stakeholders will pay the investors the amount of money equivalent to the cost incurred by the investments and activity restrictions necessary to reach point L^*. Such an amount corresponds to *area 2* (Triangle $L^* - L_{Max} - MC^*$). This result is correct if we assume, as in Coase (1960), that the bargaining will be dealt with by two negotiators (in this case the stakeholders and investors), each group being so cohesive that it acts as an individual agent. If this is not the case, the problem becomes more complicated.

Aivazian and Callen (1981) show that Coase's theorem does not always hold when three negotiators are involved, and that the larger the number of negotiators the higher the chance that the theorem is not applicable. In our particular case, it is easy to find a numerical example where the Pareto optimum equilibrium cannot be reached. Let us split the stakeholders into two categories: S_1 for owners of restaurants and shops and S_2 for owners of hotels and residences. For the sake of argument, suppose that there are four possible deals: D_1 if the centre does not open; D_2 if the centre opens between 2 pm and 5 am; D_3 if the centre opens between 8 pm and 5 am; and finally D_4 in a case where the centre opens between 11 pm and 5 am Within this context, the following actions will take place if the centre opens:

- S_2, the only agents interested in acoustic isolation, will pay for it.
- Either S_1, S_2 or both will pay the local police for their extra efforts, which will increase with the length of opening time.
- Investors will decide the opening times according to their own interests or, if they are paid enough, according to the interests of either S_1 or S_2 or even both.

Table 11.1 illustrates the expected yearly net gains of each deal for each agent, in relation to D_1. Overall, it shows that:

- The centre has a zero or net positive effect for S_1, which increases as the opening time coincides with the busy hours for shops and restaurants.
- The centre has a net negative effect for S_2, which are forced to pay the expenses of acoustic isolation and in some cases of the police, in addition to welfare losses arising from the negative effect of the centre on the quiet ambience of the neighbourhood.

Table 11.1 The expected yearly net gains of each deal for each agent

			Options			
			D_1	D_2	D_3	D_4
L O S S E S	S_1	Police	0	−1400	−600	0
		Welfare	0	1900	700	0
		Total	0	500	100	0
	S_2	Police	0	0	−600	−1000
		Welfare	0	−1500	−800	0
		Isolation	0	−1200	−1200	−1200
		Total	0	−2700	−2400	−2200
	I		0	2600	2900	2600
	Total		0	400	600	400

- For the investors (I) the centre certainly has a net positive effect which is maximum for D_3, because expected marginal income is smaller than marginal costs before 8 pm and larger afterwards.
- The social benefit (the sum of the net gains for the three types of agents) is positive for all options of opening the centre (Pareto improvement) and maximum for D_3 (Pareto optimum); nonetheless, each agent has a different opinion on what deal should be taken.

According to Coase (1960), the agents will bargain and reach an agreement which corresponds to the Pareto optimum. It is easy to see that in the present case this is not true. First of all, S_2 would prefer to avoid the centre but no one else agrees. So, their second-best option is D_4, which implies that they will pay the police and, to attract I, which prefer D_3, they are ready to pay up to 200. However, I require more than 300 to change their minds. On the other hand, the preferred option for S_1 is D_2 and they are ready to pay up to 400 to convince I, which will accept anything above 300 to move to D_2 (which is not the Pareto optimum). And because S_1 do not like D_2 at all, they are ready to offer something between 400 and 500 to move I to D_1, an act that makes the investors indeed very satisfied. This deal also does not correspond to a Pareto optimum. At this time, S_1 and S_2 realise that they are running a silly competition which makes both of them losers, and that it is better to give up all offers and let I go to D_3, which in fact is the Pareto optimum. Now it is time for I to become unhappy with the prospect of losing a very good bribe. Getting 450 as a premium to move to D_2 more than compensates for the corresponding loss of 300 in their expected gains. Then they try to lure S_1, saying that they will accept 350 to go to D_2, which is a good deal for both of them. However, such solution is not stable because S_2 are not happy and will try to break the deal. The outcome of this long story is that there is not a stable deal but instead several possible ones that do not correspond to a Pareto optimum.

Coase's theorem breaks down in this fabricated case because the set of conditions necessary for a three-member stable coalition concerning the allocation of the net gains is violated. Such set is called *the core* and in the present case it is said that there is an *empty core* (for a more detailed explanation see Aivazian & Callen, 1981). If for a three-member coalition it is necessary to fabricate carefully the numbers in order to obtain an empty core, as the number of bargainers increase the chances of finding such an empty core grow. Since, in our example, we do not have three types of bargainers but a high number of agents with specific and often contradictory interests, it is certain that there are no chances of avoiding an empty core. With many agents, the Coase theorem breaks down, despite the very strong assumptions of perfectly rational agents and zero transaction costs. However, the central element of Coase (1960) is not his famous theorem but an often-neglected issue: the existence of *transaction costs*.

Adding the Idea of Transaction Costs

Transaction costs refer to all the costs which agents incur to make a contract and to enforce the application of the contract, added to all losses which arise when contracts are broken (Williamson, 1985, 1996, 2007). They include:

- The costs of acquiring and processing all the information necessary to make an optimum contract.
- The costs of collecting inaccurate information and making incorrect use of it, leading to wrong decisions. Even if a list of all possible outcomes and respective probabilities of occurrence is created, it is by definition incomplete and probabilities are difficult or impossible to calculate, mainly when it is the outcome of deceiving behaviour, strategically envisaged by competitors and agents involved in the contracts. For similar reasons, even if the net present value of all possible outcomes is calculated, it can only be achieved approximately in the best cases.
- The costs of opportunistic behaviour of contracting partners taking advantage of unpredicted events.
- The costs of irrational behaviour of contracting partners which preclude that the best deals are obtained or lead to *ex post* inefficiency in the fulfilment of contracts.

Continuing with the same example, it is easy to envisage the various sources of transaction costs which will hamper the bargaining of stakeholders and investors. For example, if investors are legally enforced to compensate stakeholders, they have incentives to overestimate their welfare losses: going back to Figure 11.1(B), we will have MCS' rather than MCS, which leads to a sub-optimal equilibrium and eventually to a curve of net benefits NB' which in turn will discourage investors to open the leisure centre. This is a case in which contracts are hampered by information asymmetries. The fact that in many transactions or investment decisions the relevant information is split between different agents, no one agent having enough information alone to make the best decision, is the key argument used by Hayek (1945) to conclude that decentralised markets, which convey all the relevant information in commodity prices, are superior to centrally planned state decision making. However, Hayek's argument is not valid when we deal with strong externalities, such as in the present case. Externalities mean that correct prices and optimal decisions do not appear unless all the relevant information is disclosed, something which is not likely to occur.

In case investors are not legally enforced to make compensations, there is a risk that many neighbours belonging to the S_2 group will refuse to pay their share of acoustic isolation costs, either because their behaviour is not driven by economic rationality or because they are making a conscious attempt to free ride. In such a case, if free riders or stubborn stakeholders are a minority, it is possible that the remaining agents are still willing to increase their shares and avoid noise nightmares. On the other hand, because this will most likely incentivise further free riding, there is a high risk that everyone will refuse to pay, leading to what can be quite a catastrophic outcome.

In addition to the disturbance to the environment caused by economic activities, negative externalities can be the result of a failure to maintain the quality of the public space. Using the same example, independently of the leisure centre, the quality of the neighbourhood can only be kept up if the owners of the buildings are willing to pay for an appropriate maintenance of their properties. In fact, in abstract they do, because this is essential to keep up the value of their own properties. Still, what happens if a number of owners, for different reasons, decide not to keep up the quality of the facade? Such an option will affect the value of their neighbours' houses and it can even lead to a situation in which everyone will no longer be interested in expensive maintenance of their properties, because the decline in their value no longer justifies it. A similar situation can be found in Portuguese forests, when the bush cleaning works to avoid summer fires are made useless because neighbours do not clean their own properties. In both cases, we have the reverse of the well-known economic concept of the *Tragedy of Commons* (Hardin, 1968), where collective property gives no incentive for each person to bear the costs of keeping assets, because free riding will destroy their own efforts. What we explain here is that, in the presence of strong externality effects, a *Tragedy of Privates* may occur, mainly because the neighbour's bad behaviour eliminates my willingness to act appropriately.

So far we have only discussed externalities related to environment nuisances. Positive externalities arising from investments in touristic assets which will benefit all the agents are even more problematic. In other words, it is easier to preserve positive externalities than to build new ones. Suppose that the building of a theme park does not generate the expected revenues which will compensate investments, but if one adds all the business potential in terms of hotels, shops, restaurants and so forth, the park represents a clear Pareto improvement. The outcome of pure market mechanisms is that such a park will not be built unless investors are willing to make a giant resort which internalises all externalities. Even in such a case, free riding in the neighbourhood cannot be avoided, which means that they will never internalise all the benefits of the park. Nevertheless, the investment in touristic attractions and the maintenance and recovery of natural or historic heritage in a whole region can never be internalised unless public authorities decide to run all the business in *Soviet style*.

In conclusion, if we add unstable bargaining outcomes to a behaviour not driven by economic rationality, plus information asymmetries, free riding and also risks associated with the tragedy of privates, we can quite straightforwardly eliminate the hypothesis that the pervasive externalities related to tourism can be efficiently internalised through market solutions and bargaining between agents. Unless we have an unshakeable faith in market mechanisms, we have to accept that, in the presence of strong externalities such as those related to tourism, markets break down. Does it mean that the state can take the place of markets, envisaging and managing the solutions which lead to Pareto optimality? To accept this also requires an unshakeable faith in state capabilities.

Following the same example, we can easily acknowledge that the state can carry out many things. For instance, the state can enforce investors who harm pleasant local environments to be responsible for their nuisances. Of course, in this case, the problem is to make a correct measurement of such nuisances and of the corresponding costs. However, the state can also eliminate several risks related to the tragedy of privates by stimulating or even forcing owners to maintain the environmental quality of their properties. This is the case where, at the limit, the state can take the place of the owners, paying or heavily subsidising the investments, but this will not only encourage free riding but also restrain the taxpayer willing to make investments whose profits will go to free riders. Is that what taxpayers think is the best use of public money? On the other hand, there are mechanisms which can enable the state to achieve the return of public investments made in private property, but they limit individual freedoms and there is a serious risk of miscalculations arising from problems such as information asymmetry. The state can also subsidise investments which are only profitable if positive externalities are taken into account, such as the theme park referred to above; these subsidies can take the form of supplying the land at low or zero costs, offering tax incentives or building infrastructure which directly or indirectly benefits the park. By doing so the state is using public money to favour only a reduced number of people. Of course there is the counter-argument that the state can force those who will benefit from the positive externalities to compensate the state through increased tourism taxes and that the park will generate employment as well as several indirect effects which will benefit the region in general. However, it is very difficult to ensure that the state contribution will compensate only the positive externalities rather than transforming public resources into private profits. Finally, the state may provide public infrastructure which, although designed for the common benefit of all the inhabitants, will have a particular impact on tourism. This is the case of roads, marinas, airports, green areas and public gardens, hospitals or even by simply ensuring a safe and clean environment.

In conclusion, the state can do a very important job by discouraging behaviours which induce negative externalities, investing in or subsidising investments in ventures that provide strong positive externalities, or even implementing an adequate policy of investment in public infrastructure. However, such a job is affected by significant limitations, such as: limited knowledge of the existing negative externalities and of shadow prices (the prices which the market would generate if externalities could be transformed into commodities and traded as such) and, in the same line of argument, limited knowledge of the existing positive externalities and shadow prices; limited technical capacity to design the best economic incentives to deal with externalities; limited legal power to force agents into behaviour which eliminates negative externalities and the tragedy of privates' outcomes (when economic incentives are not adequate or insufficient); and even all sorts of opportunistic behaviour by politicians and administrative staff, deviating public policies from the goal of maximising public welfare.

In short, as markets fail, totally or partially, when externalities occur, the state has a limited capacity to correct the situation. So, what is the solution? To choose, case by case, whether the state or the market is the mechanism which better deals with externalities could be a possible way out, but most likely is not the best one. Why not go for something else?

A Possible Way Forward: The Idea of Club Goods

Over the past few years, *Public Private Partnerships* (PPP) have become widely used in many countries to provide services and infrastructure, a trend associated with the increasing deficit constraints on national budgets due to the potential of bringing private finance to public service delivery (OECD, 2008). The idea of PPP as presented here is not related to those partnerships concocted by the state to hide or postpone deficits caused by huge investments and which are no more than a disguised form of borrowing money from private firms at harmful interest rates and unfair distribution of risks (IMF, 2004). On the contrary, we are talking about joint ventures of agents interested in the common use of assets which have strong externality effects or are even *public goods*: goods or services which cannot be restricted to a person or a group, because it is not physically or legally possible to exclude anybody from its free use. Typical characteristics of *non-rivalry* (the consumption of one individual does not detract from that of another) and *non-excludability* (it is impossible to exclude an individual from enjoying the good) are usually credited to Paul Samuelson (1954) in his well-known paper, *The Pure Theory of Public Expenditure*.

Such joint ventures will confer property rights on assets generating strong externalities, transforming public goods into *Club Goods*: 'private organizations whose members collectively consume (and often produce) at least one good or service that no one person has the capacity unilaterally to finance' (Anderson *et al.*, 2003: 175–176). Extending the examples of the traditional neighbourhood to a region with high potential to develop cultural and environmental tourism, we can envisage a club whose membership is related to the capacity to develop any action linked to tourism activities. Within this context, the club would be responsible for all investments, maintenance and operation costs attached to building and maintaining public goods and utilities related to tourism. The share of costs would be decided through a mixture of negotiation and competition:

- Licenses to operate a new restaurant or a new shop on qualified territories managed by the club and with a given capacity would be allocated to the best offers concerning the fees to be charged.
- Such offers would be a basis for negotiation of the fees to be paid by businesses already established in the territory.
- Fees and income generated by the exploitation plus the contribution of the state would provide the financial basis to start and run the club.

According to Mueller (1989), Cornes and Sandler (1996) and Anderson *et al.* (2003), there are some key characteristics that define an efficient clubbing. First is the optimal size: it is important to define the geographical and sectoral boundaries for membership of the club and the scope of club activities. In this sense, a list of sectors and territories distinguishing the cases for which membership is legally enforced or volunteered must be carefully designed and regularly revised. Second is the equation of costs and benefits: not only must fees be as close as possible to the marginal benefits expected by each member, but also a skilful process combining negotiation and competition is fundamental for the success of the club. Third, the investment and operation programmes must be as close as possible to the attainment of Pareto optimality. In fact, the capacity of the club to convince all members to disclose key private information and the management capacity to gather such information and transform it in wise, strategic and investment decisions is key to success.

Still, it is important to stress that several issues about and barriers to the fulfilment of the club's efficient conditions may emerge, such as how to choose a management board and how to define decision-making procedures which ensure that the best strategy is defined and the club action is guided by the maximisation of its members' welfare. How is it best avoid the capture of the club by a small group of powerful agents without creating a chaotic environment which hampers decision making? How is it possible to overcome all the barriers to the disclosure of private information and to the development of a culture of cooperation and mutual trust among the members? And what about the role of the state? Can the extremes of authoritarian behaviour and submission to particular interests be avoided?

The ability to answer to such questions is crucial to evaluate the reasonability of our club proposal. We believe that we have provided sufficient arguments to bring critical commentary to this arena and to issue a challenge to policy makers to engage in a more appropriate set of discussions about this subject.

References

Aivazian, V. and Callen, J. (1981) The Coase Theorem and the empty core. *Journal of Law and Economics* 24 (1), 175–181.

Anderson, G., Shughart, W. and Tollison, R. (2003) The economic theory of clubs. In C.K. Rowley and F. Schneider (eds) *The Encyclopedia of Public Choice*. New York: Springer.

Candela, G., Castellani, M. and Dieci, R. (2008) Economics of externalities and public policy. *International Economic Review* 55, 285–311.

Coase, E. (1960) The problem of social cost. *Journal of Law and Economics* 3, 1–44.

Cornes, R. and Sandler, T. (1996) *The Theory of Externalities, Public Goods, and Club Goods*. New York: Cambridge University Press.

EC (2010) *Europe, the World's No 1 Tourist Destination – A New Political Framework for Tourism in Europe*. COM(2010) 352 final. Communication from the Commission to the European Parliament, the Council, the European Economic and Social Committee and the Committee of the Regions. Brussels: European Commission.

Edgell, D., Allen, M., Smith, G. and Swanson, J. (2007) *Tourism Policy and Planning Yesterday, Today and Tomorrow*. Oxford: Elsevier.

Gray, H. (1982) The contributions of economics to tourism. *Annals of Tourism Research* 9 (1), 105–125.

Hall, C. (2008) *Tourism Planning Policies, Processes and Relationships* (2nd edn). Harlow: Pearson Education.

Hardin, G. (1968) The tragedy of the commons. *Science* 13, 162 (3859), 1243–1248.

Hayek (1945) The use of knowledge in society. *American Economic Review* 35 (4), 519–530.

IMF (2004) *Public-Private Partnerships*. Washington, DC: Fiscal Affairs Department of the International Monetary Fund (in consultation with other departments, the World Bank and the Inter-American Development Bank).

Mak, J. (2004) *Tourism and the Economy: Understanding the Economics of Tourism*. Honolulu: University of Hawai'i Press.

Mueller, D. (1989) *Public Choice II*. Cambridge: Cambridge University Press.

OECD (2008) *Public-Private Partnerships: In Pursuit of Risk Sharing and Value for Money*. Paris: OECD Publishing.

Rodrigues, O. (2000) Utilização do Território e Propriedade Fundiária. Doctoral thesis. Instituto Superior de Agronomia, Lisbon.

Samuelson, P. (1954) The pure theory of public expenditure. *Review of Economics and Statistics* 36 (4), 387–389.

Schubert, S. (2010) Coping with externalities in tourism: A dynamic optimal taxation approach. *Tourism Economics* 16 (2), 321–343.

Veal, A. (2002) *Leisure and Tourism Policy and Planning*. Wallingford: CABI.

Williamson, O.E. (1985) *The Economic Institutions of Capitalism*. New York: Free Press.

Williamson, O.E. (1996) *The Mechanisms of Governance*. New York: Oxford University Press.

Williamson, O.E. (2007) Transaction cost economics: An introduction. *Economics Discussion Papers* 2007-3. Kiel: Kiel Institute for the World Economy.

12 'Going International': Challenges and Strategies for European Tourism Businesses

Zélia Breda and Carlos Costa

Introduction

Tourism is today the world's largest commercial service sector industry. Over the past six decades, the travel and tourism industry has experienced continued development and diversification to become one of the largest and fastest growing economic sectors in the world. Its importance is particularly visible when considering the major indicators on the demand side, such as international tourism arrivals and receipts.

Whereas in 1950 the top 15 destinations absorbed 98% of all international tourist arrivals, in 1970 the proportion was 75%, and this fell to 57% in 2007, reflecting the emergence of new destinations, many of them in developing countries (UNWTO, 2008). Over time, more and more destinations have opened up and invested in tourism development, turning modern tourism into a key driver for socio-economic progress. The generalised expansion of the tourism sector, allied to an increasing dispersion of tourists and diversification of destinations, has created new challenges to enterprises that are now striving to have an international presence and to be competitive in the global market. However, the current external environment, characterised by the interdependence of economies, the globalisation of markets and the deregulation and globalisation of competition, has also opened up new opportunities that have pushed companies to adopt internationalisation strategies.

The European tourism industry presents a fragmented structure, which consists mostly of small and micro enterprises (Buhalis & Peters, 2005). Globalisation poses a big challenge to these enterprises which must strive for increasing competitiveness. One approach which helps enterprises and destinations to cope with their internal limitations and challenges posed by the transformations occurring within the global market is the development of networks and partnerships. By cooperating with other tourism industry partners, these enterprises are able to develop strategic positioning, extend competences, identify opportunities and threats and build up the capacity to operate in a competitive tourism environment (Breda *et al.*, 2004, 2006; Costa *et al.*, 2008; Williams, 1999).

Indeed, increasing competitiveness and competition requires a concentration of resources on core competencies and an articulation of the value chain in order to enhance complementarity and synergies, which for most enterprises are only within reach through cooperation relationships (Magriço, 2003). Increasingly, international operations and the internationalisation of companies require the establishment of partnerships, agreements or other forms of relationships that allow resource leverage. Cooperation is therefore crucial for the success of European firms in the global market, allowing them to assimilate skills, gain advantages of proximity, enhance international reputation, coordinate skills and reduce dimensional barriers in the internationalisation process (Simões, 1997).

Despite the relatively widespread literature on the importance of networks in the tourism sector, most of the research is towards the role and importance of the network on the destination management. There is also an interesting stream in the literature that discusses the role of networks in tourism firms' performance and competitiveness, particularly small and medium-sized businesses. However, when considering international tourism businesses, not much empirical research has been conducted, especially on the role of networks in tourism enterprises' internationalisation process. This might be related to the fact that literature on tourism internationalisation is scarce and also to the newness of the application of the network approach in tourism studies.

Given the globalised nature of the tourism sector and the growing expansion of foreign direct investment (FDI) flows, it is important to study what drives companies in their market expansion and how they engage in international markets. This chapter aims to evaluate the role of network relationships in the internationalisation process, by bringing empirical evidence to bear on Portuguese tourism enterprises. The empirical study by Breda (2010) examined 14 enterprises of different sizes and ages, with different types of ownership and on different levels of internationalisation. The small size of the sample was partly offset by the quality of the firm-level data. Through structured interviews targeting chief executives, rich information was able to be gathered, enabling a better insight to be gained into the phenomenon being researched.

Globalisation and Tourism

Tourism is very much part of the globalisation process and has gained from the broad and expanding movement towards international economic liberalisation. It can be said that it is shaped by globalisation, but globalisation is also influenced by tourism, which means that it is in many ways a driver of globalisation.

The global tourism market is composed of a multitude of small producers that co-exist along with a small number of big transnational corporations. About 95% of the accommodation and food sector is classified as small business (Buhalis & Peters, 2005), and these firms are expected to compete on an equal basis regardless of their size or country of origin. Globalisation thus does not involve only big corporations, but also a large number of small and medium-sized businesses.

According to Go and Pine (1995), a growing number of local businesses are being drawn into the global arena. The main reasons for this are the weakening of growth opportunities in some economies, pushing firms to expand into foreign markets, and the fact that corporations based in developed economies are being pulled into fast-growing markets in search of growth opportunities. Despite being in a minority, transnational companies are important because they generally set the pace and standards (Johnson, 2002), remaining a force in the worldwide hotel industry (Littlejohn & Roper, 1991), and also influencing the development and direction of the hotel industry in less developed nations (Go, 1989).

Global enterprises view the world as their operating environment and establish both global strategies and global market presence (Knowles et al., 2004). The most important effect of globalisation is thus an intensified competition through market extension. Tourism businesses operate globally and many have opted for the competitive advantage of internationalisation.

Hjalager (2007) provides a descriptive model of the globalisation of the tourism industry, aiming to understand the increasing complexity of dynamic interactions across borders (Table 12.1). The level of analysis of the model is the tourism community and its actors, and the globalisation process is seen as the result of both the business decisions of single enterprises and political decision making. The model suggests a logical progression of four stages, representing: (1) the attempt of the national tourism system to reach out to new markets; (2) the integration and incorporation of its business across borders; (3) the fragmentation and flexible relocation in space of production processes; and (4) the challenge of the industry identity and the emergence of new market types and business concepts that go beyond previous definitions of tourism (Hjalager, 2007).

The model suggests that individual firms, destinations and countries, by embracing globalisation in stages, may be able to control costs, gain market share and enjoy access to competencies and other important resources. By joining international networks, tourism agents can address institutional and investment pressures at home at several levels (Knowles et al., 2004). The growing importance of strategic alliances in creating networks of business relationships has also become a trend in tourism.

Table 12.1 Stages in the globalisation of tourism

Features	Low globalisation profile			High globalisation profile
Stage title	(1) Missionaries in the markets	(2) Integrating across borders	(3) Fragmentation of the value chain	(4) Transcending into new value chains
Logic	Access to profitable new markets for existing products	Utilisation of market access and brand profiles in foreign markets	Creating profitability in services and getting access to specified material and immaterial resources	Adding value by integrating economic logics in other sectors
Manifestations in the tourism sector	(A) Tourism board representation and operations in the markets (B) International marketing collaboration by regional/ national tourism enterprises (C) Market expansion of larger tourism corporations	(D) Transnational integration through business investments and mergers (E) Import and export of business concepts through franchising and licensing	(F) Splitting the value chain, outsourcing (G) Flexible human resourcing and enhancing of the international labour markets	(H) Development, production and marketing of knowledge (I) Sales of market positions and brand extension and spin-off (J) Tourism in global media production

Source: Hjalager (2007)

According to the model, globalisation is further enhanced by developments in information and communication technologies (ICT) and transportation opportunities. The diffusion of technologies has helped to develop the tourism industry. The most important changes have occurred through computer reservation and global distribution systems (GDS) that were originally developed by airlines (Galileo, Amadeus and Sabre), but were later adopted and personalised by major hotel companies (Johnson, 2002).

By facilitating the linkages between service providers (and consumers), ICT plays a fundamental role in the growing interdependence of markets and production activities across regions and countries, changing the nature of the competition itself. This enables opportunities for new inter- and intra-industry alliances, with horizontal and vertical integration occurring virtually, rather than physically, under each company's organisational umbrella (Olsen, 1999). The 'information revolution' and the reduction of boundaries have created new forms of service companies, not only large multinational corporations but also small niche specialists (Peric, 2005).

The globalisation process is predicted to continue and, as tourism is a global business, it will strive to achieve a balance between unification and diversification, and to adopt the positive aspects of globalisation, while emphasising particularities and attractions through localisation (Holjevac, 2003).

The Global Expansion of the Tourism System

The tourism system has been described and modelled from different perspectives, but always including demand and supply elements. Globalisation has increased the interdependence between countries, economies and people, thus affecting the tourism supply and demand in many ways. According to Smeral (1998), demand has been affected by increasing income and wealth, the aging population of the developed world, the saturation of demand for traditional destinations and mono-activity vacations, emerging new motives and changing lifestyles, and the increasing experience and knowledge of tourists. All these are important factors in explaining the nature of globalisation in tourism demand. On the supply side there is an increase in worldwide acting suppliers, as well as the impact of computerised information and reservation systems, the decreasing costs of travel, and the emergence of new destinations, supported by the hardware investments of multinational enterprises and infrastructure investments (Smeral, 1998).

Tourism demand

Over the past six decades there has been a tremendous change in the scale of travel. Tourism has experienced continued growth and diversification to become one of the largest and fastest growing economic sectors in the world. The substantial growth of the tourism activity clearly marks it as one of the most significant economic and social phenomena of the 20th century. The levels of international travel increased as a result of the factors mentioned above, coupled with some substitution of national by international travel. The number of international arrivals has grown from 25 million international arrivals in 1950, to 277 million in 1980, to 684 million in 2000, and to 980 million in 2011 (UNWTO, 2001a, 2012), corresponding to an average annual growth rate of 6.2%.

During this 60-year period, development was particularly strong in the East Asia and Pacific regions and in the Middle East, while the Americas and Europe grew at a slower pace and slightly below the world's average growth. Thus the consequences of globalisation are already evident as the variance among regional market shares in world tourism has been decreasing over time.

In 1950 Europe and the Americas represented together over 95% of worldwide international tourist arrivals. In 1990 their joint market share was 82%, in 2000 it had dropped to 76%, and in 2011 their share in world tourism had decreased to 67%. In 2002 East Asia and the Pacific overtook the Americas as the second most popular destination, representing 22% of total international arrivals in 2011. New destinations are thus gradually increasing their market share, while more mature regions, such as Europe, tend to have less dynamic growth. Growth has been particularly high in the world's emerging economies, with the share in international tourist arrivals of the developing countries steadily rising from 31% in 1990 to 47% in 2011 (UNWTO, 2012).

The World Tourism Organisation forecasts that international tourist arrivals will reach 1.6 billion in 2020 (UNWTO, 2001a). Despite a modest average annual growth rate (3.2%), Europe will remain the most popular destination (717 million international arrivals), although its market share will decline to 45%. Growth in this region will be led by central and eastern countries, where arrivals are expected to increase by 4.8% per year (UNWTO, 2001a). Given the dominance of this region, it is not surprising to find six European countries among the top 10 tourism destinations, with the United States holding the second position. However, in 2020 China is expected to replace France as the top destination.

Europe will also remain the world's largest generating region, being responsible for almost half of all the tourist arrivals worldwide, despite its low annual growth rate. East Asia and the Pacific will become the second largest outbound travel region, forcing the Americas into third place. Despite not being major sources of tourists, the other regions will experience above-average growth rates (UNWTO, 2001a). Considering the countries that will be the main producers of tourists abroad, the list will continue to include the major industrialised countries (Germany, Japan, the United States, the United Kingdom and France), with China already being the third largest source of tourists in the world market, something that was expected to happen only in 2020. Departures from Africa (especially the southern region), the Middle East and South Asia are expected to grow as well.

Tourism supply

The creation of a global society means that tourism businesses have the ability to operate globally and many have opted for a competitive strategy of internationalisation (Knowles *et al.*, 2004). Outsourcing and transnational ownership structures and investments have thus become standard, involving not only big corporations, but also small and medium-sized businesses. As an industry, tourism includes various component sectors ranging from hotels and restaurants, travel agencies and tour operators, and transport, as well as entertainment and tourist guides. All these components are closely integrated through the consumption patterns of travellers, thus having strong backward and forward linkages.

Tour operators, airlines, international reservation systems and hotels are key actors in international tourism as they strongly influence visitor flows (Endo, 2006). Despite their importance, there are no comprehensive international FDI statistics in tourism. Nonetheless, it is considered low compared to the levels of FDI in other economic activities (UNCTAD, 2007). Hotels and restaurants and car rentals represent the largest and major portion of FDI in tourism (Table 12.2), indicating that there is little FDI in important activities such as tour operations, reservations systems and airlines, partially because they undertake little FDI in their main areas of activities (UNCTAD, 2007). Many of these companies are transnationals as a result of overseas investment in tourism activities other than their own, giving rise to vertically integrated tourism firms. Vertical integration allows them to control various links in the distribution chain. Some companies have also started adopting a diagonal integration strategy to offer products and services that tourists usually purchase (Endo, 2006).

FDI is concentrated primarily in developed countries, both in terms of tourism-related FDI stocks and the locations of hotels that are part of international hotel chains (Endo, 2006; UNCTAD, 2007). The vast majority of FDI in hotels and restaurants have also been generated by developed

Table 12.2 Frequency of FDI occurrence by sector

Sector	Frequency
Hotels and similar	•••
Restaurants and similar	•••
Second homes	•••
Passenger transport rental equipment	•••
Railway passenger transport services	••
Air passenger transport services	••
Road passenger transport services	•
Water passenger transport services	•
Passenger transport supporting services	•
Travel agencies and similar	•
Cultural services	•
Sports and other recreational services	•

Notes: ••• frequent; •• occasional; • rare.
Source: Adapted from UNCTAD (2007)

countries. In this regard, Go and Klooster (2005) uphold that the tourism sector still has a continental rather than a global character. Todd (2001) also shares a similar view, stating that, although international travel is a global activity, it is dominated by relatively few countries, both as origin markets and as destinations.

The growth of mid-sized groups began to evolve during the 1980s, their consolidation intensified in the 1990s and larger groups began to enter the equities market to fund continued expansion (Go & Klooster, 2005). The result was the formation of multinational groups, being US-based firms ahead of European and Japanese ones in terms of vertical integration (Tulder, 1999, cited in Go & Klooster, 2005), showing at the time strong links with airlines and tour operators (Dunning & McQueen, 1982; Lafferty & Fossen, 2001). A significant part of globalisation strategies is mergers and acquisitions, commonly through horizontal or vertical integration.

There is thus a tendency for the emergence of integrated tourism multinationals, in order to benefit from the advantages of internal control of the various stages of transporting, accommodating and servicing tourists. This enables firms to plan, coordinate and control the flow of tourism services, providing ease of accessibility and enabling economies of scale to be exploited (Buckley & Papadopoulos, 1988). Hilton Hotels has played a prominent role in creating synergies between accommodation, gambling and entertainment, an example followed by the Hyatt Corporation in the 1990s, when it ventured into casino-hotels. During the 1990s, the Marriott organisation strengthened its food and beverage holdings and also expanded into time shares and luxury retirement communities (Lafferty & Fossen, 2001).

Global-acting airlines, hotel chains and tour operators already have branches throughout the world and cover major parts of international tourism demand with their GDS. The use of modern ICT in connection with the various forms of horizontal, vertical and diagonal integration extends the value chain (Smeral, 1998). Strategic alliances, mergers and acquisitions, which are prevalent in the international hotel industry, are additional driving forces of the globalisation process.

Networks and Tourism Internationalisation

Small and medium-sized enterprises dominate the tourism sector in Europe, mostly in the form of family-owned businesses. Similarly, they play an important role in the economy and in the development of destinations, especially in peripheral regions, because of their ability to create new jobs, their capacity to stimulate competition and their higher multiplier effect, among other socio-economic reasons (Buhalis & Peters, 2005).

As a result of the world's globalisation, vertical and horizontal integration of the industries, and the opening of the world's frontiers, competition has become fierce and has led to a growing pressure on this type of tourism enterprise (Smeral, 1998). However, on the other hand, globalisation can also be seen as an opportunity to benefit from the open world market. Increasing worldwide competition pushes companies to become more efficient and effective. Hence, firms are becoming conscious that, to compete globally, they have to interconnect with other agents in order to become more efficient in their operations, incorporate resources and reduce costs. As mentioned above, the importance of networks as facilitators in the access to knowledge, resources, markets and technology is enormous, especially in a globalised sector like tourism.

In today's networked society and economy, tourism is a networked industry by nature, where business and personal relationships exist between companies and managers in a very wide diversity of services, allowing the overcoming of problems associated with its fragmented and geographic dispersion (Scott et al., 2008; Tremblay, 1998).

The network perspective is highly appropriate in the tourism industry, as tourism destinations usually include different types of organisations of different structures and sizes, interacting and competing with each other and also shaping the destination's tourism product. This creates a dichotomy in that competition and cooperation co-exist (Pavlovich, 2003), thus being necessary 'co-opetitive' strategies. Collective actions thus become important for the development and in some cases even the survival of tourism companies and destinations.

Another reason for the network approach in tourism destinations is knowledge management. Grizelj (2003) discusses this, based on the network perspective of the virtual service company, emphasising that the knowledge-building requirement is not confined to the single travel company itself, but transcends to the virtual network the company belongs to, and may eventually lead to collective competencies of the network itself. Therefore, knowledge management within tourist destinations has to be understood as a mutual, collaborative task. A similar approach is defended by Gnoth (2007).

Firms use their networks to gain access to resources, to improve their strategic positions, to control transaction costs, to learn new skills, to gain legitimacy and to cope with technological changes (McDougall & Oviatt, 2003). Through networks it is easier to compete, both domestically and internationally, to reach economies of scale and dimension and to generate synergies (UNWTO, 2001b). Cooperation and partnerships play an important role in the internationalisation process, preventing many of the location-specific risks due to 'foreignness' and inadequate knowledge of the operating environment, as partners tend to compensate for these shortcomings, acting as information channels and interpreting market information (Etemad & Wright, 2003; Forsgren et al., 2005).

Hassid (2003) reveals that the mechanism most favoured by small firms in the services sector to acquire internationalisation-related competences is through the promotion of networking, therefore showing the importance of the development of distribution and market penetration through formal and informal links. The embeddedness of these relationships and ties has a positive impact on economic and social actions and outcomes (Etemad, 2004).

The network perspective in internationalisation thus provides an interesting opportunity to understand the entry into foreign markets by young and/or resource-constrained small business. It also posits that internationalisation is a process that takes place through networks of relationships. Social embeddedness of the network plays an important role in binding individual firms or entrepreneurs into value-adding relationships, which enable them to minimise or overcome their disadvantages of smallness and isolation, as well as to overcome problems associated with unknown markets and psychic distance (Etemad, 2004).

These inter-firm relationships, composed of personal networks connected to the individual and extended networks associated with organisations, have also been acknowledged as a driving force in internationalisation, functioning as enablers of action, thus being known as opportunity networks (Axelsson & Agndal, 2000). Not only direct partners, but also the partners of their partners affect a firm's behaviour, which means that existing relationships can be used as bridges to other networks (Johanson & Vahlne, 1990; Sharma & Johnson, 1987).

According to Etemad and Wright (2003), the key to successful internationalisation no longer lies in the firm's internal resources and management capabilities, but increasingly in the ability to understand its relative position in relation to the network and to manage inter-firm relationships to generate globally competitive value chains. Other studies have also suggested the importance of network relationships. In Granovetter's (1983) discussion of weak ties, it is argued that secondary contacts offer opportunities for renewal in ways that primary or strong ties do not; weak ties thus create access to potentially important clusters. Burt (1992) also asserts that a large number of contacts or complementary networks is preferable for the firm.

Cunningham and Turnbull (1982) asserted that personal contacts are at the heart of interaction between organisations, as it is the individual who makes contact and builds up trust between organisations (Axelsson & Agndal, 2000). In the context of entrepreneurship, personal networks have been found to play an important role in businesses (Butler et al., 2003), and family and friends were important elements in entrepreneurs' networks (Staber & Aldrich, 1995). The importance of personal networks has not been, however, much explored in business research, especially at the international level, where more attention has been given to formal business-to-business linkages (Butler et al., 2003).

Social bonds within business networks tend to strengthen business relationships. These are important for gaining information (Björkman &

Kock, 1997) and might also affect the firm's choice of foreign market and entry mode (Coviello & Munro, 1995; Johanson & Vahlne, 2003). They might be instrumental in explaining why some firms decide to internationalise and choose the market mode of entry, but they can also inhibit a firm's internationalisation.

In their study, Coviello and Munro (1995) found that the 'initial triggers' for internationalisation came from networks of firms looking for new market opportunities and with established players as potential partners. Networks also allowed firms to overcome typical industry weaknesses, and were important in accelerating access or entry into new markets. Similar results were found by Zain and Ng (2006), who revealed that network relationships trigger and motivate firms to internationalise, influence their market selection and mode of entry decisions, help them gain initial credibility, allow access to additional relationships and established channels, help in lowering cost and reducing risk, and influence their internationalisation pace and pattern.

While the internationalisation process approach suggests that, for a firm to successfully enter new international markets, surmounting country borders (economic, institutional and cultural barriers) plays an important role (Johanson & Vahlne, 1977). In the network model, barriers to internationalisation are more dependent on the firm's relationships within both domestic and international markets (Johanson & Mattsson, 1988). Forsgren et al. (2005) decided to propose a combination of both approaches, calling it network approach to internationalisation.

According to this approach, markets are bounded by institutional and cultural barriers, and are depicted as a system of business relationships among a number of players, with some of them being cross-border relationships. Contrasting with the traditional view, which stresses institutional and cultural barriers to business, this approach upholds that entry problems are not solely associated with country markets but also with the establishment and development of relationships, which can be used to surmount the country market barriers (Forsgren et al., 2005).

An inexperienced firm can benefit from others' learning-by-doing, through the firm's personal and business networks (Arrow, 1962). The firm can thus gain access to other enterprises' experiential knowledge without necessarily going through the same experiences (Eriksson et al., 1997), learning instead, through them, about business conditions and market networks.

From the network perspective, the internationalisation process is a result of the interaction between experiential knowledge development and commitment, although they concern potential and existing relationship partners, not countries (Johanson & Vahlne, 2003). Internationalisation of the firm can be achieved through the establishment of relationships in foreign country networks that are new to the firm (international extension), the development of relationships and increasing resource commitments in those networks in which the company already has a position (penetration), or connecting existing networks in different countries (Johanson & Mattson, 1988). The experienced enterprises can use their existing network position as a base for further internationalisation.

The main difference between the network approach and the internationalisation process of the firm relates to the decision-making process. Whereas in, the stage model, internationalisation is regarded as an outward extension of the firm and the outcome of its decision-making, the network approach sees it in terms of the firm's existing relationships. Another characteristic that distinguishes them is the size of firms under study, with the network perspective providing an opportunity to understand the entry into foreign markets by young and/or small businesses, not focusing just on big companies.

The Internationalisation of Portuguese Tourism Firms

The internationalisation of Portuguese tourism firms started in the late 1990s, at about the same time that outward investment experienced a boom, and accelerated in recent years. This late entry in international markets might also reflect the fact that tourism enterprises were just then starting to be mature enough to venture overseas, benefiting from their experience and from the relationships established with international companies operating in the domestic market. The small size of the country, which is an important but also mature destination in the international tourism market, and also the increasing competition might have prompted the desire to reach new markets.

Although the internationalisation of the Portuguese firms in the tourism sector started late, being dominated by a few companies and their degree of internationalisation being relatively low, a number of new projects and firms have been identified as intending to engage in foreign markets other than the traditional ones. Nonetheless, the investment has mainly been made in former colonies, particularly Brazil and some Portuguese-speaking African countries (Cape Verde and Mozambique), which are new destinations on the world tourism scene, with interesting natural attractions and warm weather throughout the year. Fundamentally, these are appealing destinations for sun and sea tourism or nature-related tourism, still relatively undeveloped in regard to tourism, allowing Portuguese firms to gain some considerable advantages, since the big international players are not seriously engaged in some of these destinations; thus the competitive pressure and dimensional demands are considerably lower. This is corroborated by the fact that for some of the hotels, their competitive advantage was precisely the fact that there was no direct competition.

There seems to be either a convergence of interests among Portuguese companies or a tendency to imitate the competition. The first option seems more likely, as through cooperation it is easier to consolidate these tourism destinations, and therefore their individual businesses. Some companies are vertically integrated in business groups, thus allowing them to control the value chain, especially through tour operators that are responsible for the creation of tourism packages. Despite competing in the destinations, these companies can cooperate at a broader level in order to allow some dimension and to develop the destination. This is suggested by the fact that in some cases, particularly in Brazil, there are other Portuguese companies in the same region, and also by the fact that in many cases the firms pointed out that one of their main difficulties relates to a lack of promotion by local governmental entities. Co-opetition thus seems inevitable and essential. This cooperation and its concerted strategies are not just inter-organisational, however; some groups strategically position their hotels in proximate locations so as to gain economies of scale and dimension. Despite this geographical concentration, results show that some of the new players will contribute to the diversification of FDI destinations. Investment will be more dispersed even in countries that do not show evident cultural affinities.

Results show that a considerable number of firms' initial foreign market selections and entry modes were triggered by opportunities presented by formal or informal networks, rather than solely by the strategic decisions of managers and their own proactive identification process. Relationships are also important in accessing local market knowledge. The networks in which firms are embedded represent a source of knowledge, either directly or indirectly capitalised, for the internationalisation of the firm. The network theory thus offers a rich perspective on how and why the international development patterns of entrepreneurial firms occur.

The internationalisation of Portuguese companies, however, is not explained solely by network relationships, given that concepts inherent in FDI theory, international new venture perspective and the stage models are also evident in their internationalisation, and they are interrelated. For example, there is support for the network perspective that internationalisation is influenced heavily by the firms' networks of formal and informal relationships (relationships involving competitors, colleagues, government, friends, and so forth), and these network relationships provide market knowledge and influence initial market selection and also mode of entry. Some firms reveal patterns of internationalisation which occurred fairly rapidly and across a number of international markets. To a certain extent, this supports the international new ventures perspective. Some of these firms were able to internationalise very quickly by linking themselves to networks. Usually, partners provided the initial trigger for foreign market selection as well as the entry mode. There is evidence of the stage models of internationalisation as foreign market entry is done in cultural proximate countries. Geographic distance does not seem to be regarded as a barrier to internationalisation. Finally, aspects of FDI are evident as the firms internationalise in a manner that maximises control and internalises firm-specific assets. Location-specific advantages emerge through various network relationships, and these advantages are particularly relevant as investments in tourism can only take place in a particular location because they utilise resources/attributes that are immobile.

Conclusions

In a globalised and interconnected world, organisations may no longer be seen in an isolated way, seeing as their success is linked to the surrounding environment. Tourism is a networked industry by nature, where business and personal relationships exist between companies and managers in a great diversity of services, allowing the overcoming of problems associated with its fragmented and geographic dispersion. Considering that the economic structure of the tourism sector is largely composed of SMEs and by more 'flat' organisational structures, the identification and creation of partner-ships and networks play an important role in the development of regional competitive advantages. The importance of networks for tourism thus seems enormous.

Through integration in business networks or the establishment of busi-ness relationships it is easier to compete, both domestic and internation-ally, to reach economies of scale and dimension and to generate synergies (UNWTO, 2001b). Cooperation and partnerships thus play an important role in the internationalisation process. Through such alliances, enterprises can avoid many of the location-specific risks due to 'foreignness' and inad-equate knowledge of the operating environment, as their local partners tend to compensate for these shortcomings (Etemad & Wright, 2003).

Hassid (2003) shows that the preferred mechanism for small companies in the service sector for the acquisition of internationalisation-related skills is through the promotion of networking. It is therefore important to develop distribution and market penetration through formal and informal links with customers, distributors, agents and other sources of information in destina-tion markets. The depth of these relationships and ties has a positive impact on the actions and results (Etemad, 2004).

The network perspective in internationalisation provides an interesting opportunity to understand entry into foreign markets by young and/or resource-constrained small businesses (Breda et al., 2008). It also posits that internationalisation is a process that takes place through networks of rela-tionships. Social embeddedness of the network plays an important role in binding individual firms or entrepreneurs into value-adding relationships, which enable them to minimise or overcome their disadvantages of smallness and isolation, as well as to overcome problems associated with unknown markets and psychic distance (Brown & McNaughton, 2003; Etemad, 2004).

It has thus been acknowledged that foreign market selection and entry initiatives can emanate from opportunities created through network contacts, rather than solely from the strategic decisions of managers in the firm. These relationships are especially relevant in culturally unfamiliar environments, given that they provide the firm with local knowledge.

Business and personal relationships can act as a bridge between actors and markets, especially when the degree of knowledge of one of them is low. Partnerships can thus fill in the gaps, transferring tacit knowledge from one partner to the other, which is essential to acquire the necessary tools in a faster and easier way.

These results have practical value for researchers and practitioners in the tourism field. In the institutional and business sphere, it may favour reflection as to what are the most relevant factors in market entry and mode of entry, and how these requirements are to be met. Companies can benefit from a better understanding of the impact of networks on international market development. Future opportunities may emanate from network relationships, so they should pay more attention to how and with whom these relationships are established and managed. In addition, managers should successfully position the firms so that they have a wide array of relationship options open to them. The existing networks, as well as their ability to establish new network relationships, should be managed as a key competitive capability.

References

Arrow, K.J. (1962) The economic implications of learning by doing. *Review of Economics and Statistics* 29, 115–173.

Axelsson, B. and Agndal, H. (2000) Internationalisation of the firm: A note on the crucial role of the individual's contact network. Paper presented at the 16th IMP Conference, Bath, UK

Björkman, I. and Kock, S. (1997) Inward international activities in service firms: Illustrated by three cases from the tourism industry. *International Journal of Service Industry Management* 8 (5), 362–376.

Breda, Z. (2010) Network relationships and the internationalisation of the tourism economy: The case of Portuguese overseas investment in the hotel sector. PhD thesis, University of Aveiro, Aveiro.

Breda, Z., Costa, R. and Costa, C. (2004) Clustering and networking the tourism development process: A market driven approach for a small backwards tourist region located in central Portugal (Caramulo). In C. Petrillo and J. Swarbrooke (eds) *Networking and Partnerships in Destination Development and Management* (Vol. 2, pp. 469–484). Naples: Enzo Albano.

Breda, Z., Costa, R. and Costa, C. (2006) Do clusters and networks make small places beautiful? The case of Caramulo (Portugal). In L. Lazzeretti and C. Petrillo (eds) *Tourism Local Systems and Networking* (pp. 67–82). Oxford: Elsevier.

Breda, Z., Costa, R. and Costa, C. (2008) Helping small businesses getting bigger: The role played by networks and partnerships in the internationalisation of small tourism enterprises. In G. Richards and J. Wilson (eds) *From Cultural Tourism to Creative Tourism: Changing Structures of Collaboration* (Vol. 2, pp. 53–64). Arnhem: ATLAS.

Brown, P. and McNaughton, R. (2003) Cluster development programmes: Panacea or placebo forpromoting SME growth and internationalization? In H. Etemad and R. Wright (eds) *Globalization and Entrepreneurship: Policy and Strategy Perspectives* (pp. 106–124). Cheltenham: Edward Elgar.

Buckley, P.J. and Papadopoulos, S. (1988) Foreign direct investment in the tourism sector of the Greek economy. *Service Industries Journal* 8 (3), 370–388.

Buhalis, D. and Peters, M. (2005) SMEs in tourism. In D. Buhalis and C. Costa (eds) *Tourism Management Dynamics: Trends, Management and Tools* (pp. 116–129). Oxford: Elsevier Butterworth-Heinemann.

Burt, R.S. (1992) *Structural Holes: The Social Structure of Competition*. Cambridge, MA: Harvard University Press.

Butler, J.E., Brown, B. and Chamornmarn, W. (2003) Informational networks, entrepreneurial action and performance. *Asia Pacific Journal of Management* 20 (2), 151–174

Costa, C., Breda, Z., Costa, R. and Miguéns, J. (2008) The benefits of networks for small and medium sized tourism enterprises. In N. Scott, R. Baggio and C. Cooper (eds) *Network Analysis and Tourism: From Theory to Practice* (pp. 96–112). Clevedon: Channel View Publications.

Coviello, N. and Munro, H.J. (1995) Growing the entrepreneurial firm: Networking for international market development. *European Journal of Marketing* 29 (7), 49–61.

Cunningham, M.T. and Turnbull, P.W. (1982) Inter-organizational personal contact patterns. In H. Hakansson (ed.) *International Marketing and Purchasing of Industrial Goods: An Interaction Approach* (pp. 304–316). Chichester: John Wiley.

Dunning, J. and McQueen, M. (1982) Multinational corporations in the international hotel industry. *Annals of Tourism Research* 9 (1), 69–90.

Endo, K. (2006) Foreign direct investment in tourism: Flows and volumes. *Tourism Management* 27 (4), 600–614.

Eriksson, K., Johanson, J., Majkgard, A. and Sharma, D.D. (1997) Experiential knowledge and cost in the internationalization process. *Journal of International Business Studies* 28 (2), 337–360.

Etemad, H. (ed.) (2004) *International Entrepreneurship in Small and Medium Size Enterprises: Orientation, Environment and Strategy*. Cheltenham: Edward Elgar.

Etamad, H. and Wright, R. (2003) Globalization and entrepreneurship. In H. Etamad and R. Wright (eds) *Globalization and Entrepreneurship: Policy and Strategy Perspectives* (pp. 3–14). Cheltenham: Edward Elgar.

Forsgren, M., Holm, U. and Johanson, J. (2005) *Managing the Embedded Multinational: A Business Network View*. Cheltenham: Edward Elgar.

Gnoth, J. (2007) Destinations as networking virtual service firms. *International Journal of Excellence in Tourism, Hospitality and Catering* 1 (1), 1–18.

Go, F. (1989) The international hotel industry: Capitalizing on change. *Tourism Management* 10 (3), 195–200.

Go, F. and Klooster, E. (2005) Managing globalization. In D. Buhalis and C. Costa (eds) *Tourism Management Dynamics: Trends, Management and Tools* (pp. 137–144). Oxford: Elsevier Butterworth-Heinemann.

Go, F.M. and Pine, R. (1995) *Globalization Strategy in the Hotel Industry*. London: Routledge.

Granovetter, M. (1983) The strength of weak ties: A network theory revisited. *Sociological Theory* 1, 201–233.

Grizelj, F. (2003) Collaborative knowledge management in virtual service companies: An approach for tourism destinations. *Tourism Analysis* 51 (4), 371–385.

Hassid, J. (2003) *Internationalisation and Changing Skill Needs in European Small Firms: The Services Sector*. Luxembourg: Cedefop.

Hjalager, A-M. (2007) Stages in the economic globalization of tourism. *Annals of Tourism Research* 34 (2), 437–457.

Holjevac, I.A. (2003) A vision of tourism and the hotel industry in the 21st century. *International Journal of Hospitality Management* 22 (2), 129–134.

Johanson, J. and Mattsson, L. (1988) Internationalization in industrial systems: A network. In N. Hood and J-E. Vahlne (eds) *Strategies in Global Competition* (pp. 287–314). New York: Croom Helm.

Johanson, J. and Vahlne, J-E. (1977) The internationalization process of the firm: A model of knowledge development and increasing foreign market commitments. *Journal of International Business Studies* 8 (1), 23–32.

Johanson, J. and Vahlne, J-E. (1990) The mechanism of internationalization. *International Marketing Review* 7 (4), 11–24.

Johanson, J. and Vahlne, J-E. (2003) Business relationship learning and commitment in the internationalization process. *Journal of International Entrepreneurship* 1 (1), 83–101.

Johnson, C. (2002) Locational strategies of international hotel corporations in Eastern Central Europe. PhD thesis, University of Fribourg, Fribourg.

Knowles, T., Diamantis, D. and El-Mourhabi, J.B. (2004) *The Globalization of Tourism and Hospitality: A Strategic Perspective* (2nd edn). London: Thomson Learning.

Lafferty, G. and Fossen, A.V. (2001) Integrating the tourism industry: Problems and strategies. *Tourism Management* 22 (1), 11–19.

Littlejohn, D. and Roper, A. (1991) Changes in international hotel companies' strategies. In R. Teare and A. Boer (eds) *Strategic Hospitality Management*. London: Cassell.

Magriço, V. (2003) *Alianças internacionais das empresas portuguesas na era da globalização: Uma análise para o período 1989–1998*. Oeiras: Celta Editora.

McDougall, P. and Oviatt, B.M. (2003) Some fundamental issues in international entrepreneurship. *USASBE White Papers*. Nashville, TN: US Association for Small Business and Entrepreneurship, accessed 26 August 2005. http://www.usasbe.org/knowledge/whitepapers/mcdougall2003.pdf.

Olsen, M. (1999) Macroforces driving change into the new millennium: Major challenges for the hospitality professional. *International Journal of Hospitality Management* 18 (4), 371–385.

Pavlovich, K. (2003) The evolution and transformation of a tourism destination network: The Waitomo Caves, New Zealand. *Tourism Management* 24 (2), 203–216.

Peric, V. (2005) *Tourism and Globalization*. Paper presented at the 6th International Conference of the Faculty of Management Koper, Congress Centre Bernardin, Slovenia, 24–26 November.

Scott, N., Baggio, R. and Cooper, C. (2008) *Network Analysis and Tourism: From Theory to Practice*. Clevedon: Channel View Publications.

Sharma, D. and Johnson, J. (1987) Technical consultancy in internationalisation. *International Marketing Review* 4, 20–29.

Simões, V.C. (1997) Internacionalização das empresas portuguesas: Que papel para a cooperação? *Economia & Prospectiva* 1 (2), 17–31.

Smeral, E. (1998) The impact of globalization on small and medium enterprises: new challenges for tourism policies in European countries. *Tourism Management* 19 (4), 371–380.

Staber, U. and Aldrich, H. (1995) Cross-national similarities in the personal networks of small business owners: A comparison of two regions in North America. *Canadian Journal of Sociology* 20 (4), 441–465.

Todd, G. (2001) World travel and tourism today. In A. Lockwood and S. Medlik (eds) *Tourism and Hospitality in the 21st Century*. Oxford: Butterworth-Heinemann.

Tremblay, P. (1998) The economic organization of tourism. *Annals of Tourism Research* 25 (4), 837–859.

UNCTAD (2007) *FDI in Tourism: The Development Dimension.* New York: United Nations.

UNWTO (2001a) *Tourism 2020 Vision: Global Forecasts and Profiles of Market Segments.* Madrid: World Tourism Organization.

UNWTO (2001b) *The Future of Small and Medium-sized Enterprises in European Tourism Faced with Globalization.* Madrid: World Tourism Organization.

UNWTO (2008) *Tourism Highlights* (2008 edn). Madrid: World Tourism Organization.

UNWTO (2012) *Tourism Barometer* (Vol. 10). Madrid: World Tourism Organization.

Williams, P.W. (1999) Strategic partnership development in small and medium sized tourism enterprises. *Tourism Review* 54 (4), 20–35.

Zain, M. and Ng, S.I. (2006) The impacts of network relationships on SMEs' internationalization process. *Thunderbird International Business Review* 48 (2), 183–205.

13 Business Environment and Accommodation Policies in Europe

Theodoros Stavrinoudis, Paris Tsartas and Andreas Papatheodorou

Introduction

Europe is the most important tourism destination globally, accounting for approximately 42% of global arrivals. According to the United Nations World Tourism Organization (UNWTO), five European Union (EU) member states were among the 10 top countries worldwide in terms of international tourist arrivals in 2008. EU citizens account for a significant percentage of overnight stays in the EU, a fact that reveals its potential as a generator of both tourism demand and supply. The EU hosts approximately 1.6 million enterprises engaging in the broader tourism sector, with 92% of those employing fewer than 10 individuals (HOTREC, 2008b). The accommodation sector in the EU accounts for, approximately, 260,000 enterprises, the majority of which are based in three countries, that is, France, Italy and Germany (HOTREC, 2008b). In 2010, 147,000 hotels were located in the EU accounting for 5.2 million rooms (Travel Daily News, 2010). According to Eurostat, 2.3 million people were employed in European hotels in 2006; however, employment was concentrated in a small number of countries and characterised by a large percentage of inadequately trained part-timers. The accommodation sector contributed 1.16% to the European GDP in 2006 (De Voldere *et al.*, 2009).

Tourism in Europe, and consequently hotel enterprises in the EU, today face various challenges, the most important being the following:

- the reduction of seasonality;
- the increase of employment in quality and quantity;

- the improvement of the product offered and the increase in competitiveness;
- the launching of entrepreneurial actions to protect the environment;
- the diversification of its client base. (Tourism Sustainability Group, 2007)

On these grounds, this chapter aims to present first the main features of the contemporary international business environment of the accommodation sector. Then it examines the EU policies implemented in the context of the accommodation industry and studies their implications for the sector. In particular, the major EU Regulations, Directives and Communications influencing the external operational environment of European hotels are analysed and their repercussions for the general entrepreneurial framework and competitive conduct are thoroughly examined.

The Business Environment of the EU Accommodation Sector

Economic issues

The EU accommodation sector is characterised by a notable dualism; on the one hand, there is a multitude of small and medium-sized enterprises, whereas on the other hand there is a limited, but continuously rising, number of national or international chains (Stabler *et al.*, 2010). In several countries the number of small and medium-sized (SME) accommodation establishments exceeds 90% as there are low barriers to entry. The prevailing tendency is that of concentration, mainly horizontally, either via the enlargement of large hotel chains or by means of collaboration between two or more SMEs (clustering and networking) (De Voldere *et al.*, 2009; Smeral, 1998). The larger units (often chains) present a high degree of concentration in the large urban centres while the market structure is more dispersed in the regional summer holiday tourist destinations (De Voldere *et al.*, 2009). Especially in the major receiving countries of the south, hotel enterprises operate in conditions of intense seasonality, a fact that among other factors affects their operational period and financial performance.

At the same time, the accommodation sector is directly affected by globalisation, following the general trend observed in the tourism sector related to the continuous expansion of vertical and horizontal integration practices (Koutoulas & Stavrinoudis, 2006), franchising and outsourcing. Globalisation creates opportunities in the European continent, raising tourism appeal (Tsartas & Stavrinoudis, 2010). It has led, though, to a dramatic increase in the power of the middlemen to the detriment of tourism producers (i.e. the European hotels), intensifying competition and facilitating buyer access to cheaper destinations. The accommodation sector operates under conditions of intense competition to a significant degree, but it still depends on a small number of multinational businesses (tour operators), which operate under oligopoly conditions and even monopoly for some destinations. Especially difficult is the position of accommodation establishments located in traditional tourist destinations, mainly small and medium-sized hotels, whose survival is threatened by international hotel chains (Stabler *et al.*, 2010).

The EU accommodation sector is challenged by the emergence of new tourist destinations in third countries, which reinforce their presence by affecting total supply and prices. Moreover, the demand for the accommodation sector in the EU is to a significant degree internal, that is, mainly originating from other EU countries. This constitutes a weakness, since an economic recession in the member states, especially those of the Eurozone, may have immediate and seriously negative repercussions on the performance of hotels. In fact, the sector is adversely hit by the current economic conditions and the rise in fuel prices, which affects the demand and the operational costs of hotels (De Voldere *et al.*, 2009; European Travel Commission, 2009). In 2010, the financial crisis resulted in a drop of business confidence, thus impeding the access of hotels to cheap funding sources. Increasing layoffs and unemployment, and of course decreases in available income, have inevitably led to a reduction in the demand for hotel services. Although short-haul travel and domestic tourism show an upward trend, an important degree of wariness is recorded among individual buyers and companies (European Travel Commission, 2009) related to a demand for better value for money.

Differences in the VAT rate applied to products and services offered by the European accommodation sector is another important feature with potentially distortive effects. Across Europe, various efforts are undertaken to reduce VAT for hotel enterprises to counter among other factors the extent of the informal economy (De Voldere *et al.*, 2009; HOTREC, 2008a). In addition, entrepreneurs hesitate about planning and realising additional investments in the sector (De Voldere *et al.*, 2009; European Travel Commission, 2009). Moreover, the reinforcement of business practices such as all-inclusive packages and low-cost operations has a direct impact on the profitability of hotels (European Travel Commission, 2009). Still, the gradual appreciation of the dollar against the euro may positively affect inbound tourism, leading to an increase of demand for hotel services in the EU.

Working in hotel enterprises is characterised by a number of peculiarities and difficulties (e.g. rolling shifts, low wages), a fact that makes it less attractive and increases personnel turnover, thus prohibiting hotels from investing in the creation of a coherent training culture and the acquisition of personnel skills (Smeral, 1998). Human resources employed in hotels are expected to possess ever-increasing knowledge and skills, to face the increasing challenge of differentiating the product offered, a demand that is often not met by the existing programmes of education and training. A significant number of employees in the sector do not have the necessary educational background and training, while capable and specialised executives often abandon the sector to work in other industries. It is not rare to see cultural clashes because of labour mobility within the EU.

The political, legal, sociocultural and technological context

The EU accommodation sector faces intense challenges from external, often uncontrollable factors, such as the increased perceived threat level from terrorism activities, epidemics (such as H1N1) and others. Moreover, the change from government to governance, a framework of changes that runs through all modes of political action and public administration at a regional, national and EU level, affects the operational environment of the accommodation sector by requiring more transparency in the commercial transactions undertaken (Borras, 2003).

The legal environment of the EU does not pose any significant barriers to entry in the accommodation sector, as explained in the next section of this chapter. Free labour mobility within the EU and flexible forms of employment among other factors create a liberal operational framework. On the other hand, hotel establishments located in environmentally sensitive areas are required to develop environmentally responsible methods of operation and production. Following the 2007 Davos Process, it is imperative that hotels adjust to the new conditions created as a result of climate change, the greenhouse effect and the continuous demand to invest in renewable energy sources.

The EU accommodation sector generates important benefits from increases in life expectancy and the more pronounced presence of senior citizens and people with special needs in tourism activities. An increased emphasis is placed by tourists on matters of health, nutrition and exercise during their vacation, a fact that has led to new products and the demand for hotel businesses to adjust their service characteristics accordingly. New information and communication technologies and primarily the internet have greatly affected the operational environment of hotels, allowing even small units to acquire direct distribution channels with customers circumventing the intermediaries. More customers book their accommodation through the internet at an international level, while we also see a rise of self-tailored tours (European Travel Commission, 2009). In spite of these interesting market developments, employment in the accommodation sector is often perceived with a negative bias, which deprives hotels of highly educated human resources (De Voldere et al., 2009).

Major EU Policies and Their Relevance to the Accommodation Sector[1]

This section presents the main EU policies that affect the organisation, operation and competitiveness of the accommodation sector. The main difficulty in discussing these policies stems from the absence of an integrated European policy framework on accommodation. Fragments of such a policy can be discerned in a plethora of other EU policies. Concerning tourism, the renewed strategy of Lisbon aims to achieve two main objectives, that is, to reinforce employment and the competitiveness of the EU tourism industry and to promote sustainable tourism development. Emphasis should be accorded to the integration of measures affecting tourism via the promotion of better regulations, the simplification of legislation and the coordination of policy making. Securing funding for sustainable development, possibly by implementing a Local Agenda 21, will further reinforce viable forms of tourism, new technologies, innovative SMTEs and related networks, cross-border tourism cooperation and strategies of high added value. Moreover, the focus should be on creating new jobs and companies, undertaking actions to improve the quality of human resources in tourism, mainly via training and education, facilitating employment mobility, and promoting Europe collectively as a unique tourism destination, via the European Tourist Destination Portal (EC, 2006).

Regulations about the internal market, standards and classification

The most important objective of these Regulations is to create a 'genuine' internal market for services via the reduction of barriers, the facilitation of the installation of service providers in member states, the free provision of services among them, the improvement of quality and the standardisation of the services offered. Via this policy, it is possible to create better competitive conditions and to improve the business environment.

The European Committee for Standardization (CEN) and the International Organization for Standardization (ISO) decided to collaborate in this context. Technical Committee 228 established seven working groups in the field of tourism and related services: diving, health tourism (spa, thalassotherapy etc.), information and reception services in tourism information offices, golf, beach, natural protected areas and adventure tourism. Another Directive moves in the same direction, aiming at the creation and implementation by member states of a unified methodology on tourism data collection.

Regulations on consumers, consumer protection and the applicability of the law

These regulations are directly related to the multinational character of the EU and the globalised market of goods and services. They concern matters of visa granting, while many aim to protect the buyers' rights from illegal or unethical practices (e.g. sales practices) by enterprises. They cover other areas of activity of the accommodation sector such as packaged tours, timeshares, etc. They also set the framework for the resolution of commercial disputes among enterprises or citizens and enterprises located in different countries.

Regulations on labour matters and entrepreneurship

These regulations seek to settle matters concerning employees and the maintenance of minimum quality standards by enterprises with respect to employment and human resources. Such matters are working hours, new forms of employment (part-time work), safety and security specifications for enterprises (these mainly pertain to hotel customers), the provision of advisory support to employees, the equal treatment of employees regardless of differences (religion, sex, etc.), the facilitation of the integration of highly qualified employees from countries outside the EU, the management of undeclared work and other matters. The regulations on entrepreneurship include actions – policies that reinforce company formation (also via the establishment of European limited companies), with an emphasis on small to medium-sized enterprises which in any case comprise the majority of tourism and hotel businesses. Business taxation matters as well as the protection of the environment are also addressed in this context.

The Effect of EU Policies on the Accommodation Sector of the EU

The implications of the main EU policies in the accommodation sector are analysed hereafter, based on the examination of selected Directives, Regulations and Communications. In particular, Directive 2006/123 affects the international macro-environment (because of the size of the market of the EU), but mainly the external operational environment of hotel enterprises, via the implementation of a unified market, the reinforcement of trade and the liberalisation of markets. It aims to remove any barriers to entry, and promotes the free installation of service providers and the free exchange of services within the EU. Lifting barriers to entry can facilitate the foundation and relocation of accommodation (via the 'centres of unified service' and the implementation of unified printed forms), the free and unimpeded access of entrepreneurs to information, the supply of accommodation and the reinforcement of employment. At the same time, it can lead to an increase in demand and to easier consumer access to information on supply in the accommodation sector. It attempts to improve the quality of services by motivating enterprises to adopt quality assurance procedures. Competition in the accommodation sector is intensified and expanded into more countries.

These policies, however, mainly refer to the large hotel chains and have little or even negative effects on small to medium-sized ones.

The policies of the EU directly affect entrepreneurship in the accommodation sector via the possibility, with Regulation 2157/2001, of founding a European limited company (Societas Europaea). This refers to enterprises active at a Community level, even those arising from a merger. This intervention is capable of affecting the market structure and competitive conduct in the internal European accommodation market since it reinforces the foundation of larger, internationally oriented enterprises. This may lead to an increase in mergers and the creation of strong groups in a sector currently dominated by SMEs.

Of great importance and immediate effect are the EU policies in matters of taxation. Directive 2006/112 is of great interest, since it aims to establish a common VAT system. The accommodation sector is directly affected (e.g. hotel products and services can be classified under a reduced VAT regime) since VAT has a direct influence on the sales price of the hotel service, thus affecting the demand and to a great extent the sector's competitiveness in the EU. Its repercussions are important for the cost of production and distribution of the hotel product, for inflation and for the growth rate of the European economy in general. This Directive therefore affects the external as well as the legal environment (tax legislation) of the European accommodation sector.

Directive 95/57 constitutes a focused sectoral intervention on the operational environment of EU hotels by consolidating the fragmented and usually erroneous collection of tourism statistics by the national tourism authorities. The existence of a unified, uniform and up-to-date tourism statistics database is a valuable source of information on tourism enterprises in matters of supply and demand. In this way, accommodation establishments can better define their place in the market, evaluate competition and formulate more effective operational strategies. Such policy interventions can affect other variables of the external environment of the accommodation sector, such as the price, the cost of production and sale of the product, the characteristics of the human resources working in tourism, etc.

The European Parliament also affects the sociocultural environment of the accommodation sector. This is achieved by the establishment of a system to award an eco-badge (Regulation 1980/2000) to products and services so that these can be easily identified by customers and/or professional purchasers. Along these lines, the Decision of the Committee of 9 June 2009 defines the prerequisites to award this eco-badge for tourism accommodation services using specific criteria (energy and water consumption, waste output, use of renewable resources, etc.). The social trend for environmental protection is reinforced and the notion of corporate social responsibility on environmental matters is broadened. The accommodation sector thus has enough information and guidance to proceed with the production and sale of services with appropriate specifications. It is made easier to differentiate, modernise and enrich the supply with a simultaneous capability to focus on a segmented and environmentally sensitive customer market.

Another related policy intervention is the Announcement of the Committee COM (2007) 621 dated 19 October 2007 about the 'Agenda for sustainable and competitive European tourism'. This recognises the structural connection between tourism and the natural, cultural and social environment of the destination areas as well as its contribution to the social and financial prosperity of the local population. Based on a sustainable approach, the accommodation sector (especially small to medium-sized hotel enterprises) can protect and promote its main resources, increase its competitiveness, take better advantage of the multiplying effects of tourism, and seek new innovative ideas, often via local, national and/or international cooperation with other enterprises or even institutions that produce knowledge (universities, research centres, etc.).

Regulation 810/2009 on the instauration of a community code of visas for transit or stay in the EU has an effect on the demand for tourism as well as on the formulation of its cultural and social environment. Other policies with legal content are on the field of protecting consumers and market operations. These aim to correct market distortions arising from illegal or unethical entrepreneurial practices. Illustratively, Directive 2008/122 discusses the protection of consumers by timeshare contracts and similar products. The homogenisation of the legal and regulatory directives of the member states is done in a way that promotes the advantages of the internal market for consumers and enterprises alike. At the same time, the accommodation establishment owners integrated into the system are also protected, thus being less at risk of being defrauded by sellers and being defamed, avoiding negative repercussions for their own hotel products, while the establishment of codes of conduct is also encouraged.

Other Directives focus on the proper operation of the tourism market. For example, Directive 2005/29 aims to reduce uncertainty, protect customer interests and encourage the development of travel and tourism within the EU. In particular, the sector is protected from aggressive tactics of unfair competition; brand-name and quality products are also protected, while at the same time more effective and often less expensive marketing techniques are adopted. Special emphasis is put on organised travel (Directive 90/314) which constitutes the predominant source of tourism demand, securing an important number of stays for hotel enterprises. The establishment of common market regulations also motivates tourists from countries outside the EU who seek a stable, safe and secure operational framework in the accommodation sector.

The EU policies on labour mobility have an important impact on the employment conditions in hotels. The entry and stay prerequisites for skilled workers and their families (Directive 2009/50) affect the sociocultural environment of hotels as well. The most important effect, though, concerns the ability of accommodation establishments to improve the quality characteristics of human resources and to attract specialised personnel to enrich and differentiate the product supplied, making it more competitive in comparison to third countries. Skilled workers from other countries can also bring expertise and know-how from their home countries. Of interest is the right granted under conditions to foreign university students to work in the EU; this also applies to foreign researchers aiming at knowledge dissemination and the transmission of skills.

Similarly, Directive 2009/38 reinforces employee participation in negotiations with enterprises. Despite the fact that this Directive concerns a small number of accommodation establishments, its international character can affect hotel enterprises in the EU as well as their employees. If this initiative is indeed implemented, it can increase the degree to which employees identify themselves with enterprises and the effectiveness of their participation in the decision-making processes. Directive 2008/104 is about workers seeking temporary employment through agencies. It regulates matters of labour market flexibility and enhances the capabilities of hotels to meet their needs in human resources. However, important issues arise with respect to the protection of employee rights and the development of a coherent organisational culture in the hotels of the EU.

A more important policy intervention, however, is COM (2007) 628 final on combating undeclared employment and undeclared enterprises. Among other matters, it settles the framework of labour supply, taxation and tax evasion, protection of employment and the social rights of the employees. Its importance is underlined by the fact that undeclared employment is mainly used in the accommodation sector for circumstantial posts of low specialisation to reduce labour costs. Non-registered accommodation establishments are also widely encountered, especially in the main tourist-receiving countries of the EU; they result in unfair competition and a reduction in government income from taxes and also have negative repercussions for the overall quality of the tourism product.

The conditions of working hours (e.g. work, rest, night shift hours) are set by Regulation 2003/88 and their implementation in the operational environment of the accommodation sector is very important, since many hotels operate on a 24-hour basis, demanding night shifts, work on public holidays and other considerations. This Regulation has an effect on labour supply and job satisfaction, which is of particular importance in the case of hotels, because of the intensely seasonal nature (on an annual or weekly basis) of employment, among other factors. The multinational character of labour in tourism increases the importance of Regulation 2000/78 (which aims to provide a general framework for the equal treatment of employees irrespective of religion, age, sexual orientation and other factors) and of Regulation

2000/43 on the equal treatment in the workplace of employees with different racial or ethnic descent. Respectively, Regulations 1999/70 and 97/81 are related to fixed-term and part-time employment, which are widely used in the accommodation sector; the regulations propose agreements between professional organisations aiming on the one hand to improve the quality of work offered and on the other to avoid distinctions and abuse against workers under different employment regimes.

Regulation 89/391 aims to establish minimum hygiene and safety standards for employees. Its implementation may result in improved job satisfaction and motivation of workers, with positive implications for the service quality of the accommodation sector. Finally, certain aspects of EU policies affect the technological environment of hotels; for instance, Recommendation 86/666 settles fire safety issues in hotels, enforcing the introduction of measures and precautions that increase safety for both employees and customers. Similarly, Directive 2002/91 promotes the energy efficiency of buildings, with important implications for tourism accommodation.

Conclusions

This chapter has discussed the various policies implemented by the EU in the context of tourism accommodation. Some of these policies draw special attention to the liberalisation of the accommodation sector and the intensification of competition. Still, in a market traditionally dominated by small and medium-sized enterprises, such interventions need to be carefully planned to avoid exhausting the kernel of the productive sector and its main competitive advantages. Large-scale interventions are targeted at tourism having established a direct association with people, either as customers or personnel. Important steps have been taken – and will continue in the future – to boost tourism demand, to establish a feeling of safety and security among tourists buying tourism products and services, and to achieve better value for money. Particularly essential are interventions to regulate employment issues in the accommodation sector, as these affect the working conditions and the exchange of know-how and expertise among EU member states, as well as the qualifications of the junior employees and researchers involved. The financial crisis which started in the late 2000s seems to have put significant pressure on the fundamental pillars of the EU, with some analysts questioning the very essence of its existence. Still, many of the problems may have actually emerged as a result of inadequate policy coordination in the past and the lack of deeper integration. In this context, it is strongly recommended that all EU member states abide by the various common policies to create a better and stable business environment favouring among other matters the encouragement of investment in tourism infrastructure and the growth in tourism demand.

Appendix: EU Legal Documents Related to the Accommodation Sector

- Directive 2006/123/EC of the European Parliament and of the Council of 12 December 2006 on services in the internal market.
- Directive 95/57/EC on the collection of statistical information in the field of tourism.
- EN 13809: 2003/EN ISO 18513:2003 on the terminology of hotels and other types of accommodation.
- EN 15288-2:2003 on safety requirements for the operation of swimming pools (hotel pools included).
- Regulation (EC) 810/2009 of the European Parliament and of the Council of 13 July 2009 establishing a Community Code on visas.
- Directive 2008/122/EC of the European Parliament and of the Council of 14 January 2009 on the protection of consumers in respect to certain aspects of timeshare, long-term holiday product, resale and exchange contracts.
- Regulation (EC) 593/2008 of the European Parliament and of the Council of 17 June 2008 on the law applicable to contractual obligations (Rome I).
- Directive 2005/29/EC of the European Parliament and of the Council of 11 May 2005 concerning unfair business-to-consumer commercial practices in the internal market and amending other Council Directives.
- Council Directive 90/314/EEC of 13 June 1990 on package travel, package holidays and package tours.
- Council Directive 2009/50/EC of 25 May 2009 on the conditions of entry and residence of third-country nationals for the purposes of highly qualified employment.
- Directive 2009/38/EC of the European Parliament and of the Council of 6 May 2009 on the establishment of a European Works Council or a procedure in Community-scale undertakings and Community-scale group of undertakings for the purpose of informing and consulting employees.
- Directive 2008/104/EC of the European Parliament and of the Council of 19 November 2008 on temporary agency work.
- Communication COM (2007) 628 final from the Commission to the Council, the European Parliament, the European Economic and Social Committee and the Committee of the Regions on stepping up the fight against undeclared work.
- Directive 2003/88/EC of the European Parliament and of the Council of 4 November 2000 concerning certain aspects of the organisation of working time.
- Council Directive 2000/78/EC of 27 November 2000 establishing a general framework for equal treatment in employment and occupation.

- Council Directive 2000/43/EC of 29 June 2000 implementing the principle of equal treatment irrespective of racial or ethnic origin.
- Council Directive 1999/70/EC of 28 June 1999 concerning the framework agreement on fixed-term work concluded by ETUC, UNICE and CEEP.
- Council Directive 97/81/EC of 15 December 1997 concerning the Framework Agreement on part-time work concluded by UNICE, CEEP and ETUC.
- Council Directive 92/85/EEC of 19 October 1992 on the introduction of measures to encourage improvements in the safety and health at work of pregnant employees and employees who have recently given birth or are breastfeeding.
- Council Directive 89/391/EEC of June 1989 on the introduction of measures to encourage improvements in the health and safety of employees at work.
- Council Recommendation 86/666/EEC of 22 December 1986 on fire safety in existing hotels.
- Council Directive 2006/112/EC on the common system of value added tax and two more Directives (2008/8/EC and 2009/47/EC) amending the aforementioned Directive.
- Council Regulation 2157/2001 of 8 October 2001 on the Statute for a European company (SE).
- Commission Decision 2009/578/EC of 9 July 2009 establishing the ecological criteria for the award of the Community eco-label for tourist accommodation service.
- Communication from the Commission (COM (2007) 621 final) of 19 October 2007 on an Agenda for a sustainable and competitive European tourism.
- Directive 2002/91/EC of the European Parliament and of the Council of 16 December 2002 on the energy performance of buildings.
- Regulation (EC) 1980/2000 of the European Parliament and of the Council of 17 July 2000 on a revised Community eco-label award scheme.

Note

(1) HOTREC (2009) has proved especially helpful in the preparation of this section. Also, please see Appendix.

References

Borras, S. (2003) *The Innovation Policy of the European Union. From Government to Governance.* Cheltenham: Edward Elgar.
De Voldere, I., Myncke, R., Jans, G., Staelens, P., Vincent, C., Nuñez, C., Briene, M., Ronner, E., Verheyen, J. and Devet, J.M. (2009) Study on the competitiveness of the EU tourism industry, with specific focus on the accommodation, tour operator and

travel agent industries. Final report. Brussels: Directorate-General Enterprise and Industry, European Commission.

EC (2006) *Communication from the Commission. A Renewed EU Tourism Policy: Towards a Stronger Partnership for European Tourism.* Brussels: Commission of the European Communities.

European Travel Commission (2009) European tourism 2009 – trends and prospects. Quarterly Report, Q3/2009. Brussels: European Travel Commission.

HOTREC (2008a) *Reduced VAT Rates: A Must for a Sustainable European Hospitality Industry.* Brussels: HOTREC.

HOTREC (2008b) *EU Regulatory Challenges and the Hospitality Industry.* Brussels: HOTREC.

HOTREC (2009) *Some 60 European Union Measures Affecting the European Hospitality Industry.* Brussels: HOTREC.

Koutoulas, D. and Stavrinoudis, Th. (2006) Timeless evolution and strategic guides of development of Greek tourism under conditions of international expansion and magnification of the European tour operators. In V. Angelis and L. Maroudas (eds) *Economic Systems, Development Policies and Business Strategies in the Era of a Planetary Market* [in Greek] (pp. 763–789). Chios: University of the Aegean.

Smeral, E. (1998) The impact of globalization on small and medium enterprises: new challenges for tourism policies in European countries. *Tourism Management* 19 (4), 371–380.

Stabler, M.J., Papatheodorou, A. and Sinclair, M.T. (2010) *The Economics of Tourism* (2nd edn). London: Routledge.

Tourism Sustainability Group (2007) *Actions for more Sustainable European Tourism.* Brussels: Tourism Sustainability Group.

Travel Daily News (2010) EU reaches 5.2 million rooms, 17 June. http://www.traveldailynews.com/news/article/37537.

Tsartas, P. and Stavrinoudis, Th. (2010) European enlargement, opportunities and threats for the Greek tourist destinations and the Greek tourist enterprises [in Greek]. *Geographies* 16, 32–51.

Part 4
Policy

14 Mapping the EU's Evolving Role in Tourism: Implications of the New EU Tourism Competence

Emese Panyik and Constantia Anastasiadou

Introduction

Few would argue that the existence of international trading areas and agreements has not impacted profoundly on the organisation and development of international tourism. Perhaps nowhere is this more obvious than in the case of the European Union (EU), where tourism development is influenced by a number of policies ranging from immigration to regional development and competition policies (Halkier, 2010; Hall, 2008). Until very recently, the approach of the EU to tourism could be described as a pursuit for the determination of, and the attempt to assume, supranational competences in the area of tourism, and the definition of legitimate policy tools of intervention. To this end, a number of Community initiatives have been undertaken to leverage supranationality for tourism development, although in the absence of a coherent community policy.

For the first time in the history of the EU, the Lisbon Treaty, which entered into force in 2009, established a direct legal base for Community measures with supporting competence in the area of tourism (Council of the European Union, 2007b). This new political framework may mark a major shift in the approach of the Community to tourism.

Given the range of Community policies and financial instruments influencing tourism development, the impact of the EU on tourism planning is perhaps irrefutable. However, there is a dearth of studies examining the complex tourism policy environment and development strategies of the EU over the past decade. The purpose of this chapter is thus to explore how the role of the EU has changed in tourism over the course of this period leading to the Lisbon Treaty, by examining the development priorities assigned in key policy documents. On the basis of this analysis, the aim is to address the potential implications of the EU's competence for tourism and to discuss future perspectives of tourism development at a European level.

To this end, the chapter is divided into four sections. First, it begins by briefly discussing the evolution of the EU's approach to tourism, followed by a discussion of the present organisational structure and tourism policy environment, the stakeholders who are involved in formulating and shaping Community initiatives in tourism. Next follows an in-depth analysis of critical issues emerging from the tourism policy documents. The chapter concludes by a reflection on the potential implications of acquired competence for the future of tourism policy and planning in the EU.

Evolution of EU Tourism Policy Approach: Priority Setting in Retrospect

At the time of the establishment of the European Community, mass tourism was still in its infancy; thus no provisions were made for tourism in the Treaty of Rome in 1957 (Davidson, 1998). Tourism was considered as essentially a locally delivered activity and a responsibility of each member state, requiring intervention at local, regional and national government levels (Barnes & Barnes, 1993; Lickorish, 1991).

In recognition of the rapid growth of tourism activity in the 1970s and the inter-relationship between tourism and a large number of Community policies, the first Commission communications on tourism (EC, 1971, 1982) reflected emerging issues related to the length of the tourism season, the working conditions of tourism employees, transport and the protection of tourists. The importance of the Community was recognised in areas that require supranational coordination, notably environmental protection, statistical data collection, tourism promotion and financial assistance through the regional development funds.

The year 1990 was designated the 'European Year of Tourism', with the aim of emphasising the role of tourism and developing a coherent and integrative policy approach (European Council, 1988). Despite its modest budget, limited scale and inefficiency of action, the initiative became the main source of inspiration for increased Community involvement in tourism (Davidson, 1998). Specifically, at the end of the programme, the ministers of tourism approved a new, three-year 'Community action plan to assist tourism' (1992–1995). The programme aimed at the strengthening of public–private cooperation, the diversification of tourism products, the expansion of the tourist market and cross-border cooperation, and was elaborated in full consultation with representatives of the European tourism industry (EC, 1991).

Although the Treaty of Maastricht in 1992 included, for the first time, 'measures in the sphere of tourism' in the list of Community activities foreseen in support of the Community's overall objectives, there was no particular guidance for a community tourism policy. Thus, tourism remained a marginal policy area separated from the major policies with ad hoc measures and a very limited budget (Lickorish, 1994, cited in Davidson, 1998).

The Commission's subsequent communication, the 'Green Paper on Tourism' in 1995, was dedicated explicitly to the role of the EU in tourism development, with the aim of stimulating conversation among stakeholders on the level of involvement the EU institutions should acquire. One of the scenarios envisaged in the Green Paper was the incorporation of a specific chapter on tourism in the EU Treaty, but no agreement was reached as to whether more EU staff and funds should be assigned to tourism matters, or whether a tourism competence should be included in the Treaty.

The range of responses to the Green Paper by member states and private sector stakeholders demonstrated the diversity of opinion as to whether an increased involvement by the EU institutions was necessary or desirable. Furthermore, the endeavour to establish a coherent and coordinated tourism strategy came to a standstill when the Commission withdrew the First Multi-annual Programme to assist European Tourism ('Philoxenia', 1997–2000) after the Council of Ministers could not reach unanimity on the proposed programme, despite the favourable opinion of the European Parliament and other European institutions. The withdrawal of the Philoxenia initiative coincided with the exposure of mismanagement in the European Commission's Tourism Unit, which triggered a chain of events that eventually led to the resignation of the EU Commission in the late 1990s (Anastasiadou, 2004). As a result of these events there was very limited activity in tourism in the ensuing years.

To reinvigorate interest in tourism, attention shifted away from an explicit policy to the contribution of tourism in EU employment. A 'High Level Group on Tourism and Employment' was set up, composed of qualified tourism experts from all member states, followed by the establishment of five working groups over 2000 and early 2001, to address five key areas at the intersection of tourism and employment (information, training, quality, sustainability and technology). The working groups' reports formed the basis of the Commission Communication 'Working together for the future of European tourism', but the concrete outcomes of this process were overall limited (Anastasiadou, 2004). Ultimately, the Communication simply proposed the uptake of discretionary measures in support of the five key areas by member states, regional authorities and tourism businesses.

In the past decade, a number of communications (EC, 2001, 2003, 2007a) have focused on highlighting the EU's potential as an initiator and coordinator of action between member states, regional authorities and public and private stakeholders. This gradual change of focus from policy to coordination is expressed by the changing priorities, the identification of several stakeholders and the redefinition of role(s) of the EU institutions which are discussed later in this chapter.

However, the most exciting development is undoubtedly the inclusion of tourism among the EU policy areas in the Constitutional Treaty in 2007, which entered into force on 1 December 2009. Accordingly, 'the Union can carry out actions to support, coordinate or supplement Member States' actions in the field of tourism'. Although it was referred to as 'a revolution in tourism policy' by the Vice-President of the European Commission during the European Tourism Stakeholders Conference in Madrid in April 2010, this new EU competence gives the EU moderate powers to legislate in support of existing national initiatives on tourism and does not allow it to harmonise national legislation. However, instead of the former requirement of unanimity, new decisions are now subject to qualified majority voting and the co-decision process (joint approval by the Council of Ministers and the European Parliament), which certainly make decision making easier and faster. The inclusion of a specific reference to tourism in the Lisbon Treaty provides a blueprint for an EU policy and gives an indication of the types of actions that may be henceforth undertaken jointly (Anastasiadou, 2006).

Tourism Stakeholder Influences on Policy Priorities

The EU tourism policy takes place within a policy environment that is characterised by the existence of multiple venues and several players that wish to influence the decision-making process. The EU institutions, member states, industry and civil society groups are the key stakeholders in the tourism policy environment who do not share the same levels of power.

For a long time the EU institutions in their majority were in favour of more formalised roles and responsibilities for tourism. However, the lack of a legal basis and a specific competence had constrained their involvement and the adoption of concrete actions (Anastasiadou, 2008a). The lack of a tourism framework at the EU level disabled dialogue among interested parties and, ultimately, involvement in tourism remained in a state of limbo; stakeholders were not involved because there was no legal basis and then there was no legal basis because there was not enough interest in tourism (Anastasiadou, 2008a, 2008b). The absence of a specific competence for tourism has meant that the growth of tourism has been the responsibility of national and subnational governments. At the supranational level, the EU institutions have created additionality for tourism by looking after one of the more neglected parts of the tourism system – the tourist (Anastasiadou 2008a, 2008b), and have initiated a range of measures to support them (see, for example, consumer protection measures such as the EC Package Travel Directive).

Time and again, the effectiveness of the EC's Tourism Unit in representing the interests of tourism has come under question because of its small size and lack of resources (Anastasiadou, 2006, 2008b). The exposure of mismanagement of funds in the Tourism Unit in the late 1990s led to its restructuring under the DG Enterprise and the drastic cutback of its budget with the added implication that for a long time it performed very rudimentary functions (Anastasiadou, 2004).

The European Parliament has provided a platform for civil society and business interest organisations to meet with representatives from the EU institutions. Notably, the Tourism Intergroup is an informal working group comprising MEPs that share an interest in tourism. It meets on a monthly basis and holds occasional discussions with industry representatives (Markson, 2008). In addition, the EP was instrumental in the establishment of the European Tourism Industry Network (ETIN), an umbrella group of tourism interest organisations.

The Committee of the Regions (CoR), which aims to involve local and regional authorities in the EU's decision-making process, and the European Economic and Social Council (EESC), the membership of which is drawn from economic and social interest groups, are consultative bodies that enable their members to express their views on legislation and other EU issues. Over the years, both bodies have explicitly expressed their support to tourism as an economic activity and their desire for a more active involvement of the EU in tourism (CoR, 1999; EESC, 2005). The EESC, in particular, has been described as tourism's biggest ally (Greenwood, 1995) and had repeatedly advocated in favour of the inclusion of tourism in the Treaties (EESC, 1999: 5). However, they have both exerted limited influence on policy making due to their consultative role. Consequently, they are perhaps the weakest players in the EU tourism policy environment.

Member states, however, have been divided in their approach to tourism and the EU in part because of the variation in the level of the importance of tourism as an economic activity. Consequently, some are more willing to see greater EU involvement but there is a strong sentiment that a common approach to tourism may result in more regulation (Downes, 2000). Member states have perceptual, pragmatic and financial reasons for not wishing to see a formal competence, while the style of political administration and the dominant political philosophy in the management of tourism at the national level ultimately condition expectations of involvement in tourism at the supranational level (Anastasiadou, 2006, 2008a). Until recently, the consensus of all member states was necessary for any tourism proposals to materialise and consequently member states were the most powerful players in the EU tourism policy system. The inclusion of tourism as a complementary competence in the Treaty of Lisbon highlighted that it was possible to define a competence for the EU that all member states could agree on after all. This competence has been carefully crafted so that it transfers a degree of power to the EU institutions without the need for harmonisation or increased regulation for the member states.

Given the nature of tourism activity, it is not surprising that a large number of business interests and civil society organisations, including peak European industry associations such as the Confederation of National Associations of Hotels, Restaurant Association Cafés and Similar Establishments in the European Union and the European Economic Area (HOTREC) and the International Bureau of Social Tourism (BITS) are also trying to influence policy making. One can also not overlook the influence of other business interests such as the World Travel and Tourism Council (WTTC) which, although not entirely focused on Europe, has come to acknowledge the importance of the EU. Furthermore, loose networks and umbrella groups exist of specific membership such as the Network of European Private Entrepreneurs in the Tourism Sector (NET). The annual European Tourism Forum is the main platform for interaction between the industry and the institutional stakeholders. Some groups might also participate in the EP Tourism Intergroup meetings, but this is a more informal gathering and of course all groups attempt to influence policy through direct exchanges with the representatives of the EP and the EC.

On the whole, tourism business groups tend to be reactive to the initiatives and changes instigated by the EU institutions and are involved in a type of hazard management rather than a strategy towards the EU institutions. Instead of a policy, a strategy or a framework for tourism, they simply wish to exert some control over the impact of policies and legislation stemming from the institutions (Anastasiadou, 2008b). Within this context, they aim to gain greater recognition of 'tourism interests' when policy making is taking place, and to limit damage to the sector from obtrusive EU legislation. Business interest groups have become acknowledged as important players in the consultation stages of EC communications not as an outcome of their lobbying efforts but rather because of the desire for greater inclusion of business interests and civil society organisations in the EU tourism policy-making process.

It is evident from the above discussion that in the complex tourism policy environment the distribution of power and influence between stakeholders is uneven. The existence of a multitude of stakeholders might also go some way to explain the fluctuating approach and changes in tourism priorities which are evident in the EU's approach to tourism planning.

Mapping Current Planning and Development Trends

In order to map the tourism development strategies of the EU, the main reference documents issued by the Commission during the past decade have been analysed (EC, 2001, 2003, 2006, 2007a, 2010). The analysis follows a two-stage qualitative methodology split between the authors. First, an ana-lytical framework was designed comprising six predefined themes based on the tourism planning literature, which has been systematically applied on the documents. Second, and in parallel, a qualitative coding process was used to identify the key themes emerging from the communications following the methodology described by Miles and Huberman (1994), which resulted in eight recurrent themes representative in all documents. The main difference between these approaches is that the first uses *a priori* concepts as analytical aspects, whereas the second draws only on new emergent themes. The two different angles through which tourism strategies are viewed allowed for the triangulation of the results and highlighted critical issues in the EU's role in tourism planning and development as emerging from the Commission's communications.

Shifting priorities in tourism planning

Set against the policy environment and the stakeholder dynamics dis-cussed earlier, Table 14.1 illustrates how the EU approach to tourism plan-ning has gradually changed from promoting direct intervention to that of coordination and the facilitation of activities. It also demonstrates how gradually a wider range of stakeholders has been acknowledged and their active participation in the policy-making process has been encouraged. Encouraging the participation of business interests and other stakeholders in the decision-making process is a means of ensuring the legitimacy of EU interventions (Anastasiadou, 2011).

The approach to planning has gradually moved from a purely economic approach to an economic approach that places added emphasis on environ-mental and social sustainability, competitiveness and job growth. The Communications reflect the changing priorities of the EU in the last 10 years and the influence of other policy priorities as is also evidenced from their titles (a gradual shift of focus from employability, to sustainability, partner-ship and competitiveness). In this way the influence of changes in the wider EU policy environment is clear to see. Sustainability, which constitutes a cross-cutting priority for the EU, is a key priority for European tourism. In addition, the EU's Open Method of Cooperation[1] is also visible in the recent tourism strategy (EC, 2010), which makes extensive reference to the estab-lishment of networks and partnerships between stakeholders, coordination of activity in areas of common interest and exchange of best practice infor-mation (Anastasiadou, 2011).

In the absence of a tourism competence, the approach to implementa-tion has always been collaborative. However, the acknowledgment and par-ticipation of different stakeholders has gradually changed. Since 2001, the incorporation and participation of industry and other stakeholders in the policy process has been more actively encouraged (EC, 2001), with the EC

Table 14.1 The changing EU approach to tourism planning

Pre-defined themes	Objective(s) of tourism development	Approach to planning	Approach to implementation	Implementation instruments	Stakeholders identified	Type and level of EU involvement
EU Communications		Boosterism, economic, spatial/ territorial and social approach as in Hall (2000: 20–24)	Top-down, bottom-up, collaborative, as in Hall (2008)	Financial, voluntary, regulatory, legislative, etc., as in Hall (2008)	National governments, regional, local authorities, private sector, business interests and civil society) as in Anastasiadou (2008)	Coordinator, facilitator, organiser, stimulator, legislator, etc. High/low, active/ passive, as in Hall (2008)
Working together for the future of European tourism (2001)	Increase the basic knowledge of tourism; competitiveness; improve the sustainable development of tourism in the EU and its contribution to job creation	Economic with some awareness of sustainability issues	Cooperative approach and partnership; emphasis on the establishment of networks between stakeholders	Annual European Tourism Forum	'Open coordination' between member states, tourism industry, civil society and the Commission	Facilitator, initiator – actions to be implemented by other stakeholders
Basic orientations for the sustainability of European tourism (2003)	Promote the sustainability of European tourism	Sustainable tourism planning	Bottom-up 'cooperative and proactive multi-stakeholder approach' partnership	Continuation of status quo; strengthening of existing measures; establishing a Tourism Sustainability Group	Reference to 'other stakeholders' – citizens, tourists, destinations, regional and local authorities, civil society organisations	EC providing linkages between stakeholders and tourists; awareness raising and dissemination of best practices

Document	Aim	Approach	Type	Instruments	Actors	EU role
A renewed EU tourism policy: towards a stronger partnership for European Tourism (2006)	Improve the competitiveness and sustainability of the European tourism industry; create more and better jobs through sustainable growth	Economic approach with some awareness of sustainability issues	Bottom-up	Better regulation; policy coordination; improved use of available financial instruments; establishing a European Agenda 21 for tourism; financing of European Tourism Destination Portal	Destinations, local authorities, knowledge actors, European Tourism Forum, member states	Consultative, coordinator, facilitator, funder
Agenda for a sustainable and competitive European tourism (2007)	Improve the competitiveness of the European tourism industry; create more and better jobs through sustainable growth	Economic approach with some awareness of sustainability issues	Bottom-up	Continuation of status quo; mobilisation of existing financial instruments	Destinations, local authorities, knowledge actors, European Tourism Forum, member states	Coordinator; awareness raising and dissemination of best practice; facilitator
Europe, the world's No. 1 tourist destination – a new political framework for tourism in Europe (2010)	Competitiveness; sustainable, responsible, high-quality tourism; consolidate the image of Europe; maximise the potential of EU financial instruments	Economic approach with some awareness of sustainability issues	Collaborative	Financial, voluntary (extension of tourist season; tourism exchange mechanism; charter for sustainable tourism; marketing: a Europe brand, joint promotional actions, VisitEurope.com)	Increased industry participation	Coordinator

undertaking a facilitator role and stimulator for the development of partner-ships and networks between interested stakeholders. This fully reflects the promotion of a multi-level governance environment that is characteristic of all EU policy domains.

In terms of implementation instruments, the earlier documents (EC, 1995, 2001) envisaged active EU interventions through joint activities and marketing campaigns, but more recent communications (EC, 2007a, 2010) have shifted more towards promoting a facilitating role for the EC and voluntary instruments, such as networks and partnerships between inter-ested stakeholders, and 'soft' law measures.

Emerging themes in tourism development

Table 14.2 presents the eight key themes that have emerged from the coding process as key areas of tourism development strategies prevailing in the past decade. In defining the EU's role in tourism development, a funda-mental argument has been the major contribution of tourism to the EU's economy both in terms of demand and supply. Its importance as an eco-nomic and social factor for development of the Community is reflected in the long-term steady growth rate of the sector, which has been stronger than the average economic growth over an extended period of time.

In order to assign policy priorities at the EU level, particular emphasis has been placed on recognising the challenges facing the European tourism industry. From an international perspective, the increasing competition trig-gered by the emerging destinations in eastern Asia and the Pacific has led to a considerable loss of market share in Europe since the early 1970s. Further-more, the seasonality of the European tourism industry generates specific, adverse working conditions such as precarious employment and dispropor-tionate employment patterns of labour. Also, the dominance of small and medium-sized enterprises (SMEs) has been identified as a disadvantageous feature which, coupled with the heterogeneity of tourism, makes it is diffi-cult for the supply-side actors to establish a common platform of interest and cooperation.

Besides their struggle to manage marketing, to use new technologies and to access capital, the SMEs are increasingly challenged by the detri-mental effects of the growing trend towards concentration in the sector, in particular vertical integration in the hotel sector and in travel and trans-port services.

It was also recognised that conflicting priorities exist between the approaches of the sender countries (mainly in the north) and receiver coun-tries (mainly in the south) to sustainability. While the former appear to give priority to the environmental problems linked to tourism, the quality of services and the preservation of natural and cultural heritage, the main focus of the latter is the quantitative growth of private businesses, often at the

Table 14.2 The emerging themes in EU tourism development

The importance of tourism in the EU	Challenges of the European tourist industry	Legitimacy of tourism policy	Community added value in tourism	EU policy tools	Actions with regard to related policies	Stakeholder participation	Strategic directions of development
• *Demand:* the world's number one tourist destination (40% of international tourist arrivals in 2008). • *Supply:* the third largest socio-economic activity in the EU (accounts for 5.5% of EU GDP). • *Growth rate:* long-term and steady, stronger than the average	• Considerable loss of market share of Europe from 1970 onwards due to increasing competition; • Seasonality of the industry triggers specific, adverse working conditions; • The dominance of SMEs; • Heterogeneity and concentration in the sector; • Conflicting priorities between sender and	• References made by EU Treaties on tourism (e.g. Article 3t of the Maastricht Treaty, 1992); • The role of tourism in fulfilling the objectives of the major EU policies); • Adherence to the principle of subsidiarity.	• *Subsidiarity:* synchronising actions, resources and stakeholders between various levels of intervention ranging from Community to local levels. • *Complementarity:* developing complementary support mechanisms under Community instruments. • *Reciprocity:* providing the opportunity to exchange experiences and	• Reinforcing intermediary coordination (Advisory Committee on Tourism, Tourism Sustainability Group); • The application of the Open Method of Coordination; • Voluntary and regulatory instruments for sustainable tourism; • Creation and application of IT tools and networks; • Mainstreaming measures affecting tourism (impact	• *Regional and rural development policy:* diversifying tourism on the supply side and expanding it in less developed regions through Structural Funds. • *Transport policy:* sustainable mobility, passenger rights and safety and transport quality • *Competition:* concentration of businesses, vertical integration and state aid. • *Internal market:* suppressing national barriers to free movement of services within the EU and freedom to provide tourist services.	• Enabling an integrated, pro-active and multi-stakeholder approach to tourism in service of sustainability; • Stimulating interaction between stakeholders within and between destinations; • Preventing and reconciling the conflict of interests between private and public interests;	• Achieving balance between quantity (particularly with regards to mass tourism) and profitability (in particular the per capita profit expected); • Promoting stakeholder access to Community instruments; • Developing strategic guidelines and

(continued)

Table 14.2 (*Continued*)

The importance of tourism in the EU	Challenges of the European tourist industry	Legitimacy of tourism policy	Community added value in tourism	EU policy tools	Actions with regard to related policies	Stakeholder participation	Strategic directions of development
economic growth.	receiver countries; • External factors.		compare best practices between member states • *Promotion:* (1) promoting sustainable tourism at the international level; (2) promoting the concept of European citizenship; (3) providing international promotion through events.	assessment, screening, simplifying existing regulation and policy co-ordination); • Strategic planning and monitoring; • Risk management; • Measurement of carrying capacity; • Establishment of a voluntary tourism exchange and online information exchange mechanism; • Promotion of public–private partnerships (CALYPSO Programme).	• *Consumer protection:* addressing the issues of rights derived from signature of the contract, unfair commercial practices and distance sales. • *Maritime policy:* economic diversification into tourism in coastal areas with declined economic activities, incomes and increased unemployment linked to fisheries and shipbuilding • *Equal opportunities:* making tourist activities accessible to certain target groups, in particular young people, old people, those living on the threshold of poverty, the unemployed and disabled people.	• Stimulating a convergence of policy approach between member states; • Establishing forums for public participation at the early stages of planning (European Tourism Forum, Tourism Sustainability Group); • Initiating co-operation with international organisations (UNWTO, OECD).	measures at the European level to achieve a sustainable model for tourism; • Establishing harmonised criteria for the accessibility of tourist sites and facilities to disabled tourists; • Promoting sustainable inter- and intra-destination mobility.

expense of the public supply elements, as a response to excessive demand. In this regard, the failure of the EU to reconcile the latent conflicts between the dimensions of growth, tourist satisfaction and heritage protection has been acknowledged. At the managerial level, the major obstacles to implementing sustainable initiatives are inappropriate priority setting and poor communication. On the one hand, managerial priorities are focused at the local market whereas, on the other hand, messages formulated at high level do not effectively reach local and regional actors, communities and the tourists.

Lastly, external factors ranging from the terrorist attacks on the USA (2001), the foot and mouth epidemic (2001) and the oil slicks (2003) to the financial crisis (since 2008) and, more recently, the intense volcanic activity in Iceland (2010), have highlighted the vulnerability of European destinations and air transport as well as the volatility of tourist behaviour.

In defining the role of the EU in tourism development, the Green Paper on Tourism (1995) set out two main objectives: to ensure that proper consideration is given to the tourism dimension of Community policies, and to combine the three poles of the tourism concept – growth, tourist satisfaction and heritage protection – in the most effective way possible. The analysis revealed that the source of argumentation for the legitimacy of EU tourism policy in the policy discourses of the Commission during the past decade has been threefold: first, the references made by the EU treaties directly or indirectly on tourism; second, the role of tourism in fulfilling the objectives of the major EU policies; and third, the compatibility of adherence to the principle of subsidiarity with the need for Community-level action in the area of tourism. Within this context, subsidiarity can be applied not only to lower levels but also to central coordination of actions, resources and stakeholders between various levels, both horizontal and vertical, of intervention in areas of common interest spanning across borders. In particular, the leverage of coordinative community action lies in the supranational potential to synchronise the financial support available for tourists and enterprises from Community to local levels and to create a common platform of interest for tourism suppliers.

The analysis of policy priorities highlighted that in addition to subsidiarity, there are three principal forms of EU added value: complementarity, reciprocity and promotion (see Table 14.2). Considering the first, the EU can create a favourable environment for tourism and develop complementary support mechanisms under Community instruments based on its own exclusive competences (e.g. internal market, consumer protection). Examples of these Community actions with regard to related policies are listed in Table 14.2. Reciprocity allows for the opportunity to exchange experiences and compare best practices between member states. Lastly, the marketing of Europe as a set of destinations, the promotion of European citizenship and the endorsement of sustainable tourism as a matter of global responsibility through the organisation of events, the development of marketing tools and the implementation of projects are also seen as areas of further potential. While marketing Europe as a single destination was considered flawed by several tourism trade representatives (Anastasiadou, 2006, 2008a), the EU has tended to place emphasis on the variety and diversity of European destinations, which is reflected both in the online promotional strategy (http://visiteurope.com) as well as in the slogan of the European tourism brand ('Europe: a never-ending journey').

The policy tools of intervention have been designed to enable an integrated, proactive and multi-stakeholder approach to tourism, the majority of which are in the service of sustainability, such as the reinforcement of intermediary coordination, the application of 'soft law' and voluntary mechanisms, impact assessment, the measurement of carrying capacity, strategic planning and monitoring. According to the World Tourism Organization (UNWTO, 2004), the informed participation of all relevant stakeholders, as well as strong leadership are essential for consensus building, and thus, for the sustainability of tourism. In line with this argument, particular emphasis has been placed on stakeholder participation. The rationale, as well as the challenge of involvement, is the recognition of the equal value of the above-mentioned three inherently conflicting dimensions of tourism, which require combined responses from all the players concerned. Although the inability of the EU to reconcile these conflicting dimensions globally was acknowledged early on (EC, 1995), the Community's potential to prevent and reconcile the conflict of interests between private (tourist supply) and public (heritage protection and renewal and growth of the sector) interests by stimulating a convergence of policy approaches between member states was also recognised. With its emphasis on promoting networking and improving the interface between public and private stakeholders, it can be argued that much of the Community's action for tourism has contributed towards the reconciliation of private and public sector interests in tourism.

Future Directions in View of the New Tourism Competence

The latest policy document (EC, 2010) identifies four key priorities: (a) stimulate competitiveness in the European tourism sector; (b) promote the development of sustainable, responsible and high-quality tourism; (c) consolidate the image and profile of Europe as a collection of sustainable and high quality destinations; and (d) maximise the potential of EU financial policies and instruments for developing tourism. These priorities are not new but, due to the ratification of the Lisbon Treaty, there is now greater potential for the take-up of concrete measures and actions.

New tourism policy elaborates further on the coordinating role for the EU Commission. Given the political environment and the public sector budgetary cuts in European states, it is likely to lead to joint promotion campaigns and greater coordination of funding mechanisms. The budgetary implications of the tourism reference are still unclear, although the latest communication indicated that some of the measures and initiatives will be supported by the EC.

Recent initiatives to support demand have fully reflected the philosophy and priorities of the EU's tourism strategy to improve the sustainability of European tourism and deal with seasonality and the overcrowding of certain tourist destinations. These objectives correspond to the main demographic trends of an ageing population, the expansion of paid leave and shorter working hours, and the impacts of the global recession which will likely lead to the expansion of inbound weekend tourism and senior tourism, and thereby to a better distribution of tourism demand and supply.

For instance, the 'European Destinations of ExcelleNce' (EDEN) is an annual-themed competition that promotes emerging European destinations committed to environmental, cultural and social sustainability. The initiative aims to decongest over-visited tourist destinations, encourage the adoption of sustainable practices across Europe and encourage visitation to emerging destinations (EC, 2011). Each year one destination from each participating country receives an award at the annual European Tourism Forum which helps showcase these destinations to the rest of Europe.

Moreover, the basic premise of the Calypso (2009–2011) Project is that travel and tourism are a right for all European citizens and its actions promote social tourism for population groups which may not be able to afford or are not physically able to travel. The project's intended impacts are to stimulate demand in low season, safeguard tourism employment, combat seasonality, encourage cultural exchanges, stimulate European citizenship and extend tourism to more people (EC, 2011).

In both initiatives the importance of the involvement of relevant stakeholders in member states that join up to deliver the actions fully reflects the intention of previous Communications to stimulate the creation of networks and partnerships between interested parties and limit the involvement of the EC to facilitation. Although the objectives of the initiatives fully reflect the EU tourism strategy priorities for job creation, competitiveness and the promotion of sustainable practices, their scope is limited and their reach, relevance and influence on the rest of the European tourism system is perhaps questionable.

Conclusions

The aim of this chapter was to explore the evolution of the EU's role in tourism over the course of the past decade leading to the Lisbon Treaty, and to consider the potential implications of the EU's competence for the future of EU tourism.

In accordance with the subsidiarity principle, the EU has generally played a coordinative role in synchronising actions, resources and stakeholders between various levels of tourism intervention, ranging from Community to local levels. Recent initiatives such as EDEN and Calypso fully reflect the European Commission's decision to continue to take this role of facilitator and encourage stakeholder involvement and the development of networks between tourism providers in member states.

Clearly, the notion of sustainability in the EU's approach to tourism development has been inextricably linked to that of competitiveness. Sustainability is considered a condition for long-term competitiveness. Conversely, in order to meet the industry's greatest challenges, namely demographics, external competition and sustainability, the EU must focus its efforts on improving its competitiveness. Improving tourism competitiveness and sustainability may appear to be incompatible in practice; for instance, improving sustainability may lead to losses in terms of price competitiveness. However, the EU's approach aims to improve sustainability and competitiveness largely through product innovation (Halkier, 2010), hence the emphasis placed on the exchange of information and best practice.

With regard to the interdependent relationship of sustainability and competitiveness, two major conclusions could be drawn from the analysis of EU intervention strategies. Firstly, the Lisbon Treaty reference did not elevate tourism to the status of mainstream policies, in which the EU has either exclusive or shared competence. Still, as a cross-cutting sector, tourism influences and is as well influenced by many policies. Thus, the sustainability of the sector at a Community level is only attainable through reinforcing the integration of sustainability concerns into Community policies affecting European tourism. However, since sustainability is one of the key priorities and cross-cutting issues across the main policies of the EU, the challenge might actually lie in the relatively low importance attributed to tourism-related issues in other policy areas rather than solely on the integration of sustainability concerns.

Secondly, in order to preserve the competitiveness of the tourism industry against expanding external competition, the industry's ability to respond to market changes and the travel models which arise from demographic, social, economic and environmental challenges such as climate change, should improve. In this regard, in its coordinator role the EU could synchronise member states' actions aiming at increasing the flexibility of the tourism sector.

In response to the need to reconsider the system for consultation of European tourism organisations, the 'Tourism and Employment' process underlined the value of wide consultation at the early stages of planning (EC, 2001), and confirmed the literature (Gunn, 1979; Murphy, 1985) on the importance of public participation in planning at national, regional and local levels. Due to the insufficient consultation by the DGs of mainstream policies on tourism impacts prior to decision making, the first Council resolution adopted specifically in tourism in 2002 (EC, 2002) called for a broad framework of coordination between tourism and related policies. Initiatives such as the European Tourism Forum and the Tourism Sustainability Group were developed to improve the interface between the industry and other stakeholder groups at a Community level. Moreover, cooperation has been initiated with the UNWTO regarding specific UNWTO measures on sustainable tourism targeting Europe, as well as technical assistance on implementing global initiatives in sustainable tourism in Europe (EC, 2003). These Community initiatives reflect the three principal forms of supranational intervention that have proven most effective on the basis of policy documents analysed over the past decade: the EU as facilitator of cooperation and information exchange, and as promoter of sustainability.

In retrospect, it is clear that tourism has always been considered a complementary issue of mainstream Community policies such as transport, employment, regional, environmental and enterprise development. In recent years the EU's role has been largely confined to providing the initial stimulation to creating public–private partnerships and networks and to the allocation of responsibilities between private and public actors. Although the EU has added most value through the development of complementary support mechanisms for tourism under its major policy instruments, the EU competence that the Lisbon Treaty has established could herald more wide-ranging impacts.

While decision making in tourism continues to be based on soft law mechanisms such as guidelines, benchmarking and sharing of best practice, the EU tourism competence signifies a renewed policy system for tourism where unanimity has been replaced by majority voting. The decision-making process is thus simplified and this fact may act as the trigger for the expansion of initiatives to improve competitiveness and the adoption of more sustainable practices by the tourism industry.

Note

(1) The OMC is a framework for cooperation between member states that is achieved through techniques such as the use of guidelines, benchmarking and the establishment of indicators for measuring 'best practice' (Shore, 2011).

References

Anastasiadou, C. (2004) Tourism at the supranational level: The case of the European Union. Unpublished thesis. University of Strathclyde, UK.

Anastasiadou, C. (2006) Tourism and the European Union. In D. Hall, M. Smith and B. Marciszweska (eds) *Tourism in the New Europe: The Challenges and Opportunities of EU Enlargement* (pp. 20–32). Wallingford: CABI.

Anastasiadou, C. (2008a) Stakeholder perspectives on the European Union tourism policy framework and their preferences on the type of involvement. *International Journal of Tourism Research* 10 (3), 221–235.

Anastasiadou, C. (2008b) Tourism interest groups in the EU policy arena: Characteristics, relationships and challenges. *Current Issues in Tourism* 11 (1), 24–62.

Anastasiadou, C. (2011) Promoting sustainability from above: Reflections on the influence of the European Union on tourism governance, *Policy Quarterly Journal* 7 (4), 27–33.

Barnes, I. and Barnes, P. (1993) Tourism policy in the European Community. In W. Pompl and P. Lavery (eds) *Tourism in Europe: Structures and developments*. East Lansing, MI: CABI.

CoR (1999) Opinion of the Committee of the Regions of 28 June 1999 on *The Role of Local and Regional Authorities in Tourism Development and the Impact of European Union Measures in the Sphere of Tourism*. Brussels: COM-5/003.

Davidson, R. (1998) *Travel and Tourism in Europe* (2nd edn). New York: Addison Wesley Longman.

Downes, J. (2000) EU legislation and the travel industry. *Travel and Tourism Analyst* 5, 49–71.

EC (1971) *Commission des Communautes Europeennes. Projet d'inventaire des problemes du tourisme a l'echelle communautaire.* SEC(71) 357 final. Brussel: Commission of the European Communities.

EC (1982) Initial guidelines for a Community policy on tourism. *Communication from the Commission to the Council.* COM(82) 385 final, 1 July 1982.

EC (1991) *Community Action Plan to Assist Tourism.* COM (91) 97 final. Brussels: Commission of the European Communities.

EC (1995) *The Role of the Union in the Field of Tourism.* Commission Green Paper COM(95)97 final. Brussels: European Commission.

EC (2001) *Working Together for the Future of European Tourism.* Commission Communication to the Council, the European Parliament, the Economic and Social Committee and the Committee of the Regions. COM(2001) 665 final. Brussels: European Commission.

EC (2002) *Council Resolution of 21 May 2002 on the Future of European Tourism (2002/C 135/01).*

EC (2003) *Basic Orientations for the Sustainability of European Tourism.* Communication from the Commission to the Council, the European Parliament, the European Economic and Social Committee and the Committee of the Regions. COM(2003) 716 final. Brussels: European Commission.

EC (2006) *A renewed EU Tourism Policy: Towards a Stronger Partnership for European Tourism.* Commission Communication. COM(2006) 134 final. Brussels: European Commission.

EC (2007a) *Agenda for a Sustainable and Competitive European Tourism.* Commission Communication. COM(2007) 621 final. Brussels: European Commission.

EC (2007b) Treaty of Lisbon amending the Treaty on European Union and the Treaty establishing the European Community. *Official Journal of the European Union*, 2007/C 306/01. Brussels: European Commission.

EC (2010) *Europe, the World's No. 1 Tourist Destination – A New Political Framework for Tourism in Europe.* Communication from the Commission to the European Parliament, the Council, the European and Social Committee and the Committee of the Regions. COM(2010) 352 final. Brussels: European Commission.

EC (2011a) *EDEN- European Destinations of Excellence*, accessed 15 December 2011. http://ec.europa.eu/enterprise/sectors/tourism/eden-estination/index_en.htm

EC (2011b) *Low Season Tourism*, accessed 15 December 2011. http://ec.europa.eu/enterprise/sectors/tourism/calypso/index_en.htm

EESC (1999) *Opinion of the European Economic and Social Committee on Tourism Policy (own initiative opinion).* Brussels, 24 March 1999, INT/024.

EESC (2005) *Opinion of the European Economic and Social Committee on Tourism Policy in the Enlarged EU* (own initiative opinion). Brussels, 6 April 2005, INT/248.

European Council (1988) Council Decision 89/46/EEC on an Action Plan Programme for a European Year of Tourism. Luxembourg: European Council.

Greenwood, J. (1995) Tourism. In J. Greenwood (ed.) *European Casebook on Business Alliances* (pp. 128–140). London: Prentice Hall.

Gunn, C.A. (1979) *Tourism Planning*. New York: Crane Russak.

Halkier, H. (2010) EU and tourism development: Bark or bite? *Scandinavian Journal of Hospitality and Tourism* 10 (2), 92–106.

Hall, C.M (2008) *Tourism Planning: Policies, Processes and Relationships*. Harlow: Pearson Education.

Lickorish, L.J. (1991) Developing a single European tourism policy. *Tourism Management* 12 (3), 178–184.

Markson, N. (2008) The EU's role in tourism – policy and powers. *Tourism Insights*, online document. http://www.insights.org.uk/articleitem.aspx?title=The+EU%2527s+Role+in+Tourism+%e2%80%93+Policy+and+Powers.

Miles, M.B. and Huberman, A.M. (1994) *Qualitative Data Analysis: An Expanded Sourcebook*. London: Sage.

Murphy, P.E. (1985) *Tourism: A Community Approach*. New York and London: Routledge.

Shore, C. (2011) European governance or governmentality? The European Commission and the future of democratic government. *European Law Journal* 17 (3), 287–303.

UNWTO (2004) *Making Tourism More Sustainable: A Guide for Policy Makers*. UNEP and UNWTO.

15 The Role of the EU in Defining Tourism Policies for a Competitive Destination Governance

M. Manente, V. Minghetti and F. Montaguti

Introduction

Defining appropriate tourism policies is one of the most challenging tasks facing politicians and public and private stakeholders, given the characteristics of tourism as an economic phenomenon and the numerous actors it involves. The tourism product is a complex mix of non-reproducible resources (e.g. environment, beaches, heritage, etc.) and of goods and services produced by different sectors (hospitality, transport, attractions, etc.) that can be identified once and for all only when a tourist reaches a destination and experiences it (Leiper, 1990; Costa & Manente, 2000; Brent Ritchie & Goeldner, 2007). Tourism activities generate costs and benefits that are not only borne or enjoyed by tourism operators, but also by tourists and by the destination as a whole (residents, local resources, other operators) (Brent Ritchie & Goeldner, 2007; Costa & Manente, 2000).

The development of a coherent and integrated system of tourism policies firstly implies mediating among all these actors and their requirements (Gunn, 1994; Manente & Minghetti, 2005). Secondly, it means taking into account initiatives specifically aimed at influencing the tourists' behaviour and the development of tourism supply (e.g. the activities of hotels, tour operators and travel agencies) as well as those addressing other components of the tourism system (e.g. transport, culture, environment), which can also affect the tourism sector. In other words, where there are policies for tourism, there are also policies addressing other objectives but which have a direct or indirect impact on tourism. Thirdly, its development cannot disregard the fact that decisions concerning tourism and other sectors are generally taken at different levels (European, national, regional and local) by policy makers having different competences and roles. Given all these elements, a coherent tourism policy should overcome the potential fragmentation/overlapping of decision makers and actions, by considering the relationships between tourism and other economic activities and particularly the effects that decisions taken in other sectors (e.g. agriculture, transport, culture, information technologies, etc.) can have on the development of tourism activities and vice versa.

This chapter discusses the importance of clearly determining competences and responsibilities among different stakeholders, focusing on the role of the European Union (EU). Secondly, it stresses the importance for regional decision makers of defining a strategic vision and being able to reconcile the fragmentation of tourism and non-tourism policies, which can both affect the evolution of tourism at local level. This aspect is crucial considering the rising role of the EU in promoting, through different financing channels, local initiatives not directly linked to tourism, but which can affect the competitiveness of European tourist destinations.

From this point of view, in this chapter the EU policies having effects on local tourism strategies will be analysed, discussing the risks of friction between global and local actions.

The analysis derives from a research work CISET carried out for the European Parliament in 2007 on the fragmentation of the European Tourism Policy (European Parliament, 2007).

Community Policies for Tourism and Destination Governance

The request to analyse European policies and their effects on tourism and on local governance strategies was motivated by different elements.

Before the coming into force of the Lisbon Treaty at the end of 2009, the Community did not develop tourism policies (the Maastricht Treaty stated that tourism was not a competence of the EU). Nevertheless, it was responsible for a range of initiatives that could heavily affect both the tourism industry and the development of tourism destinations (a tourism policy de facto). However, the European Commission itself and the Parliament acknowledged that the activities of the Commission had an impact on tourism. Foreshadowing a new attribution of competences in this field, the Commission specified the objectives of its policies as follows: 'to improve the competitiveness of the European tourism industry and create more and better jobs through the sustainable growth of tourism in Europe and globally' (COM (2006) 134 Final).

A second element is that the amount of financial resources that the EU offers to member states – through the Regional Development Programme and other funds – affects both general and tourist development of different regions and areas and influences the investment policies at national and local level.

A third aspect concerns the geographical size of the decision maker (EU) and its tourist importance (the EU area is the first world tourism destination), which implies that any initiative taken influences both single tourist destinations and the equilibrium of the global tourism market: for example, agreements on the access for extra Community air carriers to intra-Community routes can have an impact on both the competitiveness of the origin country and of all member states.

Consequently, even when the EU had no competences on tourism, it had the power to drive or change destination policies and strategies developed by private actors, acting at global level but with important effects also locally.

For all these reasons, local governments should take into account EU policies and actions when they plan or develop tourism policies.

Community Policies for Tourism: Interactions and Effects on Tourism

The general framework

Besides mediating among the requirements of different destination actors, a proper tourism policy should promote the competitiveness and sustainability of the destination (Brent Ritchie & Crouch, 2003). The EU defines competitiveness and sustainability as the main objectives of its action, as stated in the document *A Renewed EU Tourism Policy: Towards a Stronger Partnership for European Tourism* (COM (2006) 134 Final).

The investigation carried out on the initiatives delivered by different policy areas of the Commission between 2005 and 2007 (legislative and non-legislative acts, like Communications, Regulations, Directives, Proposals, White Papers, etc.) (European Parliament, 2007), highlighted that all of them potentially impact on the competitiveness and sustainability of tourism and destinations. In particular, they can:

- affect the competitiveness and sustainability of the whole EU system (e.g. policies concerning greenhouse gas emissions ceilings);
- affect the behaviour of demand inside or outside the EU (e.g. consumer protection measures, exchange rates, enlargement of the EU);
- influence a number of economic sectors, including tourism (actions focused on promoting the access and use of ICTs by small and medium-sized enterprises (SMEs));

- be specifically intended for industries linked to tourism (e.g. policies regulating the use of some kind of fuels, which can affect the transport fares and then the final price of the travel or of the holiday package);
- be aimed at developing infrastructures, financial capital, human knowledge, etc., which contribute to enhancing the competitiveness of tourism as well as other economic sectors at global and local level (e.g. policies aimed at improving the railway system or at enlarging airport capacity or, more, at empowering the education level);
- benefit industries competing with tourism for basic resources (e.g. policies aimed at strengthening the competitiveness of a rural product and, for that purpose, envisaging measures that can cause a change in the landscape of some tourist destinations);
- affect areas where tourism is a key economic sector (e.g. regional policies addressing peripheral regions such as Andalusia in Spain);
- be intended for resources essential to tourism (e.g. environmental protection or cultural heritage);
- address industries related to or supporting tourism (e.g. festivals, events, sport);
- be specifically intended for the tourism industry as a whole or for specific groups of tourism businesses (e.g. Code of Conduct for Global Distribution Systems (GDS) and Computerised Reservation Systems (CRS));
- be specifically developed for promoting tourism as driver of growth in some areas, regions, cities, etc. (e.g. policies aiming at developing angling tourism in order to ensure fishers and additional source of income).

These examples also prove that EU policies can directly or indirectly affect all the main components of the tourism system (local resources, enterprises, demand, etc.).

From this point of view, EU policies can be divided into two main groups as follows:

(a) *Policies that are not directly intended for tourism.* These policies affect tourism in two different ways. They can act on some components of the tourism system with the goal of developing, protecting, etc. the component itself (e.g. local resources) or as part of a policy planned for another economic sector and so indirectly influencing the development of tourism (e.g. funding the building of a new railway system to enhance the freight transport). Their influence on the tourism industry or on the tourism development of a destination can be positive or negative.

(b) *Policies intended for, and addressed to, tourism as an economic activity.* This group of policies act on some elements of the tourism system with the implicit or explicit goal of affecting the tourism system itself (i.e. funding the improvement of the transport system to support the development of some kind of tourism in certain areas).

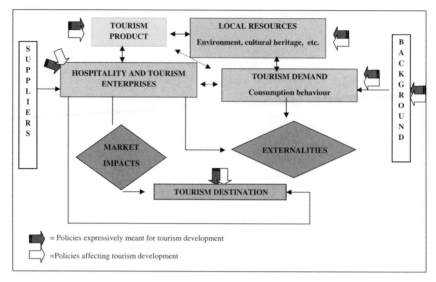

Figure 15.1 The tourism system and the two groups of policies
Source: Adapted from Costa *et al.* (2001)

Figure 15.1 shows the elements of the tourism system (Costa *et al.*, 2001) on which the two groups of policies can act.

The investigation carried out by CISET for the European Parliament showed that between 2005 and 2007 the policy areas more active in terms of number of proposals or recommendations with direct and indirect effects on tourism were agriculture, regional policies, fishing and maritime activities, transport, information society, culture, environment, immigration and monetary policy.

There are other policy areas from which initiatives impacting on tourism can originate, but the amount and importance of their proposals may vary significantly from one area to another over the time. For example, measures for customer protection undoubtedly have a central role in affecting tourists' behaviour. However, proposals in this field were made before 2005 and then declined between 2005 and 2007.

In order to identify the initiatives with the highest impact on tourism and rank them according to the previous two categories, the following criteria have been defined:

(1) *proposals not intended for tourism – exogenous policies –* but with relevant impact on it (e.g. measures aimed at reducing the sulphur content of marine fuels, which can influence the fuel costs for cruise ships sailing on the Mediterranean or other European seas);

(2) *proposals not intended for tourism,* but which contribute to *shaping the framework within which decisions directly affecting tourism development are*

taken (e.g. policies on the use of fuels, like the National Emission Ceilings, the Emissions Trading System, which shape a series of constraints for the tourism industry (and not that industry alone); these proposals should be taken into consideration by destinations when planning their development;

(3) *proposals intended for tourism and which define its role within the overall socio-economic development* (e.g. regional policies focusing on tourism as a potential driver of economic development for the poorest areas);

(4) *proposals intended for tourism and which affect the nature and development of the tourism product* (e.g. maritime policies that identify ecotourists as a valuable segment for coasts and islands and allocate financial resources for tourism infra- and super-structures addressed to this particular segment).

Criteria (1) and (2) basically refer to policies (a) (indirectly intended for tourism), while criteria (3) and (4) refer to policies (b) (policies directly intended for tourism).

This distinction is important in order to analyse the interactions between different actions and their effects on the destination, taking into account the principles of competitiveness and sustainability.

The analysis of the EU proposals and of their interactions, according to the criteria previously defined, showed that there are three potential critical aspects, which can generate a fragmentation/overlapping of actors and actions:

(A) *proposals/actions developed by different policy areas and concerning the same component of the tourism system* (local resources, demand, industry and enterprise) *but having diverging objectives*. These policies can be included both in category (a) (not addressing tourism) and (b) (addressing tourism). An example of this kind of fragmentation is given in the section on 'Interactions between environment and transport policies and effects on tourism';

(B) *proposals/actions developed by different policy areas and concerning different components of the tourism system but having common objectives*. An example of this kind of fragmentation is given in the section on 'Interactions between the European Regional Development Fund and the Culture Programme and their effects on tourism';

(C) *proposals/actions developed by different policy areas and concerning the same component of the tourism system and having common objectives* (fragmentation no. 3). An example is given when two services of the Commissions, e.g. the Maritime Affairs area and the Regional Policy area, adopt different measures – through the European Fishing Fund (EC Regulation No. 1198/2006) and the Cohesion Fund (EC Regulation No. 1184/2006) to develop the local transport system along coastal areas. These two actions together represent de facto one policy for the development of tourism transport. Although this policy is implemented by each service with the objective of enhancing the competitiveness of coastal areas as tourism destinations, this frequently happens without any coordination between the two actions, which would be useful to prevent the overlapping of initiatives.

Figure 15.2 describes the EU policy areas, the interrelations among their decisions/proposals and the type of fragmentation/overlapping that can take place.

Given these considerations, it is important to understand whether and to what extent the fragmentation of decisions can create conflicts, inconsistencies and opposing actions, frustrating the achievement of the competitiveness and sustainability goals and of a coherent EU tourism approach. The accomplishment of these objectives requires a tourism policy contributing to enhance the competitiveness and sustainability of each component of the tourism system (local resources, environment, enterprises, etc.), as well as of the tourism system as a whole, taking into account the fact that a system is not just a sum of different components, but also the relationships between them. Secondly, the policy has to ensure the coherence of each action to the final goal, but also the coherence of different actions and proposals (regulations, recommendations, directives, etc.) according to a common objective.

The level of coherence and interaction of EU policies affecting tourism will be analysed in the following sections, using two examples. The first one is related to proposals/actions developed by different EU policy areas (Environment and Transport) and concerning the same component of the tourism system (air transport) but having diverging objectives (policies (a)). The second one refers to proposals/actions developed by different policy areas (Regional Development and Culture) and concerning different components of the tourism system (supply, infrastructure and culture) but having common objectives (policies (b)).

For each of these, the interactions between the different measures will be discussed and the potential effects of fragmentation at destination level highlighted.

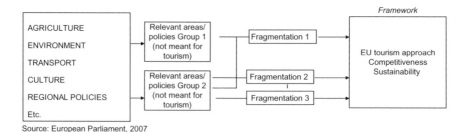

Source: European Parliament, 2007

Figure 15.2 Fragmentation, interaction among policies and the general framework
Source: European Parliament (2007)

Interactions between environment and transport policies and effects on tourism

In 2006 the Environment policy area proposed to include civil transport in the EU Greenhouse Gas Trading System. This was a decision not intended for tourism but with potential impact on it. At the same time, the Transport area launched an initiative aimed at developing regional airports, which was implicitly developed to promote tourism.

How do both proposals act on tourism? Does their joint application ensure a coherent approach according to the principles of tourism competitiveness and sustainability?

The first Communication of the Commission (COM (2006) 818) – which became a Directive in 2008 (2008/101/CE) – aims at reducing greenhouse gas emissions produced by civil air transport within the EU Greenhouse Gas Trading System. Starting from 2011, the initiative will address the emissions produced by civil flights within the EU and, from 2012, by all flights departing from and arriving at European airports. Airline companies will be involved in the Trading System: they will be allowed to sell excess allowance when they are able to reduce emissions, or to buy supplementary allowance when they increase their emissions beyond the fixed allowance. According to the assessment made by the Commission itself on the consequences of this measure, the average air fare within Europe is estimated to increase by about 2% and the growth in the number of passengers is expected to be lower than in the absence of the Directive, in the medium to long term. The higher the share of incoming tourists arriving by air of total tourists at a destination, the heavier will be the impact of an increase in air fares on tourism development at the local level.

The second Communication (COM C 312/01/2005), published by the Transport policy area, is aimed at enhancing the competitiveness of air transport at the European level by:

- reducing congestion levels at European hubs;
- creating a greater number of access points for intra-European flights;
- empowering those small regional airports (less than 1–1.5 million passengers per year) to attract airline companies (e.g. low cost companies) to peripheral destinations, thus also creating the conditions for tourism development.

From the tourism policy perspective, the initiative taken by the Transport area acts as a strategy directly addressing tourism supply. In addition, to the extent that the action promotes new or emerging destinations, it is coherent with the objective of increasing the competitiveness of European tourism. It has to be noted that the initiative can also benefit small airports located in popular tourism destinations, like Pisa in Tuscany and Sevilla in Andalusia, where the development of local airports has resulted in an additional demand. The risk is, on the one hand, that the additional number of tourists will continue to gravitate around congested areas (e.g. Florence, Costa del Sól), worsening the local carrying capacity, and on the other hand, that the environmental impact of air transport (gas emissions, noise pollution, etc.) can contaminate a wider area.

What it is crucial is trying to understand the combined effects of both proposals for European tourism as well as for the competitiveness and sustainability of European tourism destinations. Climate changes will probably translate into stricter environmental policies. In this situation, any initiative addressing the development of a network of regional airports can collide with a scenario of potential decreasing air mobility, whereas the increase in flight fares due to fuel allowances and more conscious travel behaviour discourages some tourists from travelling by plane. Developing big infrastructures in peripheral areas which welcome a lower number of passengers than was initially expected generally implies a lower income to cover investment costs. In addition, it does not ensure medium- to long-term benefits for the airports and the surrounding areas.

Interactions between the European Regional Development Fund and the Culture Programme and their effects on tourism

The second example analyses how a group of policies having the same objective (supporting the development of tourism in some areas) can generate a patchwork of incomplete initiatives, whose interaction has not been envisaged or managed. The effects of a lack of strategic vision have been discussed here, assessing how this approach is coherent with the principles of competitiveness and sustainability.

The first policy refers to the provisions in the European Regional Development Fund (ERDF) and Cohesion Fund in the period 2007–2013 (EC Regulations Nos 1080/2006, 1083/2006, 1084/2006) and the rules related to these Funds.

The Programme for Regional Development (policy (b)) addresses tourism as one of the key sectors for socio-economic development of the poorest areas within the EU27. Through the ERDF and the Cohesion Funds, the European policy – although taking into account the priorities of members states – supports investments for the improvement or development of tourism supply: creation of infrastructures, transport systems, preservation of environmental and cultural heritage, development of tourist services, etc.

These are initiatives explicitly intended for tourism. However, they address basically local resources and infrastructure. Less attention is paid to other important elements of the tourism system, such as events, communication, distribution systems, etc. These elements are considered as the competence of other policy areas of the European Commission and then objects of other specific policies. For example, where cultural heritage can be preserved through the ERDF, its exploitation should be supported through cultural programmes, events and other initiatives within the Culture Programme 2007–2013 (policy (b)).

This Programme, established with the Decision No. 1855/2006/CE, does not refer to tourism as a driver of a cultural resources-based economic development. Furthermore, even if the necessity to ensure a link with other EU measures has been highlighted – in particular with the EFRD – there is no further reference to coordination with Regional Policies, not even those focused on the exploitation of cultural resources.

This fragmentation of European policies implies that:

- the Regional Policy area has defined a part of the tourism development strategy (preservation of cultural resources), which is as yet incomplete;
- the Culture Programme has not been able to add important elements in order to complete the development framework.

The interaction between these initiatives can support the competitiveness and sustainability of European tourism destinations, but also hamper them by dispersing investments on a series of uncoordinated initiatives.

The task to complete the action and ensure the strategic coherence of different initiatives can be entrusted to national and regional governments, but such a fragmentation can be difficult to manage for local administrators.

Conclusions

A coherent tourism policy, aimed at enhancing the competitiveness and sustainability of a destination, has firstly to overcome the fragmentation/overlapping of actions carried out by different decision makers, who can act on tourism indirectly and through exogenous measures.

From this perspective, the analysis highlights that the European Community, even without any specific competence on tourism yet (i.e. before the ratification of the Lisbon Treaty), was an actor able to implement a number of policies with an important impact on tourism development both at global and local level. From the destination point of view, the Community – now the EU – is a player whose activities stay behind local policies and address investments. Therefore, it should be taken into account in order to define local actions. Its influence will increase from now on, following the ratification of the Lisbon Treaty.

However, the different services of the Commission generally act separately and this fragmentation can generate conflicts among their decisions or a lack of coordination of actions having the same objective. Notwithstanding the effort made by the EC for creating a common reference framework, as stated in COM (2006) 134, critical situations can arise, motivated firstly by the complexity of the tourism sector, just its nature requires a coherent policy to accomplish the objectives (competitiveness and sustainability) fixed by the EC itself.

At the destination level, as shown by the examples discussed previously, developing a fruitful relationship with the EU implies:

- defining tourism policies not only taking into account the objectives and requirements of residents and other stakeholders, but also the European guidelines;
- identifying the prevailing guidance between policies that seem potentially or effectively in conflict among themselves, so as to appropriately drive the tourism development;
- mapping European policies in a strategic framework that allows the local decision makers and stakeholders to seize the opportunities the EU offers to accomplish their objectives of local development (in terms of investments, removal of entrance barriers, opening of new markets, etc.).

The lack of internal and external coherence of some EU policies directly and indirectly linked to tourism requires that decision makers implement a clear and proper tourism programme, in order to keep down the risk of fragmentation of public actions and investments at national and local level and to manage the requirements of different stakeholders.

The ability of regions and destinations in general to identify and follow a strategic vision and, at the same time, to coordinate the implementation of European policies at the local level, can represent an important competitive advantage in the near future.

References

EU Documentation

COM (2005) C 312/01 Communication from the Commission, Community Guidelines on financing of airports and start-up aid to airlines departing from regional airports. *Official Journal of the European Union* C 312, 09.12.2005.

COM (2006a) 134 Final, Commission of the European Communities, Communication from the Commission. *A Renewed EU Tourism Policy: Towards A Stronger Partnership For European Tourism* 17.03.2006. http://ec.europa.eu/enterprise/sectors/tourism/documents/communications/commission-communication-2006/index_en.htm.

COM (2006b) 818 final – 2006/0304 (COD). Proposal for a Directive of the European Parliament and of the Council Amending Directive 2003/87/EC in order to include aviation activities in the scheme for greenhouse gas emission allowance trading within the Community, 20.12.2006. http://eur-lex.europa.eu/LexUriServ/site/en/com/2006/com2006_0818en01.pdf.

Council Regulation (EC) No. 1084/2006 of 11 July 2006 establishing a Cohesion Fund and Repealing Regulation (EC) No. 1164/94. *Official Journal of the European Union* L 210/79, 31.7.2006.

Council Regulation (EC) No. 1083/2006 of 11 July 2006 – General Provisions in the European Regional Development Fund, the European Social Fund and the Cohesion Fund and repealing Regulation (EC) No. 1260/1999. *Official Journal of the European Union* L 210/25, 31.7.2006.

Directive 2008/101/EC of the European Parliament and of the Council of 19 November 2008 amending Directive 2003/87/EC so as to include aviation activities in the scheme for greenhouse gas emission allowance trading within the Community. http://eur-lex.europa.eu/LexUriServ/LexUriServ.do?uri=CELEX:32008L0101:EN: NOT.

EC Decision 2006/944/EC of 14 December 2006 determining the respective emission levels allocated to the Community and each of its Member States under the Kyoto Protocol pursuant to Council Decision 2002/358/EC (notified under document number C(2006) 6468). *Official Journal of the European Union* L 358, 16.12.2006.

EC Decision No. 1855/2006/CE of the European Parliament and the Council of 12 establishing the Culture Programme 2007–2013. *Official Journal of the European Union* L 372, 27.12.2006.

Regulation (EC) No. 1080/2006 of the European Parliament and of the Council of 5 July 2006 On the European Regional Development Fund and Repealing Regulation (EC) No. 1783/1999. *Official Journal of the European Union* L 210/1, 31.7.2006.

SEC (2006) 1684, Commission Staff Working Document. Accompanying document to the Proposal for a Directive of the European Parliament and of the Council, amending Directive 2003/87/EC so as to include aviation activities in the scheme for greenhouse gas emission allowance trading within the Community Impact Assessment of the inclusion of aviation activities in the scheme for greenhouse gas emission allowance trading within the Community (COM(2006) 818 final). http://www.ipex.eu/ipex/cms/home/Documents/doc_SEC20061684FIN;jsessionid=9A417D68246E6D3 2994603D442E36067.

Other references

Brent Ritchie, J.R. and Crouch, G.I. (2003) *The Competitive Destination: A Sustainable Tourism Perspective*. Wallingford: CABI.

Brent Ritchie, J.R. and Goeldner, C.R. (eds) (2007) *Tourism Principles, Practices, Philosophies* (10th edn). New York: J. Wiley & Sons.

Costa, P. and Manente, M. (2000) *Economia del turismo*. Milan: TUP (Touring University Press).

Costa, P., Manente, M. and Furlan, M.C. (2001) *Politica Economica del Turismo*. Milan: TUP.

European Parliament (2007) *The Fragmentation of EU Tourism Policy*. Policy Department for Structural and Cohesion policies, IP/B/TRAN/IC/2007-004. Brussels: European Parliament.

Gunn, C. (1994) *Tourism Planning: Basic, Concepts, Cases* (3rd edn). New York: Taylor & Francis.

Leiper, N. (1990) *Tourism Systems*. Palmerston North, New Zealand: Massay University Press.

Manente, M. and Minghetti, V. (2005) Managing the destination as a system: Actors, strategies and policies. In E. Buhalis and C. Costa (eds) *Tourism Business Frontiers: Consumers, Products and Industry* (pp. 228–237). London: Butterworth-Heinemann.

16 Tourism Policy and Knowledge Processes in European Tourism

Henrik Halkier

Introduction

Tourism is currently subject to political expectations that could point in different directions. On the one hand, much tourism takes place in areas with few alternative sources of income – coasts, mountains, countryside – and therefore is seen as a means to provide employment and growth in communities that would otherwise be difficult to sustain (Halkier, 2010a; Hall, 2008). On the other hand, the EU 2020 strategy specifically seeks 'to enhance the competitiveness of the European tourism sector' (EC, 2010: 19) in order to retain Europe's leading position in international tourism in face of intensifying global competition. In an ideal world this would result in tourism destinations becoming part of the knowledge economy through extensive innovation in experiences and services, and in the real world this is likely to be challenging to achieve.

Since the 1990s tourist destinations across Europe have been subject to increasing competitive pressures due to the rise of e-trade in tourist services (package holidays, transport, accommodation, destinations, attractions) and the advent of new business models in transport (budget airlines) that have created new and readily available alternatives for tourists who have hitherto been repeat visitors to nearby destinations (Halkier, 2010a). But still tourism has often been seen as slow to change compared to other parts of the economy (Hjalager, 2002): many of the core products have remained largely unchanged, and the capacity for innovation in small firms providing personal services is rather limited. It is only recently that a small but growing literature on innovation in tourism has started to emerge (for a comprehensive overview, see Hall & Williams, 2008), and in this literature the role of public policy in relation to innovative activities has rarely been examined in a systematic manner.

The contribution of this chapter focuses on the relationship between tourism policies and knowledge processes in European tourism. Tourism policy has often been subject to rather simplistic ideal-type conceptualisation with limited attention to implications for knowledge and innovation, and therefore the first part of the text consists of an attempt to conceptualise key aspects of tourism policy and knowledge processes in tourism development. Having developed a conceptual framework, the second part of the text presents results from a comparative empirical study of five European destinations, from Scandinavian coastal cool, via rural and urban destinations in middle Europe, to Mediterranean mass tourism.[1] The empirical analysis focuses on sources of inspiration for policy practices, the internal policy learning processes at the destinations as well as extra-regional interactions, and the possible long-term impact of policy initiatives on knowledge processes among public and private tourism actors in the destinations. On the basis of the analysis, conclusions are drawn with regard to the knowledge implications of current tourism policies, and strategies for the further integration of tourism development in the mainstream knowledge economy are discussed.

Tourism Policy and Knowledge Processes: A Conceptual Framework

Tourism policy is an area of public policy where several approaches have co-existed for a sustained period of time, possibly because they all take as their point of departure the complex nature of the tourism product which involves delivering a heterogeneous set of services to customers originating elsewhere (Halkier, 2010b). The relatively sparse academic research on tourism policy has predominantly relied on typologies of a fairly basic nature revolving around a series of ideal-type policy paradigms with a built-in (vague) assumption of progress over time. These paradigms are primarily based on different types of expansive objectives as in, for example, the common distinction between 'boosterism', 'economic' and 'sustainable' strategies for tourism development (e.g. Fayos-Sola, 1996; Hall, 2008), which effectively means 'more of the same' via 'more of most' to 'more of the best'.

While this generational typology of tourism policy may have an intuitive heuristic appeal, its usefulness in empirical analysis is more doubtful, simply because the same goals can be pursued in very different ways that may or may not involve innovation with regard to experiences, services and market communication. Bearing in mind that the small but rapidly growing literature on innovation within tourism has identified the building of networks within destinations spanning a wide range of actors as a widespread prerequisite for lasting change (Dredge, 2006; Hall & Williams, 2008; Hjalager, 2002), a more fine-grained approach is required in order to identify differences and similarities between strategies for destination development.

Inspired by an institutionalist perspective on public policy (Halkier, 2006; Halkier & Cooke, 2010), this text will take a more differentiated approach which focuses on the strategic changes sought by public policy, the instruments through which change is being promoted, and the knowledge implications of public intervention. The conceptual framework is summarised in Table 16.1 and elaborated in the following.

Strategy covers both the *general direction of change* and the specific targets that will have to change in order to achieve policy aims. Because tourism involves activities undertaken away from home, change can be sought in both the experiences/services at the place visited and/or the way in which these are communicated to potential visitors. An onsite information strategy which basically attempts to inform existing visitors about existing offers and thereby increase repeat visits involves little, mainly incremental, change, while a promotion strategy which seeks to convince new potential visitors of the attractions of the destination depends on changes in communication practices. Alternatively, a product innovation strategy tries to change services that contribute to the tourist experience in order to make them more attractive to potential tourists, often different from current visitors. The more widespread, comprehensive and systemic product innovation is, the greater the need for concurrently refocusing promotional efforts and engaging in a branding strategy that repositions the destination in the competition for potential visitors through coordinated efforts with regard to both product and promotion (Therkelsen *et al.*, 2010). In order to move in a particular strategic direction, policies will have to bring about change in the behaviour of social actors. This involves choosing *specific targets of change*, both the institutions (individuals, firms or the entire system of the destination/locality) and the type of capabilities that will change: tangible 'hardware', immaterial 'software' or relational 'orgware'.

In order to bring about change, public bodies will employ *policy instruments* that provide access to additional resources – often information, finance

Table 16.1 Tourism policy: A basic conceptual framework

Dimension	Sub-dimensions	Variables
Strategy	General direction of change	Onsite info/promotion/innovation/branding
	Target institutions	Individuals/firms & organisations/system
	Target capabilities	Hardware/software/orgware
Policy instruments	Resources	Authority/information/finance/organisation
	Rules	Mandatory/conditional/voluntary
Knowledge impact	Knowledge types	Analytical/synthetic/symbolic
	Knowledge phases	Exploration/examination/exploitation

Source: Elaborated on the basis of Halkier (2006) and Halkier and Cooke (2010)

or organisational support – on more or less stringent conditions. The range of resources that can potentially be employed is wide, and in practice the choice depends on what is available to policy makers and perceived as attractive by the actors targeted.

Finally, *knowledge impact* refers to the economic purpose of knowledge activities and the nature of knowledge involved (Asheim *et al.*, 2007; Manniche, 2010). Knowledge phases express the extent to which a particular knowledge activity is oriented towards creating economic benefits: is existing knowledge being exploited for production or marketing purposes, for example? Are potential solutions being examined, or is a phenomenon being explored with no particular economic application in mind? Knowledge types refer to the nature of the knowledge involved, i.e. has it been produced through science-based analytical methods in research laboratories, for example, or through try-and-fail synthetic methods such as engineering or organisational development, or does it reflect cultural symbols and values in society?

Compared to the prevailing typologies, this conceptual framework makes it possible to analyse tourism policy by systematically identifying differences and similarities between the different ways in which destination development is being addressed, for instance by distinguishing between different general strategic aims, different specific targets and instruments to bring about change, and the different knowledge implications of public intervention. While a promotion-oriented strategy will rely on informational resources to target potential visitors, its effectiveness will, among other things, depend on information about target group preferences. Conversely, a product innovation strategy can attempt to make private firms invest in new facilities, and it will therefore have difficulties in being successful unless it relies on updated knowledge about the development activities of competing destinations. In short, such an approach to the study of tourism policy will make it possible to account in a much more subtle way for the complexities and variations in policy making.

Research Design: Comparing Policies in European Destinations

As part of a major European project on knowledge dynamics in regional development, *EURODITE*,[2] 10 case studies of change within the tourism sector have been undertaken in five different destinations across Europe. This design makes it possible to consider a wide variety of tourisms in order to explore common themes and policy characteristics, but it does not of course pretend to be an exhaustive survey of tourism and public policy in Europe.

The case studies were undertaken according to a common so-called 'knowledge biography' method (Butzin *et al.*, 2007) through which innovation processes are investigated in depth by identifying the interactions of key actors throughout the entire lifespan of an innovative change process, and their institutional and geographical settings. The reports of the individual case studies, listed in the Appendix below, have been analysed in order to identify the public policies that have influenced processes of change within tourism (Halkier, 2009), and the key characteristics of these policies have been established on the basis of the conceptual framework outlined in the preceding section. All in all this makes it possible to identify policies that have made a difference in terms of innovation and assess their implication for knowledge processes within and outside tourist destinations.

Case studies have been undertaken in European destinations that are situated both in countries with high levels of outbound tourism (Denmark, The Netherlands, Germany, Sweden) and with high levels of inbound tourism (Turkey). Furthermore, if the Butler destination lifecycle is taken as a proxy (Butler, 1980; Weaver & Lawton, 2002), the five destinations represent different stages of development: North Jutland (DK) is a stagnating destination, Antalya (TR) in the late development or early consolidation stage, and Skåne (SE), Achterhoek (NL) and Ruhr (D) in the early involvement stage. Finally, as illustrated by Table 16.2, the case studies represent different types of tourism in terms of organisation (individual/collective) and with regard to the core experience (cultural/natural) that attracts visitors to a particular destination. This makes it possible to gauge whether the policies employed differ according to different ways of getting in contact with prospective visitors (directly or through commercial intermediaries) and the extent to which core experience products are more or less amenable to creative reconstruction by public and private stakeholders.

For each of the case studies the characteristics of the policy initiatives involved have been classified on the basis of the conceptual framework outlined above, making it possible to draw conclusions with regard to the knowledge implications of current tourism policies, i.e. in what ways policies influence the generation and use of different types of knowledge by key actors and organisations, and thereby provide the basis for future research on a more extensive scale.

Destination Development Strategies

Given the character of tourism as an activity ordered or planned in advance of and away from the destination at which services/experiences are eventually produced and consumed, tourism policies are typically geared towards affecting either the core experiences/services that attract tourists to a particular destination, or the way in which this experience is communicated to potential tourists, by maintaining service offers and/or communication as they are or by promoting more or less extensive changes.

Table 16.2 Destination change processes present in case studies by type of tourism

Organisation of travel	Attraction Cultural	Natural
Individual	○ Branding of Antalya as a cultured city through a combination of place marketing and sea-front redevelopment ○ Development of Ruhr industrial heritage visitor trail through networking ○ Development of Ruhr football visitor trail through networking ○ Development of film-based tourism in Skaane through marketing of new cultural assets ○ Development of North Jutland museums through network of new-media based experiences	□ Development of rural tourism in Achterhoek through training and advisory services □ Extension of season in North Jutland through DMO network □ DMO development in North Jutland in order to promote all-year tourism
Collective	● Development of football training tourism in low season in Antalya through infrastructure	■ Development of coastal tourism in Antalya through access to land for hotel construction and place marketing

Note: The four changes process identifiers (○, ●, □, ■) are used in Tables 16.3–16.6 to show the distribution of policy characteristics by types of tourism in the case studies undertaken.
Source: Elaborated on the basis of Halkier (2009)

Table 16.3 summarises the options available and the distribution of the case studies, and it is immediately evident that the main strategic focus has been on product development. Although marketing strategies also occur in relation to well-established tourist destinations, comprehensive branding strategies only occur in cases where comprehensive changes to existing services are linked to attempts to change external perceptions of the destination as a whole (Antalya, Skaane and Ruhr becoming places of culture rather than, respectively, sun-fuelled hedonism, rural idyll and industrial grind). While the low-profile or indirect nature of onsite information strategies probably explains why this kind of experience facilitation is not well represented in the case studies (in Ystad/Skaane tourist

Table 16.3 General strategic aims of tourism policies in case studies

Service/experience	Communication Continuity	Change
Continuity	Onsite information strategy: ○	Promotion strategy: ■ □
Change	Innovation strategy: ● ○ ○ ○ ■ □ □ □	Branding strategy: ○ ○ ○

Note: The four changes process identifiers (○, ●, □, ■) given in Table 16.2 are used to show the distribution of policy characteristics by types of tourism in the case studies undertaken. Each change process may involve several policy initiatives and hence be classified more than once.

information about film locations was prompted by visitor demand), the limited emphasis on marketing strategies is likely to reflect a selection of cases focusing on change processes. Likewise, the focus on innovation strategies rather than branding does not mean that the new services have not been marketed; it merely implies that the new tourism experiences have tended to be niche products which have not (yet) led to more extensive efforts to associate the destination as a whole with the new form of tourist activity. Still, the emphasis on developing new tourist experiences rather than new forms of communication raises the question about the extent to which these new attractions reflect documented trends in tourist demands or are speculative producer-driven initiatives, something that will be discussed in more detail below.

A crucial question in public policy is how general aims are translated into specific objectives for change, i.e. what capabilities are going to change where, as a result of public intervention aiming to, for example, attract a different kind of tourist. Table 16.4 summarises the nine basic options, and it is immediately obvious that the policies making a difference in the case studies include the complete range of both target institutions and capabilities. Moreover, it is also clear that, while some policies concentrate on bringing about one particular form of change – e.g. networks between

Table 16.4 Targets of change in case studies

Target institutions	Target capabilities Hardware	Software	Orgware
Individuals		■ □ □ ○ ○ ○	
Firms/organisations	■ □ ○ ○	● □	○ ○ ○
System	● ○ ○		□ □

Note: The four changes process identifiers (○, ●, □, ■) given in Table 16.2 are used to show the distribution of policy characteristics by types of tourism in the case studies undertaken. Each change process may involve several policy initiatives and hence be classified more than once.

specialised football attractions – others involve a series of coordinated changes, such as infrastructure and marketing in the re-branding of Antalya, a combination of regional funding for film projects and targeted international marketing of Skaane as a destination for specialist cultural tourism, or a combination of IT investment, staff training and networking in order to integrate North Jutland museums into the experience economy.

It is, however, also interesting to note which capacities and institutions are *not* being targeted, despite their obvious relevance for some of the development strategies pursued:

- increasing the number of individuals with relevant skills available through attraction of specialist labour (targeting 'individual hardware') was clearly relevant in Antalya to support the growth in tourism from Russia in particular;
- development of knowledge institutions in order to support tourism development would have been relevant in both mature (North Jutland, Antalya) and emerging (Ruhr) destinations; and
- creation of professional networks between tourist employees has not been a major priority in any of the case studies, although it might have furthered acceptance of change in the North Jutland museums, for example.

In the two first cases it could be argued that this problem has to some extent been addressed by other actors (hotels, tour operators, universities, museums), and the role of public policy would merely have been to improve the quality or quantity of new staff, training courses, etc.

In a situation with increasing competition between destinations, timing and quality – getting new services right before competitors – is, however, of great importance, because customer satisfaction and excitement is an important part of the creation of the image of destinations (e.g. Baloglu & McCleary, 1999). In short, supporting existing development trends by working 'with the grain of the market' is perhaps particularly important with regard to tourism, but the three examples above underline both the importance of involving a wide range of partners outside the tourism sector itself, and also taking into account the possibility that not all targets of changes are equally enthusiastic about changing their activities in order to support a strategy aimed at tourism development.

Policy Instruments

In order to bring about desirable changes in tourism, policy makers employ a range of instruments which combine resources and rules: in order to make

Table 16.5 Policy instruments employed in case studies

Policy rules	Policy resources			
	Authority	Information	Finance	Organisation
Mandatory	■ ○			
Conditional		□ ○	■ ○	□ □ ○ ○ ○
Voluntary	■ □ ○ ○			● ○

Note: The four changes process identifiers (○, ●, □, ■) given in Table 16.2 are used to show the distribution of policy characteristics by types of tourism in the case studies undertaken. Each change process may involve several policy initiatives and hence be classified more than once.

actors behave in ways conducive to policy goals, resources are made available on more or less stringent conditions. Table 16.5 provides an overview of the 12 basic types of policy instrument and identifies the main instruments employed in the case studies.

Although all four types of policy resources and three types of policy rules have been employed in the case studies, it is also clear that some instruments clearly occur more frequently than others. Mandatory measures and the use of authority and finance as policy resources are relatively rare, and they are only found in the form of land-use planning regarding industrial heritage in Ruhr, funding for film projects in the Skaane region that can be exploited for touristic purposes, and the promotion of hotel construction in Antalya, where planning has been combined with financial incentives to developers. This makes four types of policy instruments the most common in the case studies:

- conditional access to information in the form of specialist training and advice, targeting rural tourism entrepreneurs in Achterhoek and museum professionals in North Jutland;
- unconditional access to information in the form of marketing and branding efforts in Antalya and North Jutland;
- unconditional access to organisational capacity through general infrastructure supporting football tourism in Antalya and industrial heritage tourism in Ruhr; and
- conditional access to organisational capacity, by far the most frequently used policy instrument, in the form of network creation and facilitation which is recorded in all regions except Achterhoek.

On the basis of this, some important conclusions can be drawn with regard to tourism policy. Clearly conditional measures dominate, making it necessary for policy makers to be able to offer tourism actors relevant resources on attractive terms, and at the same time most policy measures are of a nature that requires policy makers and the implementing organisation to have specific knowledge about tourism as an economic activity; otherwise, neither specialist advice nor network building would be possible to set in motion. Moreover, while mandatory measures play a limited role, making information and organisational resources with no strings attached is also a widespread practice. In other words, the policy instruments employed are of an inherently knowledge-intensive nature, and hence in order to be successful, they presuppose that policy makers and their staff have access to this information.

Tourism Policies and Knowledge Dynamics

In terms of knowledge types, it could be expected that synthetic and symbolic knowledge types dominate tourism-related knowledge dynamics (see, e.g. Halkier, 2010b). Synthetic organisational knowledge is a critical resource particularly in rural/coastal tourism destinations, depending on visitors travelling individually, and symbolic cultural knowledge such as market intelligence and product knowledge about, for example, local attractions is necessary to sustain international competitiveness. As illustrated by Table 16.6, the knowledge impact of public policy only concerns synthetic and symbolic forms of knowledge while, unsurprisingly, science-based analytical knowledge is absent as none of the case studies focuses on, for example, space tourism. However, the emphasis is very strongly on exploitation of knowledge: examination is only a major aspect in three of the 10 policies identified, while exploration is completely absent.

Looking further into the impact of tourism policies on knowledge dynamics, it would appear that a 'division of knowledge labour' exists in the case studies, so that the more or less purposeful production of new knowledge tends to be undertaken by private or non-government tourism entrepreneurs, such as bringing together football or film actors, or identifying demand

Table 16.6 Tourism policy impact on knowledge types and phases

| | Knowledge types | | |
Knowledge phases	Analytical	Synthetic	Symbolic
Exploration			
Examination		○○□	□
Exploitation		○○○○○□□●■	○○○○○□□●■

Note: The four changes process identifiers (○, ●, □, ■) given in Table 16.2 are used to show the distribution of policy characteristics by types of tourism in the case studies undertaken. Each change process may involve several policy initiatives and hence be classified more than once.

patterns among new types of visitors. In contrast to this, the knowledge impact of public policy focuses on making existing knowledge available to a larger number of (small) actors who would otherwise have remained unenlightened due to the absence of a perfect market in information. This implies that the vast majority of policies increase the use of knowledge while only a few increase production of knowledge about products or markets.

The geographical impact of tourism policies on knowledge dynamics is also worth noting. The majority of policies intensify interactions internally in the destinations/regions, while only three of them increase extra-regional knowledge interactions – something which is particularly striking in light of the interregional and indeed international character of tourist flows which suggest a rather inward-looking producer-oriented perspective. All in all, policies primarily stimulate the local use/adaptation of external knowledge, with a significant minority involving production of knowledge and more distance interactions. Policies are in other words primarily stimulating local/regional knowledge dynamics.

Two conclusions would seem to follow from this finding. Firstly, market intelligence depends on more or less tacit knowledge created in SMEs by interaction with tourists or (less widely circulated) through formalised market research of large organisations such as tour operators, and thus many tourism development initiatives are bound to be producer driven in the sense that very limited efforts have been made to investigate the potential demand for new services and attractions. Secondly, while making existing knowledge more widely available is of course a very valuable role for public policy, greater efforts in terms of stimulating creative knowledge production in SMEs, DMOs and public knowledge institutions might be an important additional way of stimulating tourism development and innovation.

Given that the impact of tourism policies is to stimulate the use or adaptation of existing knowledge rather than the production of new knowledge, it is hardly surprising that the geography of tourism policy knowledge contains an important element of distance interactions. While the knowledge processes directly stimulated by tourism policies predominantly take place within the destination, the knowledge used by policy-making bodies is often extra-regional in the sense that it draws on practices developed in national networks (knowledge about rural tourism imported to Achterhoek; knowledge about tourism trends and organisational patterns imported to North Jutland; knowledge about coastal tourism imported to Antalya) or international practice (knowledge about preservation and apprehension of industrial heritage). However, given the international nature of tourism and the geographical distance between service providers and visitors, it is again noticeable that only rarely is the gathering of specific market information part of tourism policy, either as preparation for or as part of particular policy initiatives.

Tourism Policy and Knowledge Dynamics: Conclusions and Perspectives

Given the spread of case studies between different forms of tourism, it has been possible to analyse tourism policies in a variety of contexts which, despite their differences with regard to the core tourism experience, are all subject to increasing competitive pressures. In this situation, knowledge about international customer and product trends becomes increasingly crucial in order to make innovation commercially successful, but at the same time, especially for small private and public actors, such knowledge is difficult to access (in so far as it has been produced by large private tour operators, for example) and difficult/costly to produce, except in the form of tacit knowledge picked up through interaction with existing customers and partners.

The analysis of public policies involved in the 10 case studies demonstrated that:

- Policies generally focus on the development of new services and mostly combine these with promotional efforts so that from this perspective combinatorial knowledge is clearly important.
- Symbolic knowledge is clearly seen as important, but nonetheless policy efforts often concentrate on synthetic (especially) organisational knowledge. In particular, the efforts with regard to market intelligence and emerging trends about visitor preferences are surprisingly limited, despite the fact that the distance between producers and consumers of tourism services is an inherent characteristic of this particular form of economic activity.
- Policies generally target critical software and orgware resources in relation to their particular form of tourism, although it is noticeable that some targets (especially in-migration of specialist staff and involvement of public knowledge institutions) were not present, despite their obvious relevance in terms of bringing commercially relevant knowledge into the process.
- Both the policy instruments favoured and the importance of ongoing network relations clearly demonstrate that current tourism policies are knowledge intensive, and they therefore depend on qualified knowledge inputs in order to successfully make a difference in tourism development.
- Although using the experience of, for example, similar attractions is common place, the absence of systematic information about the demand-side is striking, and thus product development initiatives rely on tacit knowledge garnered by individual actors in meetings with previous visitors to the region, something that is clearly better at maintaining path dependencies than at supporting those new departures which are often at the heart of tourism policy initiatives.

It is, moreover, interesting to note that no systematic pattern of co-variation seems to exist between the characteristics of policies influencing particular types of tourism, whether organised individually or collectively, or based around cultural or natural attractions. Although further research is clearly needed, it would nonetheless seem to suggest that from a tourism policy perspective neither the character of the resource at the heart of the experience nor the more or less direct access to potential visitors makes much of a difference to the public policies influencing innovation processes within destinations, and thus in practice this implies that the repertoire of policy instruments available for different kinds of tourism is indeed a wide-ranging one.

All in all, many policy initiatives are taking place within the field of tourism that particularly further internal knowledge dynamics in regions and destinations. However, in the light of increased international competition driven by new business models, global information flows, and growing customer flexibility, the analysis nonetheless suggests that some key areas of tourism knowledge-related policy will be in need of more attention in the coming years if destinations are going to enhance or even maintain their position:

- Increased emphasis on the creative generation of market intelligence, of a more specific character and focusing on emerging trends in order to be able to inform service development activities, something which would have to involve both private partners and public knowledge institutions;
- Greater attention to systematic use of extra-regional knowledge resources, including increased use of private consultancy services as knowledge intermediaries with regard to synthetic and especially symbolic knowledge about consumer trends, in order to move towards an evidence-based form of policy making that is closer to both producers and consumers of tourism experiences;
- Efficient destination management organisations, well networked both locally and nationally, incorporating both public and private partners as well in the wider experience economy, and capable of handling diverse and complex knowledge, appear to be a prerequisite to address public-sector localism and private-sector short-termism.

In short, room for improvement would seem to exist, not least with regard to knowledge-explicit initiatives that can address the basic asymmetry between producers and consumers of tourism as an international personal service experience for increasingly mobile visitors. This is indeed a challenge for destination development initiatives across Europe because, while knowledge is a source of competitive advantage, the willingness to share strategic knowledge is likely to differ between actors, both in the private and the public sector.

Acknowledgements

Thanks are due to Karina Madsen Smed and Pennie F. Henriksen for commenting on earlier versions of the text. Responsibility for the final text, as ever, rests with the author.

Notes

(1) The empirical part of the paper draws on the joint research of partners in the *EURODITE* 6th Framework Programme Integrated Project.
(2) The objective of the *EURODITE* project was to investigate regional trajectories to the knowledge economy by showing how knowledge is generated, developed and transferred within and among firms or organisations and their regional contexts. The project was funded by the EU's 6th Framework Programme.

References

Asheim, B., Coenen, L. and Vang, J. (2007) Face-to-face, buzz and knowledge bases: Socio-spatial implications for learning, innovation and innovation policy. *Environment & Planning C: Government and Policy* 25, 655–670.

Baloglu, S. and McCleary, K. (1999) A model of destination image formation. *Annals of Tourism Research* 26 (4), 868–897.

Butler, R.W. (1980) The concept of a tourist area cycle of evolution: Implications for management of resources. *Canadian Geographer* 24 (1), 5–12.

Butzin, A., Helmsträdter, E., Larsson, A., MacNeill, S., Vale, M. and Widmaier, B. (2007) *Guidelines to the WP6 Firm Level Case Studies*. Birmingham: EURODITE.

Dredge, D. (2006) Policy networks and the local organisation of tourism. *Tourism Management* 27 (2), 269–280.

EC (2010) *Europe 2020. A Strategy for Smart, Sustainable and Inclusive Growth*. Com(2010) 2020, 3.3.2010. Brussels: European Commission.

Fayos-Sola, E. (1996) Tourism policy: A midsummer night's dream? *Tourism Management* 17 (6), 405–412.

Halkier, H. (2006) *Institutions, Discourse and Regional Development. The Scottish Development Agency and the Politics of Regional Policy*. Brussels: PIE Peter Lang.

Halkier, H. (2009) WP8 policy cloud intermediate report: Tourism. WP8 Seminar, Brussels.

Halkier, H. (2010a) EU and tourism development: Bark or bite? *Scandinavian Journal of Hospitality and Tourism* 10 (2), 92–106.

Halkier, H. (2010b) Tourism knowledge dynamics. In P. Cooke, C.D. Laurentis, C. Collinge and S. MacNeill (eds) *Platforms of Innovation: Dynamics of New Industrial Knowledge Flows* (pp. 233–250). London: Edward Elgar.

Halkier, H. and Cooke, P. (2010) Knowledge and policies for regional development: European trends. In H. Halkier, M. Dahlström, L. James, J. Manniche and L.S. Olsen (eds) *Knowledge Dynamics, Regional Development and Public Policy* (pp. 17–26). Aalborg: EURODITE, Department of History, International and Social Studies, Aalborg University.

Hall, C.M. (2008) *Tourism Planning: Policies, Processes and Relationships* (2nd edn). Harlow: Pearson Prentice Hall.

Hall, C.M. and Williams, A. (2008) *Tourism and Innovation*. Abingdon: Routledge.

Hjalager, A-M. (2002) Repairing innovation defectiveness in tourism. *Tourism Management* 23, 465–474.

Manniche, J. (2010) Types of knowledge and learning. In H. Halkier, M. Dahlström, L. James, J. Manniche and L.S. Olsen (eds) *Knowledge Dynamics, Regional Development and Public Policy* (pp. 78–85). Aalborg: EURODITE, Department of History, International and Social Studies, Aalborg University.

Therkelsen, A., Halkier, H. and Jensen, O.B. (2010) Branding Aalborg – building community or selling place? In G. Ashworth and M. Kavaratzis (eds) *Towards Effective Place Brand Management: Branding European Cities and Regions* (pp. 136–155). London: Edward Elgar.

Weaver, D. and Lawton, L. (2002) *Tourism Management* (2nd edn). Milton: Wiley.

Appendix: EURODITE Reports on Which the Empirical Analysis is Based

Berg Schmidt, P. and Halkier, H. (2008) *Knowledge Dynamics in Regional Tourism. The Case of North Jutland, Denmark*. EURODITE WP5 Final Report. Aalborg: Aalborg University.

Butzin, A. and Widmaier, B. (2009) *Tourism in the Ruhr Area*. Final EURODITE WP5 Report. Gelsenkirchen: Institut Arbeit und Technik.

Butzin, A. and Widmaier, B. (2009) *Tourism Development in the Ruhr Area: Knowledge Dynamics, Activities, Trends*. Final EURODITE WP6 Report. Gelsenkirchen: Institut Arbeit und Technik.

Dahlström, M., S.Östberg, S., *et al.* (2009) *Harnessing Complementary Resources - Knowledge Dynamics in New Media in Skåne*. Stockholm: Nordregio.

Dahlström, M., Östberg, S., *et al.* (2009) *Firm-level Knowledge Dynamics in Moving Media in Skåne: Cross-sectoral Innovations in Game Development and Film Tourism*. Stockholm: Nordregio.

Dulupcu, M.A. (2009) *Tourism in Antalya, Turkey*. Final WP5 Report. Isparta: Sleyman Demirel University.

Dulupcu, M.A. (2009) *Tourism Case Studies in Antalya, Turkey*. Final WP6 Report. Isparta: Sleyman Demirel University.

Halkier, H., Henriksen, P.F., *et al.* (2009) *Knowledge Dynamics in Tourism in North Jutland: Case Studies of Knowledge Events Within Coastal and Cultural Tourism*. EURODITE WP6 Final Report. Aalborg: Aalborg University.

Vaessen, P. (2009) *Agro-tourism in the Achterhoek Region (Netherlands)*. Final EURODITE WP5 Report. Nijmegen: Radboud University.

Vaessen, P. and Dankbaar, B. (2009) *Firm Knowledge Dynamics in the Field of Agro-tourism in the Achterhoek Region (Netherlands)*. Final EURODITE WP6 Report. Nijmegen: Radboud University.

17 European Transport Policy and Tourism

D.K. Robbins and J.E. Dickinson

Introduction

Transport is an important economic component in the European Union (EU), responsible for around 7% of GDP and 5% of employment (COM, 2009b). It is also an essential component of the tourism industry, both for tourism activity within the EU and for tourism to and from the EU.

European transport policy is the responsibility of the Directorate for Energy and Transport (DG TREN) within the European Commission (EC). As is the case with most governments in the EU, transport is in a different administrative department from tourism, which is the responsibility of the Directorate for Enterprise and Industry (DG ENTERPRISE). This in itself is not a problem; the EC should be able to integrate policies and strategies between Directorates, although it does mean that leisure and tourism is not the primary concern of policies developed by DG TREN, even though such travel is significant.

It is estimated that tourism accounts for 15–20% of all passenger km in the EU (Peeters *et al.*, 2007). However, policies developed by DG TREN can significantly impact on tourism, particularly on the price and capacity of transport systems, which in turn impacts on the size of the tourism market and patterns of tourism demand.

There have been a number of studies to promote closer integration of tourism and transport policy. Concertour is an example of a project to improve the competitiveness of European tourism; its aim is to create synergies between transport, research and tourism sectors in Europe (see Concertour, 2008 for more details). The Concertour Project organised a number of workshops and conferences and identified scope for improved coordination between DG TREN and DG ENTERPRISE.

European Transport Policy: The Past 10 Years

The EC set out its agenda for transport policy from 2001 through to 2010 in a White Paper published in 2001 (COM, 2001), updated in a mid-term review (COM, 2006). The key objectives over the last 10 years are shown in Table 17.1. These illustrate the wide range of stakeholders with valid, yet potentially conflicting expectations, whose interests must be considered. Whereas there is a clear consumer focus for many of the objectives such as improvements to safety and improved passenger rights, others focus on workers' rights, reducing the externalities of transport for the benefit of residents as a whole rather than solely transport users, and the development of appropriate infrastructure.

Table 17.1 European transport policy objectives, 2001–2010

Policy objective	Progress
Social and economic cohesion by promoting the competitiveness of European industry	Significant contribution to the Lisbon Agenda for growth and jobs
Market opening	Most advanced in air transport. EU creating a level playing field but differences in taxation and subsidies need to be addressed
Trans-European transport networks (TEN-T) (first adopted in 1996) to improve coordination in the planning of infrastructure projects	Substantial progress with around one-third of necessary investments (€400 billion)
Reduction of air pollution and road accidents	Application of ever stricter Euro emissions; target to halve road casualties by 2010 not achieved but substantial progress made standards
Improved security	Not referred to in 2001 White Paper, but following attacks on 9/11 an EU security policy was developed for most modes
Strengthening passengers' rights	Legislation on aviation and rail
Social policy with regards to transport workers	Legislation on working time, level of training and mutual recognition of diploma qualifications
Comply with targets of the EU-SDS	The MAIN policy area where further improvements are necessary

Source: Adapted from COM (2009b)

Table 17.2 Main modes of transport for holiday trips of 4+ nights by residents in the EU-27, 2008 (%)

Mode	Domestic holidays	International holidays	Total holidays
Car	76	28	56
Rail	12	3	9
Bus/coach	6	6	7
Air	4	58	26
Sea	2	4	3
Total	100	100	100

Source: Eurostat (2010)

Market share

European tourism travel is dominated by private cars and air. Table 17.2 shows the mode of transport used for holidays of four nights or longer. The private car dominates domestic tourism transport and contributes a large share for short international trips on the European mainland, although air transport/travels dominate international tourist trips.

There are significant variations in modal share among the EU-27 countries (see Eurostat, 2010), reflecting both spatial and economic factors. Air accounts for over 50% of trips from UK and Eire, both island member states, and is also very high for Denmark, Estonia and Latvia but is very low for Bulgaria. The private car has over a 50% share for virtually every other member state. Rail has a relatively low share for holiday tourism although it is higher for Poland (18%) and France (13%), the latter benefiting from a large land area and a well-established high-speed TGV network. Bus and coach have a low market share although market shares of over 20% are recorded in Bulgaria and Slovakia. Sea as a main mode of transport is rare with the exception of Greece, where travel to and from island destinations results in 18% of the modal split. Domestic tourism is the largest market, while short-haul trips dominate the international market (Table 17.3).

The policies of the last 10 years have reinforced the dominance of air and private car, which have grown more quickly than other modes. The private

Table 17.3 Number of tourism journeys by EU-25 citizens in 2000 (%)

Type of journey	%
Domestic	61
Intra – EU 25	29
Europe outside EU	4
Inter Continental	6
Total	100

Source: Peeters *et al.* (2007)

car has a number of advantages for shorter holiday journeys due to its flexibility, both in terms of route and departure time, and its availability at the destination. Furthermore, it is usually the cheapest option; the cost of an additional journey in a car already owned by a household is small. For a more detailed discussion of the inherent advantages of the car see Robbins and Dickinson (2007). Likewise, the deregulation of air services in the EU has seen a dramatic rise in the air share, as is discussed later.

One clear link between both private car and air is that neither pay the full cost of the externalities they impose. An objective of the 2001 White Paper was to internalise the cost of transport externalities, broadly on a principle that the polluter pays. Progress to date is slow. The private car can impose a number of external costs including air pollution, noise, visual intrusion, accidents and the high economic costs of congestion as well as CO_2 emissions. However, there is no comprehensive policy to charge car drivers differential prices for using the busiest roads at the peak times of day, even though this is when externalities are at their greatest. There are isolated instances where motorists do pay more, such as motorway tolls or congestion pricing in central London and Stockholm, but it falls far short of a comprehensive road pricing strategy where those who generate the greatest external costs pay the most.

Likewise, aviation also benefits from low levels of taxation. The Chicago Convention of 1994 means that there is no taxation on aviation fuel. The Commission argues that progress is being made to create a level playing field for all modes of transport with smarter pricing policies (COM, 2009b), of which the most notable is the planned inclusion of aviation in the EU emissions trading scheme (ETS) from 2012 (Article 172(2) of EC Treaty).

Rail meets the full cost of providing the fixed infrastructure (tracks, signalling, terminals) as well as the running costs of the vehicle and, even with government subsidy, can appear comparatively expensive.

Aviation

One area where the EC claims significant success is 'market opening' (COM, 2009b) the competition, generated by new entrants to the market which, it is claimed, improve efficiency and reduce costs and prices. The process is at its most advanced in air transport. The extent of market opening for other transport differs considerably between mode and country.

The creation of a deregulated market for aviation was completed prior to the publication of the 2001 White Paper. Pressure for a deregulated market in Europe came from the very high scheduled air fares and high airline cost structures that were perceived to be a product of a highly regulated market that prevented competition. Most international routes were limited to a maximum of two airlines, charging exactly the same fares and in many cases pooling the combined revenue for the route. The inspiration for an alternative approach emerged from North America, where deregulation of the US domestic market in 1978 appeared to bring about lower airline costs, lower fares and increased passenger numbers.

There were three liberalisation packages commencing from July 1987 with the important third and final package partly implemented from 1 January 1993, with full implementation completed on 1 April 1997. Seventh freedom rights, namely European airlines' ability to fly between other member states without starting or ending at a home airport (for example, a UK airline flying between Paris and Rome), were automatic from 1993. However, the position regarding eighth freedom rights (cabotage) were more complex. Consecutive cabotage, allowing airlines to fly between destinations within another member state, following or preceding a flight from the home country (for example, a UK airline flying London–Rome–Naples) were possible, but still covered by regulations controlling capacity. Complete deregulation of capacity on domestic routes and the introduction of standalone cabotage (for example, a UK airline flying Rome–Naples), were introduced from 1 April 1997. For a fuller review of the provisions of the third package, see French (1992), and Select Committee on EU (2003). For a more detailed review of the freedoms of the air see Page (2005).

The most significant impact of the single deregulated aviation market for Europe over the last 15 years is the emergence and explosive growth of low-cost carriers (LCCs). Table 17.4 shows their growth on routes to and from the UK. Initially copying a business model developed in the US by Southwest Airlines, LCCs such as Ryanair, Easyjet and Air Berlin have became the market leaders for short-haul European services, taking passengers away from both full service airlines and charter airlines, as well as generating additional passengers through some very low fares. Their development and growth was made possible by the third package, and it is noticeable how Ryanair, established in 1985, did not expand from its four traditional routes between the UK and Ireland until 1997. An examination of the current route network of this Eire-registered company demonstrates a large number of routes taking advantage of seventh freedom rights and indeed a small number utilising eighth freedom rights, most notably within the UK (see Ryanair, 2010). Likewise, Easyjet was founded in 1995 and has shown rapid growth since that time.

Table 17.4 UK airport traffic development, 1990–2005

Year	Traditional scheduled passengers (million)	Low-cost scheduled passengers (million)	Charter passengers (million)	Total passengers (million)
1990	78	0	25	103
1995	95	2	33	130
2000	125	17	38	180
2005	117	76	35	229

Source: Dennis (2007)

Charter airlines, for whom all restrictions on the sale of seats have only been removed under the third package, have nevertheless lost significant market share. However, charter airlines have tended to fare better on longer routes of between four and five hours' duration, where their product offering of a greater range of aeroplane types and some frills such as a meals may seem more attractive. An interesting recent development has been the rapid expansion of LCCs into this mid-haul market over the last two years; intense competition can be expected in this market, which is critical for the Charter airlines' longer term survival.

Although there have been isolated attempts to develop long-haul LCCs (Oasis between UK and Hong Kong and Zoom between UK and Canada), the business model has not transferred well to the long-haul market for reasons well explained by Francis *et al.* (2007).

EU–US Open Skies agreement

The full cabotage arrangements have created a single aviation market for Europe. However, the arrangements for flights to and from the EU are still governed by Bilateral Air Service Agreements (ASAs), which derive from the rules laid out in the Chicago Convention of 1944. In 2003 EU members operated some 1500 ASAs; the UK alone had 149 (Select Committee on EU, 2003).

However, the EC is keen to develop more liberalised, if not completely deregulated, markets on long-haul routes to and from the EU. Two separate issues emerge from this aspiration. First is the development of 'Open Skies' agreements, which will differ from more traditional bilateral ASAs in that there are no constraints on capacity or the number of airlines allowed to fly a route and no controls on the fares charged. Indeed, prior to 2008 eight member states had signed 'Open Skies' agreements between their countries and the US.

The second requirement is to replace multiple agreements between EU member states and other countries with a single agreement covering all flights to and from the EU and those countries. Such a development gives exclusive competence to the EC to negotiate these agreements, taking such powers from individual governments.

The EU–US Open Skies agreement was the first such agreement and came into force at the end of March 2008. This replaced the multiple bilateral ASA agreements and the eight Open Skies agreements between EU countries and the US. Prior to the EU–US Open Skies agreement, EU carriers could fly directly to the US only from their own country, whereas US airlines could fly generally from any Open Skies EU country to any US point. This distorted competition on trans-Atlantic routes in favour of US airlines and also limited competition between EU airlines on trans-Atlantic routes.

The EU–US Open Skies agreement is as follows:

- Removed restrictions on route rights so any EU airline can fly from any EU city to any US city.

- Any US airline can fly into any EU airport and from there on to a third destination.
- EU airlines can fly between any US city and any city in a non-EU country which is a member of the European Common Aviation Area (ECAA).
- US airlines can own 49% of the voting rights in European Airlines whereas European Airlines can only hold 25% of the voting rights in US airlines (Pitfield, 2009).

For a more detailed review see the 2009 Special Issue of *The Journal of Air Transport Management* 15.

The current agreement continues to favour US airlines. It allows cabotage for US airlines in the EU whereas European airlines have no access to routes in the US domestic market. The differing regulations over foreign ownership of European and US airlines is also unbalanced, although the second stage of the EU–US Open Skies agreement, signed in June 2010, seeks to address this.

Access of US airlines to European routes is a problem that predates both the EU–US Open Skies agreement and the EU single market. It arises because the US aviation market is a single domestic market, whereas the EU was a multi-state market where individual member states retained the privileges of independent nation states negotiating international bilateral agreements with nation states outside the EU. The granting of fifth freedom rights by European member states on international routes within Europe seemed a good idea, as it increased competition on these routes. However, it effectively granted US airlines access to the European market without gaining any reciprocal access to the US domestic market, and now places the EC in a much weaker negotiating position.

Rail transport

Usage of Europe's railways has grown significantly over the last decade, but not at the same rate as air. However, many sources identify a reversal of the relative decline in the rail share (COM, 2009b; Mintel, 2008) and even talk of a renaissance of rail (Dickinson & Lumsdon, 2010).

A major contributor has been the dramatic growth of high-speed rail lines. The first, the 'Train a Grand Vitesse' (TGV) line between Paris and Lyon, was developed between 1976 and 1981, but investment has increased dramatically in recent years with three new lines opened in 2007. With continuing investment the network is expected to double to 4000 km by 2020 (Mintel, 2008). There is increasing evidence of rail winning larger shares for business travellers on high-speed rail journeys of up to four hours and on leisure journeys of up to six hours. For instance, rail now carries around 71% of London–Paris traffic (Mintel, 2008).

One area where rail operates at a disadvantage over air is the ability to book through tickets on international journeys, particularly online (see

Dickinson *et al.*, 2010 for more detailed examples). Rail operators are beginning to address this and develop integrated systems, although there is much to be done. The establishment of Railteam, an alliance of Europe's seven high-speed rail operators, aims to provide better coordinated services with better connecting services and much better coordinated online ticketing systems.

The EC has attempted market opening in rail (Directives EC 2001/14 and EEC 91/440), although there are substantial variations of interpretation and practice between member states. The underlying concept of separating the ownership of the track and signalling from the ownership of the trains was first tried in the UK from April 1994 (Railways Act of 1993); however, in most countries including the UK there has been little open access to train operators, so although there has been a move towards privatisation and increased private investment, competition between train operators operating on the same route has been rare.

European Transport Policy: The Next 10 Years

A new White Paper setting the agenda for the next 10 years is eagerly awaited and scheduled for publication in 2010, although its content is already clear from recent EC publications and consultation documents (COM, 2009b). 'The environment remains the main policy area where further improvements are necessary' (COM, 2009b: 11) and will be the overriding focus of transport policy for the next 10 years. Figure 17.1 illustrates the problem. Despite the failure of the Copenhagen summit to agree specific multilateral targets for greenhouse gas (GHG) emission reductions, Europe is committed to a 20% reduction in GHG emissions over 1990 levels by 2030 (COM, 2009a), and has proposed reductions of 60–80% by 2050 (COM, 2007). Progress has been made in all sectors between 1990 and 2006, with the exception of transport, where emissions have continued to rise. By 2006 transport accounted for around 23.8% of all GHG emissions in the EU-27 and 27.9% of all CO_2 emissions, and this is set to continue to grow. While technological advances have reduced energy intensity for all modes, thereby reducing the GHG emissions per passenger km, the amount of travel has increased so rapidly as to outweigh any technological gain. However, transport has been identified as playing a key role in achieving future emission reduction targets (COM, 2009b).

Reduced dependency on fossil fuels

The first proposal is for transport to reduce its dependency on fossil fuels. Currently, transport is 97% dependent on fossil fuels (COM, 2009b), whereas the Commission has set a binding target for a 10% share from renewable energy sources. The scope to achieve this will differ for various modes of transport but options include biofuels and electric propulsion.

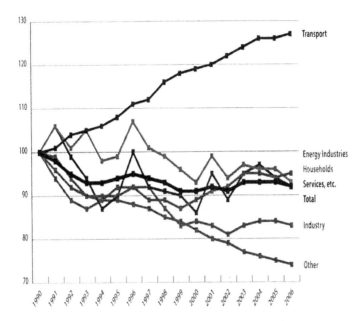

Figure 17.1 GHG emissions in the EU-27, by sector (1990 = 100)
Source: Based on COM (2009a, 2009b)

Electric propulsion

The emissions per passenger km for rail can vary greatly and are dramatically reduced by electric propulsion. However, the source of electricity generation is equally important. In France, emissions are low as 86% of electricity generation is from nuclear power (UIC/CER, 2008) and likewise in Austria (OBB) where 86% of energy comes from hydropower (Dickinson & Lumsdon, 2010). Although there are wide variations between countries, only around 50% of the European network is currently electrified and the capital cost of electrification makes significant increases in this share unlikely in the current economic climate.

There remain significant barriers to the mass adoption of electric cars. There are currently around 1000 electric cars in the UK, although this may significantly increase with the launch of production models by several main manufacturers in 2010. The most significant barrier remains cost, with an estimated price of €40,000 for a car with a 300-km range – around double the cost of a conventional vehicle. The battery alone is more expensive than the rest of the car. These vehicles do have very low operating and maintenance costs (around 25% of a conventional vehicle), making them attractive for high annual mileage fleet cars where the high capital cost can be recouped. However, they are not suited to long journeys, due to their limited range.

A second barrier to their mass adoption is the lack of associated infra-structure, particularly recharging points. Furthermore, there are some technical issues over the length of time recharging will take, with potential fast charging using a D/C power source taking 15–30 minutes.

Although technically feasible, with prototypes demonstrating their viability, production models of hydrogen cars are still some way from commercial product, and are unlikely to make a significant impact prior to 2050 (RAC, 2002). The cost of production of the fuel cells, which uses expensive metals such as mercury, is currently prohibitive.

Biofuels

There has been some progress in the use of biofuels for aviation. Following an inaugural flight by Virgin Atlantic between London (Heathrow) and Amsterdam in February 2008 where one of the four engines was powered by a biofuel manufactured from Brazilian babassu nuts, a number of other experimental flights have been undertaken by Air New Zealand, KLM, Continental and JAL, trialing a range of biofuel sources including algae, babassu, switchgrass and jatropha in combination with regular jet fuel. In June 2010 a demonstration flight by a Diamond Aircraft DA42 New Generation plane was the first to be powered by 100% algae biofuel at the ILA Berlin Air Show. These second-generation biofuels have different properties from first-generation biofuels, most notably that they do not freeze at low temperatures, an important consideration for aviation fuel (BBC, 2008).

A more critical evaluation of biofuels has highlighted concern over the land take required for their growth, either taking agricultural land away from food production, or accelerating the rate of global deforestation as has been the case of palm olive production in the Amazon Basin. Second-generation biofuels have a significantly lower land take, with algae being the most efficient of all the options. Nevertheless, it is unrealistic for biofuel production to be able to service the full fuel requirement of aviation, or indeed more than a relatively small share; for this reason most commercial airlines have opted to develop systems combining biofuels with regular jet fuel. Biofuels are yet to be certified for use on commercial flights, although KLM have expressed a desire to introduce biofuels for commercial flights in 2011 (Reuters, 2010).

Biofuels have been available for road transport for many years, but again questions have been raised, particularly for the commercial operation of bus and coach fleets. The recycling of waste products such as used cooking oil is clearly desirable, but this is a minor source. Much of the mass-produced bio diesel is from first-generation biofuels, with potential adverse effects on agriculture production. Increasingly, bus operators are arguing that the use of biofuels needs much greater technical evaluation, with anecdotal evidence growing that their use is associated with rising maintenance costs, reduced vehicle reliability and increased problems of freezing fuel tanks in winter conditions.

Vehicle efficiency

The second approach is to reduce emissions by technological advances to traditional methods of propulsion. Airline emissions per passenger km have more than halved over the last 40 years, with the Airbus A380 achieving around 75 g per passenger km as a result of economies of scale. Continued improvements are expected with Boeings new 787 (Dreamliner) set to reduce fuel consumption and CO_2 emissions by 20% over existing planes, due to the lightweight construction using carbon fibre technology.

Car engine technology is improving fuel consumption by between 1% and 1.5% per annum, resulting in similar reductions in emissions (RAC, 2002). The EC policy of stricter emission controls over the past 10 years may have accelerated this trend. The average emissions of a European car are around 200 g per vehicle km, although the newest small models can be as low as 100 g per vehicle km. A 1998 voluntary agreement between the EC and car manufacturers stating average emissions for new vehicles should not exceed 140 g per km by 2008–2009 was superseded by a statutory target of 130 g per km by 2012 (Regulation EC No 443/2009).

The benefits of lower emissions for new cars take time to be fully effective, as older vehicles are replaced, sometimes by newer second-hand vehicles. Recent scrappage schemes for cars over 10 years old, operated in both Germany and the UK, primarily for economic rather than environmental reasons, may have marginally accelerated the replacement of inefficient older vehicles.

Levels of transport demand

The third approach is to tackle levels of transport demand. Here lies the greatest threat for a growing and economically prosperous tourism industry. An aim of the 2001 White Paper was to 'decouple transport growth from GDP growth' (COM, 2009b: 11) and some degree of success has been claimed for passenger transport. Passenger transport growth averaged 1.7% per annum between 1995 and 2007, whereas GDP grew at 2.5% per annum. Reduced travel can be achieved through a number of means, such as reducing the need for business travel through video conferencing, or reducing commute journeys with more home working. Such approaches can represent increased efficiency, and a reduction of transport CO_2 emissions, with no associated reduction in economic activity, but leisure and tourism trips are different. Reduced demand for travel may shrink this sector. While some efficiencies can be achieved by holidaying closer to home, or by travelling less often but staying longer, by and large reduced demand for tourism travel will result in fewer tourists, fewer visitor nights (indeed current trends are for an increase in the number of short breaks and a falling average length of stay) and lower visitor spend. Furthermore, destinations which are 'long haul' from the main tourism-generating countries will be disproportionately affected, including developing countries heavily dependent on tourism.

Interestingly, it has proved much more difficult to decouple the demand for freight transport (average growth of 2.7% per annum) from GDP growth. There is insufficient space to include a wide-ranging discussion on the impact of tourism on freight transport here; nevertheless, mass tourist destinations, with inflated temporary populations during the peak season, will require additional logistics and distribution resources to deliver food and essential services. A reduced tourism industry will create reduced GDP and reduced demand for logistic services.

Modal shift

The final approach is to achieve modal shift, predominantly away from air and car to more sustainable modes of public transport. Table 17.5 shows the relative CO_2 emissions for different modes of transport, although these are averages and will vary with vehicle occupancy.

Further trends for 2010–2020

As outlined in the introduction, tourism accounts for a minority of transport activity. Other trends which DG TREN has identified that it must take into account (COM, 2009b) when devising transport policies for the next 10 years are:

- an ageing population;
- net migration to the EU and increased internal migration within the EU;

Table 17.5 Mode-specific CO_2 emission factors for transport

Mode	Emission factor (kg/passenger km)*
Air	
<500 km	0.183
500–1000 km	0.134
1000–1500 km	0.130
1500–2000 km	0.121
>2000 km	0.111
Car	0.121
	(0.180 v/km)
Rail	0.033
Coach	0.027
Ferry	0.066

*An average based on various sources (Eurostar, 2008; Friends of the Earth, 2010; National Express, 2008; Peeters et al., 2007)

- increasing scarcity of fossil fuels;
- increased urbanisation;
- global trends such as geopolitical instability and strong economic growth in some developing countries.

Conclusions

European Transport policy over the last 10 years has seen a focus on deregulation, increased competition and open markets. The modes of transport that have thrived are air, where competitive pressures have led to much reduced fares and passenger growth, and the car, particularly for domestic transport. Despite significant levels of investment in new high-speed links, rail has not won significant market share increase, although this may be changing.

A second objective of the 2001 White Paper was to internalise the cost of transport externalities, broadly based on a principle that the polluter pays. In practice this has been unsuccessful, with air and car being undertaxed, resulting in low prices contributing to their high market share and rapid growth. Rail, on the other hand, meets the full cost of providing the fixed infrastructure (tracks, signalling, terminals) as well as the running costs of the vehicle and, even with government subsidy, can appear comparatively expensive. The EC argues that progress is being made to create a level playing field for all modes of transport with smarter pricing policies (COM, 2009b) and air fares are likely to rise following the planned inclusion of aviation in the EU ETS from 2012. Likewise, road freight vehicles will pay more. However, strategies to have differential pricing for car users using different types of roads at different times of day or in different types of area (comprehensive electronic road pricing), although considered in both the UK and the Netherlands, are 20 years or more away from implementation, if ever.

The overriding European transport policy objective of the next White Paper will be to develop sustainable transport policies, with a key objective of reducing CO_2 emissions.

References

BBC (2008) Airline in first biofuel flight. BBC News, 24 February 2008, accessed 27 October 2010. http://news.bbc.co.uk/1/hi/7261214.stm.

COM (2001) *European Transport Policy for 2010: Time to Decide.* White Paper, Cmnd 370. Luxembourg: European Commission.

COM (2006) *Transport White Paper Mid-term Review.* Cmnd 314. Luxembourg: European Commission.

COM (2007) *Limiting Global Climate Change to 2 Degrees Celcius. The Way Ahead for 2020 and Beyond.* Cmnd 354. Luxembourg: European Commission.

COM (2009a) *Adapting to Climate Change: Towards a European Framework for Action.* White Paper, Cmnd 147. Luxembourg: European Commission.

COM (2009b) *A Sustainable Future for Transport – Towards an Integrated, Technology-led and User-friendly System.* Luxembourg: European Commission.

Concertour (2008) Available at http://concertourproject.eu/.

Dennis, N. (2007) We're all going on a summer holiday! Impact of the low-cost scheduled airlines on charter operations and the inclusive tour holiday market. European Transport Conference, Leiden, Netherlands, October.

Dickinson, J. and Lumsdon, L. (2010) *Slow Travel and Tourism.* London: Earthscan.

Dickinson, J.E., Robbins, D. and Lumsdon, L. (2010) Holiday travel discourses and climate change. *Journal of Transport Geography* 18 (3), 482–489.

Eurostar (2008) *Greener Than Flying.* Eurostar website, accessed 19 June 2008. http://www.eurostar.com/UK/uk/leisure/about_eurostar/environment/greener_than_flying.jsp.

Eurostat (2010) *Tourism Statistics in the European Statistical System.* Luxemberg: European Commission.

Francis, G., Dennis, N., Ison, S. and Humphries, I. (2007) The transferability of the low cost model to long-haul airline operations. *Tourism Management* 28 (2), 391–398.

French, T. (1992) The European Commission's Third Air Transport Liberalisation Package. *Travel & Tourism Analyst* 5, 5–22.

Friends of the Earth (2010) *Aviation and Global Climate Change.* Friends of the Earth website document, accessed 24 July 2010. http://www.foe.co.uk/resource/reports/aviation_climate_change.pdf.

Mintel (2008) *Rail Travel – Europe.* London: Mintel.

National Express (2008) Carbon emissions calculator. National Express website, accessed 14 February 2010. http://www.nationalexpress.com/coach/OurService/CarbonEmissionsCalculator.cfm.

Page, S. (2005) *Transport and Tourism* (2nd edn). Harlow: Pearson.

Peeters, P., Szimba, E. and Duijnisveld, M. (2007) European tourism: Transport and the main environmental impacts. *Journal of Transport Geography* 15 (2), pp 83–93.

Pitfield, D.E. (2009) The assessment of the EU–US Open Skies Agreement: The counterfactual and other difficulties. *Journal of Air Transport Management* 15, 308–314.

RAC (2002) *Motoring Towards 2050.* London: RAC Foundation.

Reuters (2010) KLM want to offer biofuel flights from 2011. Reuters News item, 18 March 2010, accessed 27 October 2010. http://www.reuters.com/article/idUSLDE62H28E20100318.

Robbins, D.K. and Dickinson, J.E. (2007) Can domestic tourism growth and reduced car dependency be achieved simultaneously in the UK? In P. Peeters (ed.) *Tourism and Climate Change and Mitigation: Methods, Greenhouse Gas Reductions and Policies.* Breda: NHTV.

Ryanair (2010) Route map. Ryanair website, accessed 27 October 2010. http://www.ryanair.com/en/cheap-flight-destinations.

Select Committee on EU (2003) *Open Skies or Open Markets.* Seventeenth Report of the House of Lords, accessed 27 October 2010. http://www.publications.parliament.uk/pa/ld200203/ldselect/ldeucom/92/9203.htm.

UIC/CER (2008) *Rail Transport and the Environment: Facts and Figures.* International Union of Railways and Community of European Railway and Infrastructure Companies, accessed 27 October 2010. http://www.uic.org/homepage/railways&environment_facts&figures.pdf.

Part 5

Methods and Techniques

18 Strategies for Positioning Tourism Destinations: Trend Analysis

Maria João Carneiro, Carlos Costa and John Crompton

Introduction

Marketing is a powerful tool in destination competitiveness, namely through product development, packaging and innovation (Ritchie & Crouch, 2003). The image that potential visitors hold of tourism destinations became an important field of research in tourism (e.g. Echtner & Ritchie, 1993; Gallarza *et al.*, 2002; Gartner, 1993; Pike, 2002). Assessing destinations' image is very important for designing tourism strategies, given the potential impact that image may have in the satisfaction and consequent loyalty of visitors to destinations. When choosing destinations to visit, potential visitors often compare the images they have of several tourism destinations in order to select the destination(s) that best fit their requirements. The majority of the research on destination image (e.g. Crompton, 1979; Echtner & Ritchie, 1993) only focuses on assessing the image of one destination, and makes it impossible to understand how potential visitors compare and select tourism destinations. In order to overcome this problem, research on the positioning of tourism destinations has increased in the last decades (e.g. Bartikowski *et al.*, 2009; Pike & Ryan, 2004).

However, continuous changes, namely concerning the increasing competition among tourism destinations, the growing difficulty of differentiating tourism destination and the increasing requirements of potential visitors (Ritchie & Crouch, 2003) have created new challenges for tourism destinations' competitive positioning. The majority of previous papers on destinations' positioning focus on the discussion of the positioning concept, on the process for elaborating positioning strategies (e.g. Aaker & Myers, 1987;

Kotler, 1997; Moutinho, 1995) or on the analysis of the positioning of specific tourism destinations (e.g. Bartikowski *et al.*, 2009; Pike & Ryan, 2004). This chapter aims to identify trends in strategies for positioning destinations, namely concerning the bases used for achieving competitive positions and the type of cooperation developed among destinations to achieve those positions. A literature review on marketing, especially on the promotion and positioning of tourism destinations, has been undertaken to accomplish these objectives. This work has been complemented with the consultation of websites designed to promote tourism destinations.

The Concept of Positioning

According to Embacher and Buttle (1989), a destination's image is the group of conceptions and ideas that people, individually or collectively, have of the destination. Similarly, Crompton (1979: 18) argues that the image a person has of a tourism destination corresponds to a 'sum of beliefs, ideas, and impressions that a person holds of a destination'. Evaluating a destination's image is highly important and may provide directions to an efficient management of that destination. However, potential visitors hold several destinations' images in their minds and their decisions are frequently based on the comparison of images of several destinations. Assessing the image of only one destination is, thus, rather limited, not allowing a full understanding of how these comparisons are made.

Positioning analyses overcome this limitation by enabling an assessment of the images of several destinations and an understanding of how these destinations compare with one another, according to the perspective of potential consumers (Aaker & Myers, 1987). According to Ries and Trout (1986: 2), positioning is a communication approach 'for the purpose of securing a worthwhile position in the prospects' minds'. Moutinho (1995: 325) states that positioning is 'the act of formulating a competitive position for the product', but argues that this may be achieved by designing a detailed marketing mix to the product. Kotler (1997: 295) corroborates this idea by defining positioning as 'the act of designing the company's offerings and image so that they occupy a meaningful and distinctive competitive position in the target customers' minds'. According to Kotler (1997: 294–295), the objective of positioning a product in the consumers' minds is to ensure that potential consumers consider this product as being distinctive and superior to the competitors' products in something they value. Taking into consideration the perspectives of Moutinho (1995) and Kotler (1997), a competitive position – the aim of positioning – can be achieved by designing an appropriate offering, that is, an appropriate marketing mix to the product, with all the elements of this mix being important determinants of the position to reach in customers' minds.

As suggested by Aaker and Myers (1987), reaching a competitive position in customers' minds requires, among other features, the identification of the following: competitors of the products; features that potential customers use to evaluate the product; the importance customers assign to the several features; and consumers' perspective on the performance of the product and of respective competitors in the several features referred to above. Other authors (e.g. Urban & Star, 1991) have referred to the importance of monitoring the position in customers' minds, in order to ensure the maintenance of a competitive position in their minds.

According to Ennis (1982), one of the most important things for reaching a competitive position is to choose an appropriate selling proposition, which requires choosing the best-selling idea for promoting the brand in the target market. This requires identifying the most suitable associations to establish with the product. In the scope of positioning, Ennis (1982) suggests that selling ideas must be created by establishing an association between the product and one of the following: specific attributes where the product has a good performance, potential benefits the product may provide, or both. Authors such as Wind (1982) and Aaker and Myers (1987) corroborate this perspective, highlighting the importance of product attributes and benefits as potential bases for product positioning. However, Wind (1982) and Aaker and Myers (1987) also point to other options of bases of positioning available, such as associating the product with a specific use, specific users, or even a combination of several positioning bases.

In tourism, the requirements for a destination to reach a competitive position in the potential visitors' minds may change over time, partially due to changes in the competing environment, namely growing competition and new competition rules that result from processes such as globalisation. Modifications in consumers' needs and requirements, resulting from trends such as higher travel experience and desire to have a deeper experience of the destination, also put challenges into the definition of the most appropriate positioning, frequently requiring new positioning strategies. Challenges for positioning tourism destinations and trends observed in the positioning of destinations are presented and discussed in the next section.

Trends on Destinations' Positioning

Tourism destinations are physical spaces in which visitors undertake leisure and business activities away from home. Despite tourism destinations having physical and administrative boundaries, their competitiveness is defined by the images and perceptions people hold of them. As remarked by several authors and organisations (e.g. Leiper, 1993; WTO, 2004), destinations are complex amalgams of different tourism businesses. These places sometimes encompass a wide variety of tourism attractions and supporting

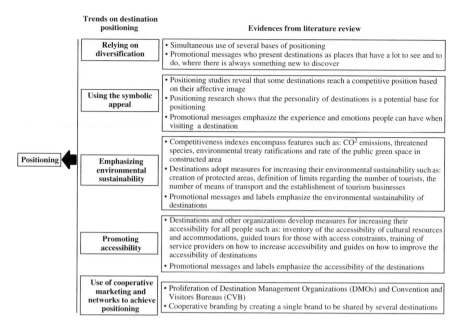

Figure 18.1 Trends on destination positioning

services and experiences, delivered and managed by several stakeholders, from municipal authorities, hotel managers and tourism attractions' managers to host communities. This situation raises several problems in achieving a competitive position, as a consequence of the disaggregation of the tourism sector and inherent difficulties in the coordination and creation of a coherent image of the destination. However, these circumstances, namely the diversity of tourism attractions, may also provide the opportunity to develop different positioning strategies. Flexibility is required so that destinations, over time, adapt to the threats and opportunities they face. The following sections reveal some trends observed in recent years in the positioning of tourism destinations, also summarised in Figure 18.1.

Relying on diversification

The advantages and disadvantages of using a unique or several selling propositions to position products have been discussed over the past decades. Promoting a tourism product based on several features (e.g. several characteristics of the product) may facilitate competing in the market, given that potential consumers may easily recognise more advantages in buying the product. However, this strategy may also lead to the creation of a confused idea about the product in customers' minds and to distrust, leading consumers to suspect that the product cannot have so many advantages (Kotler, 1997).

Frequently it is very difficult to identify a single characteristic where a tourism destination presents a better performance than the competing destinations and which enables the customer to differentiate it. This situation has probably contributed very often to the simultaneous use of several bases of positioning in the case of destinations. Miller and Henthorne (2006) analysed the slogans of Caribbean destinations presented on their official tourism promotion websites. Only a small percentage (12%) of the destinations used a unique selling proposition (USP) approach. This was, for example, the case of Dominica, which adopted the slogan 'The nature island of the Caribbean' (Miller & Henthorne, 2006: 55), and of the US Virgin Islands, with the slogan 'America's Caribbean' (Miller & Henthorne, 2006: 55).

Therkelsen and Gram (2010), in their analysis of the Visiteurope website, also highlight the difficulty of finding unique elements to promote Europe. They state that the promotional strategy underlying the website emphasises several features that are common to several European regions – history, culture and nature – and the diversity of features that can be found in all the European territory. Some slogans used for promoting Europe such as 'Europe: a never-ending journey' (ETC, 2011) also intend to create an image of these territories as places that have a lot to see and to do, where there is always something new to discover. The brand 'Allgarve', used in several promotional messages in order to promote the Algarve (located in the south of Portugal) (Algarve Tourism Board, 2011), is a good example of a communication strategy designed to evoke the idea of a wide range of attractions and opportunities in the Algarve. This brand strategy aims to point out that Algarve is not only characterised by good 'sun and beach', but encompasses a wide range of other tourism attractions. Previous examples highlight a trend for positioning destinations based on diverse features of tourism destinations over adopting USP approaches. The diversified range of resources of tourism destinations has proved to be a frequently adopted basis of positioning.

Using the symbolic appeal

As Echtner and Ritchie (1991) advocate in their seminal work, the image people hold of tourism destinations encompasses both functional and psychological features. Whereas the functional images are characterised by measurable or physical features, psychological images correspond to impressions or feelings. Taking into consideration the difficulty of differentiating functional and psychological attributes, these authors proposed a continuum that goes from the more functional attributes (e.g. natural attractions, price levels) to the more psychological ones (e.g. quality of service, fame/reputation). Gartner (1993) also remarks that a destination image is composed of three components: (i) the cognitive image, largely corresponding to beliefs about the destination; (ii) the affective image, associated with the motives for choosing the destination; and (iii) the conative image, regarding behaviours in relation to the destination.

As Echtner and Ritchie (1991) remark, earlier works on the image of tourism destinations focused almost exclusively on functional attributes. The first research on the positioning of tourism destinations (e.g. Hu & Ritchie, 1993) was also confined, almost exclusively, to the assessment of the cognitive image of the competing destinations. Probably due to recognising that destinations are having more difficulties in achieving competitive positions only based on functional attributes, in positioning studies across the years, researchers (e.g. Balogu & Mangaloglu, 2001; Pike & Ryan, 2004) have increasingly tried to compare destinations both on their cognitive and affective dimensions.

When evaluating the affective image, the main focus has been to assess whether the destination is pleasant, arousing, exciting and/or relaxing. In the study of Baloglu and Mangaloglu (2001), the relaxing dimension of the tourism destinations is revealed to be extremely efficient in differentiating two Mediterranean countries – Italy and Greece – from two other Mediterranean countries – Turkey and Egypt. While (in the opinion of US-based tour operators and travel agents) the former countries are more relaxing, the latter are more distressing. In a study of five domestic holiday areas on New Zealand's North Island among Auckland's residents, Bay of Islands is considered more pleasant and exciting, whereas in contrast Mt. Maunganui seems to be more unpleasant and boring (Pike & Ryan, 2004).

Certain researchers (e.g. Bartikowski *et al.*, 2009) opt for assessing the positioning of the destinations based on their personality. Bartikowski *et al.* (2009) assessed the personality of several cities. In that study, Barcelona, London, New York and Sidney emerged as sophisticated, exciting and sincere destinations.

In the orientation to a more symbolic appeal, it may also be noticed that there is a growing trend towards promoting tourism destinations based on the experience visitors may have at the destination. Hudson and Ritchie (2009), referring to Canada, provide an interesting explanation of the need to rethink the promotional strategy for promoting Canada in this perspective. The previous strategy to promote Canada was found to be too narrow and focused on a limited number of elements – nature and geographical assets, safety, cleanliness and beauty – not powerful enough to motivate the visit of a lot of visitors. The need to put the emphasis on the experience visitors may have on visiting Canada led to the adoption of the slogan: 'Canada: keep exploring'. Some promotional messages are even clearer about the experience people may get when visiting a certain territory. For example, Visitwales (Welsh Assembly, 2011), promotes South Wales Valleys as a place where people can have an experience marked by warm welcomes, magic, male voice choirs, stunning scenery and energy.

Emphasising environmental sustainability

As the World Commission on Environment and Development (WCED, 1987) states, 'sustainable development is development that meets the needs of the present without compromising the ability of future generations to meet their own needs'. The threats posed by the uncontrolled development of some tourism regions, the increasing requirements of potential visitors on quality and environmental preservation and the threat posed to tourism resources due to the growing competition among tourism destinations give rise to a high concern about ensuring the environmental sustainable development of destinations. Zhang *et al.* (2011) argue that some early competitiveness models ignore some sustainability dimensions such as those related to environmental quality. However, this situation is changing, and environmental sustainability is gaining importance in tourism destination competitiveness.

The World Travel and Tourism Council (WTTC) considered, among several indices for assessing countries' competitiveness, an environmental index which includes CO_2 emissions, ratification of environmental treaties and other features on environmental development (Gursoy *et al.*, 2009). This index, in conjunction with a social development index (which encompasses the number of television sets, personal computers and daily newspapers, among other indicators) was important to distinguish a group of countries – Jordan, Egypt, Yemen, Morocco and Saudi Arabia – from another group of countries – Bahrain, Kuwait, Israel, Lebanon and United Arab Emirates. While the former group of countries performs well on environmental features, the latter has a good social development index score. However, no countries had good performance in both indices. Nowadays, the World Economic Forum (WEF, 2009) also assesses countries' competitiveness on travel and tourism through an index that encompasses an environmental sustainability dimension. The environmental dimension is very similar to that of the WTTC and encompasses features such as CO_2 emissions, threatened species and environmental treaty ratifications. The tourism destination competitiveness framework proposed by Zhang *et al.* (2011), used for assessing the competitiveness of 16 cities of the Yangtze River Delta, also incorporates aspects regarding socio-economic development (e.g. paved road area per capita, possession of public vehicles per 10,000 persons) and environment quality and preservation (e.g. rate of consumption of treated waste water, amount of public green space in constructed areas).

It may also be observed that, in the promotion of several destinations, there is already a high emphasis on their environmentally sustainable development. On the webpage of the International Ecotourism Society (TIES, 2011) it is possible to find a list of places that are considered 'ecodestinations', which include geographical areas of several countries from Costa Rica and

Brazil to African countries. As previously stated, as remarked by Miller and Henthorne (2006: 55), Dominica promotes itself as 'The nature island of the Caribbean'. On the official site of Costa Rica (Instituto Costarricense de Turismo, 2011), one of the main menus is called 'sustainability in Costa Rica' and gives access to information about certification for sustainable tourism including, for example, tourism accommodation that holds this kind of certification.

Fernando Noronha in Brazil is one of the tourism destinations that has been trying to achieve a competitive position through sustainable environment strategies. Government contributions to ensure the sustainable development in this destination include (de Oliveira, 2003): creation of protected areas, definition of limits regarding the number of tourists and the number of flights to the territory, and also restrictions on the establishment of tourism businesses in the region.

Promoting accessibility

The Global Code of Ethics defined by the World Tourism Organization (WTO, 1999) suggests, in Article 7, that all people should have a right to tourism and an equal right to enjoy the resources in their own country and foreign countries. The European Economic and Social Committee (EESC, 2006) also reinforces the importance of social tourism, whose aim is to promote the right to tourism for people who have partial or total inability to exercise that right due to some condition (e.g. financial constraints, reduced mobility, physical or mental disability). Darcy et al. (2010) argue that the percentage of disabled people is increasing but also remark that, worldwide, proactive actions have already been developed to cope with this challenge, namely, to develop more accessible infrastructure. In Europe, research has been developed in order to create an e-tourism platform for accessible tourism in Europe (Michopoulou et al., 2007).

There has also been an effort to increase the accessibility of several destinations to disabled people. Darcy and Dickson (2009) documented several initiatives to promote accessible tourism in Australia. These initiatives included not only the development of specific tours for people with access constraints, but also action to improve the accessibility of tourism providers' supplies. These actions include the development of toolkits for tourism service suppliers designed to improve their accessibility and specific training to these suppliers.

Lousã, a destination located in the mountain area of Serra da Lousã, has also been developing a plan in order to be considered an accessible tourism destination. This plan, supported by national and EU funds, involves, for example, the creation of a label used by the companies that compromise themselves in order to perform concrete actions to increase their accessibility to disabled people (ENAT, 2010).

Seniors are also one of the segments that experience more constraints in their participation in tourism. Aware of the need to increase the seniors' accessibility, the World Health Organization has published a guide with guidelines on how to improve seniors' accessibility to cities (WHO, 2007). This guide identifies the characteristics of an ideal city for seniors, the features that should be changed to increase this accessibility and, additionally, the positive impacts of these changes to seniors.

Use of cooperative marketing and networks to achieve positioning

The tourism industry is highly fragmented, being controlled by a high number of diversified tourism suppliers. Consequently, in a destination, as D'Angella and Go (2009) argue, tourism suppliers face many difficulties, namely a lack of financial resources for promotion and the complexity of providing an experience of the destination as a whole. In this context, co-operative marketing at the destination level, involving the several tourism suppliers of the destination, becomes crucial, so that tourism destinations achieve a competitive positioning. Destination management organisations (DMOs) help to overcome some problems of tourism suppliers at the destination level, due to their significant role as coordinators of tourism suppliers of the destination and as marketers of the whole destination (Dwyer & Kim, 2003). Hence, DMOs assume a crucial role in the positioning of destinations by acting as facilitators, promoting cooperation and directing the tourism development process at a destination.

More specialised organisations, such as convention and visitors bureaus (CVB), have also been proliferating worldwide, contributing to this co-ordinated promotion at the destination level. In an effort to identify the roles of a CVB, Wang (2008) suggests that some of its major functions are to develop an attractive image of its region as a destination for meetings, to manage the destination, taking into consideration the needs of both visitors and tourism meetings' suppliers, to represent the interests of meetings' suppliers of the region, and to position the region as an attractive tourism destination for meetings. This reinforces the significant role that CVB may have in cooperative marketing at the destination level for effectively positioning the destinations as convention destinations.

Cooperative marketing is also visible in the effort to promote Europe through the Visiteurope destination portal, described by Therkelsen and Gram (2010). The aim of the EU, while developing this initiative, is to create both a supranational European brand and a communication tool, in order to enhance and energise national brands and to position Europe more efficiently in the marketplace. On the website, Europe's diversity is illustrated by constantly changing photos in specific parts of the site. A great effort was also undertaken to identify elements that may characterise Europe as a tourism destination: (i) functional characteristics (e.g. beaches, mountains, museums, monuments); (ii) psychological characteristics (e.g. welcoming atmosphere); and (iii) elements of uniqueness (e.g. traditions for fine cuisine and wine). The creation of a supranational brand is also observed in the process analysed by Lemmetyinen and Go (2010), of creating a cruise passing through 10 countries of the Baltic area. Meetings for sharing experiences about cruising activities and for coordination, together with the creation of the brand 'Baltic cruise' and a logo with 10 pearls representing the 10 countries involved, were just some of the actions required to develop this initiative.

Trends and Challenges

The development trends observed both in the market and supply sides of the tourism industry, as well as the evolution of the socio-economic and environmental domains where tourism operates are making the competitive positioning of destinations increasingly difficult and challenging. The growing diversity of tourism supplies all over the world and the higher requirements of the tourism market will force the development of positioning strategies based on synergy and complementarity. Identifying complementary tourism products (e.g. specific cultural and rural tourism products) that may be developed in the same tourism area or in neighbouring areas becomes essential for increasing the attraction power of the territories. Complementarities and synergies should be found, not only inside the tourism industry, but also by searching partners outside it, as in the case of industrial tourism, with excellent examples in Wales. Creating synergies should also 'cross' the usual geographic areas of cooperation (Therkelsen & Gram, 2010). In a EU whose geographical limits are changing due to the inclusion of new countries, those responsible for tourism development will have to learn how to cooperate with other countries, including emergent countries. Identifying new synergies and ways of cooperating in tourism products' development in the future will largely rely on immaterial imagery and on the supply of tourism experiences with attractive sets of positive emotions.

The growing and fierce competition among tourism destinations also demands more proactive and efficient modes of operation in the tourism sector. The creation of CVBs and DMOs (Dwyer & Kim, 2003; Wang, 2008) highlights the need to develop new, specialised and proactive structures in tourism promotion, to assist those involved in the tourism industry.

Finally, another high challenge is the 'development with conservation'. Climate change, lack of planning in development and several other reasons are threatening these natural resources. The high dependence of the tourism industry on natural resources, both as tourism attractions (e.g. big mountains and lakes in central Europe), and on other scopes (e.g. tourism transportation; Gursoy et al., 2009), demands the identification of strategies (e.g. the use of renewable energy sources, reducing consumption of certain resources) to enable the preservation of resources along with tourism development.

Conclusions and Implications

Being aware of the changes occurring in the tourism industry worldwide is a critical factor for initiating an efficient positioning process of tourism destinations. However, identifying how tourism destinations may profit from opportunities and minimise the threats they face is also a big challenge in this process. Being aware of the strategies that can lead to efficient positioning and which may help destinations to achieve a distinctive and superior position in relation to competitors in the eyes of prospective consumers is of crucial importance in the present competitive environment.

Usually, the positioning of destinations has been based on the diverse set of destinations' resources rather than on a single characteristic of the destination. This results from the high difficulty of finding a characteristic of a destination where the destination differentiates from competitors and presents a comparatively better performance. This does not mean, however, that destinations should not position themselves based on only one single feature. This strategy may be used where possible. Nevertheless, the challenge for most destinations is to identify a diversified set of resources that may be used to achieve a competitive position.

This chapter shows that, across the years, in the positioning of destinations there was a clear shift from more cognitive promotional messages towards more affective ones. Higher reliance on psychological features rather than exclusively focusing on functional attributes is a major trend in destinations' promotion. Broadening the promotional content and stimuli used to attract potential visitors to tourism destinations seems unavoidable. When promoting destinations, marketers do not rely only on the functional attributes of destinations, but should rather emphasise the experience and emotions people can have when visiting.

The scarcity of some natural resources and the requirements of potential visitors for environmental conservation lead to a real challenge for destination managers in order to position destinations as environmentally sustainable places. Minimising CO_2 emissions, protecting threatened species, environmental treaty ratifications, and limiting the number of visitors and of means of transportation in the destination, are just some of the potential measures to achieve a more environmental sustainable position.

Making the destination more accessible to all, namely through the inventory of accessible resources, specific guided tours for the disabled and the training of service providers, is also a visible trend among tourism destinations. Finally, the development of positioning strategies through cooperative marketing is advised. As observed throughout this chapter, many destinations develop positioning strategies conjointly with other destinations, profiting from a critical mass of financial and tourism resources that facilitates the achievement of a competitive positioning. Diverse resources, symbolic appeal, environmental sustainability, accessibility to all and cooperative marketing correspond to important elements in current positioning strategies.

References

Aaker, D.A. and Myers, J.G. (1987) *Advertising Management* (3rd edn). Englewood Cliffs, NJ: Prentice-Hall.

Algarve Tourism Board (2011) Visit Algarve website, accessed 2011. http://www.visitalgarve.pt/.

Baloglu, S. and Mangaloglu, M. (2001) Tourism destination images of Turkey, Egypt, Greece, and Italy as perceived by US-based tour operators and travel agents. *Tourism Management* 22 (1), 1–9.

Bartikowski, B., Merunka, D., Ouattara, A. and Valette-Florence, P. (2009) Les villes ont-elles une personnalité? *Marketing Touristique* 197, 49–64.

Crompton, J.L. (1979) An assessment of the image of Mexico as a vacation destination and the influence of geographical location upon that image. *Journal of Travel Research* 18 (4), 18–23.

D'Angella, F. and Go, F.M. (2009) Tale of two cities' collaborative tourism marketing: Towards a theory of destination stakeholder assessment. *Tourism Management* 30, 429–440.

Darcy, S. and Dickson, T.J. (2009) A whole-of-life approach to tourism: The case for accessible tourism experiences. *Journal of Hospitality and Tourism Management* 16, 32–44.

Darcy, S., Cameron, B. and Pegg, S. (2010) Accessible tourism and sustainability: A discussion and case study. *Journal of Sustainable Tourism* 18 (4), 515–537.

de Oliveira, J.A. (2003) Governmental responses to tourism development: Three Brazilian case studies. *Tourism Management* 24, 97–110.

Dwyer, L. and Kim, C. (2003) Destination competitiveness: Determinants and indicators. *Current Issues in Tourism* 6 (5), 369–414.

Echtner, C.M. and Ritchie, J.R.B. (1991) The meaning and measurement of destination image. *Journal of Tourism Studies* 2 (2), 2–12.

Echtner, C.M. and Ritchie, J.R.B. (1993) The measurement of destination image: An empirical assessment. *Journal of Travel Research* 31 (4), 3–13.

EESC (2006) *Opinion of the European Economic and Social Committee on Social Tourism in Europe*. Brussels: European Economic and Social Committee.

Embacher, J. and Buttle, F. (1989) A repertory grid analysis of Austria's image as a summer vacation destination. *Journal of Travel Research* 27 (3), 3–7.

ENAT (2010) *Projects and Good Practices*. European Network for Accessible Tourism, accessed 2011. http://www.accessibletourism.org/?i=enat.en.enat_projects_and_good_practices.

Ennis, F.B. (1982) Positioning. *Advertising Age* 53 (11), 43–46.

ETC (2011) European Travel Commission website, accessed in 2011. http://www.visiteurope.com/home.aspx.

Gallarza, M.G., Saura, I.G. and García, H.C. (2002) Destination image – towards a conceptual framework. *Annals of Tourism Research* 29 (1), 56–78.

Gartner, W.C. (1993) Image formation process. In M. Uysal and D.R. Fesenmaier (eds) *Communication and Channel Systems in Tourism Marketing* (pp. 191–215). New York: Haworth Press.

Gursoy, D., Baloglu, S. and Chi, C.G. (2009) Destination competitiveness of Middle Eastern countries: An examination of relative positioning. *Anatolia* 20 (1), 151–163.

Hu, Y. and Ritchie, J.R.B. (1993) Measuring destination attractiveness: A contextual approach, *Journal of Travel Research* 32 (2), 25–34.

Hudson, S. and Ritchie, J.R.B. (2009) Branding a memorable destination experience. The case of 'brand Canada'. *International Journal of Tourism Research* 11, 217–228.

Instituto Costarricense de Turismo (2011) Official website of Costa Rica, accessed 2011. http://www.visitcostarica.com/.

Kotler, P. (1997) *Marketing Management – Analysis, Planning, Implementation, and Control* (9th edn). Englewood Cliffs, NJ: Prentice Hall.

Leiper, N. (1993) Defining tourism and related concepts: Tourist, market, industry, and tourism system. In M.A. Khan, M.D. Olsen and T. Var (eds) *VNR's Encyclopedia of Hospitality and Tourism* (pp. 539–558). New York: Van Nostrand Reinhold.

Lemmetyinen, A. and Go, F.M. (2010) Building a brand identity in a network of Cruise Baltic's destinations: A multi-authoring approach. *Brand Management* 17 (7), 519–531.

Michopoulou, E., Buhalis, D., Michailidis, S. and Ambrose, I. (2007) Destination management systems: Technical challenges in developing an etourism platform for accessible tourism in Europe. *Information and Communication Technologies in Tourism* 7, 301–310.

Miller, M.M. and Henthorne, T.L. (2006) In search of competitive advantage in Caribbean tourism websites: Revisiting the unique selling proposition. *Journal of Travel & Tourism Marketing* 21 (2/3), 49–62.

Moutinho, L. (1995) Positioning strategies. In S.F. Witt and L. Moutinho (eds) *Tourism Marketing and Management Handbook – Student Edition* (pp. 325–333). London: Prentice-Hall.

Pike, S. (2002) Destination image analysis – a review of 142 papers from 1973 to 2000. *Tourism Management* 23 (5), 541–549.

Pike, S. and Ryan, C. (2004) Destination positioning analysis through a comparison of cognitive, affective, and conative perceptions. *Journal of Travel Research* 42 (4), 333–342.

Ries, A. and Trout, J. (1986) *Positioning: The Battle for Your Mind* (1st revised edn). New York: McGraw-Hill.

Ritchie, J.R.B. and Crouch, G.I. (2003) *The Competitive Destination: A Sustainable Tourism Perspective*. Wallingford: CABI.

Therkelsen, A. and Gram, M. (2010) Branding Europe – between nations, regions and continents. *Scandinavian Journal of Hospitality and Tourism* 10 (2), 107–128.

TIES (2011) International Ecotourism Society website, accessed 2011. http://www.ecotourism.org/.

Urban, G.L. and Star, S.H. (1991) *Advanced Marketing Strategy: Phenomena, Analysis, and Decisions*. Englewood Cliffs, NJ: Prentice-Hall.

Wang, Y. (2008) Collaborative destination marketing: Roles and strategies of convention and visitors bureaus. *Journal of Vacation Marketing* 14 (3), 191–209.

WCED (1987) *Our Common Future*. World Commission on Environment and Development, accessed 2011. http://www.un-documents.net/ocf-02.htm#I.

WEF (2009) *Travel & Tourism Competitiveness Report*. Geneva: World Economic Forum.

Welsh Assembly (2011) Visit Wales website, accessed 2011. http://www.visitwales.co.uk/regions-of-wales/areas-holiday-destinations-in-wales/south-wales-valleys/.

WHO (2007) *Global Age – Friendly Cities: A Guide*. Paris: World Health Organization.

Wind, Y. (1982) *Product Policy: Concepts, Methods and Strategy*. Reading, MA: Addison-Wesley.

WTO (1999) *Approval of the Global Code of Ethics for Tourism*. Resolution A/RES/406(XIII): Madrid: World Tourism Organisation.

WTO (2004) *Indicators of Sustainable Development for Tourism Destinations: A Guidebook.* Madrid: World Tourism Organisation.

Zhang, H., Gu, C-L., Gu, L-W. and Zhang, Y. (2011) The evaluation of tourism destination competitiveness by TOPSIS and information entropy – a case in the Yangtze River Delta of China. *Tourism Management* 32, 443–451.

19 Tourism Satellite Accounts: An Overview

Stephen L.J. Smith

Background

In the eyes of government, tourism is important because, in addition to other potential effects, it can be a major source of employment, GDP growth, export earnings and foreign direct investment. As a result, governments have sought tools to provide reliable and valid measures of the magnitude of the sector. Numerous ad hoc tools have been developed in many nations; however, these have not been widely accepted because they are inconsistent with accepted macro-economic measures. Moreover, many of these tools are flawed by inappropriate or unreliable data sources and methodology, as well as inconsistent definitions of core concepts.

A key challenge to measuring the magnitude of tourism as an economic activity is that it is not an industry as the term is normally used by economists and national statisticians. An industry, generally speaking, is a group of businesses producing a relatively homogeneous product using relatively homogeneous technology. Tourism lacks such homogeneity. For example, tourism involves diverse products such as some form of transportation by which consumers move around, some form of temporary accommodation, food services, attractions and activities and other services.

In the late 1970s, French national statisticians outlined an analytical conceptual framework that would become known as a satellite account ('satellite' because the framework was envisioned as a satellite – or extension – to the System of National Accounts (SNA) (UNWTO, 1999). Satellite accounts were seen as a strategy for measuring the economic magnitude of activities, such as tourism, that are important but do not fit neatly into existing industrial classifications. This early work drew the attention of a number of governments and agencies, including the UNWTO, OECD and Eurostat.

The UNWTO commissioned a report in 1982 on how the measurement of tourism could be done in a way consistent with the principles and methods of SNA (UNWTO, 1999). No actions followed the presentation of the report, but it is still considered to be a seminal work outlining a strategy for the international harmonisation of tourism concepts and statistics.

The Tourism Committee of OECD picked up the concept of what would become known as Tourism Satellite Account (TSA) and discussed some of the challenges associated with measuring tourism in their *Manual on Tourism Accounts* (OECD, 1991). Also in 1991, the UNWTO convened what would become known as the 'Ottawa Conference', at which international agreement on core concepts was achieved. A key definition was that of 'tourism': the activities of persons temporarily away (for less than one year) from their usual environment for any purpose other than the pursuit of remuneration from within the place visited. Certain other forms of international movement such as travel by refugees or diplomatic personnel were also excluded (UNWTO, 1993).

One of the papers presented at the Ottawa Conference was a proposal for TSAs (Wells, 1991). This proposal was a refinement of earlier work by the Canadian National Task Force on Tourism Statistics (Statistics Canada, 1988). Building on the 1991proposal, Statistics Canada published the first TSA in 1994 (Lapierre & Hayes, 1994). Other international tourism and statistical agencies also began to develop conceptual frameworks for TSAs. These efforts led to the approval by the UN Statistical Commission (1993) of 'Recommendations on Tourism Statistics' which became the foundation of a conceptual framework for TSAs (UNWTO, 1994) and, finally, a recommended methodological framework (RMF). Initially, the first details of the RMF proposed by the UNWTO and parallel proposals by Eurostat and OECD differed in subtle but important details. The various approaches were reconciled and an updated RMF was approved by the UN Statistical Division, other statistical bodies and the UNWTO (UN Statistical Division, 2008).

TSAs are 'works in progress' in that their development is long term and reflects different stages of completeness. Eurostat (2009) recognises four levels of development: (1) 'regularly updated fully-fledged national TSAs'; (2) 'comprehensible fully-fledged national TSA pilot studies' (essentially a complete draft of a TSA, but lacking a system for regular updates); (3) 'first compilation started with empirical results' (an even more preliminary stage in which empirical work has begun to produce tentative but incomplete results); and (4) 'first compilation started with no empirical results' (essentially the first stages of conceptual and methodological development work). Table 19.1 summarises the state of TSA implementation by member states of the EU as of 2009 (Eurostat, 2009).

In addition to the work of official statistical organisations, the World Travel and Tourism Council (WTTC), in cooperation with the Wharton Econometric Forecasting Associates (WEFA), produced what they called a 'simulated TSA'. Despite its label, the WTTC/WEFA approach is more of an economic impact model than a tool for measuring the magnitude of tourism.

Table 19.1 TSA development in EU member states

Regularly updated fully-fledged TSA	Comprehensible fully-fledged nationals TSA pilot studies	First compilation started with empirical results	First compilation started with no empirical results
Austria	France	Belgium	Bulgaria
Cyprus	Germany	Italy	Luxembourg
Czech Republic	Greece	Romania	Malta
Denmark	Ireland		
Estonia	Latvia		
Finland	Slovakia		
Hungary	Slovenia		
Lithuania	United Kingdom		
Netherlands			
Poland			
Portugal			
Spain			
Sweden			

Source: Eurostat (2009)

WTTC/WEFA employed concepts and data that diverged substantially from the UNWTO approach and, as a result, cannot meaningfully be labelled a TSA. A summary of these differences can be found in Smith and Wilton (1997).

Core Concepts

TSAs are built on a foundation of interrelated concepts. Chief among these are 'tourism', 'tourism commodities' and 'tourism industries'. As noted previously, tourism refers to the activities of persons temporarily away from their usual environment for any of a wide variety of purposes (UNWTO, 1993). The primary exclusion from the concept of tourism is travel for the primary motivation of earning income from the place visited. Thus, a business trip in the course of one's duties for an employer, such as calls on clients, would be considered to be tourism. However, travel by an independent salesperson, to make earn income directly from on-site sales, would not be considered to be tourism. Similarly, anyone who commutes to a place of work outside his or her usual environment would not be considered to be engaged in tourism. 'Visitor' is used as the generic term to refer to persons engaged in tourism; 'tourist' refers to a visitor who stays overnight in a destination; someone who does not stay overnight is referred to as a 'same-day visitor'.

Table 19.2 Forms of tourism

Fundamental forms

Domestic tourism	Trips taken by residents of a nation within the borders of that nation (the 'reference nation')
Outbound tourism	Trips taken by residents of a nation to destinations outside the reference nation
Inbound tourism	Trips taken by residents of other nations to destinations within the reference nation

Hybrid forms

National tourism	Domestic plus outbound tourism; in other words, all trips taken by residents of a nation regardless of the destination
Internal tourism	Domestic plus inbound tourism; in other words, all trips taken by in a reference nation regardless of the nation of residence of the visitor
International tourism	Inbound plus outbound tourism; in other words, all trips that cross an international border

A key feature of this definition is that tourism is a demand-side concept: it is something people do, not something businesses produce. Thus, the construction of cruise ships or airports, maintenance of border-crossing facilities, the operation of a visitors' information centre – as important as these activities are to tourism – are not tourism per se. They are 'upstream' or ancillary activities to tourism services. Only activities engaged directly in by persons during a tourism trip (or by businesses working directly on behalf of a visitor, such as a travel agency) are considered to be tourism.

Six forms of tourism (or types of visitors) are recognised within the RMF. Three of these are fundamental; three are hybrids of the fundamental forms (see Table 19.2).

Tourism commodities

The second core concept is that of tourism commodities. A tourism commodity is any good or service for which a significant portion of demand comes from visitors. In other words, if tourism did not exist, tourism commodities would disappear or at least be produced in significantly reduced quantities. The purchase of these commodities by visitors is 'tourism consumption'.

The threshold of demand for a commodity to be considered a tourism commodity is a matter of judgment. In Canada, for example, the threshold is 20%. This rule-of-thumb is based on two observations: (1) approximately 20% of all commercial food services in Canada come from people engaged in tourism; (2) food services are considered to be an essential commodity for tourism (Statistics Canada, 2010).

The commodities ('consumption products') used in the EU in the construction of TSAs are:

- Accommodation services (temporary accommodation for visitors as distinguished from vacation home ownership).
- Food and beverage services.
- Railway passenger transportation services.
- Road passenger transport services.
- Water passenger transport services.
- Transport equipment rental services.
- Travel agencies and reservation services.
- Cultural services.
- Sports and recreational services.
- Country-specific tourism characteristics **goods** (goods specific to tourism in a given country other than those identified above).
- Country-specific tourism characteristics **services** (services specific to tourism in a given country other than those identified above).

Certain payments that visitors might make in the course of a trip are excluded from the concept of tourism consumption. These include:

- Taxes and duties not directly charged against products.
- Interest payments on credit or loans used to make purchases during a trip.
- Purchase of assets such as land, art works, antiques, or jewellery.
- Transfer payments such as donations or money given to friends or family by the visitor during a trip.
- Goods purchased for resale or use in a production process, such as chemicals or equipment purchases by a business representative during a trip for use by his/her employer.

Certain forms of tourism consumption are 'collective consumption'. These services are available simultaneously to all visitors (and usually residents) of a destination. Use of these services is often passive or implicit, not requiring an active decision to consume them; nor can these services be withheld from someone who does not wish to benefit from them. In other words, tourism collective consumption services are a form of public good: security, legislation such as consumer protection, and tourism promotions. These services offer real benefits but the consumption of them by one person does not diminish their supply to another person. There is generally no practical way to assign a market value to collective consumption. As a result, while TSAs may, in principle, recognise the existence of collective consumption, no value is normally estimated for these services.

Two categories of commodities merit further comment. The first is consumer durables such as automobiles, boats or camping equipment. In principle, one could assign a proportion of the total cost of the durable to each trip during which the durable was used. In practice, however, data to permit this allocation are often difficult to obtain and thus consumer durables are excluded from most TSA calculations. One exception to this might be the purchase of an item, such as an automobile purchase for an extended road trip, that is sold at the end of a trip. The difference between the original purchase price and the sale price reflects the value of that durable for the purposes of a specific trip.

Another conceptually complicated category is privately owned vacation homes. To illustrate this complexity: if the vacation home is rented on a commercial basis, the value of the rent can be treated just as a measure of the value of other another form of commercial accommodation. However, if the vacation home is used by the owner, some non-market estimate of the value of the accommodation service could be made. According to National Accounting principles, the second home is generating 'housing services' whether or not the owners use the second home at any given time. Second home ownership also involves home repairs. When minor repairs are done by the owner and involve minor expenditures, such as do-it-yourself plumbing, expenditures are considered to be tourism consumption. The purchase of consumer durables for the home, such as furniture, would be treated as consumer durables, and thus subject to the same treatment as other durables. Substantial repairs, such as repairing a roof, are considered to be an 'intermediate expenditure' incurred for production of accommodation services (as other business expenses), and would not be counted as a tourism expenditure.

Tourism industries

The third core concept is 'tourism industries'. While there is no single holistic 'tourism industry', there are multiple tourism industries. A tourism industry is any industry whose characteristic product – the product that defines the identity of an industry – is a tourism industry. For example, the hotel industry is the industry that produces hotel stays. Other examples of tourism industries are: the cruise industry; food service industries such as restaurants; recreation and entertainment industries such as performing arts companies; and the travel agency and tour operator industry.

Other complications

A dilemma in measuring the economic magnitude of tourism is that not all tourism commodities are consumed by visitors. For example, people often patronise restaurants in their hometown. Expenditures by non-visitors on tourism commodities should not be counted as tourism expenditures.

Further, visitors will consume no-tourism commodities, such as groceries, during a trip. These commodities are not tourism commodities because the great percentage of demand for groceries does not come from visitors. One of the key tasks of TSAs is to identify what portion of spending on tourism commodities is truly related to tourism, and what portion is not. Similar, some estimate of visitor spending on non-tourism commodities is needed if one is to accurately measure the magnitude of tourism as an economic sector.

An aspect of tourism often of interest to governments is the level of investment in tangible non-financial assets such as infrastructure or equipment. These investments are known as 'tourism gross capital formation'. The growth in gross fixed capital is closely correlated with the level of tourism activity as a demand phenomenon – both the numbers of visitors and value of their spending.

Gross fixed capital items that have some bearing on tourism can be classified into three broad categories. The first are tourism-specific fixed assets. These are assets that would be produced in substantially reduced volumes in the absence of tourism, such as passenger aircraft.

The second category is non-tourism-specific fixed assets. These are assets purchased by tourism enterprises because they are useful but which are also purchased by other types of enterprises. Computer hardware is an example.

Infrastructure is the third form of fixed asset formation. Infrastructure normally results from public investment, and involves roads, water and sewerage systems, and so on. Tourism is a minor consumer of such infrastructure, but could not exist without it. There are also some forms of infrastructure that are more heavily dependent on tourism, such as airports and train stations. Investment in cultural and sports facilities can represents a hybrid form of infrastructure development. A major tourism event such as a world's fair or major international sports event may be the stimulus for the initial investment, but the infrastructure becomes used by a broader group of people.

TSA Structure

The basic structure of a TSA is shaped by the SNA. Very simplistically, an SNA can be thought of as a series of giant spreadsheets that provide data on inputs and outputs of commodities by every industry in an economy, as well as measures of final demand (e.g. by household, governments, or exports) of each commodity. There are three 'spreadsheets' of relevance to tourism: (1) the consumption account; (2) the production account; and (3) the goods account.

The consumption account describes demand for tourism commodities by broad categories of consumer, such as private households, government and exports. The value of each tourism commodity by each category of consumer is reported in the various cells of the 'spreadsheet'. The value of consumption reported by the TSA reflects tourism-specific consumption – spending by persons directly engaged in a tourism trip. Expenditures of tourism commodities by non-visitors, such as meals consumed at restaurants by locals, are excluded from the TSA.

The production account presents the value of output by tourism industry as well as some non-tourism industries (such as retail trade) by commodity. Thus, the product account provides data on the value of accommodation services, transportation services, and so on, produced by each industry. The TSA reports the total value of tourism commodities as well as key non-tourism commodities consumed by visitors, such as retail goods. These expenditures are often grouped in a TSA as 'other visitor spending' or 'other commodities'.

Finally, the goods account links the consumption and the production accounts together, illustrating how much of each industry's output is consumed by persons directly engaged in tourism (Smeral, 2006). Further, analysis of the accounts allows the value-added of each commodity arising from a production chain to be calculated (Smeral, 2005).

The data required to construct these accounts come from a variety of sources. Demand data typically are derived from visitor or household surveys that ask questions about consumption of commodities during the course of an individual trip that meets the definition of a tourism trip. Demand data sources also need to distinguish tourism spending by form of tourism: domestic tourism, inbound tourism and outbound tourism. As a result, nations that have developed tourism statistical systems typically use a number of different types of surveys such as household surveys or border-crossing surveys to collect data. Adequate demand-side data can be particularly challenging and expensive to develop, and represents one of the major impediments to the development of a TSA.

Production data describe (1) the consumption of goods and services required to produce tourism commodities (for example, how much money is spent on the purchase of fuel by the passenger airline industry) and (2) the value of the commodities produced by tourism industries. The goods account reports the portion of the output of tourism industries that is consumed by visitors, as a percentage of total industry output. This percentage is sometimes referred to as the 'tourism ratio'. For example, in Canada, the tourism ratio of passenger air service is typically in excess of 90%, whereas the tourism ratio for food service averages 20% (Statistics Canada, 2010).

Benefits of TSAs

The overarching goal of a TSA is to measure the magnitude of tourism as an economic sector. Equally important, though, is the context in which this measurement occurs. As noted above, tourism is not a traditional industry.

However, policy makers and national economists are often interested in understanding the magnitude of tourism in comparison to conventional industries. Thus, the TSA is designed to create, in effect, a 'synthetic' industry in the sense that it provides a credible measure of tourism as an area of economic activity that utilises conventions consistent with national accounting rules and thus allows tourism to be directly compared to conventional industries.

TSAs also provide insights into other matters of interest. For example, patterns of consumption of visitors within an economy can be identified and tracked: what types of visitors (domestic or international) spend how much on various tourism commodities. TSAs provide a measure of the relative importance of domestic, inbound (exports) and outbound (imports) forms of tourism in a national economy. They also provide an overview of the importance of different types of tourism commodities in terms of overall tourism demand: what percentage of total tourism spending in a nation is attributable to accommodation services, food services, and so on.

More generally, TSAs promote international consistency in defining, collecting and reporting tourism statistics. One of the strategic goals of international agencies in promoting TSAs is to develop a measurement system that permits comparisons of the magnitude of tourism in any given national economy to other national economies. An extension of this goal builds on the recognition that TSAs are 'data hungry'. Thus, the framework can stimulate improvement in the collection of tourism statistics. Indeed, the development of a TSA presumes a significant investment in a national statistical system that provides data on the value of tourism spending/receipts by commodity, volumes of visitors, production/consumption patterns of industry outputs of tourism commodities by industry, and the relative importance of tourism consumption as a component of the demand for specified commodities.

A few words about what TSAs are not intended to do might also be helpful. They cannot be used to develop marketing plans. They offer no insights into market segments, effective marketing mixes or communication strategies with potential markets. TSAs also do not provide guidance for product development or planning. They can offer insights into what industries are linked with other industries, but they do not provide any insights into consumption trends by potential visitors for specific products. Finally, although TSAs provide credible and defensible statistics on the magnitude of tourism as an area of economic activity, they do not – by themselves – resolve or avoid political fights among government agencies and industry sectors. TSAs also have certain limitations, which are briefly discussed in the following section.

Some Limitations

Although TSAs are shaped by the rules of SNAs (UNWTO, 1999), there are a few aspects of TSAs that diverge from SNAs. Business travel is considered

Table 19.3 Effects of business travel and indirect value added on TSA estimates

Macroeconomic metric	€ million	Percentage GDP
Direct value added		
Including business trips by residents	14,443	5.4
Excluding business trips by residents	13,581	5.0
Direct and indirect value added		
Excluding business trips by resident	22,289	8.2

to be a form of tourism in a TSA. However, SNAs treat expenditures by firms on business travel as an intermediate input – a cost of services required for the production of their final output. The difference is due to the fact that tourism is fundamentally a demand concept, not a production concept. In other words, TSAs consider business travel to be a form of final consumption whereas conventional National Statistical Accounting considers business travel to be an expense.

Further, TSAs look only at direct effects associated with spending on tourism services by consumers. They do not directly report 'upstream' linkages – economic exchanges in a production chain for a tourism product. In other words, TSAs do not directly measure the value of activities such as construction or insurance needed to produce final tourism products. As a result, the value of tourism GDP will be underestimated.

The potential magnitude of these effects can be seen in Table 19.3, which summarises the effects of including or excluding business travel as well as adding indirect value-added for tourism in Austria, 2007. When business trips by residents of Austria are included (as is the convention in TSAs), tourism's contribution to Austrian GDP is 5.4%. Excluding these expenditures (in effect, considering business tourism to be an expense for firms, not an output of the tourism sector) reduces tourism's contribution to the national GDP to 5.0%. Adding indirect effects associated with tourism production, but excluding business travel, increases tourism's contribution to the Austrian GDP to 8.2%.

Future Developments

As noted above, TSAs should be considered 'works in progress'. The potential functionality of TSAs is substantial, albeit limited by time, money, technical expertise and data. Some of the more important developmental initiatives under consideration by TSA developers include the following.

Updates to SNAs often occur only once every three to five years because of the substantial resources required for their updating. This usually is not a problem because the general relationships of production and consumption across a national economy usually change slowly. However, the construction and calibration of a TSA can also take years. Thus, even once a basic TSA is in place, it can still often take several years to update the TSA using the latest release of the SNA. In other words, TSA results can be based on conditions five to eight years in the past. If one is interested in the overall structure of the tourism sector and the relationships among tourism industries, this is usually a manageable delay. However, for policy and industry-tracking purposes, something more current is needed. Some system of indicators, based on a TSA but which can be updated frequently, is often required. One example of such a system is Canada's 'National Tourism Indicators', a set of tables based on TSA relationships but which is updated quarterly with the latest results from visitor surveys (Delisle, 1999).

TSAs are usually developed only at the national level. However, many analysts are interested in seeing TSA-type data at a subnational level. There are two basic approaches to developing such accounts: top-down and bottom-up. 'Top-down' refers to taking a national TSA and apportioning results by subnational regions. Such an approach guarantees that if one were to reverse the method, the aggregate national figures would be consistent with the original data. However, such an approach requires a high level of precision in national data to permit disaggregation to subnational units. Available tourism data in many nations may prevent or severely restrict the potential for a top-down TSA.

A bottom-up TSA involves the creation, *de novo*, of a regional TSA. In other words, one follows the principles of developing a TSA but uses only subnational data. This is often a feasible approach if data exist at a subnational level, although the methodological and data requirements are as great as those for a national TSA. Further, unless all subnational units in a nation have compatible data, subnational TSAs cannot be reliably combined to form a national TSA. Such aggregation is often not the goal of those who develop subnational TSAs, so the problem may not be relevant. A subnational TSA may be approximated using regional data and a social accounting matrix (a tool whose description is beyond the scope of this chapter). The result is not truly a TSA, but can often provide basic information on the structure and magnitude of a local tourism sector that is satisfactory for local decision makers, including the magnitude of tourism expenditures and revenues across a range of tourism commodities and industries (Smith *et al.*, 2003).

TSAs are, in principle, capable of supporting a number of modules – specialised 'add-ons' that extend the basic coverage of a TSA into other policy domains. Such modules are grounded in the basic structure and concepts of a TSA, but expand coverage into topics that may be of interest to policy makers. At the time of writing, these modules exist only as experimental or demonstration tools, but they do point the way for possible developments in the next generation of TSAs. Three examples are:

- *Labour market module*: a set of tables reporting the number of employees and payrolls. One particular challenge for measuring labour markets in tourism is that, compared to other sectors, tourism has a high proportion of part-time and seasonal labour, as well as high turnover rates. Being able to accommodate complex labour patterns is a special problem in tourism labour force studies.
- *Foreign direct investment (FDI) module*: in many nations, tourism offers opportunities for foreign investment directly into enterprises, whether through purchasing a company, acquiring shares, participating in an equity joint venture, or through other mechanisms. FDI can provide operating capital for firms, but can also result in economic leakages or in loss of national control over key resources. An FDI module could allow better tracking of the magnitude and impacts of FDI.
- *Associated industry modules*: certain forms of economic activity overlap with tourism, but involve activities that fall outside the scope of tourism. An example is the meeting and convention industry. This industry is a part of the tourism sector, but analysts interested in the meetings and convention industry are also concerned with topics that are not captured by TSAs, such as spending by locals on meetings as well as economic impacts of the industry. Separate accounts for 'associated' industries allow measurement of these activities that extend and broaden the scope of conventional TSAs.

Conclusions

The development of a functioning TSA is, in some ways, comparable to Galileo's construction of his telescope. Galileo did not invent the telescope, but he was the first to begin to exploit its power to reveal truths his contemporaries did not fathom. He used the telescope to begin to understand the very fabric of the solar system and, over the last 400 years, fired a scientific and intellectual revolution. TSAs reveal patterns of tourism production and consumption that have not been available. As these tools are refined and analysts gain more experience in using and interpreting the results, they will lead – not only to new understandings – but new questions. TSAs will revolutionise our perceptions and understanding of not just the magnitude of tourism, but its very nature.

References

Delisle, J. (1999) The Canadian National Tourism Indicators: A dynamic picture of the Satellite Account. *Tourism Economics* 5, 331–343.

Eurostat (2009) *Tourism Satellite Accounts in the European Union, Vol. 1: Report on the Implementation of TSAs in 27 EU Member States.* Luxembourg: Eurostat.

Lapierre, J. and Hayes, D. (1994) The Tourism Satellite Account. *National Income and Expenditure Accounts, Second Quarter,* xxxiii–lviii, cat. 13-001. Ottawa: Statistics Canada.

OECD (1991) *Manual on Tourism Economic Accounts.* Paris: OECD.

Smeral, E. (2005) The economic impact of tourism: Beyond satellite accounts. *Tourism Analysis* 10, 55–64.

Smeral, E. (2006) The Tourism Satellite Accounts: A critical assessment. *Journal of Travel Research* 45 (1), 92–98.

Smith, S.L.J. and Wilton, D. (1997) TSAs and the WTTC/WEFA methodology: Different satellites or different planets? *Tourism Economics* 3, 249–263.

Smith, S.L.J., Tatarinov, A.A., Trekhlab, P. and Poshnagov, S. (2003) *Tourism as a Factor of Regional Economic Development in Russia: An experience of Measuring the Role of Tourism in a Regional Economy.* Sochi: Sochi State University Press.

Statistics Canada (1988) *Final Report: The National Task Force on Tourism Data.* Ottawa: Statistics Canada.

Statistics Canada (2010) *National Tourism Indicators.* Cat. 17-009-X. Ottawa: Statistics Canada.

UN Statistical Commission (1993) *System of National Accounts 1993.* New York.

UN Statistical Division (2008) *Tourism Satellite Account: Recommended Methodological Framework.* New York: United Nations Statistical Division.

UNWTO (1993) *Recommendation on Tourism Statistics.* Statistical Papers Series M, No. 83. New York: UNWTO.

UNWTO (1999) *Tourism Satellite Account (TSA): The Conceptual Framework.* Madrid: UNWTO.

Wells, S. (1991) *A Proposal for a Satellite Account and Information System for Tourism.* Ottawa: Statistics Canada.

World Tourism Organization (UNWTO) (1994) International Recommendations on Tourism Statistics. Madrid, Spain: World Tourism Organization.

20 Using Network Analysis to Improve Tourist Destination Management

Rodolfo Baggio, Noel Scott and
Chris Cooper

Introduction

Tourism is a fragmented, geographically dispersed sector with many small specialist businesses contributing to an overall product experience. In most tourist destinations formal organisations have little actual power to enforce destination-wide coordination and instead rely on the cooperation and trust of their members and the wider community. This coordination relies on a set of peer-to-peer relationships that is considered here as a network. Most destinations encompass a network of tourism suppliers and the benefits of such networks include a more profitable tourism destination (Buhalis, 2000). The study of these networks offers a number of insights useful for the planning and management of destinations. Network analysis methods provide a means of visualising complex sets of relationships and simplifying them, and so can be useful in developing collaboration within a destination, increasing the support of actors who span political or geographic boundaries, and supporting the formation of group cohesion and identity (Cross *et al.*, 2002). The use of standard methods for the analysis of networks enables the structure of inter-organisational relationships to be compared between destinations over time, and also allows the study of dynamic situations within a destination and to provide recommendations as to how the relationships and overall efficiency of the network can be improved.

Given the importance of such network forms of organisation for the functioning of a tourism destination, it is somewhat surprising that there has not been more study of tourism networks and practical use of network analysis methods. In tourism, many of the main resources of a tourism destination are community 'owned' and are used jointly to attract tourists. Such collective action does not necessarily require a network organisation but in situations characterised by a general lack of resources and where decisions related to tourism are seen to lie outside the government mandate, the response is often a network of interested actors.

In analysing these systems of destination organisations, there are three basic elements of interest: actors, relationships and resources (Knoke & Kuklinski, 1991). The actors of any network are the actors who develop and maintain effective relationships displaying varying degrees of formality and complexity, ranging from close, cooperative relationships to the more distant. Actors can be members of many networks but the cost involved in engaging with a network limits membership. Actors gain power from their position within a network; the more centrally located, the stronger the power and influence of that organisation within the destination (Pavlovich, 2003). Actors must be identified within some boundary, often a particular discourse domain or a geographic destination. The second element required to understand networks is the relationships (ties) between actors. Strong ties encourage conformity, acceptable action and inclusion and so they enable destination cohesion. Weak ties, on the other hand, can exclude other actors and tend to act as bridges to those actors who are external to the network. As such, they play an important role in importing new information into the network and therefore underpin innovation. An optimally efficient network comprises both weak and strong ties; a dominance of either type will weaken a network. Such networks of relationships are important for sharing or diffusing resources such as social support, operational integration and the acquisition of knowledge at both the destination level and within value chains.

In this chapter, we review recent network research in tourism and highlight a number of areas where the authors consider that further application of the network concept will benefit tourism planning.

Policy and Inter-organisational Network Analysis

Network analysis has in the past proven useful in two areas relevant for tourism planning: analysis of policy development and improving inter-organisational network effectiveness. An inter-organisational network may be conceived as a political economy concerned with the distribution of two scarce resources, money and authority, and actors in the political economy pursue an adequate supply of resources (Benson, 1975). Networks are seen increasingly as the source of policy rather than it being promulgated by a central authority. Methodologically, policy analysis typically relies on thick qualitative description of relationships between actors (either individuals or groups) and eschews quantification (Rhodes, 2002), although other authors recommend the use of formal social network methods (Christopoulos, 2008). Policy analysis seeks to provide a theoretical explanation as to why policy changes occur (Tyler & Dinan, 2001) and networks are one means of co-ordination between these actors in its development. Van Waarden (1992) indicates that the main concepts involved in studying policy networks are actors and agencies, network functions and structure, characteristics of institutions, rules and power.

In tourism many authors using the policy network analysis tradition rely on 'thick' description to understand the complexity of the policy approach (Dredge, 2006a, 2006b; Pavlovich, 2001). Tyler and Dinan (2001) have examined the nature of policy networks regarding tourism in the UK using this approach, as have Treuren and Lane (2003) in discussing planning in tourism and how it is contingent on network alliances. Dredge (2005, 2006b) has sought to facilitate the integration of qualitative and quantitative approaches in developing a four-level framework for investigating policy networks.

Inter-organisational networks may form for a number of purposes such as obtaining resources, promotion or examination of common areas of interest or even to adjudicate in areas of dispute (Lovelock, 2001). Until recently, researchers examining the competitive advantage of firms have focused on internal resources as sources of competitive advantage. However, the network literature highlights the importance of external resources available to the firm through its linkages (McEvily & Marcus, 2005). The strategic network perspective considers that the embeddedness of firms within networks of external relationships with other organisations holds significant implications for their performance (Gulati et al., 2000). Researchers have highlighted the importance of collaborative advantage for organisational advantage (Dyer & Singh, 1998) and for business activities such as marketing (Pillai, 2006).

Gulati and Gargiulo (1999), who studied how a firm's alliance network shapes alliance formation decisions, introduced the notion of network resources. The concept of network resources is consistent with resource advantage theory. In this theory, a competence is a distinct package of basic resources. Specifically, competencies are viewed as socially complex groupings of tangible and intangible resources that work together. Intangible resources include formal and informal social structures. Thus, resource advantage theory allows for the impact of structure in social relations on competition, an idea ignored in neoclassical economic theory where firms are non-interacting independent entities. However, when firms form networks, they move away from being considered as atomised firms in perfect competition and networks may be considered resources that deliver advantages to firms (Watkins & Bell, 2002). The resources and competencies developed through relationships include access to diverse knowledge (Burt, 1992), pooled resources and cooperation (Uzzi, 1996), and third-party endorsements (Stuart et al., 1999).

Inter-organisational network analysis has been used to understand the collective nature of organisational action, constraint and coordination within tourism. Bramwell and Meyer (2007) have examined issues of relationships, power and agency between organisations in an East German coastal resort. Alford (1998) has discussed the establishment of a market position by regional tourist boards, in part by developing inter-sector networks in the context of sustainable tourism planning and development. Halme (2001) considers networks important in developing sustainability in tourism due to the isolation of individual actors. Network analysis of organisational actors has also been undertaken in the study of events (Stokes, 2006).

In addition to policy and inter-organisational analysis, networks have been used to study knowledge management (Cooper, 2006) and learning (Beesley, 2005), governance (Yuksel & Yuksel, 2005), social capital (Vernon et al., 2005), network density (Pforr, 2006), partnerships (Dredge, 2006a), personal relationships (McGehee, 2002), collaboration (Mottiar & Tucker, 2007) and innovation (Novelli et al., 2006).

Recent Analysis of Tourism Destination Networks

Managing tourism networks is challenging due to the possible conflicts that may arise from the different views, values and attitudes held by the diverse components of the complex system of a destination. Governance of a complex system such as a tourist destination requires an adaptive attitude, rather than a rigid deterministic, authoritarian style. The proposal of using adaptive management to deal with a complex system derives from the work of 1970s ecologists (Holling, 1978). It calls for an experimental path to management building on the idea of exploring alternative possibilities, implementing one or more of them, monitoring the outcomes, testing the predictions and learning which one most effectively allows the achievement of management objectives. The cycle then closes by using the results of the actions to improve knowledge and adjust subsequent management activities. This approach has been adopted in different complex systems, including tourism destinations, with encouraging results (Agostinho & Teixeira de Castro, 2003). Thus, it is still possible to manage and understand complex systems, at least at some level. Large-scale behaviours might still be foreseeable if it is possible to describe the overall dynamics of the system including the presence of any preferred evolutionary paths. Once these have been identified, it can be possible to determine whether changes in some specific parameter can produce sudden shifts in behaviour, or at least establish a probability distribution for their occurrence (Hansell et al., 1997). Short-term predictions allow the identification of the main evolutionary paths and small *corrections* to the system behaviour that may be effective in avoiding undesired regimes.

Since the mid-1990s, a set of tools, methods and theories able to analyse and model a networked system have been developed under the discipline of network science (Watts, 2004). The structural characteristics (topology) of a network such as a tourism destination network influence the overall dynamic behaviour of the system and explain and control a number of processes from the diffusion of ideas to the robustness to external or internal shocks, to the optimisation of the relationships among the network components. An important consequence of these ideas is that the simple existence of a network in a tourism destination is not sufficient to generate effective synergies; depending on the topological structure of such networks, dynamic processes may attain different outcomes and have different effects on the evolution of the destination (Baggio et al., 2010; Scott et al., 2008).

The relevant methods and techniques have been extensively described and discussed elsewhere (Boccaletti et al., 2006) and have been applied to tourism systems (Baggio, 2008; Baggio et al., 2010; Scott et al., 2008). These studies use a number of measurements to characterise a network topology: degree (the connections each node of the network has to others) and the statistical distribution of the degrees in a network, density at a local or global level and its non-homogeneities (clustering coefficient, for example), average distance between any two nodes (average path length), efficiency (global and local) in transferring information, correlations between the degree of a node and that of its neighbours (assortativity) and modularity (extent of division in denser sub-networks, also called communities).

Using these methods, a destination network has been found to have a scale-free topology, as have many other social systems (Baggio et al., 2010; Scott et al., 2007). Destinations examined show a very low density of connections, low clusterisation and a negative degree–degree correlation (i.e. highly connected actors tend to link to low-degree actors). These features have been interpreted as symptom of the well-known tendency of tourism actors to avoid forms of collaboration or cooperation. This is an important (even if partial) result, because an undisputable identification of strategic weaknesses in the cohesiveness of the destination can be addressed by policy and management. It is also possible to detect differences in the measures of inter-organisational cohesion at different tourism destinations (Scott et al., 2008).

Beside these structural features, some dynamic characteristics of complex systems have been examined. The capability to reach a node from another one and the associated probabilities have been measured and analysed, leading to a series of important findings related to the interactions between tourism companies. The type and size of these companies strongly influences these characteristics (da Fontoura Costa & Baggio, 2009). A modularity analysis has shown that clusters of actors exist in a destination although not well defined or highly significant. This community structure goes beyond preset differentiations (by geography or type) and companies of the same type (e.g. hotels), or in the same geographical area, and tend to connect companies running different businesses or in other localities (Baggio *et al.*, 2010; da Fontoura Costa & Baggio, 2009).

One interesting use of these techniques is to identify the important actors in a destination: those who are reputed to give the most important contribution to the tourism activities. Destination management organisations or actors possessing critical resources have the highest centrality and local government bodies are perceived to hold the greatest legitimacy and power over others in destination development (Timur & Getz, 2008). Another useful analysis is a comparison between the perceived importance of organisations in a destination (obtained through a series of interviews) and their network characteristics and a set of metrics able to examine this have been developed. It has thus been possible to reliably show that the key actors are located in the core of the network and form an elite that is seen as more salient while peripheral actors are seen as less important. This suggests that destination management is controlled by a limited number of actors (Cooper *et al.*, 2009).

Network Simulation and Scenario Planning

One of the advantages of a network representation of a complex system is that it is possible to use it for performing numerical simulations. They allow *experiments* to be performed in fields where these would not otherwise be feasible for both theoretical and practical reasons. Different configurations can be designed and several dynamic processes simulated in order to better understand how these configurations influence the behaviour of the whole destination system. The credibility of these techniques is good, provided some basic requirements are met: a solid conceptual model specified for the particular circumstances for which the simulations are run (Küppers & Lenhard, 2005). Within these conditions, simulations can be effective and efficient in reproducing different types of processes and they may be considered a valuable aid in decision making (Axelrod, 2006).

Information and knowledge flows in a destination network are relevant determinants of the health of a system. Productivity, innovation and growth are strongly influenced by them, and the way in which the spread occurs affects the speed by which individual actors perform and plan their future (Argote & Ingram, 2000). A commonly used way to study the problem is that based on an analogy with the diffusion of a disease (Hethcote, 2000). It has been demonstrated that the structure of the network is highly influential in determining the basic unfolding of a dissemination process (Da Costa & Terhesiu, 2005).

A set of simple simulations have shown these effects (Baggio & Cooper, 2010). Different configurations have been used, based on the single actors' capacities to absorb and retransmit knowledge and on different network topologies. It has been proved that scale-free networks (such as those found in a tourism destination) affect the process by speeding it up. A further improvement is obtained by eliminating differences in the capability of tourism actors to transfer knowledge to other members of the community. The best results in terms of process efficiency, however, have been obtained when the network has been reconfigured (rewired) in order to increase the clustering characteristics. A very important determinant for the spread of knowledge in a tourism destination is the presence of a structured topology in the network of relations that connects the different actors, with a well-established degree of local cohesion. In other words, destination actors should be encouraged to form cooperative or collaborative clusters to raise the overall competitiveness of the destination. This is an important result for public sector bodies which can help the development of such clusters.

Another knowledge diffusion mechanism is also crucial for the success of tourism operators. The diffusion of marketing messages through traditional advertising and word-of-mouth is a well-known and studied technique. In a recent study a simulation has been set up, in which a tourism actor (a hotel manager, for example, or a whole destination) wishes to understand the possible effectiveness of traditional advertising as compared to word-of-mouth for promoting the services offered to a target market (Baggio *et al.*, 2009). By comparing the two situations, the relative effects of these two methods have been measured in terms of time needed for reaching a certain fraction of the target population and resources spent. The results show the higher effectiveness, at least in the short term, of word-of-mouth. For the classical paid advertising, a more intense effort is needed to reach the same level of informed people.

The methods discussed here can also be used as a powerful complement to scenario planning activities. Scenario planning essentially consists of conceiving stories about future situations and using them to foresee lines of actions for facing those situations. The planning process analyses possible reactions and outcomes and designs action plans based on these stories (Yeoman, 2008). Usually, some preliminary investigation grounded in qualitative analysis methods provides the building blocks for the stories. The problems identified are then discussed by experts and plans are designed (Breukel & Go, 2009).

Use of quantitative information to support the scenario-building process can be of fundamental importance and can give it a more rigorous and sound foundation. This combination has already proved to be quite effective when dealing with policy issues in other fields (Bankes, 2002). Network analysis methods, as seen in the previous section, are able to provide extensive sets of simulations. They may allow testing of different hypotheses and examination of their consequences in cases in which a 'real' experiment is impossible or impracticable. These results and their conditions can, when combined with more traditional methods, provide a useful basis on which to build scenarios.

Concluding Remarks

The general framework of networks within a complexity science perspective offers a sound basis for the study of a tourism destination. Within this framework, the structure of a system can be described in terms of its components and of the linkages that connect them. This brief review has shown that, among the many possible approaches, the study of the topological structure of a destination is able to give insights into the functioning of the system both from a static and a dynamic point of view. Modelling a tourism destination as a complex network and using the ideas, the concepts and the techniques of network science to study its topology and its evolution over time is proving to be an interesting and promising line of research. Moreover, besides the intellectual appeal, the implications that can be derived, in terms of capabilities of understanding the general behaviour and the dynamic evolution of a destination, may give tourism organisation managers a strong leverage to improve the flow of information and to target opportunities where this flow may have the most impact on business activities.

Most studies examined here have, obviously, limitations. Very simplified models and representations of tourism systems have been used, and straightforward simulations have been set up. However, this is only the beginning of a new research path, and most works have been conducted with the main goal of proving the applicability and choosing, among the hundreds of possible techniques, the most useful and effective for the field. As is well highlighted in the works described here, the most important contribution so far is of a methodological nature. A combination of models and techniques has been synthesised in order to develop a uniform set of tools for the structural analysis of a tourism destination. As noted several times, this approach must necessarily be coupled with a deep knowledge of the object of study. Both quantitative and qualitative instruments are necessary to fully exploit the potential of the methods presented here.

The use of quantitative measurement for the assessment of network properties has little meaning without a *physical* interpretation which may only come from the outcomes of more traditional qualitative investigations. For the scholar, this can greatly help in confirming these models. For those interested or involved in managing a destination, the combination of both traditional qualitative evaluations and quantitative measurements can give more strength to the decisions made and better inform the actions and policies needed.

As a final point, it is important to note that a more rigorous establishment of methodological tools, such as those described here, can be a powerful way to help a transition towards a less *undisciplined* set of theories and models in the tourism arena, and that this can be greatly beneficial for the understanding of the structure and behaviour of this system and its components, so important in today's social and economic setting.

References

Agostinho, M.E. and Teixeira de Castro, G. (2003) *Co-creating a Self-organizing Management System: A Brazilian Experience.* Paper presented at the Complexity, Ethics and Creativity Conference, London School of Economics, 17–18 September. http://www.psych.lse.ac.uk/complexity/Conference/AgostinhoCastro.pdf.

Alford, P. (1998) Positioning the destination product – can regional tourist boards learn from private sector practice? *Journal of Travel and Tourism Marketing* 7 (2), 53–68.

Argote, L. and Ingram, P. (2000) Knowledge transfer: A basis for competitive advantage in firms. *Organizational Behavior and Human Decision Processes* 82, 150–169.

Axelrod, R. (2006) Simulation in the social sciences. In J-P. Rennard (ed.) *Handbook of Research on Nature Inspired Computing for Economy and Management* (pp. 90–100). Hersey, PA: Idea Group.

Baggio, R. (2008) Symptoms of complexity in a tourism system. *Tourism Analysis* 13 (1), 1–20.

Baggio, R. and Cooper, C. (2010) Knowledge transfer in a tourism destination: The effects of a network structure. *Service Industries Journal* 30 (8); preprint at http://arxiv.org/abs/0905.2734.

Baggio, R., Cooper, C., Scott, N. and Antonioli Corigliano, M. (2009) Advertising and word of mouth in tourism, a simulation study. In A. Fyall, M. Kozak, L. Andreu, J. Gnoth and S.S. Lebe (eds) *Marketing Innovations for Sustainable Destinations* (pp. 13–22). Oxford: Goodfellow Publishers.

Baggio, R., Scott, N. and Cooper, C. (2010) Network science – a review focused on tourism. *Annals of Tourism Research* 37 (3), 802–827.

Bankes, S.C. (2002) Tools and techniques for developing policies for complex and uncertain systems. *Proceedings of the National Academy of the Sciences of the USA* 99 (suppl. 3), 7263–7266.

Beesley, L. (2005) The management of emotion in collaborative tourism research settings. *Tourism Management* 26 (2), 261–275.

Benson, J.K. (1975) The interorganizational network as a political economy. *Administrative Science Quarterly* 20 (2), 376–396.

Boccaletti, S., Latora, V., Moreno, Y., Chavez, M. and Hwang, D-U. (2006) Complex networks: Structure and dynamics. *Physics Reports* 424 (4–5), 175–308.

Bramwell, B. and Meyer, D. (2007) Power and tourism policy relations in transition. *Annals of Tourism Research* 34 (3), 766–788.

Breukel, A. and Go, F.M. (2009) Knowledge-based network participation in destination and event marketing: A hospitality scenario analysis perspective. *Tourism Management* 30 (2), 184–193.

Buhalis, D. (2000) Marketing the competitive destination of the future. *Tourism Management* 21, 97–116.

Burt, R.S. (1992) *Structural Holes: The Social Structure of Competition.* Cambridge, MA: Harvard University Press.

Christopoulos, D.C. (2008) The governance of networks: Heuristic or formal analysis? A reply to Rachel Parker. *Political Studies* 56 (2), 475–481.

Cooper, C. (2006) Knowledge management and tourism. *Annals of Tourism Research* 33 (1), 47–64.

Cooper, C., Scott, N. and Baggio, R. (2009) Network position and perceptions of destination stakeholder importance. *Anatolia* 20 (1), 33–45.

Cross, R.L., Borgatti, S.P. and Parker, A. (2002) Making invisible work visible: Using social network analysis to support human networks. *California Management Review* 44 (2), 25–46.

Da Costa, L.E. and Terhesiu, D. (2005) A simple model for the diffusion of ideas. Complex Systems Summer School Final Project papers. Santa Fe, NM: Santa Fe Institute.

da Fontoura Costa, L. and Baggio, R. (2009) The web of connections between tourism companies: Structure and dynamics. *Physica A* 388, 4286–4296.

Dredge, D. (2005) Networks and innovation in Lake Macquarie. In D. Carson and J. Macbeth (eds) *Regional Tourism Cases: Innovation in Regional Tourism* (pp. 61–68). Gold Coast: STCRC.

Dredge, D. (2006a) Networks, conflict and collaborative communities. *Journal of Sustainable Tourism* 14 (6), 562–581.

Dredge, D. (2006b) Policy networks and the local organisation of tourism. *Tourism Management* 27 (2), 269–280.

Dyer, J.H. and Singh, H. (1998) The relational view: Cooperative strategy and sources of interorganizational competitive advantage. *Academy of Management Review* 23 (4), 660–679.

Gulati, R. and Gargiulo, M. (1999) Where do interorganizational networks come from? *American Journal of Sociology* 104 (5), 1439–1493.

Gulati, R., Nohria, N. and Zaheer, A. (2000) Strategic networks. *Strategic Management Journal* 21 (3), 203–215.

Halme, M. (2001) Learning for sustainable development in tourism networks. *Business Strategy and the Environment* 10, 100–114.

Hansell, R.I.C., Craine, I.T. and Byers, R.E. (1997) Predicting change in non-linear systems. *Environmental Monitoring and Assessment* 46, 175–190.

Hethcote, H.W. (2000) The mathematics of infectious diseases. *SIAM Review* 42 (4), 599–653.

Holling, C.S. (ed.) (1978) *Adaptive Environmental Assessment and Management.* New York: John Wiley and Sons.

Knoke, D. and Kuklinski, J.H. (1991) Network analysis: Basic concepts. In G. Thompson, J. Frances, R. Levacic and J. Mitchell (eds) *Markets, Hierarchies and Networks* (pp. 173–182). London: Sage Publications.

Küppers, G. and Lenhard, J. (2005) Validation of simulation: Patterns in the social and natural sciences. *Journal of Artificial Societies and Social Simulation* 8 (4), accessed March 2006. http://jasss.soc.surrey.ac.uk/8/4/3.html.

Lovelock, B. (2001) Interorganisational relations in the protected area – tourism policy domain: The influence of macro-economic policy. *Current Issues in Tourism* 4 (2/4), 253–274.

McEvily, B. and Marcus, A. (2005) Embedded ties and the acquisition of competitive capabilities. *Strategic Management Journal* 26 (11), 1033–1055.

McGehee, N.G. (2002) Alternative tourism and social movements. *Annals of Tourism Research* 29 (1), 124–143.

Mottiar, Z. and Tucker, H. (2007) Webs of power: Multiple ownership in tourism destinations. *Current Issues in Tourism* 10 (4), 279–295.

Novelli, M., Schmitz, B. and Spencer, T. (2006) Networks, clusters and innovation in tourism: A UK experience. *Tourism Management* 27 (6), 1141–1152.

Pavlovich, K. (2001) The twin landscapes of Waitomo: Tourism network and sustainability through the Landcare Group. *Journal of Sustainable Tourism* 9 (6), 491–504.

Pavlovich, K. (2003) The evolution and transformation of a tourism destination network: The Waitomo Caves, New Zealand. *Tourism Management* 24 (2), 203–216.

Pforr, C. (2006) Tourism policy in the making: An Australian network study. *Annals of Tourism Research* 33 (1), 87–108.

Pillai, K. (2006) Networks and competitive advantage: A synthesis and extension. *Journal of Strategic Marketing* 14, 129–145.

Rhodes, R.A.W. (2002) Putting people back into networks. *Australian Journal of Political Science* 37 (3), 399–416.

Scott, N., Cooper, C. and Baggio, R. (2007) Use of network analysis in tourism research. *Proceedings of the Advances in Tourism Marketing Conference (ATMC)*, Valencia, Spain, 10–12 September.

Scott, N., Cooper, C. and Baggio, R. (2008) Destination networks – four Australian cases. *Annals of Tourism Research* 35 (1), 169–188.

Stokes, R. (2006) Network-based strategy making for events tourism. *European Journal of Marketing* 40 (5/6), 682–695.

Stuart, T.E., Hoang, H. and Hybels, R.C. (1999) Interorganizational endorsements and the performance of entrepreneurial ventures. *Administrative Science Quarterly* 44 (2), 315–349.

Timur, S. and Getz, D. (2008) A network perspective on managing stakeholders for sustainable urban tourism. *International Journal of Contemporary Hospitality Management* 20 (4), 445–461.

Treuren, G. and Lane, D. (2003) The tourism planning process in the context of organised interests, industry structure, state capacity, accumulation and sustainability. *Current Issues in Tourism* 6 (1), 1–22.

Tyler, D. and Dinan, C. (2001) Trade and associated groups in the English tourism policy arena. *International Journal of Tourism Research* 3, 459–476.

Uzzi, B. (1996) The sources and consequences of embeddedness for the economic performance of organizations: The network effect. *American Sociological Review* 61, 674–698.

Van Waarden, F. (1992) Dimensions and types of policy networks. *European Journal of Political Research* 21, 29–52.

Vernon, J., Essex, S., Pinder, D. and Curry, K. (2005) Collaborative policymaking: Local sustainable projects. *Annals of Tourism Research* 32 (2), 325–345.

Watkins, M. and Bell, B. (2002) The experience of forming business relationships in tourism. *International Journal of Tourism Research* 4, 15–28.

Watts, D.J. (2004) The 'new' science of networks. *Annual Review of Sociology* 30, 243–270.

Yeoman, I. (2008) *Tomorrow's Tourist: Scenarios & Trends*. Oxford: Butterworth Heinemann.

Yuksel, A. and Yuksel, F. (2005) Managing relations in a learning model for bringing destinations in need of assistance into contact with good practice. *Tourism Management* 26 (5), 667–679.

21 Tourism Forecasting Using Econometric Models

Haiyan Song, Egon Smeral, Gang Li and Jason L. Chen

Introduction

This chapter examines the forecasting accuracy of a range of alternative modern econometric approaches based on the work of Song *et al.* (2003). In addition, the forecasting accuracy of the Bayesian Vector-autoregressive (BVAR) model is also assessed. Two univariate time series models are used for benchmarking purposes – the seasonal integrated autoregressive and moving average (SARIMA) model and naïve no-change model. Although the forecasting accuracy of the above models has been examined, this study is different from previous research in two ways. Firstly, the forecasting accuracy of modern econometric models is assessed using quarterly rather than annual data. Secondly, individual models are estimated for an extensive range of countries/country groupings, including Australia, Austria, Belgium-Luxemburg, Brazil, Canada, the Czech Republic, Denmark, Finland, France, Germany, Greece, India, Ireland, Italy, Mexico, The Netherlands, New Zealand, Portugal, Russia, Slovenia, Spain, Sweden, Turkey, the United Kingdom and the United States. Such a large-scale empirical study should generate robust conclusions on the forecasting performance of various tourism demand models.

Furthermore, up to now, most of the discussion on and empirical studies of tourism demand forecasting models have focused on tourist arrivals rather than tourism expenditure/receipts, according to the comprehensive reviews by Witt and Witt (1995) and Li *et al.* (2005).

The contribution of this chapter is therefore twofold. First, this chapter presents the most comprehensive comparison to date of the forecasting performance of econometric models within a tourism context using quarterly data. Although the forecasting accuracy of some of the modern econometric models included in this chapter has been investigated previously, these models were often estimated using annual data. In contrast to annual data, quarterly economic time series data often exhibit substantial seasonal variation. Therefore, considerable care has to be taken when generating seasonal tourism demand forecasts.

The second contribution of this chapter is the testing of the accuracy of various econometric and time series models in forecasting tourist expenditure. Compared with tourist arrivals, forecasts of tourist expenditure/receipts are of great importance for economic planners in assessing the economic impacts of tourism on the destination economies.

The remainder of this chapter is organised as follows. Section 2 discusses the specifications of the forecasting models used in the accuracy comparison. Section 3 introduces the measures of forecast accuracy. In Section 4, the properties of the data set used in this study are examined. The assessment of forecasting performance is presented in Section 5, and Section 6 concludes the study.

Model Specifications

The selection of the forecasting models used in this study is based on the popularity of those used in past tourism forecasting research (Li *et al.*, 2005). All of the forecasting models evaluated are special cases of the general autoregressive distributed log model (ADLM):

$$y_t = \alpha + \sum_{j=1}^{k}\sum_{i=0}^{p} \beta_{ji}x_{jt-i} + \sum_{i=1}^{p} \phi_i y_{t-i} + \varepsilon_t, \tag{1}$$

where p is the lag length, which is determined by the type of data used, k is the number of explanatory variables and ε_t is the error term, which is assumed to be white noise. As quarterly data are used in this study, a lag length of four is adopted.

Error correction model

Equation (1) can be reparameterised into an error correction model (ECM) of the following form (Song & Witt, 2000: 73–74):

$$\Delta y_t = (\text{current and lagged } \Delta x_{ji}s, \text{lagged } \Delta y_t s)$$

$$- (1 - \phi_1)\left[y_{t-1} - \sum_{j=1}^{k} \beta_j x_{jt-1} \right] + \varepsilon_t. \tag{2}$$

Based on the residuals from the long-run cointegrating models estimated using ordinary least squares (OLS), the ECM presented by Equation (2) can be estimated through various procedures.

According to the review of Li *et al.* (2005), four ECM estimation methods have been used in previous tourism demand forecasting studies: the Engle and Granger two-stage approach (EG), the Wickens and Breusch one-stage approach (WB), the ADLM approach and, most frequently, the Johansen-maximum-likelihood (JML) approach. Unlike the other methods, the JML approach can detect more than one cointegration relationship among the dependent and explanatory variables. In addition, Song *et al.* (2003) found that the magnitudes of the estimated coefficients calculated using the WB method vary widely compared with those estimated using the JML approach. Song and Witt (2000) recommended that the latter approach be used whenever possible because it gives more reliable estimates of the long-run coefficients and generates more accurate forecasts. Therefore, the JML method is used in this study.

The JML-ECM, also known as the vector error correction model (VECM), results from the Johansen cointegration procedure, which is an extension of the univariate Dickey–Fuller test to a multivariate vector autoregressive (VAR) framework. The JML-ECM in this study can be formulated as

$$\nabla S(B)Y_t = \sum_{i=1}^{p-1} \Phi_i \nabla S(B)Y_{t-i} + \Phi \nabla S(B)Y_{t-p} + \Psi D_t + U_t, \qquad (3)$$

where $\nabla = (1 - B)$ denotes the first difference operator, $S(B)$ is a seasonal filter, Y_t is a $(k \times 1)$ vector of k potential endogenous variables, Φ is a $(k \times k)$ matrix of parameters, D_t is a vector of deterministic variables (such as intercept, trend and seasonal dummies) and U_t is a $(k \times 1)$ vector of errors. The parameter matrices Φ_i and Φ are the short-run and long-run adjustments to the change in Y_t, respectively.

Reduced ADLM

The dynamic econometric modelling technique advocated by Hendry (1986), known as the general-to-specific approach, is used in this study. In the initial specification of the general ADLM shown by Equation (1), all possible variables are included and the lag length is set equal to four. The least significant explanatory variable is deleted from the model, and then the simplified model is re-estimated. This process is repeated until the coefficients of all of the remaining explanatory variables are statistically significant at the 5% level (one-tailed). The final specific model should be simple in structure and possess the desirable statistical properties. That is, the final model should pass all or most of the diagnostic tests, such as the tests for autocorrelation, heteroskedasticity, misspecification and non-normality.

Time-varying parameter model

The time-varying parameter (TVP) model was developed to allow the elasticities in log-linear regression to change over time. This method is more adaptable when the assumption of constant coefficients is not valid and structural changes in econometric models need to be tackled. The TVP approach has been successfully applied in modelling and forecasting other economic activities (Brown *et al.*, 1997; Riddington, 1993; Song *et al.*, 1996, 1997, 1998; Stock & Watson, 1996; Swamy *et al.*, 1989). However, the TVP method has not received adequate attention in the tourism forecasting research. The published studies include those of Li *et al.* (2006), Riddington (1999), Song and Witt (2000), Song *et al.* (2003), Song and Wong (2003) and Witt *et al.* (2003). These studies, which use annual data, consistently show empirical evidence of the TVP model's superior performance in short-term forecasting. However, the seasonal forecasting performance of this model requires further investigation.

The TVP approach uses a recursive estimation process in which more recent information is weighted more heavily than that obtained in the distant past. With the restriction $p = 0$ imposed on the coefficients in Equation (1), the TVP model is rewritten as a state-space form as follows:

$$y_t = x_t \beta_t + \varepsilon_t, \tag{4}$$

$$\beta_t = \Phi \beta_{t-1} + \omega_t, \tag{5}$$

where y_t is a vector of tourism demand, x_t is a matrix of the explanatory variables, β_t represents the regression coefficients, ε_t refers to a vector of temporary disturbances, ω_t is a matrix of permanent disturbances and Φ is a matrix initially assumed to be known. Equation (4) is called the *measurement* or *system equation*, while Equation (5) is known as the *transition* or *state equation*, which is used to simulate how the parameters in the system equation evolve over time. If the components of the matrix Φ in Equation (5) equal unity, then each component (β_{jt}) of the transition equation becomes a random walk (RW) process:

$$\beta_{jt} = \beta_{jt-1} + \omega_{jt} \ (j = 1, 2, \ldots). \tag{6}$$

In most cases, the RW process is adequate to capture the parameter changes in various economic models (see, for example, Bohara & Sauer, 1992; Greenslade & Hall, 1996; Kim, 1993; Song & Witt, 2000). In this study, based on the RW process, a seasonal component (β_{0t}) is incorporated into the state equation to capture the seasonal fluctuation that is due to seasonal variation in the parameters. The seasonal component is specified as follows:

$$\beta_{0t} = \beta_{0t-4} + \omega_{0t}. \tag{7}$$

The rationale behind this structure is that the seasonal pattern and fluctuation of the parameters can be captured by such a specification. As shown in Equation (7), the lag period of the intercept term β_{0t} is set to four quarters, to identify the seasonal pattern of tourism demand from the same season of the previous year. To capture the variations in the parameters of the intertemporal relationship, the parameters of the other explanatory variables are assumed to be determined by their values in the previous season and the external shocks.

The TVP model can be estimated using the Kalman filter algorithm (for details of the estimation procedure, see Harvey, 1989; Kalman, 1960).

Vector autoregressive model

The vector autoregressive (VAR) model is a system estimation technique that was first suggested by Sims (1980). In contrast to the above models, which depend heavily on the assumption that the explanatory variables are exogenous, the VAR method treats all of the variables as endogenous. It has been widely used in macroeconomic modelling and forecasting. Witt *et al.* (2003) and Song and Witt (2006) have successfully applied this technique to tourism demand forecasting. It is important to include an appropriate lag structure in the specification of a VAR model as too few lags will result in the model being unable to fully represent the data generating process (DGP), whereas too many lags will result in over-fitting and lack of degrees of freedom. The criteria used for determining the lag length are the Akaike information criterion (AIC) and Schwarz Bayesian criterion (SBC) (Song & Witt, 2000: 93–94).

Bayesian vector autoregressive model

As argued by many scholars over the last two decades (Brandt & Freeman, 2006; Kadiyala & Karlsson, 1997; Rebucci & Ciccarelli, 2003; Sims & Zha, 1998; Spencer, 1993; Wong *et al.*, 2006), VAR models may suffer from the problem of over-fitting because of the large number of parameters to estimate, which causes a loss of degrees of freedom and results in inefficient estimates. To address the over-fitting problem, the Bayesian approach has been applied to the unrestricted VAR model (Doan *et al.*, 1984; Litterman, 1986). By introducing the prior probability distribution over the model parameters, the lag structure of the VAR model is restricted and the over-fitting problem can be resolved. As a result, the BVAR approach is likely to generate more accurate forecasts than the unrestricted VAR model (Rebucci & Ciccarelli, 2003).

BVAR models are virtually unused in the literature of tourism demand modelling and forecasting. The only exception is Wong *et al.* (2006), who evaluated the forecasting performance of BVAR models and their unrestricted VAR counterparts. In the present study, the forecasting performance of BVAR models is evaluated based on the Minnesota prior, in line with Wong *et al.* (2006). Given different sets of hyperparameters, three BVAR models are estimated and the best performing one is adopted for subsequent analyses. The technical illustration of the BVAR model based on the Minnesota prior is provided by Litterman (1986) and Wong *et al.* (2006).

Univariate time series models

If none of the explanatory variables plays a statistically significant role in explaining the variation in the dependent variable, then the general ADLM presented by Equation (1) is reduced to a simple autoregressive (AR) model, or to an integrated autoregressive and moving average (ARIMA) model if the residuals of the AR model can be used to explain the variation in the dependent variable. Both the AR models (and naïve no-change ones) and ARIMA models are considered to be able to generate better forecasts of economic variables than can econometric models (Ashley, 1988; Makridakis, 1986; Martin & Witt, 1989; McNees, 1986). A seasonal ARIMA and a naïve no-change model are therefore included in this study as benchmarks for the comparison of forecasting accuracy. The standard Box–Jenkins approach (Box & Jenkins, 1976) is followed to fit seasonal ARIMA models for each of the 25 destinations. In general, a seasonal ARIMA model is denoted by SARIMA (p,d,q) $(P,D,Q)^s$. A multiplicative seasonal ARIMA model can be written as

$$\varphi_p(B)\Phi_P(B^s)\nabla^d\nabla_s^D y_t = \theta_q(B)\Theta_Q(B^s)\varepsilon_t, \tag{8}$$

where B is the backward shift operator, $\varphi_p(B)$, $\theta_q(B)$, $\Phi_P(B^s)$ and $\Theta_Q(B^s)$ are polynomials in B or B^s of non-seasonal and seasonal orders p, q, P and Q, respectively, and ε_t is the white noise term. The orders p, q, P and Q are determined by the partial autocorrelation function (PACF) and autocorrelation function (ACF), respectively. The number of seasonal differences (∇_s), D, and the number of regular differences (∇), d, are used to reduce the series to stationarity so that an ARIMA model can be fitted. A comprehensive explanation of the multiplicative seasonal ARIMA model-building approach can be found in Chu (1998).

To duplicate the seasonal pattern of the previous year, the naïve no-change model used in this study assumes that the forecast for period t equals the number in period $t - 4$:

$$\tilde{y}_t = y_{t-4}. \tag{9}$$

Measures of Forecasting Performance

Two kinds of forecast accuracy are considered in this study: error magnitude accuracy and directional change accuracy.

Error magnitude accuracy measure

To assess the overall forecasting performance of each of the above models, one-, two-, three-, four- and eight-quarter-ahead forecasts are calculated and compared with the actual values of the series. The measures used for comparing forecasting accuracy are the mean absolute percentage error (MAPE) and root mean square percentage error (RMSPE), which are defined respectively as follows:

$$MAPE = \frac{1}{n}\sum_{t=1}^{n}\frac{|e_t|}{y_t} \times 100, \tag{10}$$

$$RMSPE = \sqrt{\frac{1}{n}\sum_{t=1}^{n}\left(\frac{e_t}{y_t}\right)^2} \times 100, \tag{11}$$

where n is the length of the forecasting horizon, $e_t = \hat{y}_t - y_t$ is the forecasting error, and $\hat{y}_t$ and y_t are the forecast and actual values of the dependent variable, respectively.

The most commonly used accuracy measures, the MAPE and RMSPE, do not depend on the magnitudes of the demand variables being predicted. Therefore, forecasting performance can be compared not only between different forecasting techniques but also across different countries (units) (for detailed discussion of accuracy measures, see Martin & Witt, 1989; Witt & Witt, 1992).

Directional change accuracy measure

To measure directional change accuracy, Wright *et al.* (1986) suggested using the percentage of directions of movement forecast correctly (PDMFC), which can be written as follows:

$$PDMFC = \frac{N_{PDC}}{N_{ADC}} \times 100, \tag{12}$$

where N_{PDC} is the number of directional changes predicted accurately, and N_{ADC} is the number of directional changes actually happening. It is common practice to employ the naïve no-change model, using annual data, as a benchmark. A forecasting method must correctly forecast over 50% of the directions of movement to outperform the benchmark, as the naïve no-change model forecasts no directional change; that is, it will generate neither a correct nor an incorrect forecast of the direction of change. In this study, in contrast to the usual case, the naïve no-change model cannot be regarded as a benchmark because the forecasts change inter-quarter. If the percentage of correct forecasts exceeds 50%, then a forecasting model is considered to be useful in generating forecasts of directional change. A detailed methodological description of other measures of directional change accuracy can be found in Witt *et al.* (2003) and Stekler (1994).

Preliminary Data Analysis

As mentioned, tourism demand in this chapter is measured by tourist expenditure, which is described as the expenditure of international inbound visitors excluding transport payments. The economic conditions that are relevant to tourist expenditure include income and tourism prices adjusted by exchange rates. The general tourism demand function takes the form

$$Q_{it} = f(Y_{it}, P_{it}, P_{ist}, Dummy\ Variables), \tag{13}$$

where Q_{it} is the real expenditure of inbound international visitors in country i at 2000 prices in US dollars. Y_{it} is the average income level of country i's major source markets, and is measured by the weighted average GDP of the key source markets (the tourist arrivals from which account for 70% of total tourist arrivals to country i) at 2000 prices in US dollars. Because of data unavailability, the tourist arrivals variable (rather than the tourist expenditure variable) is used for the selection of the major source markets. P_{it} represents the cost of living for tourists in country i, and is measured by the CPI of country i (2000 = 100), adjusted by the relevant exchange rate. P_{ist} represents tourism prices in substitute destinations adjusted by the relevant exchange rates, and is measured by a weighted average price index of a set of alternative destinations for country i. The alternative destinations are chosen by comparing the arrivals by country of residence in 2004. When comparing two destinations, if most of the main source markets are the same, then they are chosen as the alternative destinations. The dummy variables comprise a Gulf War dummy (DGULF = 1 in 1990Q3–91Q1, and 0 otherwise), a dummy for the introduction of the euro (for SARIMA and JML-ECM, DEURO = 1 in 1999Q1, and 0 otherwise; for other models, DEURO = 1 in 1999Q1 and thereafter, and 0 before 1999Q1), a dummy for the 9/11 terrorism attack in 2001 (D911 = 1 in 2001Q4–2002Q1, and 0 otherwise), a dummy for the SARS epidemic in early 2003 (DSARS = 1 in 2003Q1–Q2, and 0 otherwise), a dummy for the avian flu outbreak in 2004 (DFLU = 1 in 2004Q1, and 0 otherwise) and seasonal dummies.

The sample covers the period from 1980Q1 to 2007Q1.[1] The data period 1980Q1–2005Q1 is used to estimate the individual forecasting models and the subsequent period to evaluate forecasting performance. Most of the data are extracted from the *Yearbook of Tourism Statistics* published by the United Nations World Tourism Organization (UNWTO) and the International Financial Statistics Online Service website of the International Monetary Fund (IMF). The missing data are generated through extrapolation. As a standard practice, a static log-linear function is adopted for modelling tourism demand for the 25 destinations:

$$q_{it} = \alpha_0 + \alpha_1 y_{it} + \alpha_2 p_{it} + \alpha_3 p_{ist} + Dummies + u_{it}, \qquad (14)$$

where the lower-case letters represent the corresponding variables in Equation (13) in logarithmic form.

Before any relationships are estimated, the properties of the data set used are examined. The HEGY test proposed by Hylleberg *et al.* (1990) is used to test for both seasonal and non-seasonal unit roots. Regressions using nonstationary variables may be subject to the spurious regression problem. An important exception is where the nonstationary variables are integrated of order one, and the linear combinations of these $I(1)$ variables are stationary; that is, these series are cointegrated. The next step is to determine which of the regressors discussed above should be included in the cointegration regressions.

According to the results of the HEGY test (results are omitted), all of the time series have a unit root at zero frequency, which implies that these time series have nonstationary stochastic trends. Therefore, there could be common stochastic trends between the dependent and explanatory variables.

To see whether there is any relationship between the explanatory variables and the dependent variable, we first estimate Equation (14) using the data from 1980Q1 to 2005Q1 for each of the 25 destinations with all of the explanatory variables included. The model for each country is estimated using OLS.[2] The variables included in each equation are all cointegrated. Therefore, the regression relationships are nonspurious, and the inferences drawn from the F- and t-statistics are reliable.

As discussed earlier, the JML method is used in this study to test for the long-run cointegrating relationships in the 25 models. It is assumed that the time series have deterministic trends but that the cointegration equations have only intercepts. This assumption has been found to be the most commonly used specification in economics and tourism demand modelling (Song & Witt, 2000). The intervention and orthogonalised seasonal dummy variables are included in the test for cointegration relationships using the JML approach. According to the calculated maximal eigenvalue and trace statistics, only one cointegration relationship is detected in each model apart from the cases of Mexico, Turkey, the United Kingdom and the United States, in each of which two cointegration relationships are found.

Empirical Results

Error magnitude accuracy

All eight models discussed above are estimated based on the quarterly data of 1980Q1–2005Q1, and *ex post* forecasts are generated for the 2005Q2–2007Q1 period. Using Italy as an example, the estimates of the eight competing models are presented in Table 21.1.[3] Most models are well specified. Where diagnostic tests are available, the estimated models pass all of them with only three exceptions, which occur for the static regression model and reduced ADLM. Failing the diagnostic tests may lead to unsatisfactory forecasting performance. This is discussed later.

The forecasting performance of the eight models is examined here for each time horizon by ranking the methods in order of both the MAPE and RMSPE for each of the 25 destinations. A summary of the empirical results is presented in Table 21.2.

Table 21.1 Model estimates for Italy

Variable	Static regression	Reduced ADLM	TVP	VAR	BVAR	Variable	JML-ECM
Constant	2.902**	1.395*	7.814	1.126	0.348	Constant	0.018
	(2.401)	(1.966)	[4.778]	(1.212)	(0.445)		(1.430)
q_{t-1}		0.319***		0.281***	0.439***	Δq_{t-1}	0.528
		(4.233)		(3.638)	(9.731)		(4.393)
q_{t-2}		−0.126*		−0.108	−0.029	Δq_{t-2}	−0.042
		(−1.837)		(−1.081)	(−0.470)		(−0.317)
q_{t-3}				0.147	0.210***	Δq_{t-3}	0.027
				(1.455)	(4.111)		(0.191)
q_{t-4}		0.600***		0.546***	0.186***	Δq_{t-4}	−0.066
		(9.321)		(5.702)	(4.109)		(−0.555)
p_t	−2.026***	−0.953***	−0.543			Δp_{t-1}	0.171
	(−8.863)	(−3.690)	[−2.355]				(0.573)
p_{t-1}		0.416*		−0.602*	−0.132	Δp_{t-2}	0.006
		(1.675)		(−1.824)	(−0.913)		(0.022)
p_{t-2}				0.341	0.023	Δp_{t-3}	−0.028
				(0.710)	(0.223)		(−0.100)
p_{t-3}				0.101	−0.002	Δp_{t-4}	−0.126
				(0.221)	(−0.024)		(−0.422)
p_{t-4}		0.247**		0.195	0.013	Δp_{st-1}	−0.241
		(2.233)		(0.582)	(0.244)		(−0.579)
p_{st}	2.437***	0.543***	0.439			Δp_{st-2}	−0.175
	(9.472)	(2.718)	[1.728]				(−0.476)

Table 21.1 (*Continued*)

Variable	Static regression	Reduced ADLM	TVP	VAR	BVAR	Variable	JML-ECM
p_{st-1}				0.551	0.211	Δp_{st-3}	−0.198
				(1.614)	(1.355)		(−0.564)
p_{st-2}				−0.153	0.002	Δp_{st-4}	0.343
				(−0.320)	−0.019		(0.953)
p_{st-3}				−0.598	−0.011	Δy_{t-1}	−0.012
				(−1.470)	(−0.156)		(−0.029)
p_{st-4}				0.401	0.041	Δy_{t-2}	0.096
				(1.115)	(0.744)		(0.245)
y_t	0.287**	0.256*	0.120			Δy_{t-3}	0.072
	(2.108)	(1.848)	[0.731]				(0.183)
y_{t-1}				0.076	0.021	Δy_{t-4}	−0.054
				(0.284)	(0.179)		(−0.138)
y_{t-2}		−0.331**		−0.146	0.004	EC_{t-1}	−0.024
		(−2.343)		(−0.377)	(0.039)		(−1.018)
y_{t-3}				0.132	0.000	$ODUMQ1$	0.009
				(0.343)	0.000		(0.207)
y_{t-4}				−0.154	0.007	$ODUMQ2$	−0.016
				(−0.563)	(0.146)		(−0.313)
$DUMQ1$	−0.236***	0.155**				$ODUMQ3$	−0.010
	(−4.928)	(2.415)					(−0.221)
$DUMQ2$	0.376***	0.359***		0.175*	0.420***		
	(7.885)	(5.181)		(1.970)	(7.052)		
$DUMQ3$	0.685***	0.288***		0.273***	0.564***		
	(14.342)	(4.451)		(2.981)	(10.008)		
R^2	0.871	0.967		0.963		R^2	0.366
S.E.	0.168	0.088		0.097	0.107	S.E.	0.100
NORM(2)	2.157	1.532		1.055		NORM(2)	0.541
HETRO(1)	20.444***	22.705**		22.458		HETRO(1)	10.527
D-W	0.701	1.659		1.577	1.966	D-W	1.987
RESET(1)	0.304	3.108*		1.635		RESET(1)	0.581
AIC	−0.664	−1.900	−0.627	−1.658		AIC	−1.576
SC	−0.483	−1.555	−0.497	−1.154		SC	−1.004

Notes: (a) The values in parentheses and square brackets are the *t*-statistics and *z*-statistics, respectively. (b) *, ** and *** indicate that the estimates are significant at the 10%, 5% and 1% levels, respectively. (c) The diagnostic statistics: NORM(2) is the Jarque–Bera normality test; HETRO(1) is a heteroscedasticity test based on the regression of squared residuals on squared fitted values; D-W is the Durbin–Watson test for autocorrelation; and RESET(1) is the Ramsey misspecification test. AIC and SC are the Akaike information criterion and Schwarz criterion, respectively. The figures in brackets are the degrees of freedom associated with the tests.

Table 21.2 Summary of forecasting accuracy

Method	Measure	Forecasting horizon				
		One quarter	Two quarters	Three quarters	Four quarters	Eight quarters
Static regression	MAPE	16.396 (8)	16.396 (8)	16.635 (8)	16.352 (8)	16.072 (6)
	RMSPE	18.129 (8)	18.136 (8)	18.355 (8)	17.901 (8)	16.072 (6)
JML-ECM	MAPE	7.033 (4)	12.538 (7)	8.854 (4)	9.367 (6)	15.174 (5)
	RMSPE	8.606 (4)	15.452 (7)	10.401 (4)	10.613 (6)	15.174 (5)
Reduced ADLM	MAPE	7.900 (5)	8.930 (6)	9.766 (7)	10.272 (7)	16.838 (7)
	RMSPE	9.430 (5)	10.700 (6)	11.497 (7)	11.654 (7)	16.838 (7)
TVP	MAPE	5.372 (1)	5.819 (1)	6.228 (1)	6.926 (2)	9.919 (2)
	RMSPE	6.751 (1)	7.101 (1)	7.450 (1)	7.876 (2)	9.919 (2)
VAR	MAPE	7.935 (6)	8.913 (5)	9.065 (5)	9.103 (4)	17.330 (8)
	RMSPE	9.627 (7)	10.651 (5)	10.741 (5)	10.576 (5)	17.330 (8)
BVAR	MAPE	8.202 (7)	8.673 (4)	9.097 (6)	9.291 (5)	12.355 (4)
	RMSPE	9.591 (6)	10.353 (4)	10.982 (6)	10.510 (4)	12.355 (4)
SARIMA	MAPE	6.292 (2)	6.510 (3)	6.909 (3)	7.814 (3)	10.677 (3)
	RMSPE	7.562 (2)	7.781 (3)	8.217 (3)	8.720 (3)	10.677 (3)
Naïve	MAPE	6.491 (3)	6.271 (2)	6.408 (2)	6.357 (1)	8.469 (1)
	RMSPE	7.697 (3)	7.444 (2)	7.532 (2)	7.335 (1)	8.469 (1)

Note: The figures represent the average MAPE and RMSPE across 25 destinations. The values in parentheses are rankings. The MAPE and RMSPE are the same for the eight-quarter-ahead forecasts because only one forecast value could be calculated for each destination.

For the one-, two- and three-quarter-ahead forecasts, the results show that in terms of both the MAPE and RMSPE, the TVP model is the most accurate forecasting model, followed by the SARIMA model for one-quarter-ahead forecasts and the naïve no-change model for two- and three-quarter-ahead forecasts. The least accurate one-, two- and three-quarter-ahead forecasts are generated by the static regression model. The BVAR model based on the Minnesota prior does not outperform the unrestricted VAR model in the case of short-term forecasts. This finding suggests that the values assigned to the hyperparameters are crucial in a BVAR model. Rather than using rules of thumb, the hyperparameters should be estimated consistently to obtain a closer approximation to the full Bayesian estimation (Rebucci & Ciccarelli, 2003).

When lengthening the forecasting horizon to four and eight quarters ahead, the naïve no-change model's relative performance improves, and it replaces the TVP model to top the competition. The TVP model still generates the second most accurate forecasts, followed by the SARIMA model. The BVAR model's performance increases compared to that in short-term forecasting. As with the short-term forecasts, the static regression model generates the least accurate forecasts at the horizon of four quarters. With regard to eight-quarter-ahead forecasts, the ranking of the unrestricted VAR model dramatically sinks to the bottom of the competition, followed by the reduced ADLM with the second worst performance and then the static regression model. It seems that the superior performance of the BVAR model over its unrestricted counterpart is evident in longer term (at least two years ahead) forecasting. It should be noted that the level of forecast accuracy decreases significantly as the forecasting horizon extends from one year to two years, which indicates that there is increasing uncertainty about the long-term future and makes the accurate prediction of long-term tourism demand difficult.

In general, the TVP model provides the most accurate short-term forecasts, whereas the naïve no-change model provides the best long-term ones. Over all of the forecasting horizons examined, the TVP, naïve no-change and SARIMA models are always ranked the top three among the competition.

The superior performance of the TVP model suggests that it approximates well the underlying DGP of a demand series. The actual underlying DGP of a time series is an unknown function of a variety of complex factors. Forecasting models are at best only crude approximations of actual DGPs (Bhansali, 2002). The evolution of a nonconstant DGP is characterised by both structural change and regime shifts (Clements & Hendry, 1998). By introducing time-varying parameters and taking into account potential structural change, stochastic trends and seasonality, the TVP model is able to capture well the dynamic characteristics of the underlying DGPs. In contrast, the unrealistic assumption that the data are generated by a constant, time-invariant process, in other words, that the economic structure does not change over time, leads to the forecast failure of the static regression model. The changes in the DGP beyond the sample period may be caused by some factors that are not incorporated into an econometric model, which may result in inaccurate forecasts. Because the effects of various causal factors on a demand variable are likely to take place in a gradual fashion, the TVP model can still precisely forecast the demand for the near future, but its predictive power diminishes as the forecasting horizon lengthens. However, the naïve no-change model, as the most parsimonious approximation of the actual DGP, also nested in other econometric models, performs well in longer term forecasting. This is probably because it does not contain any 'misleading' causal information, which is valid only for the observed sample period but not beyond that. In other words, the effects of all causal factors that explain the actual DGP during the forecasting period are balanced, even though they are entirely omitted from the model. In contrast, among econometric models, the unaccounted significant effects of missing causal factors leads to relatively high forecast error. In addition, the naïve no-change model is not subject to the model misspecification problem, which is a possible reason for the forecast failure of some econometric models.

To determine whether there is any significant difference in the forecast accuracy between the models, the Morgan–Granger–Newbold (MGN) and Harvey–Leybourne–Newbold (HLN) tests are applied (Diebold & Mariano, 1995; Granger & Newbold, 1977; Harvey et al., 1997; Newey & West, 1987, 1994). The MGN test is applicable only to one-step-ahead forecasts, whereas the HLN test can be employed for multiple-step-ahead forecasts. Table 21.3 summarises the results of the HLN test between the top two models (i.e. the TVP and naïve no-change models) and the other competitors, respectively. These results provide statistical evidence of the superior forecasting performance of the TVP and naïve no-change models. In particular, the TVP model significantly outperforms all of the other competing models at least at the 5% significance level in one-quarter-ahead forecasting. The MGN test confirms this finding.[4]

The superior performance of the TVP model over its competitors in short-term forecasting suggests that it is essential to take structural instability into account when generating tourism demand forecasts (Song & Witt, 2000). This empirical result is consistent with the findings of previous research into international tourism forecasting, which uses annual data to assess forecasting accuracy and in which the TVP model outperforms its competitors in the short run (see, for example, Song & Witt, 2000; Song et al., 2003). A new finding in this study is that, with the proper treatment of seasonality (i.e. by incorporating a seasonal component into the state equation), the TVP model is able to accurately forecast seasonal tourism demand.

The finding of the excellent forecast accuracy of the naïve no-change model in the long run confirms the empirical results obtained by Martin and Witt (1989), Song and Witt (2000), Kulendran and Witt (2001) and Song et al. (2003). In addition, the empirical finding that the naïve no-change model generates more accurate long-term tourism demand forecasts than does the SARIMA one partially supports the findings of Chan (1993), Kulendran and Witt (2001) and Song et al. (2003).

The static regression model tends to generate relatively inaccurate forecasts of international tourism demand for all forecasting horizons. The main reason for its poor forecasting performance is that the model does not have a dynamic structure and thus is unable to adequately capture fluctuations in quarterly tourism demand series, which are likely to be more evident than those in annual time series.

Directional change accuracy

The empirical results of the percentage of directions of movement forecast correctly (PDMFC) are presented in Table 21.4. For the one-, two- and three-quarter-ahead forecasts, all of the models perform well, with the TVP

Table 21.3 HLN tests for equal forecast accuracy

Method	One quarter ahead		Two quarters ahead		Three quarters ahead		Four quarters ahead	
	TVP	Naïve	TVP	Naïve	TVP	Naïve	TVP	Naïve
Static regression	6.253***	5.522***	5.537***	5.268***	5.386***	5.224***	4.698***	4.770***
JML-ECM	2.625***	0.815	1.570	1.549	2.473**	2.370**	1.980**	2.370**
Reduced ADLM	3.816***	1.711*	3.345***	2.520**	3.090***	2.817***	2.521**	2.820***
TVP	–	–2.132**	–	–1.014	–	–0.472	–	1.983**
VAR	3.486***	1.621	2.601**	2.127**	2.025**	1.890*	1.715*	2.133**
BVAR	3.561***	1.882*	3.165***	2.638***	2.632***	2.506**	1.849*	2.288**
SARIMA	2.113**	–0.300	1.632	0.420	1.289	0.743	1.251	1.802*
Naïve	2.132**	–	1.014	–	0.472	–	–1.983**	–

Note: ***, ** and * indicate the 1%, 5% and 10% significance levels, respectively. The positive statistics suggest that the TVP or naïve no-change models (in columns) outperform the competing models (in rows). Because of the extremely small number of eight-quarter-ahead forecasts, the HLN test was not conducted.

Table 21.4 Directional change forecasting accuracy (percentage of directions of movement forecast correctly)

Method	One quarter ahead	Two quarters ahead	Three quarters ahead	Four quarters ahead	Eight quarters ahead
Static regression	87.0 (8)	83.4 (8)	87.3 (8)	56.8 (6)	48.0 (7)
JML-ECM	93.5 (5)	93.7 (4=)	88.7 (7)	59.2 (3)	44.0 (8)
Reduced ADLM	91.0 (7)	89.7 (7)	91.3 (4=)	61.6 (2)	64.0 (2=)
TVP	95.5 (1)	94.3 (3)	93.3 (1)	53.6 (7)	56.0 (4=)
VAR	93.0 (6)	94.9 (1=)	90.0 (6)	70.4 (1)	64.0 (2=)
BVAR	95.0 (2=)	92.6 (6)	92.0 (3)	58.4 (4=)	56.0 (4=)
SARIMA	95.0 (2=)	94.9 (1=)	92.7 (2)	58.4 (4=)	68.0 (1)
Naïve	94.0 (4)	93.7 (4=)	91.3 (4=)	50.0 (8)	50.0 (6)

Note: The values in parentheses are rankings.

and SARIMA models generally ranked on the top. The differences among the models, however, are not significant. All of them have fairly similar performance in that the PDMFC for each model exceeds 80% for short-term forecasts. Given the obvious seasonality of tourism demand, the models are unlikely to make an incorrect forecast of directional change within one year as long as seasonality has been properly treated. Performance drops quickly, starting from the horizon of four quarters; however, the directional change

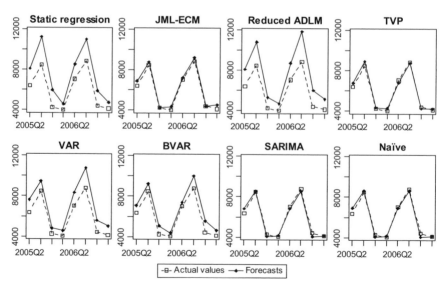

Figure 21.1 Multi-step forecasts of the eight competing models for Italy (2005Q2–2007Q1)

accuracy of all models is still acceptable (i.e. with PDMFCs above 50) for the four-quarter-ahead forecasts, except for that of the naïve no-change model. As the forecasting horizon lengthens to eight quarters, the PDMFCs of two more models, the static regression model and JML-ECM, fall below 50. The VAR and SARIMA models perform the best for the horizons of four and eight quarters, respectively. With regard to the naïve no-change model, as seasonal fluctuations are obvious, it performs well in one- to three-quarter-ahead forecasting. Because of the model specification, the naïve no-change model cannot predict any directions of movement as the horizon extends to four and eight quarters. The static regression model always generates the least accurate forecasts, as the line at the bottom of Figure 21.1 suggests.

Concluding Remarks and Future Research Directions

The relative forecasting accuracy of six econometric models has been evaluated in this study using quarterly data. These models comprise a static regression model, an ECM based on the JML approach, a reduced ADLM, an unrestricted VAR model, a BVAR model and a TVP model. In addition, two univariate time series models – a SARIMA model and a naïve no-change model – have been included in the comparison. The forecasting performance of the various models has been assessed using international tourism demand data in terms of aggregate tourist expenditures in 25 countries/country groupings.

The TVP, SARIMA and naïve no-change models are the three top-performing models over all forecasting horizons examined. For the short-term (one-, two- and three-quarter-ahead) forecasts, the TVP model is the most accurate forecasting model. The least accurate short-term forecasts are generated by the static regression model. In terms of directional change accuracy, the performance of all of the models in short-term forecasting is fairly similar. They all perform well and could be considered useful in generating forecasts of directional change. As the forecasting horizon extends to four and eight quarters, the TVP model is outperformed by the naïve no-change model in terms of the error magnitude accuracy. As with the short-term forecasts, the static regression model generates the least accurate forecasts at the four-quarter-ahead horizon, and the unrestricted VAR model is outperformed by all of the others in eight-quarter-ahead forecasting. In terms of directional change accuracy, the VAR and SARIMA models outperform the others in four- and eight-quarter-ahead forecasting, respectively. The naïve no-change model cannot predict any direction of movement, and the static regression model always exhibits below-average performance in directional change forecasting.

Taking both the error magnitude and directional change accuracy measures into consideration, the TVP, naïve no-change and SARIMA models all perform consistently well in short-term forecasting, and the TVP model appears to be the best one. These models can all be applied for both error magnitude and directional change forecasting in the short term. However, although the naïve no-change model outperforms the others in terms of error magnitude accuracy in the long term, it should not be applied for directional change forecasting as the horizon lengthens. This implies that the choice of a forecasting model in practice depends on which accuracy measure is of concern. Many tourism practitioners such as airline operators are keen to know whether there will be more or fewer visitors next year than this year. This information will help them to decide whether or not they should increase capacity or staffing (Frechtling, 2001). If that is the primary purpose for longer term forecasting, then the VAR model should be considered rather than the naïve no-change model.

The superior performance of the TVP model in short-term forecasting suggests that it is essential to take structural instability and stochastic seasonal fluctuations into account when forecasting tourism demand. It also indicates that the TVP model is a successful approximation of the actual nonconstant, time-variant DGP.

The frequency of the top performance of the destination-specific models suggests that the TVP model consistently performs well across different market conditions. One option for dealing with the difficulty in choosing an optimal forecasting model is to combine the forecasts generated by various models. Based on different modelling techniques and assumptions, the TVP, naïve no-change and SARIMA models all demonstrate superior forecasting performance, and contain different information about the actual DGP. In view of the forecast combination literature and past empirical evidence (for example, Bates & Granger, 1969; Winkler, 1989), combining the forecasts of these models is likely to lead to even more accurate results. This is worth further investigation in future research.

Notes

(1) Because of the unavailability of data, the sample range is adjusted for some destinations. The estimation and forecasting periods are also adjusted accordingly.
(2) The estimation results are not presented because of space constraints, but are available from the authors upon request.
(3) Because of space constraints, the estimation and forecasting results of other cases are not reported here, but are available from the authors upon request.
(4) The results are not presented because of space constraints, but are available from the authors upon request.

References

Ashley, R. (1988) On the relative worth of recent macroeconomic forecasts. *International Journal of Forecasting* 4 (3), 363–376.

Bates, J.M. and Granger, C.W.J. (1969) The combination of forecasts. *Operational Research Quarterly* 20 (4), 451–468.

Bhansali, R.J. (2002) Multi-step forecasting. In M.P. Clements and D.F. Hendry (eds) *A Companion to Economic Forecasting* (pp. 206–221). Malden, MA: Blackwell Publishers.

Bohara, A.K. and Sauer, C. (1992) Competing macro-hypotheses in the United States: A Kalman filtering approach. *Applied Economics* 24 (4), 389–399.

Box, G.E.P. and Jenkins, G.M. (1976) *Time Series Analysis: Forecasting and Control* (2nd edn). San Francisco, CA: Holden-Day.

Brandt, P.T. and Freeman, J.R. (2006) Advances in Bayesian time series modeling and the study of politics: Theory testing, forecasting, and policy analysis. *Political Analysis* 14 (1), 1–36.

Brown, J.P., Song, H. and McGillivray, A. (1997) Forecasting UK house prices: A time varying coefficient approach. *Economic Modelling* 14 (4), 529–548.

Chan, Y-M. (1993) Forecasting tourism: A sine wave time series regression approach. *Journal of Travel Research* 32 (2), 58–60.

Chu, F-L. (1998) Forecasting tourist arrivals: Nonlinear sine wave or ARIMA? *Journal of Travel Research* 36 (3), 79–84.

Clements, M.P. and Hendry, D.F. (1998) *Forecasting Economic Time Series*. Cambridge: Cambridge University Press.

Diebold, F.X. and Mariano, R.S. (1995) Comparing predictive accuracy. *Journal of Business & Economic Statistics* 13 (3), 253–263.

Doan, T., Litterman, R. and Sims, C.A. (1984) Forecasting and conditional projection using realistic prior distributions. *Econometric Reviews* 3 (1), 1–100.

Frechtling, D.C. (2001) *Forecasting Tourism Demand*. Oxford: Butterworth-Heinemann.

Granger, C.W.J. and Newbold, P. (1977) *Forecasting Economic Time Series*. Orlando, FL: Academic Press.

Greenslade, J.V. and Hall, S.G. (1996) Modelling economies subject to structural change: The case of Germany. *Economic Modelling* 13 (4), 545–559.

Harvey, A.C. (1989) *Forecasting, Structural Time Series Models and the Kalman Filter*. Cambridge: Cambridge University Press.

Harvey, D., Leybourne, S. and Newbold, P. (1997) Testing the equality of prediction mean squared errors. *International Journal of Forecasting* 13 (2), 281–291.

Hendry, D.F. (1986) Empirical modeling in dynamic econometrics. *Applied Mathematics and Computation* 20 (3–4), 201–236.

Hylleberg, S., Engle, R.F., Granger, C.W.J. and Yoo, B.S. (1990) Seasonal integration and cointegration. *Journal of Econometrics* 44 (1–2), 215–238.

Kadiyala, K.R. and Karlsson, S. (1997) Numerical methods for estimation and inference in Bayesian VAR-models. *Journal of Applied Econometrics* 12 (2), 99–132.

Kalman, R.E. (1960) A new approach to linear filtering and prediction problems. *Transactions of the ASME – Journal of Basic Engineering* 82 (Series D), 35–45.

Kim, C-J. (1993) Sources of monetary growth uncertainty and economic activity: The time-varying-parameter model with heteroskedastic disturbances. *Review of Economics and Statistics* 75 (3), 483–492.

Kulendran, N. and Witt, S.F. (2001) Cointegration versus least squares regression. *Annals of Tourism Research* 28 (2), 291–311.

Li, G., Song, H. and Witt, S.F. (2005) Recent developments in econometric modeling and forecasting. *Journal of Travel Research* 44 (1), 82–99.

Li, G., Song, H. and Witt, S.F. (2006) Time varying parameter and fixed parameter linear AIDS: An application to tourism demand forecasting. *International Journal of Forecasting* 22 (1), 57–71.

Litterman, R.B. (1986) Forecasting with Bayesian vector autoregressions: Five years of experience. *Journal of Business & Economic Statistics* 4 (1), 25–38.

Makridakis, S. (1986) The art and science of forecasting: An assessment and future directions. *International Journal of Forecasting* 2 (1), 15–39.

Martin, C.A. and Witt, S.F. (1989) Forecasting tourism demand: A comparison of the accuracy of several quantitative methods. *International Journal of Forecasting* 5 (1), 7–19.

McNees, S.K. (1986) Forecasting accuracy of alternative techniques: A comparison of U.S. macroeconomic forecasts. *Journal of Business & Economic Statistics* 4 (1), 5–15.

Newey, W.K. and West, K.D. (1987) A simple, positive semi-definite, heteroskedasticity and autocorrelation consistent covariance matrix. *Econometrica* 55 (3), 703–708.

Newey, W.K. and West, K.D. (1994) Automatic lag selection in covariance matrix estimation. *Review of Economic Studies* 61 (4), 631–653.

Rebucci, A. and Ciccarelli, M. (2003) Bayesian VARs: A Survey of the Recent Literature with an Application to the European Monetary System. IMF Working Paper No. WP/03/102. Washington, DC: International Monetary Fund.

Riddington, G.L. (1993) Forecasting ski demand: Comparing learning curve and varying parameter coefficient approaches. *Journal of Forecasting* 18 (3), 205–214.

Riddington, G.L. (1999) Time varying coefficient models and their forecasting performance. *Omega: The International Journal of Management Science* 21 (5), 573–583.

Sims, C.A. (1980) Macroeconomics and reality. *Econometrica* 48 (1), 1–48.

Sims, C.A. and Zha, T. (1998) Bayesian methods for dynamic multivariate models. *International Economic Review* 39 (4), 949–968.

Song, H. and Witt, S.F. (2000) *Tourism Demand Modelling and Forecasting: Modern Econometric Approaches*. Amsterdam: Pergamon.

Song, H. and Witt, S.F. (2006) Forecasting international tourist flows to Macau. *Tourism Management* 27 (2), 214–224.

Song, H. and Wong, K.K.F. (2003) Tourism demand modeling: A time-varying parameter approach. *Journal of Travel Research* 42 (1), 57–64.

Song, H., Liu, X. and Romilly, P. (1996) A time varying parameter approach to the Chinese aggregate consumption function. *Economics of Planning* 29 (3), 185–203.

Song, H., Liu, X. and Romilly, P. (1997) A comparative study of modelling the demand for food in the United States and the Netherlands. *Journal of Applied Econometrics* 12 (5), 593–608.

Song, H., Romilly, P. and Liu, X. (1998) The UK consumption function and structural instability: Improving forecasting performance using a time-varying parameter approach. *Applied Economics* 30 (7), 975–983.

Song, H., Witt, S.F. and Jensen, T.C. (2003) Tourism forecasting: Accuracy of alternative econometric models. *International Journal of Forecasting* 19 (1), 123–141.

Spencer, D.E. (1993) Developing a Bayesian vector autoregression forecasting model. *International Journal of Forecasting* 9 (3), 407–421.

Stekler, H.O. (1994) Are economic forecasts valuable? *Journal of Forecasting* 13 (6), 495–505.

Stock, J.H. and Watson, M.W. (1996) Evidence on structural instability in macroeconomic time series relations. *Journal of Business & Economic Statistics* 14 (1), 11–30.

Swamy, P.A.V.B, Conway, R.K. and LeBlanc, M.R. (1989) The stochastic coefficients approach to econometric modeling Part III: Estimation, Stability Testing and Prediction. *Journal of Agricultural Economics Research* 41 (1), 4–20.

Winkler, R.L. (1989) Combining forecasts: A philosophical basis and some current issues. *International Journal of Forecasting* 5 (4), 605–609.

Witt, S.F. and Witt, C.A. (1992) *Modeling and Forecasting Demand in Tourism*. London: Academic Press.

Witt, S.F. and Witt, C.A. (1995) Forecasting tourism demand: A review of empirical research. *International Journal of Forecasting* 11 (3), 447–475.

Witt, S.F., Song, H. and Louvieris, P. (2003) Statistical testing in forecasting model selection. *Journal of Travel Research* 42 (2), 151–158.

Wong, K.K.F., Song, H. and Chon, K.S. (2006) Bayesian models for tourism demand forecasting. *Tourism Management* 27 (5), 773–780.

Wright, D.J., Capon, G., Pagé, R., Quiroga, J., Taseen, A.A. and Tomasini, F. (1986) Evaluation of forecasting methods for decision support. *International Journal of Forecasting* 2 (2), 139–152.

Part 6

Vision

22 Futurecast: An Exploration of Key Emerging Megatrends in the Tourism Arena

Luiz Moutinho, Shirley Rate and Ronnie Ballantyne

The tourism industry continues to push forward, ever expanding in its importance to the European economy and increasingly involving more and more participants. Despite one of the most severe recessions since WWII, and the ongoing global economic uncertainty, the industry continues to represent the third largest socio-economic activity in the European Union (EU). On an international scale, the EU remains the world's number one tourist destination, accounting for more than half of all global arrivals (ETC, 2011). However, it is an industry facing major challenges. The World Tourism Organisation (UNWTO) estimates that recovery for the sector will be slower in Europe than in other regions of the world. Indeed, the industry is facing escalating global competition with emerging countries offering new destinations and attracting a growing number of tourists. Furthermore, their populations are growing in size and economic power, thus becoming more transient themselves, which will inevitably drive changes in global consumption and product innovation.

Thus, as the European tourism market becomes increasingly dynamic and complex in nature, new markets will emerge and tourism consumers will become more sophisticated, with motivations and preferences in constant flux. The already rapid pace of change in the business environment continues to accelerate, prompted and amplified by such economic instability added to a variety of other interrelated factors including technological innovations, evolving consumer expectations and dramatic demographic shifts. This turbulent environment poses significant challenges to the tourism provider. For example, there will be greater emphasis on individual and self-determined holidays and on educational and active recreational pursuits. On one hand, increasing environmental awareness will affect planning policies and tourist demand. On the other hand, nature, which is the critical resource of tourism, will become more scarce and fragile; the quality of the natural environment is essential to tourism as such an ecological and more sustainable long-term approach to tourism planning is postulated. Understanding this new business environment and in particular identifying key trends and movements, including importantly the new consumer or indeed the new tourist, is pivotal to the formulation, development and maintenance of successful management strategy.

To effectively compete in such a world, an increasing number of tourism planners recognise that one of the most fundamental means of creating value for themselves and their stakeholders is to develop and nurture a marketing orientation – whereby marketing planning and decision making is based on a thorough understanding of an organisation's goals and capabilities, its customers and competitors, and the business environment in which it operates. Increasingly, the flexibility and the degree of reactivity to the changing business environment are becoming fundamental determinants of not only success but indeed survival. Successful new strategic tourism planning initiatives will require that decision makers not only understand historic and contemporary trends and movements in the business environment but will require the ability to predict new key emerging developments and shifts. This will lead to the development of innovative and effective strategies.

The unique attributes of the tourism industry – the complexity involved in supplying its services, the network of players and industries which make up a service offering, and its proximity to the customer in delivering the service, make the tourism business environment somewhat more complex than other sectors. It has been proposed, therefore, that in scanning the tourism business environment, the long-standing methodology of PEST analysis falls short of providing a comprehensive snapshot of such a dynamic sector. Instead, an approach which better fits the nature of the tourism industry and allows a more robust analysis is the SCEPTICAL framework (Moutinho *et al.*, 2011). This framework considers environmental influences in terms of:

Social factors
Cultural factors
Economic factors
Physical factors
Technical factors
International factors
Communications and infrastructure factors
Administrative and institutional factors
Legal and political factors

The aim of this chapter is, in drawing on the philosophy of this framework, to examine some of the distinguishable and important megatrends in the tourism environment. While such trends have been documented before, commentators have been criticised for listing issues which lack overall coherence, relevance and guidance (Dwyer, 2005). In addressing this, the objective of this chapter is to synthesise those trends which have converged, resulting in unprecedented changes in tourist consumer behaviour. The aim of this chapter is not to present a definitive picture of all past, present and future developments within the business arena but to illuminate those elements that continue to gain in size and momentum towards the creation of the 'new tourist'. In addition and importantly, the chapter traces some of the more novel developments in the sector that are now beginning to emerge in response to these trends. These new developments may only be present as 'weak signals' in terms of environmental scanning; currently, however, they are likely to accelerate and dominate in the coming years. This chapter will also focus on the future – bridging the gap between more traditional management approaches and the exploration of new paradigms of thought. By isolating and exploring these new paradigms and techniques in conjunction with tracing and understanding key trends and developments in the new business environment, the tourism strategist gains invaluable decision-making intelligence that allows him or her to 'Futurecast'. In effect, tourism operators will have the ability to 'see' events before they occur – allowing strategic decision makers to develop innovative and effective strategic tourism initiatives. Moreover, this approach allows companies not only to anticipate major shifts in the environment, but also to try to influence these changes.

This chapter is divided into five main sections which identify trending topics for consideration: first, the *New Tourist* which considers some of the key geo-demographic trends which are influencing the nature of the market; second, the *New Socioquake*, which examines some of the current social and cultural trends affecting tourism behaviour; third, the *New e-Generation* which explores how innovation and the advancement of technology has impacted on attitudes in the tourist sector; and, fourth, the *Rise of the Prosumer*, which considers the consumer behaviours of the new e-generation. Finally, the chapter outlines *Evolutions and Revolutions in Branding*, which investigates those paradigm shifts necessary for tourism marketers to successfully engage with the new tourist.

The New Tourist

European tourism faces major challenges with regard to social and cultural developments which are affecting the nature of tourism demand. These have come about due to a number of key influences. Perhaps one of the most apparent of these is the demographic shifts affecting both advanced and emerging market economies. Demographic shifts towards lower fertility and falling mortality, added to improvements in life expectancy, have created an increase in the proportion of populations over the age of 60.

Worldwide, this cohort currently represents an estimated 10% of the population, with an increase to 22% expected by the year 2050 (Office for National Statistics, 2010). Changes in age structures like this result in fundamental shifts in the nature of demand for tourist products as well as presenting new tourist behaviours and expectations. The older population is healthier and wealthier and enjoying longer retirement than its predecessors. This 'golden mafia', a demanding consumer group, puts travel high on the agenda in their time-rich years. Younger at heart, anti-materialistic and more experienced and confident travellers than previous generations, these consumers seek experiential travel with an emphasis on self-improvement, such as volunteerism, educational travel, health, wellness and sporting programmes, as well as off-the-beaten-track, authentic and adventurous experiences (Deloitte LLP, 2010).

While this market should be an imperative for tourism providers, the 16–35 market still accounts for more than 20% of global tourism (ETC, 2011). This is due to a combination of social influencers including rising incomes, extended social networks, the tendency to start families later and the growth of single-person households, which has led to an increase in travel by the youth market (ETC, 2006). Furthermore, this market should be of particular interest to tourism providers in the EU as its own youth market begins to dwindle – in developed regions, growth of older populations can be more than double the global average while younger cohorts quickly decline (Office for National Statistics, 2010). Meanwhile, as emerging economies such as the BRIC countries (Brazil, Russia, India and China) continue to grow, the reality of almost 2 billion new middle-class potential tourists by 2030 (Deloitte, 2011) has the very real potential to entirely alter the shape of the tourism sector in the EU.

Most important, however, is that the tourism sector recognises that such new markets consuming in such unique competitive marketplaces bring with them a new and challenging set of values and behaviours. As EU countries are forced to enter a more competitive global environment, where their consumers have more choice of newer tourism destinations, they face a new type of tourist. This tourist is more knowledgeable, more experienced, more demanding and has higher expectations than ever seen before. Evolutions in technology have provided them with more power and control and the industry is witnessing more sophisticated and complex consumer demands. This has resulted in the emergence of the *'Prosumer'* – the consumer who takes control in designing unique, customised and more economical travel experiences meeting their specific set of needs. The nature of this consumer will be explored in greater detail later in the chapter. The tourism operators that will prosper in such challenging marketplaces are those that dispense with archaic, outdated and irrelevant marketing practices and truly listen to, shape conversations with and engage with this new tourist.

The New Socioquake

Within any business context, operators are at the mercy of social and cultural forces which influence values, perceptions, preferences and behaviours. However, facing the tourist industry now is the 'New Socioquake' which reflects the future of social values, but also the pace at which they infiltrate borders and become global trends. The diffusion of information for events and trends across global locations is becoming shorter due to technological innovations in communications technology. Popcorn (2002) describes a number of such trends which have the potential to cause a socioquake – that of 'affluenza' is perhaps most pertinent to the tourist sector. The more affluent people across the globe become, the more complex life becomes and the more roles people play, which has created unparalleled pressures and demands and as such a growing disillusionment with wealth. The unending search for happiness through products and services is conflicting with the inner need for a simpler life, producing the fast-spreading virus, affluenza (Hamilton & Deniss, 2006).

Importantly for tourism, this trend is leading towards a boycott of the materialistic values of the past and a pursuit instead for more meaningful consumption. A process of 'Rehumanisation' is being witnessed – consumers seeking personal fulfilment through experiential consumption, consistent with Maslow's self-actualisation concept (Yeoman et al., 2007) and aligned with this, a high sensitivity to ethical, social and environmental impacts of individual behaviours. The new luxury is not related to wealth but time, simplicity and a richness of experience that creates long-lasting memories. The sector is seeing a move away from ostentation and conspicuous consumption, although luxury will always have a place in the market, and instead a move towards a growing demand for tourism which fulfils these back-to-basic needs. This new 'Transumer' is motivated more by the capacity of products and services to serve as a gateway to experiences. These experiences must be authentic – tourists wish to be involved as participants, not spectators (Dwyer et al., 2009). Their new consciousness of the needs of others has led to a more altruistic attitude; it is not where you holiday but what you do when you are there (Forum for the Future, 2009). As a result, the industry is facing new and growing demands for volunteer tourism which incorporates real experiences in real communities where the consumer can volunteer, contribute or support that community. The concept of mass tourism offering shared, off-the-shelf package holidays is quickly becoming a quaint memory of the industry's history.

This new consumer consciousness has also brought about a growing awareness of the impact of travel and tourism on the physical environment. What has been experienced in other sectors in the way of ethical consumption is being mirrored in the tourism industry in the guise of sustainable tourism. The facts are stark. The impact of tourism in fragile and sensitive environments is dramatic; as the industry is set for phenomenal global growth, over-crowding in natural environments will inevitably lead to further damage (Yeoman *et al.*, 2006). Consumers are better educated about the finite nature of natural resources and the need to preserve them. Their new-found power and that of pressure groups and environmental experts is such that tourist operators are being forced to consider integrating tourism planning with community planning and socially responsible decision making into tourism product development (Dwyer, 2005). According to a report by Forum for the Future (2009), the industry has no choice but to urgently find and implement strategies to reduce carbon and waste and increase energy efficiency, yet it is one of the least prepared sectors for the decline in the resources it relies upon.

Those vanguard tourist producers, viewing sustainability as a lens for product innovation, brand relevance, growth and value creation will undoubtedly be rewarded by this new consumer movement. For example, investing in new transport and fuel technologies, focusing on yield rather than growth, resourcing scenario planning and crisis management, identifying opportunities for local but authentic experiences, managing over-crowding with the pop-up hotel or floating resort and considering new technologies to deliver alternative forms of entertainment are all possible future-proofing strategies. However, juxtaposed to this new consumer concern for the environment is the contradictory demand for air travel, nature tourism, the lust for discovery – new and untouched destinations, unique and authentic experiences and the curiosity about and willingness to pay a premium to see fast-disappearing attractions – all of which exacerbate the problem. Indeed, recent findings are indicating a reluctance to make any dramatic change in consumer behaviours to protect the environment (Miller *et al.*, 2010). Ryan (2002), however, argues that tourists switch roles – while they may not all be eco-tourists all of the time, more choice of 'sensitive' products will lead to a gradual shift in attitudes. Like any other market offering, the value that is perceived remains a critical determinant of choice; 'values-plus-value' is expected to become the new consumer mantra (Deloitte LLP, 2010). Tourism businesses that recognise they have a vested interest in protecting their environments and that engage with governments, regulators and tourist communities to help educate and influence consumer behaviours by providing competitive offerings are the true forward-thinkers.

The New e-Generation

There is no question that new technologies have made significant impacts on all sectors in terms of the way products and services are researched, developed, distributed, marketed and sold. Equally, new technology is arguably the biggest influencer on recent consumer behaviour shifts. Nonetheless, repeatedly, studies show that technology investment in the tourism industry significantly lags behind other sectors. It has been argued that this is due to the structure of the industry, made up largely of small and medium-sized enterprises. Yet findings from Dwyer *et al.* (2009) indicate that practitioners are aware that thanks to technology, such enterprises can compete with larger ones on a more level playing field. Similarly, a study of practitioners by Formica and Kothari (2008) suggests the industry is also aware of the substantial investment required in both the technology itself and the manpower to utilise it. With a recorded 2 billion people globally online in 2010, a figure that is to double by 2015 (Deloitte LLP, 2010), 77% of people owning mobile phones sending 6.1 trillion text messages in 2010 and spending a quarter of all online time social networking (e-Consultancy, 2011), tourism operators must utilise these ever-evolving channels to engage and interact with their consumers.

Technological revolutions can without doubt be viewed as a threat. Advances in new forms of media like the internet have allowed the acquisition of immeasurable amounts of information, from pricing to availability to scandals and product recalls. 'Infolust' is the new virus whereby consumers expect anytime anywhere information, increasingly demanding instant gratification, a trend which is being exacerbated by developments in mobile technology. This access to information has resulted in increased expectations of the service delivered by tourist businesses. Social media drives greater transparency and tourist operators are under more pressure to maintain standards and services that are promised. Negative experiences can be relayed to vast audiences and the impact of sites like TripAdvisor has been a very powerful one for many businesses. Indeed, the basis of holiday choice is no longer the tourist operator, travel agent or brochure, but the word of other tourists. 'Twinsumers', those people who share tastes and attitudes, are the only trustworthy source of information. The intangible nature of the product has always encouraged consumers to use word-of-mouth as a decision criterion, but the internet has allowed the creation of endless forums for e-word-of-mouth to prosper (Buhalis & Law, 2008). Virtual communities, blogs, social networking sites and review pages give a platform for online opinion leaders from anywhere across the globe which has inevitably changed the nature of travel information and consequently consumer knowledge and perceptions (Litvin *et al.*, 2008). Consumers are in control and brand 'authority' is gone. Empowered to create and tailor the product themselves, it is the consumers who now own the brand (Deloitte LLP, 2010).

The savvy tourist operator is one that accepts these new developments and trends as challenges rather than threats and considers the many opportunities that can be harnessed in a bid to engage with their consumers. Indeed, advances in technology have enhanced the desire to travel (Forum for the Future, 2009); the challenge is keeping up with changeable needs and increasing demands. At a very minimum, tourism providers must deliver distribution systems that allow seamlessness and immediacy in the booking process as well as control in packaging and personalising the product. Hilton is among those operators who place this as a high priority, having devised an app for the iPhone which allows guests to manage their bookings (Deloitte LLP, 2010). New technologies can be used to augment the product itself. Airlines continue to lead the way, utilising smartphone technologies to allow effortless check-in and joined up journeys. Only the most advanced hotels are focusing on in-room technology to enhance the consumer experience, taking the form of windows that turn into televisions, beds that rock guests to sleep and floors that light up when walked on in the dark – the key is understanding what adds real value. Very advanced technologies such as virtual reality offer the tourism sector exciting opportunities to exploit the demand for entertainment and education as well as providing alternative and sustainable means of seeing protected sites (Guttentag, 2010). The 'virtual window' which beams destinations into your home is more likely to create a desire for travel than substitute for it altogether.

Of most immediate concern is that tourist organisations place communication and engagement with their consumers as a priority. Websites are a critical element of driving bookings, but tourism marketers need to look beyond this, recognising the importance of online and application design for mobile devices as increasingly consumers use these as a primary means of internet use. Furthermore, tourist operators need to find and talk to consumers where they are; the ability to build and manage trust-based relations with customers, building reputation and credibility is a critical aspect of addressing the new power relationships. Social networking is fast becoming a mainstream marketing tool. With over 500 million users of the leading site, Facebook, spending over 700 billion minutes of time a month on the site, it is clear that these platforms are the future for building awareness, gathering data, listening and building consumer relationships. With the continued resistance to mass communications with artificial, exaggerated messages, businesses need to engage consumers with relevant, real and credible conversations to humanise the brand. Providing forums and communities in which consumers can talk, generate and share content is one of the few ways of truly bonding with the consumer in an attempt to create brand advocates rather than critics.

The Rise of Prosumption

As cited previously within the chapter we are now witnessing the creation of the New Tourist. Not only are demographic shifts occurring, but key shifts in consumer expectations, participation and consumer consciousness are taking place. The emerging consumer is no longer easily categorised by a classic segmentation typology but is an individual, a human being who has become a sophisticated 'high frequency' traveller, who is technologically literate and who has the ability to adapt to and function in multicultural environments. Consumers want their real experiences reflected and connected to their very specific and personal needs – not a generally perceived notion of their needs. The new empowered tourist enabled by the internet will seek out authentic, customised, environmentally aware and friendly tourism experiences; specialist niche interest activities and independently customised tourism will flourish. As such, tourism providers must become truly customer centric – they must listen to the 'voice of the consumer'. They must become about understanding them implicitly, in real time and moreover on their schedule. As mentioned, the rise of prosumption begins to challenge classic top-down or 'outbound' marketing and management philosophies of 'we market to you' or 'telling and selling', to a 'bottom-up' experience whereby the consumer can become a more active participant in the overall brand experience as opposed to a passive receiver of information and products. As such the New Tourist is no longer content in terms of simply waiting for new products and services to arrive and will continue to demonstrate a more active behaviour in consumption, thus blurring the traditional boundaries of producer and consumer and importantly allowing for shifts in business thinking – facilitating developments of new paradigms of marketing and, importantly, branding.

Prosumption presents real opportunities for tourism providers in the EU and is viewed as a megatrend that the tourism industry must respect and turn to its advantage. The very nature of tourism determines a degree of inseparability that indeed the consumer must be present for the tourism experience to occur. However, historically consumers had little ability or power to truly customise and shape their tourism experience to best suit their need, wants, desires and indeed their dreams. Customer-made products and experiences will continue to accelerate in the 21st century. The phenomenon of corporations creating goods, services and experiences in close cooperation with experienced and creative consumers, tapping into their intellectual capital, and in exchange giving them a direct say in (and rewarding them) what actually gets produced, manufactured, developed, designed, serviced or processed will increasingly become the norm across many business sectors including the tourism arena. The web has given rise to a more powerful consumer – liberating and empowering them, but at a deeper level there is a consciousness paradigm. The new consumer is searching for real value and needs to know what is behind the brand name and promise. By encouraging and facilitating co-creation, the dimensions of the brand become more transparent to the consumer and indeed the consumers themselves become the authors of the brand experience – thus leading to greater trust and more involved, stronger relationships between organisations and individuals. In summary, the continued growth of prosumers challenges traditional business logic where:

- Firms create value unilaterally;
- Consumers are passive;
- Products and services represent the value.

Prosumption brings new frame of reference by:

- Focusing on the customer–company interaction as a new value creation;
- Co-creating value through customer and company;
- Taking into consideration that value is unique to each customer and is associated to personalised experiences;

Prosumption is then transforming the customer–company relationship by allowing consumers to co-construct their own unique value. This new type of operation is turning the 'supply chain' into a 'demand value chain', by reversing the flow of marketing from 'company to customer' to 'customer to company'. Enlightened providers of tourism will collaborate with consumers to build a dialogue and exchange process that creates value for both parties. This shift in thinking moves the emphasis from what marketers do to consumers to what consumers want from marketing. The UK-based travel company Trailfinders has been a pioneer in this arena. Trailfinders have positioned themselves as travel experts – challenging the traditional role of the travel agent – marketing expertise and knowledge and in particular trust and security and offering consultation rather than simply booking facilities, while delivering tailor-made travel services worldwide. Trailfinders seeks to get to know their client and through expert consultation suggests and recommends tailor-made customised unique itineraries for customers.

Evolutions and Revolutions in Branding

Brands have become omnipresent in today's marketplace. Consumers have become accustomed to using brands as essential guides to help navigate the over-cluttered multiple-choice, multiple-destination, multiple-experience world in which we live. Brands have historically facilitated short cuts in consumer decision making, allowing consumers to develop decision-making heuristics – reducing time and effort by identifying reputable and trusted sources of consumer value. Within the tourism arena, destinations, travel companies, accommodation, food and entertainment providers alike have all come to be marketed very much like traditional product-based brands with particular brand dimensions and personality traits highlighted and exaggerated in advertising claims. Tourism operators have sought to position their brands distinctively in the hearts and minds of their target audience, thus facilitating the development and maintenance of the brand tribe or brand community. Nevertheless, the classic branding paradigm is becoming tired and may now be beginning to lose its edge. As cited above, the rise of the empowered consumer suggests that in the future the most successful brands will be those that abandon the traditional top-down approach – 'we market to you' – in favour of bottom-up strategies, adopting true consumer centricity whereby the consumer is an active participant in the design of the overall brand experience. In effect, tomorrow's megabrands will be the consumer's agent as opposed to producer's, pioneering a transformation from trademarks to trust marks using trust-based marketing.

The challenge for strategic decision makers is that consumers in the future will want less not more, sense not nonsense and above all they want companies to inject 'simplicity marketing'. The time when brands preached and consumers listened is no longer as dominant as it once was. This means repositioning tourism brands to survive in an environment of savvy, cynical, marketing-literate consumers no longer seeking solace in false brand gods, hype and spin. In a society where brands are now becoming 'mental pollutants' and the traditional 'marketing medicine' (e.g. I buy therefore I am and to buy is to be perceived) is increasingly diagnosed as a 'disease', we are now witnessing the era of the demarketing chic. Brands can become negative baggage as they are undermined by the very values they own in the mind of the consumer. The deferential consumer, conditioned to 'salivate' and desire upon being 'buzzed' by brands, has been buried along with the golden era of marketing. Consumers are already becoming increasingly brand immune and in some cases they are developing 'brand allergies'. The classic model of interruption and annoyance is ending – consumers are no longer willing to be forced to absorb brand messages. As a consequence, brands may then be losing control of their own image.

The new realities of branding are then upon us. Innovative companies are dispensing with the mass economy tactics of old and replacing them with tactics more suited to the consumer economy. Strategic tourism planners must then recognise that markets consist of human beings and not segmentation typologies. Markets can no longer be treated as pure demographics, geo-demographics or psychographics in terms of segmentation bases with brands to fit. Markets actually consist of human beings, each with unique needs and desires. This awareness, coupled with less passive and savvier consumers, prompts the need for a new model of brand relations – the 'brain to brain' model. Companies must adopt an intelligent and integrated marketing and management approach that seeks to establish and nurture 'intelligent dialogue' with customers, a mutually satisfying experience whereby meaningful back-and-forth communication improves the consumer's perception of the resolution experience. Ironically, this may mean a return to classical marketing: solving peoples' problems at a profit period. As brands evolve to ensure an intelligent dialogue with customers, ever greater demand for (emotional) authenticity and value will be desired by consumers. The emotional value is the economic value or momentary worth of feelings when consumers positively (or negatively) experience branded products and services. Emotional value, as much as quality or any other product attribute or dimension of an organisation's worth, can make or break a business. If companies do not handle well consumers' emotional needs and wants, brands are at risk. Incorporating emotional design into the development and branding of the tourism product is becoming a necessity for tourism and travel providers. Today and in the future, marketers want to extend their contact with customers through time. In effect, the brand must become not a product or a service but an invitation, an invitation to an emotionally satisfying and enduring relationship. The brand promise is about the quality of that relationship. Branding must then become more than seduction and emotional manipulation or indeed the construction of artificial needs and desires – it is about the fostering and promotion of trusting relationships and being intelligent, caring and having human common-sense to satisfy real existing human needs.

We are only at the very beginning of a new journey from 'brand building' and 'customer relationship management' to the consumer agency. This new vision is driven less by knowing about consumers and more by understanding them. Consumers are now beginning to view themselves as citizens not only of countries but of corporations and brands and as citizens they have a 'say' in how that organisation behaves.

Futurecasting Tourism

Perhaps more than most sectors, the tourism industry is experiencing unprecedented change at an extraordinary pace. Trends and changes in the environment are converging to create an entirely new tourist consumer. This consumer represents a new geo-demographic, shirking the materialistic values of previous generations, placing new importance on people, societies and environments and expecting businesses to follow suit. This new consumer will not accept mass marketing or communications or the one-product-fits-all approach – they want personalised treatment, real, true and authentic lives and products and services to function as a gateway to this. This new consumer lives in a 24-hour information society where new technologies play a bigger role than that of the mighty television. They have education, knowledge and understanding of the tourism sector and all it offers and are savvier about product portfolios than the operators themselves. This new consumer will only respond to trustworthy, truer brands – brands that understand their personal needs and fit into their lifestyles.

For tourism operators to survive, traditional methodologies of environmental scanning fall short of allowing appropriate strategy development.

Using the SCEPTICAL framework, relevant and timely intelligence can be identified, gathered and utilised to 'FUTURECAST' – map future scenarios and potential situations for which they can be better prepared than competitors. Futurecasting will allow tourist operators to indentify the need for and incorporate new and relevant paradigms of consumer-centricity within their business models as the only means of future-proofing their profits. The New Tourist is the new author of the brand and the tourism industry has to take a much more active role in engaging with this consumer and delivering platforms upon which value-based, experiential and co-created offerings can be developed. The businesses that can achieve this will be best positioned to seize future opportunities in a volatile market.

References

Buhalis, D. and Law, R. (2008) Progress in information technology and tourism management: 20 years on and 10 years after the internet – the state of etourism research. *Tourism Management* 29, 609–623.

Deloitte LLP (2010) *Hospitality 2015: Game Changers or Spectators?* London: Deloitte LLP.

Deloitte LLP (2011) *Consumer 2010: Reading the Signs.* London: Deloitte Global Services.

Dwyer, L. (2005) Trends underpinning global tourism in the coming decade. In W.F. Theobald (ed.) *Global Tourism* (3rd edn; pp. 529–545). Burlington, MA: Elsevier.

Dwyer, L., Edwards, E., Mistills, N., Roman, C. and Scott, N. (2009) Destination and enterprise management for a tourism future. *Tourism Management* 30, 63–74.

e-Consultancy (2011) *Internet Statistics Compendium.* London: eConsultancy.

ETC (2006) *Tourism Trends for Europe.* Brussels: European Travel Commission.

ETC (2011) *European Tourism 2010: Trends and Prospects.* Brussels: European Travel Commission.

Formica, S. and Kothari, T.H. (2008) Strategic destination planning: Analysing the future of tourism. *Journal of Travel Research* 46, 355–367.

Forum for the Future (2009) *Tourism 2023: Four Scenarios, a Vision and a Strategy for UK Outbound Travel and Tourism.* London: Forum for the Future.

Guttentag, D.A. (2010) Virtual reality: Applications and implications for tourism. *Tourism Management* 31, 637–651.

Hamilton, C. and Deniss, R. (2006) *Affluenza: When Too Much is Never Enough.* Sidney: Allen & Unwin.

Litvin, S.W., Goldsmith, R.E. and Pan, B. (2008) Electronic word-of-mouth in hospitality and tourism management. *Tourism Management* 21 (3), 458–468.

Miller, G., Rathouse, K., Scarles, C., Holmes, K. and Tribe, J. (2010) Public understanding of sustainable tourism. *Annals of Tourism Research* 37 (3), 627–645.

Moutinho, L., Ballantyne, R. and Rate, S. (2011) The new business environment and trends in tourism. In L. Moutinho (ed.) *Strategic Management in Tourism* (2nd edn, pp. 1–19). Wallingford: CABI.

Office for National Statistics (2010) *Population Trends* 142, Winter.

Popcorn, F. (2002) *Dictionary of the Future.* New York: Hyperion.

Ryan, C. (2002) Equity, management, power sharing and sustainability – issues of the 'new tourism'. *Tourism Management* 23, 17–26.

Yeoman, I., Munro, C. and McMahon-Beattie (2006) Tomorrow's world, consumer and tourist. *Journal of Vacation Marketing* 12 (2), 174–190.

Yeoman, I., Brass, D. and McMahon-Beattie, U. (2007) Current issues in tourism: The authentic tourist. *Tourism Management* 28, 1128–1138.

23 Perspectives and Trends on Knowledge Management: European Agencies and Initiatives

Christine Scherl and Chris Cooper

Introduction

European tourism is undergoing fundamental structural change driven by technology, changing systems of governance and the demands of the knowledge economy (Buhalis, 2000; Scott *et al.*, 2008). As part of this change, the tourism sector has begun to embrace the notion of knowledge management (KM) and, in particular, the imperative of knowledge transfer. Tourism has come late to KM, yet the generation and transfer of tourism knowledge is essential for sustainable innovation at destinations and this in turn underpins competitiveness (Cooper, 2006). This chapter examines knowledge transfer for tourism within a European dimension and focuses upon the agencies and policies involved.

Across the European regions, knowledge is increasingly seen as the engine of economic growth (OECD, 2001). Yet KM has received little attention in the tourism literature. However, the network structure of destinations lends itself to a KM approach and particularly to the processes of sharing knowledge. There is no doubt that the generation and use of new tourism knowledge for innovation and product development is critical for the competitiveness of destinations. Indeed, despite the fact that researchers, consultants, industry and government are constantly generating new tourism knowledge, destinations have been slow to harness that knowledge. As a result, Hjalager (2002: 473) states that policy for KM is an issue that must be addressed if tourism is to be 'a professional and respected stakeholder in economic life'.

The fact that tourism lags behind other economic sectors in KM has impacted upon the evolution of policy. Initially, to fill the policy void, informal governance structures developed within many European destination networks, acting as an alternative to the public sector. As tourism has slowly embraced the knowledge economy, European governments and international agencies have begun to respond by developing policy initiatives, including those at the destination level, in order to deal with the process of knowledge creation and transfer. Effectively, these policies grapple with the issues surrounding the nature of knowledge as a public good. These issues include:

- access to knowledge;
- the removal of barriers to knowledge transfer and adoption; and
- the need to encourage private enterprise to share knowledge.

This chapter demonstrates that many European agencies apply policies through the network concept by intervening at the level of knowledge creating or receiving nodes (the organisation), or facilitating knowledge flow and transfer around the network (Scott *et al.*, 2008).

For Europe, the production and distribution of knowledge are increasingly significant processes determining economic performance and competitiveness at the regional and destination level. However, it might be expected that regionally, their impact will be differential. This may be due to the fact that interaction between organisations varies according to the social and spatial configuration of each region, as well as the particular policy environment. Here the issue of just what is the most appropriate geographical scale for policy intervention is important. For example, the OECD (2001) has published an influential report on knowledge policy at the regional level emphasising a shift from the national to the subnational level in terms of innovation and knowledge policy. However, given the fact that the success and impact of policy may vary according to the region itself, it begs the question as to whether the region (or destination) is the best level at which apply knowledge and innovation policy. In fact, to be successful, there needs to be a careful application of general policy principles to particular economic and social regional circumstances at the destination level.

In Europe, this regional shift is due to the growth of urban and regional development authorities – as well as private/public sector partnerships. As we demonstrate in this chapter, at the European regional level, policy intervention for knowledge development and transfer in tourism is needed to ensure:

- Learning takes place at both the individual and the organisational level.
- The interaction between organisations takes place at the destination level in terms of knowledge sharing; otherwise they may have no incentive to do so. The most supportive environment for this is one of collaboration

and consensus with public/private partnerships creating 'networked destination governance'.
- An equitable distribution of benefits around the destination, including the host community.

The remainder of this chapter is devoted to an analysis of the key agencies and initiatives in Europe that are involved with KM and tourism.

European Agencies and Their Initiatives on Knowledge Management

OECD: Policy and research on tourism and knowledge management

Across Europe, tourism is a highly knowledge-intensive industry in a rapidly growing international economy. As a result, the sector's development is of prime concern to multinational agencies over and above national governments. Here, the Organisation for Economic Cooperation and Development (OECD) has a tourism section, which comes under the Centre for Entrepreneurship, SMEs and Local Development. The OECD Tourism Committee cooperates with international organisations including the European Union (EU), the UN World Tourism Organisation (UNWTO) and the International Labour Organisation (ILO) to coordinate tourism policies of member states. As such, the tourism committee supports governments with policy issues, in particular the integration of tourism policies with other policy areas, helping tourism to respond to new developments and challenges caused by globalisation and social change. In this vein, the OECD is rethinking the approach to (tourism) policy and (tourism) businesses by suggesting that 'policies which engage human capital, innovation, and entrepreneurship in the growth process alongside policies to mobilise labour and increase investment, are likely to bear the most fruit over the long term' (OECD, 2001: 8). This approach applies to the tourism sector in every sense but depends upon tourism stakeholders to take advantage of the knowledge-based economy.

Innovation and KM activities – initially the focus of the technology-intensive industry – are also important in the service sector (OECD, 2001). With the evolving knowledge-based economy, the OECD has called for more sophisticated indicators, which go beyond research and development, to gauge the scale of the knowledge economy. In order to compete in the changing economy, the OECD advocates an innovation-based tourism policy to promote dynamic destinations where KM is harnessed as an important mechanism of innovation. This requires creative entrepreneurs, highly skilled specialists, well-trained managers, tourism-specific knowledge, and support systems that are supplementary to research and development expenditure (OECD, 2006). Here, there is an emphasis on tacit knowledge shared through the support of 'learning on the job' and 'hands-on learning' rather than relying on the formal training and academic degrees with which codified knowledge is taught. Consequently, education and vocational training is high on the agenda when it comes to KM implications.

As noted in the introduction, tourism has lagged behind other sectors in its adoption of KM, in part because tourism is dominated by small and medium-sized enterprises (SMEs) and is both a fragmented and heterogeneous industry. Tourism therefore faces the challenges of these characteristics as well as the unique characteristics of the tourism sector itself (OECD, 1996). To better understand tourism and its contribution to employment and the economy in general, the OECD, together with Eurostat, the UN Statistical Division and UNWTO, have developed the Tourism Satellite Account (TSA). This methodology captures valid and comparable statistics of both demand-driven and supply-driven results, to ease the comparison of European member states and provide a clearer picture of the industry (OECD, 2008). However, variables such as investment are not included in the comparison. It remains to be seen if this international benchmarking approach achieves the acceptance of tourism in general and assists in placing it more centrally in economic life. In fact, across European tourism there are still significant regional differences, which are hard to compensate. The international benchmarking tool may provide transparency, but inter-regional collaboration, where potentially tourism expenditure is evenly distributed, is far from reality. Similarly, the knowledge base across European tourism regions differs with respect to the target of becoming a knowledge-based tourism economy. While there were intensive bursts of particular innovations, such as spa tourism a decade ago, the tourism sector still relies upon existing knowhow rather than investing in long-term innovation.

The EU and knowledge management

In 2005, the Lisbon strategy stressed 'jobs and growth', with knowledge as a focal point of the strategy (EC, 2006a; Rodrigues, 2009). In the global environment, the EU has the ambition to become the most competitive knowledge-based economy. As part of the information age, the knowledge-based economy recognises the value of knowledge as a resource, which needs to be managed systematically in order to nurture growth. The knowledge economy is thus based on the production, distribution and use of knowledge. The Lisbon strategy incorporates priorities such as (i) growth of knowledge, (ii) human capital, and (iii) research that generates the basis for the EU's future strategy to develop a 'smart and green' economy, where knowledge can indeed create competitive advantages. The main implication of the knowledge-based economy is that knowledge creation and learning are the source of prosperity and economic growth. Effectively, there is a greater emphasis on human resources, explicitly human qualifications (skills and competencies), which trigger competitive advantages and become the route to long-run economic growth.

In order to meet the Lisbon goal, the EU has focused particularly on research, education and innovation (EC, 2006b). Moreover, knowledge exchange has become paramount, particularly through the development of information and communication technology (ICT) and knowledge networks throughout EU member states (EC, 2007a). These gradually changing economic structures break down barriers to knowledge and experience sharing and thus promote transparency. Further, to mobilise tourism stakeholders in the difficult process of producing and sharing knowledge, the Commission supports conferences and studies of best practice examples and requests National Annual Reports. All tourism representatives are invited to participate at the Annual Tourism Forum, launched in 2002, to strengthen knowledge transfer among member states and to improve the interface of tourism stakeholders.

Europe as a tourism destination has a long history and thus considerable expertise in the field compared to the expanding international tourism market of, say, Asia or other emerging destinations. As new destinations emerge, new products are developed and innovation implemented. Europe's tourism industry, however, adheres to popular success strategies and reluctantly embraces strategic innovations. In this vein, with tourism as a key international economic driver in the 21st century, the European Commission has drafted the Communication 'Working Together for the Future of European Tourism' (EC, 2001). These working groups have elaborated questions about information, quality, training and sustainability – the four potential factors that will contribute to more and better employment and growth through tourism. Consequently, the evolving European tourism policy aims to forge stronger partnerships in European tourism. Therefore, a Tourism Sustainability Group was set up to implement the 'Agenda for a sustainable and competitive European tourism' (EC, 2007a). This commitment was launched in 2007 to guide European tourism policy makers to, for example, use and share the latest knowledge available. On a continuous basis, initiatives and programmes are being introduced with respect to KM tools applicable for tourism. In particular, the 'European Year of Creativity and Innovation 2009' aimed to create awareness of the importance of upgrading skills and promoting innovation following the Lisbon strategy. The reality, though, is that its factual implementation is meagre at best in tourism. Tourism needs clear guidelines, institutions and structures similar to the transport sector. Here, the White Paper initiated in 2002 has been continuously updated and linked with future strategies; compared to tourism, transport in the EU has its own policy area.

Knowledge management and policy invention

The European framework for tourism encompasses various European policy areas that contribute to tourism, because the EU does not have competence in tourism. As a result, tourism is viewed as a policy area for member states, with the Commission supporting policy and projects in close cooperation with individual national or regional authorities. However, a variety of distinctive European policy and programme areas, including education, vocational training and regional policy, offer considerable potential for fostering KM in tourism (EC, 2010). The EU's regional policy is relevant to tourism regions with poor economic performance, to ensure knowledge development and transfer in particular with respect to technological change. Here, the regional structural funds target particular regions in need of tourism-related infrastructure and services. At the regional level, policy intervention especially promotes SMEs, information technology applications and human capital, with the latter having great potential in the knowledge-based economy (Wanhill, 2000; Commission of the European Community, 2006). In particular, it is at the regional scale where we see proximity between producers, users and knowledge mediators and their interaction is the driver to foster innovation (Commission of the European Communities, 2006; Wanhill, 2000). Here, continuing training and lifelong learning are fundamental in fostering innovation and regional competitiveness. There are two ways that spatial knowledge transfer can occur through the internationalisation of tourism, so increasing the mobility of both the tourists and professionals. On the one hand, increasing numbers of tourists from different nationalities (with different languages and cultural norms) require a particular form of knowledge and knowledge transfer through, for example, qualification or migrant workers. On the other hand, labour mobility acts potentially as a boundary-spanner mechanism for unfamiliar knowledge as well as knowledge spillover through the sector's high staff turnover (Shaw & Williams, 2009). The EU's education and training policy includes various programmes supporting tourism with respect to the integrative lifelong learning programme. Here, the mobility programmes for apprentices or vocational trainees have great potential for tourism.

In addition to the structural funds, there are various other financial instruments available for the tourism industry. It is acknowledged that the industry contributes heavily to employment and to regional growth through its dominance of SMEs. Belonging to this category, there are some examples of other policy initiatives available for tourism. In particular, knowledge creation and production in tourism may benefit from research-related initiatives supported through the 7th Framework Programme (7FP) either with respect to research on ICT, or else to strengthen the innovation capacities of SMEs. Without the development of absorptive capacity, SMEs remain disadvantaged in knowledge transfer and innovation. Along with the 7FP, the Competitiveness and Innovation Framework Programme (CIP) supports various community programmes, *inter alia* to boost the innovative capability of SMEs through the active promotion of ICT applications. Through the joint creation of European tourism networks, the initiative aims to enhance the sustainable and competitive performance of SMEs (EC, 2007b). Essentially, there is a need in the tourism sector to create awareness of European initiatives and ideally public–private partnerships and to encourage more proposals that are successful. The Enterprise Europe Network (EEN) is part of the CIP and assists SMEs in particular to get access to information and advice about all EU initiatives. Even though the heterogeneous initiatives are divided into small sections and intended to support the tourism industry, successful implementation of KM and innovation has not yet taken place. Therefore, a multiple initiative tailored to the tourism sector would be the most fruitful. Here, regional disparities challenge the development of a uniform initiative.

Knowledge management initiatives and the social dimension

In the knowledge-based economy, the human resource, thought of as knowledge workers, has great potential to achieve growth. In particular, the tourism industry as an employer has a rather negative image due to the low level of qualified and trained employees, allied to high staff turnover partly caused through seasonality and unstable demand. This challenges the building of a knowledge base in tourism enterprises. Yet the tourism industry is highly knowledge intensive due to the nature of the service product with its special attributes of intangibility, inseparability, perishability and heterogeneity (Pizam, 2007; Zeithaml *et al.*, 2008). However, the preconceived assumption that overly small scale tourism businesses are not knowledge intensive may be a reason why it has been neglected in tourism and KM research (Shaw & Williams, 2009). Rather, low absorptive capacity and low-level knowledge-intensive employment in SMEs may hinder tourism businesses to absorb the knowledge and find innovative solutions. To compete in the emerging European knowledge-based economy, stronger tourism destinations and enterprises are required that comprise primarily knowledge-intensive SMEs in highly diverse sectors.

The European Commission has developed a major KM initiative for tourism in its programme of tourism-learning areas. The Commission has imported the learning area into the tourism industry in response to the question of how to upgrade skills through improved training (EC, 2001). The idea is originally based upon the manufacturing context in the early 21st century's knowledge-intensive capitalism, where Florida (1995) defines:

> learning regions[...] function as collectors and repositories of knowledge and ideas, and provide an underlying environment or infrastructure which facilitates the flow of knowledge, ideas and learning. (Florida, 1995: 528)

Table 23.1 Social and technological dimensions

Social dimensions	Technological dimensions
Human resource	Information and communication technology
Qualified, skilled staff	World wide web
Training	Web 2.0
Tourism learning areas	**Destination portals**

The regional approach is driven by two conditions. First, it is a territorial space where tacit knowledge is of primary importance for competitive advantage and, second, proximity is a precondition of informal knowledge transfer, led by trust and common value. According to the European Commission (EC, 2006a) tourism learning areas are networks, clusters or partnerships which benefit from proximity or are involved in a particular thematic issue. The programme aims to enhance tourism skills (such as ICT) and knowledge (such as health and wellness) in order to create sustainable development and enhance competitiveness through innovation. Related tourism stakeholders, training and research institutes and government agencies should be involved to share their knowledge and experience. Recently, a handbook of tourism learning areas was developed which explains the approach to developing competitive and innovative regions through a network of training institutions and tourism stakeholders (EC, 2006a). In order for KM to be successful, organisations need to consider both soft and hard factors as outlined in Table 23.1. Jarrar (2002) proposes that 90% of knowledge is managed through people and only 10% with the aid of technology.

Knowledge management initiatives and the technology dimension

ICTs have influenced both the building and management of tourism networks and the rationalisation of business processes. In the new area of information societies, the rate of change of business processes has increased. Gradually, technology has become central to knowledge transfer and exchange. The development of information technology, in particular the world wide web and web 2.0, opens up access to crucial customer and competitor knowledge, and different market segments, which become increasingly important. ICTs allow innovative tourism destinations to create the tourism experience by coordinating and linking individual service components to satisfy changing consumer needs. Here, ICTs are used as a KM tool to gather and use information and knowledge from consumers to develop tourism products and build up core competencies (OECD, 2006). In tourism, this technological innovation has developed effective models for knowledge sharing and transfer by developing knowledge portals. At the European level, the European Tourist Destination Portal (http://www.visiteurope.com) complements and adds value to national and regional efforts. Web portals allow destination-based tourism stakeholders to be part of the service chain and create synergies as well as common competencies and knowhow (Baggio *et al.*, 2007) and thus link the social and technology dimensions (as illustrated in Figure 23.1). This virtual network provides a platform for the exchange of information and partnership building to create packages and allow stakeholders to benefit from marketing and promotion. The portals navigate the tourist through the destination offer, satisfy their information needs and open up access for information to new markets.

The European Travel Commission (ETC) is an independent association, encompassing European National Tourism Organisations (NTO). It aims primarily to promote Europe and its diverse tourism offer as a single tourism destination and to increase the visibility of European tourism. Whereas each

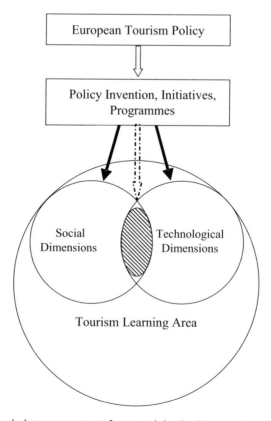

Figure 23.1 Knowledge management framework in the European tourism context

national authority contributes to the overall image, continuous competition remains among member states for tourism demand and expenditure. However, if the European regional portal is to assist NTO members to exchange knowledge and work together collaboratively, organisations such as ETC need models of knowledge sharing for their members.

Across Europe, we can identify three key initiatives here:

(1) *The European Knowledge Management Forum* was initiated by the European Information Society to influence 'KM made in Europe' (Hearn *et al.*, 2002). This independent KM community unifies experts from industry, government and research to work on a common European KM framework, terminology and implementation. This virtual cluster initiative and website publishes KM-related projects, and provides a platform to contribute to a number of special interest group discussions. However, little contribution has been made by and to the tourism sector. Since 2006 the forum was continued commercially, however there was no real engagement or use and thus the site was closed. Nevertheless, experiences and case studies have been published (Kazi *et al.*, 2009) and knowledge management forums at a local level continue to exist (c.f. Community of Knowledge, Germany). In the following, thematic approaches exemplify persistent and promising models for knowledge sharing in tourism.

(2) *Ecotrans for Sustainable Tourism Issues* is a virtual tourism network with tourism experts in sustainability, environment and regional development, launched in the 1990s (http://www.ecotrans.org). This network seeks to promote best practice in sustainability and to share knowhow and publication on these issues. In recent years, these projects have stagnated and another push is to be awaited.

(3) *DestiNet* is an information portal on sustainability using the learning area approach (www.destinet.eu). This working partnership has been established by the European Environment Agency, UNWTO and the UN Environment Project in order to provide a broad knowledge base for quality-assessed sustainable information for European tourism stakeholders. Compared to other portals it is quite active and provides regularly updated knowledge and best practice examples.

Knowledge management and best practice national initiatives

Arguably, member states can promote initiatives to encourage innovation (OECD, 2006). While innovation or tourism development is not initiated by the state, the government can support innovative industry-wide tourism projects. Here we can identify two projects:

(1) The Swiss programme 'Promotion and Cooperation in Tourism' (http://www.inno-tour.ch) supports projects which involve several institutions

in order to activate innovation sharing, to create cooperation and quality management, and to support structural changes, training and market research. The OECD classifies this innovation programme as a successful proactive instrument that can be used to grow a mature tourism destination and encourage it to remain competitive as a destination, rather than as a single organisation (OECD, 2006).

(2) An innovative network approach has been taken by the Spanish Tourism Organisation with the Spanish Destination Networks initiative. This follows Spain's aim to diversify from mass to cultural and rural tourism. To do so, the Spanish policy supports informal destination networks in order to achieve diversification. In addition, the Spanish government places emphasis on tourism education, research and support for the tourism industry as one of the main contributors to the economy. Rather than relying on local networks, which are beneficial for providing general information, the government supports non-local networks, with a knowledge flow of sector-specific knowhow and therefore providing international benchmarking (Ivars Baidal, 2004).

Based on the Spanish example, it is not surprising that larger tourism organisations are more innovative than smaller enterprises. This is explained by the lack of entrepreneurial spirit and the motivation of SMEs, who are often lifestyle entrepreneurs. However, inter-organisational relationships among independent organisations foster innovation and are a potential determinant of adapting information technology and training initiatives, and for acquiring knowledge from various sources, in particular external knowledge (Sparrow, 2001; Sundbo et al., 2007). The tourism learning handbook provides additional best practice examples of successful implementation of learning areas (EC, 2006a). There is some evidence that tourism can obtain considerable potential capacity from taking advantage of European innovation-based initiatives to become a knowledge-based economy.

Conclusions

Europe is losing market share in the international tourism market, as newer destinations in regions such as the Asia/Pacific innovate and develop new products. Innovation is the key to Europe's future success in tourism markets. The basis for such innovation is the generation, transfer and use of new tourism knowledge. We have shown in this chapter that there are a number of initiatives contributing to innovation in tourism across Europe. However, these initiatives tend to be isolated and betray the lack of a coherent European policy for KM in tourism. To be successful, a new policy environment will be required to ensure and to facilitate the sharing and adoption of tourism knowledge across destination networks. These policies will encourage the use of effective models of knowledge creation and transfer, allowing destinations to respond flexibly and quickly to threats as they develop destination knowledge stocks. In other words, the Commission's 'learning area' becomes a reality for tourism destinations, characterised by processes of mutually reinforcing interaction and cooperation between stakeholders delivering a collaborative and competitive destination.

References

Baggio, R., Corigliano, M. and Tallinucci, V. (2007) The websites of a tourism destination: A network analysis. In M. Sigala, L. Mich and J. Murphy (eds) *Information and Communication Technologies in Tourism 2007 – Proceedings of the International Conference in Ljubljana, Slovenia* (pp. 279–288). Wien: Springer.

Buhalis, D. (2000) Marketing the competitive destination of the future. *Tourism Management* 21 (1), 97–116.

Commission of the European Communities (CEC) (2006) Regions and Cities for Growth and Jobs: An overview of Regulations 2007-2013 on Cohesion and Regional Policy. *Inforegion Factsheet 148*. Brussels: CEC DG-Regional Policy.

Cooper, C. (2006) Knowledge management and tourism. *Annals of Tourism Research* 33 (1), 47–64.

EC (2001) *Working Together for the Future of European Tourism*. COM(2001) 665final. Brussels: European Commission.

EC (2006a) *Innovation in Tourism – How to Create a Tourism Learning Area – The Handbook*. Luxembourg: Office for Official Publication of the European Communities.

EC (2006b) *Amended Proposal for a Decision of the Parliament and the Council Concerning the 7th Framework Programme of the European Community for Research, Technological Development and Demonstration Activities (2007–2013)*. COM(2006) 364final. Brussels: European Commission.

EC (2007a) *Agenda for a Sustainable and Competitive European Tourism*. COM(2007) 621final. Brussels: European Commission.

EC (2007b) *A Contribution to More Growth and More and Better Jobs*. COM(2007) 474 final. Brussels: European Commission.

EC (2010) *Europe, the World's No 1 Tourist Destination – a New Political Framework for Tourism in Europe*. COM(2010) 352final. Brussels: European Commission.

Florida, R. (1995) Toward the learning region. *Futures* 27 (5), 527–536.

Hearn, P., Bradier, A. and Jubert, A. (2002) *Building Communities: Organizational Knowledge Management within the European Commission's Information Society Technologies Programme*. ITcon 7 (Special Issue *ICT for Knowledge Management in Construction*), 63–68.

Hjalager, A.M. (2002) Repairing innovation defectiveness in tourism. *Tourism Management* 23, 465–474.

Ivars Baidal, J.A. (2004) Tourism planning in Spain – evolution and perspectives. *Annals of Tourism Research* 31 (2), 313–333.

Jarrar, Y.F. (2002) Knowledge management: Learning for organisational experience. *Managerial Auditing Journal* 17 (6), 322–328.

Kazi, A.S., Wolf, P., and Troxler, P. (2009) *Supporting Service Innovation Through Knowledge Management: Practical Insights* & Case Studies. Liestal: Swiss Knowledge Management Forum.

OECD (1996) *The Knowledge-based Economy*. Paris: OECD.

OECD (2001) *Cities and Regions in the New Learning Economy*. Paris: OECD.

OECD (2006) *Innovation and Growth in Tourism*. Paris: OECD.

OECD (2008) *Tourism in OECD Countries 2008: Trends and Policies*. Paris: OECD.

Pizam, A. (2007) Does the tourism/hospitality industry possess the characteristics of a knowledge-based industry? *International Journal of Hospitality Management* 26, 759–763.

Rodrigues, M.J. (2009) *Europe, Globalization, and the Lisbon Strategy*. Cheltenham: Edward Elgar Publishing.

Scott, N., Baggio, R. and Cooper, C. (2008) *Network Analysis and Tourism: From Theory to Practice*. Clevedon: Channel View Publications.

Shaw, G. and Williams, A. (2009) Knowledge transfer and management in tourism organisations: An emerging research agenda. *Tourism Management* 30, 325–335.

Sparrow, J. (2001) Knowledge management in small firms. *Knowledge and Process Management* 8 (1), 3–16.

Sundbo, J., Orfila-Sintes, F. and Sørensen, F. (2007) The innovative behaviour of tourism firms: Comparative studies of Denmark and Spain. *Research Policy* 36, 88–106.

Wanhill, S. (2000) Small and medium tourism enterprises. *Annals of Tourism Research* 27 (1), 132–147.

Zeithaml, V.A., Bitner, M.J. and Gremler, D.D. (2008) *Services Marketing: Integrating Customer Focus Across the Firm*. Boston, MA: McGraw-Hill Irwin.

24 Technology-enabled Tourism Destination Management and Marketing

Dimitrios Buhalis and Joanna Matloka

Introduction to Tourism Destinations

Destination marketing is crucial at each of the development stages and should facilitate profitability and the overall good of all destination stakeholders. The marketing priorities, immediate and long-term goals will vary depending on the different stages of the destination development. Marketing activities should be tailored to the desired goals and target market profiles. While offline activities still consume a large part of destination marketing budgets, more and more destination management organisations (DMOs) explore online marketing and technological solutions that go along with them as a main channel facilitating or substituting for traditional marketing media.

The purpose of this chapter is to analyse the importance of information and communication technologies (ICTs) and discuss a range of online marketing solutions available for destinations.

ICTs for Marketing of Tourism Destinations

Information is the lifeblood of tourism, and ICT provides the backbone for facilitating the industry (Sheldon, 1997). The emphasis on technology has been evident for the last 20 years. In particular, since the emergence of the internet the effects of ICTs have been transformational. A wide range of tools and services were developed to facilitate interaction between different players around the world (Buhalis & Law, 2008). The internet, in particular, supports targeting niche markets in distant geographical locations. New marketing tools were provided, and as ICT development has progressed the tools have become more affordable and user friendly, allowing organisations to take full advantage and re-engineer and facilitate the entire process of marketing tourism products and destinations (Buhalis, 1998).

Academics unanimously agree that the role of ICT is critical for the competitiveness of tourism organisations and destinations (Poon, 1993; Sheldon, 1997). The internet in particular can greatly facilitate marketing in the tourism industry, for example by allowing direct communication between supplier and customer, stopping price discrimination practices and leading to more equal competition between companies with different backgrounds (Law, 2000). It can also reduce the dependence of particularly peripheral and insular destinations on intermediaries – who too often over-exercise their negotiation power (Buhalis, 1998), and increase their visibility. The ability to attract new and sophisticated tourism demand is determined by providing information regarding local facilities and attractions together with enabling the reservation of a range of tourist products.

Although ICT on its own is not necessarily a source of sustainable competitive advantage, its integration into tourism organisations is one of the keys to success (Gretzel et al., 2000). Failing to at least establish online presence results in a competitive disadvantage (Buhalis, 2003). Despite that, research has shown that both DMOs and small and medium-sized tourism enterprises (SMTEs) encounter numerous challenges to ICT adoption and integration. Barriers to ICT implementation for DMOs include limited resources, the lack of proper management, insufficient knowledge, a lack of communication, legal regulations and restrictions, and ownership issues (Gretzel et al., 2000).

Representation and the provision of timely and accurate information which is relevant to consumers is the key to successful marketing efforts. Reaching customers with information-rich messages at negligible cost is possible for DMOs thanks to the web (Gretzel et al., 2000; Wang & Fesenmaier, 2006). According to UNWTO (2008) the benefits of destination e-marketing include: the delivery of vast amounts of information in a user-friendly way; brand building; two-way interaction between DMOs, suppliers and customers; and cost-effectiveness in conveying information and products on sale directly, cheaply and at short notice. Despite the potential to be explored, most DMOs were rather slow in establishing a sophisticated presence online. However, the role of ICT was finally recognised, and from 1996 onwards many DMOs started taking the web seriously (UNWTO, 1999).

Web marketing has gradually become the mainstream (Fesenmaier et al., 2003) and it is recognised that eventually all destinations around the world will develop their online presence and practice e-marketing. This, however, will vary from advanced and fully integrated systems to simple individual websites. Online destination marketing through DMO websites has already become part of the strategy for most DMOs. However, as the web is a medium different from any other, it should also be used to do things differently rather than just cheaply and more quickly. Marketing strategies should follow the web nature and build on personalisation, experience, involvement and permission instead of mass communication or one-time selling. Innovative concepts rather than the application of existing advertising models to the online world can result in competitive advantage (Gretzel et al., 2000).

One of first innovations used by destinations for the purpose of online marketing was destination management systems (DMSs). The basic version of DMS consists of the product database and customer database and a mechanism connecting the two (Buhalis, 1993, 2008). It enables the coordination of a whole range of products and services offered by the local suppliers and promotes them on the global scale. It also allows travellers to create a personal destination experience. Yet it is recognised that in reality most destinations are not able to develop well-functioning DMS due to lack of experience, technology and resources (Buhalis, 2000, 2003).

ICT-enabled tourism consumption

Tourism is an information-intensive industry and its organisations rely very much on communicating with tourists to market their products (Poon, 1993). Information search as the essential part of the decision-making process was revolutionised with the emergence of the internet (Fodness & Murray, 1997) which has grown to be one of the most effective media for tourists to look for information and buy tourism products (Werthner & Klein, 1999).

Each tourist is different and has his own set of experiences, motivations and desires (Niininen et al., 2007). Fesenmaier et al. (2006) argue that 'popular' products are no longer attractive in the tourism context, since tourists seek variety and intend to avoid crowds, preferring to go where others do not. This implies that the new tourism trends that emerged due to ICT embedment should bring a higher demand for both long-tail destinations and their long-tail suppliers, provided that the right information is available to the tourists.

The number of choices for consumers has been dramatically increased thanks to ICT. Before the internet, choice was limited to either recognised brand names or local organisations (Buhalis & Law, 2008). ICT has enabled travellers to access reliable and accurate information and to dictate how and which promotional messages and incentives they respond to (King, 2002). Tourists are increasingly becoming 'more independent, involved and discriminatory in the itinerary planning process' (King, 2002: 105). More and more 'fully independent travellers' (FICT), 'Free and Easy Travellers' (booking only flight and hotel) and other types of tourists travel wherever they wish, creating a demand for 'special interest travel destinations' (Lew, 2008). Frequently the products are dynamically packaged, often at the time of consumption, by tourists themselves who depend heavily on electronic media obtaining information and communicating their needs (Buhalis, 2003). Poon's (1993) New Tourist – independent, adventurous, eager to experience something different and wanting to be in charge – was taken to another level and proliferated by the internet.

Online Marketing for Destinations

Understanding the process of online information search from the consumer's point of view is extremely important and crucial for the improved design of online marketing strategies (Hwang *et al.*, 2006). The online search for travel information is the critical stage impacting on the whole process of travel planning (Xiang & Fesenmaier, 2006). The choice of the destination in particular is the most important choice during the process (Jeng & Fesenmaier, 2002). Since the decision to visit (thus purchase) a destination is based on information which is available to tourists, the internet has become the new battleground of marketing (Rita, 2000). While at the early stage of online expansion the main objective was to establish online presence, now the challenge is far greater. Not only do destinations have to get their product through, reaching relevant users, but they also need to make the message engaging and as customised as possible.

Search engine optimisation

One of the main internet problems is the amount of choice it brings (Buhalis & Law, 2008). The quantity of information available online is handled by tourists with the use of search engines. The search engine market is vastly dominated by Google, yet in a few markets Bing and Yahoo! still own a considerable market share, while a few regional markets have local search engines (Yandex in Russia, Baidoo in China) which stand in competition against Google.

Search engine optimisation (SEO) is not related to paid advertising and aims to rank websites among the first natural search results. Search engine spiders crawl the web, indexing world wide web content and its relevance for specific search queries. Although the engine algorithm is not only kept secret but also dynamic, it has been established that main elements considered by the spiders are the amount of relevant outbound links driving traffic to the website in question. Other factors include HTML tags, URL and website structure. The ultimate goal of SEO is to rank as the first result for the most relevant search queries. An example of a destination which is search engine optimised well is London, which comes up first or within the top three results for many queries (e.g. 'london', 'london attractions', 'what to do in london', etc.).

Search engine marketing

SEO is a timely process and it usually takes few months before desirable results are achieved. During this period destinations may support themselves with paid advertising in order to ensure their presence on the first page of search results. Destinations can bid on keywords relevant to search related to their business and pay for them on a CPC (cost per click) or a CPM (cost per thousand impressions) basis. Paid search engine advertising is displayed in the form of text advertisements on the right-hand side of the search results and on the top of the page and it is not dependent on natural search engine optimisation. This means that, despite the fact that search engines might not consider the website content the most relevant to the search query, the advertisers still have a chance to establish their presence among the first page search results.

The position of the ads as well as CPC very much depends on the click through rate (CTR) of each of the ads, and therefore on the ratio of clicks each ad receives against the number of impressions it was served. Unless most of the relevant keywords are targeted and the ad is engaging and catches the attention of the user, the CTR is not good enough to get the ad to the first page results, regardless of the bid. Wöber (2006) suggested that a solution to the problem of low travel search precision should be domain-specific search technologies, i.e. specialised search engines and web portals.

One of the reasons why search results are not meeting tourist needs might be wrong semantic representation of destinations and their SMTEs. They often focus on 'selling' keywords (for example, 'price', 'free', etc.) which may not match the search words used by potential travellers, which are more experiential and subjective (for example, 'good' or 'different'). Pan and Fesenmaier (2006) examined the 25 most frequently used keywords in the travel search and discovered that only eight of them match both semantic models. The study by Xiang et al. (2009) found, however, that while the domain is mostly represented by a small number of keywords there is also a long tail of words reflecting unique experiences offered at destinations which also represent the individual and specific needs of tourists.

Display advertising and affiliate marketing

An alternative to the text advertisements which are used in search engine marketing (SEM) are banners or image/flash/rich media advertisements displayed on web pages. Advertising space is available on most of the websites. Website owners sell their advertising space through networks such as Google Content Network or affiliate networks. Many travel websites sell their traffic through Google Content Network (e.g. Expedia) and allow advertisers to use their space. Advertisers who chose Content Network as their source of traffic can choose between the CPC and CPM models. They can target their audience through the website category demographics of users who visit the website or by keywords. By advertising on such websites, destinations as well as all other tourism and non-tourism related organisations can reach users browsing or booking for holidays.

The same websites can also sell their advertising space through affiliate networks which specialise in broader targeted performance marketing. The CPM and CPC models are usually available to get adverting space through affiliate networks which specialise in cost per lead (CPL), cost per sale (CPS) and cost per acquisition or action (CPA) (Duffy, 2005). In the case of this model, apart from the cost of setting up the program, advertisers pay only a previously agreed price for each action (new lead, subscriber, etc.) or a percentage of the price of the product or service sold by the affiliate network.

The popularity of affiliate marketing has grown among tourism companies and organisations over the past years. In the case of DMOs which usually do not sell actual holidays but only provide information, the measurable 'actions' or 'leads' can be to sign up to a newsletter, to register for a competition, a contact request, etc.

The main advantages of affiliate marketing are increased exposure of the brand to potential new markets and audiences at little or no financial risk, since the cost is charged only when the desired action occurs. However, for this very reason, unless the offer is very attractive and converts well it will not be picked up by website publishers, who tend to select the offers that allow them to make the biggest profit on the traffic they have on their sites. Furthermore, advertisers which choose affiliate marketing may potentially be exposing their brand to damage (Daniele *et al.*, 2009) since they have limited control over which websites are used as the advertising space for their banners.

Social media

The most recent and breakthrough forms of ICT development are Web 2.0 and social media, with great personalisation and marketing potential.

The term was developed by technology publisher Tim O'Reilly in 2004; however, there was no agreed definition of it until now. Most people, including O'Reilly, believe that the Web 2.0 revolution is more about the change in consumer attitudes and behaviour rather than the technology itself. The Web 2.0 websites tend to be collaborative, inclusive, creator/user centric, unsettled and information intensive.

Although few businesses have fully discovered the potential of Web 2.0 as a marketing channel, social media presents a great marketing opportunity for the tourism industry and an emerging channel for marketers. Despite the novelty of the topic, there are already numerous academic papers specifically examining different issues of Web 2.0 developments in the tourism context. There is research regarding the virtual tourist community (Wang *et al.*, 2002), users' reviews and recommendations (Yoo & Gretzel, 2008), and electronic word-of-mouth (WOM) (Litvin *et al.*, 2008; Murphy *et al.*, 2007).

In the case of destinations, the most relevant social media that can be used for marketing purposes are user generated content (UGC) sites and communities and social networks.

User-generated content: TripAdvisor and other review websites

Zhang *et al.* (2009) found that reviews and recommendations can come from third parties, other consumers or travel companies and can be presented in the form of text-based or symbolic recommendations, numerical ratings or narrative reviews.

Yoo and Gretzel (2008) discovered that online travel reviewers turned out to be mostly motivated by supporting the service providers, concerns for other consumers, and a need for positive self-enhancement or enjoyment. Most importantly, using reviewing for venting negative feelings was not found to be an important motive. Litvin *et al.* (2008) determined that when making purchase decisions, WOM and interpersonal influence are the most important information source. Murphy *et al.* (2007) noticed that, when travelling for longer periods and with less experience of destinations, respondents were more likely to take advantage of the recommendations of other travellers or friends and relatives. Despite that, the hypothesis that travellers' destination image would be affected by WOM was not supported.

Chung and Buhalis (2008) demonstrated that the three main factors appreciated as benefits by community members are information acquisition, social-psychological and hedonic benefits. The benefit of information acquisition is composed of obtaining up-to-date information, efficient information search, convenience in finding information, sharing experiences and having trust in the community. Hence functional, social and psychological needs were the reasons for participation in virtual tourist communities (Wang *et al.*, 2002).

One of the most recognised travel communities is TripAdvisor. Founded in February 2000, this allows users to search travel entities by destinations which are also reviewed. Apart from providing tourists with authentic reviews generated by travellers, TripAdvisor provides destinations (as well as hotels and attractions) with first-hand feedback on the products and services. Used wisely, these allow marketing departments to engage in conversation with tourists and respond to their concerns and feedback, as well as to learn how to make their products and services more appealing and increase the level of customer satisfaction.

Social networks

Social networking is the fastest growing section of the internet. The biggest and most innovative social network is Facebook, allowing enterprises across the globe to create a free-of-charge Facebook page which is a company or organisation profile in the social world. The page is created the same way as a standard user profile and is an opportunity for destinations to create an online forum for potential, present and past visitors and a medium to exchange not only information and opinions but also photos and videos. It also allows destinations to present their offer and communicate with their 'fans', as well as to aggregate media-rich content such as photos, videos and applications.

In addition, incredibly detailed segmentation-based marketing is also emerging as a major strength of Facebook. Not only demographics and context are taken into consideration when segmenting a targeted audience, but also lifestyle and preferences as expressed by users in their likes and their online behaviour. Considering that the platform has over 845 million users, DMOs should take the opportunity to increase their online presence and approach tourists interested in the destination through this Web 2.0 channel.

Facebook also provides a paid advertising option. Similarly to Google, Facebook advertisers can choose between CPC and CPM models. After clicking on the ad, the user can be taken either to the Facebook page or application of the advertiser, or to a Facebook-independent website of the advertiser (e.g. DMO site). Users can be targeted by location, native language, sex, age, education or interest. The format of ads is standardised, allowing advertisers to customise them only with photos and messages written in a standardised font.

A vast majority of destinations have been present on Facebook, taking advantage of the numerous marketing opportunities offered by this channel. By building strong fan communities, destinations have an opportunity to use Facebook as a customer service, information, promotion and communication channels and to put customers at the centre of their business. Due to its fast growth and continued reinvention Facebook allows brands to come up with creative ideas for new ways to engage users through applications, stories or competitions. This gives a chance to destinations to gain competitive advantage by being original and to stand out from their competitors. The latest Facebook releases such as timeline pages for brands and timeline applications are opportunities to strengthen or establish the brand in the new marketing environment.

One of the main concerns of destinations and other tourism sectors regarding social media marketing is the measurement of return on investment (ROI) through these channels. Although the size of the social media community reflects the brand's strength, this does not always transfer into direct sales. Despite that, there are more and more technologies available in the market that allow for the measurement of conversions external to social media coming from social media traffic. Moreover, considering that the main goal of DMOs is not direct sales but promotion of the brand, eventually leading to sales of the products and services of the local stakeholders, social media should be one of the main marketing channels to be considered in marketing planning.

Mobile platforms and smart phones for destinations

Smart phones are the latest medium for advertising and are only in the infancy of their advertising potential. Many of the most tech-savvy tourism enterprises have developed their own smart phone applications for the iPhone, Blackberry and Android-based devices. Many free apps (which are effectively widgets) are available for smart phone users. These are provided by hotels (Hilton), meta search engines (Kayak), Airlines (British Airways, Lufthansa, American Airlines), travel communities (TripAdvisor), travel guides (Lonely Planet) and more. There are also many applications developed for specific destinations and these often take advantage of location services, supporting context-based services. London is an example of a destination which is well served by numerous applications developed by various destination stakeholders. With the use of free applications, a tourist is able to fully explore London on his own without any previous research or preparation. Increasingly, augmented reality is coming to mobile phones and applications, such as Layer on iPhone which enables users to use real time augmented reality applications. Layer recently announced the addition of 3D capabilities to its augmented reality browser platform. With 3D, developers can tag real-life objects with 3D text, place 3D objects in real-world space, and create multi-sensory experiences. The addition of 3D enables Layer developers to create more realistic and immersive augmented reality experiences for mobile devices.

Hence, London visitors and guests can easily move around the city using a complex system of public transport, buses and the underground. Alternatively, they can wander around the city with an accurate GPS system and Google Maps with a compass that arranges the view of the map according to the direction the user is moving in. While exploring the city, tourists can now find tourist enterprises (hotels, bars, restaurants), events and attractions matching their personal interests and preferences. This can be achieved through an all-in-one mobile device such as an iPhone, which works as a mobile online content aggregator, with a GPS system providing content relevant to the user's location and preferences. The integration of current information on location through Google's Buzz or geo-targeted Twits will also enhance the currency of the destination information.

Destinations which for various reasons have not developed their own applications can still make themselves available to smart phone users through one of bigger players such as meta-search engines (e.g. Kayak or Booking.com), or UGC sites like TripAdvisor. Finally, destinations which have their own Facebook Fan Page can also communicate with those of their Facebook fans who visit Facebook though their mobile devices rather than desktop computers. Finally, Google campaigns can be targeted through smart phone users for specific applications. Although extraordinary roaming charges remain a barrier for consumers to use mobile platforms abroad, the regulation of mobile charges as well as the proliferation of local wireless networks will encourage more consumers to use such platforms in the future. A range of new business models is also emerging in the marketplace to provide sustainable business benefits for organisations that develop and manage such technologies.

Conclusions

The online world offers unlimited opportunities for destination marketing. For destinations which are interested and can afford investment in paid advertising, the internet can provide them with worldwide exposure both through narrow audience targeting (e.g. Facebook allowing accurate demographic and lifestyle targeting or Google Search allowing the targeting of users searching for specific keywords) and wide branding exercises (e.g. Google Content Network). For destinations with particular goals in mind (such as subscription to a newsletter or booking a trip) CPA or lead-dominated affiliate marketing offer opportunities to reach these goals for an agreed price.

Destinations which care for online marketing yet cannot afford or do not find paid advertising relevant can build their online presence through social media where they are invited to present themselves to an audience for free. Regardless of their marketing efforts, most destinations will increasingly find themselves marketed online by their visitors. UGC provides destinations with discussion of their brand, media-rich content, and feedback from visitors which should be the basis for the improvement of the services and products destinations offer. Depending on the product and service quality of any given destination, UGC can also work as free and effective marketing or damaging negative advertising.

Increasingly, online marketing is growing for many destinations to become the most relevant track to obtain competitive advantage through the widest possible ways of communicating, inspiring and serving their existing and prospective clientele. Those destinations that understand and utilise the emerging tools and methods will be able to engage in long-lasting beneficial relationships and benefit all their stakeholders.

References

Buhalis, D. (1993) Regional Integrated Computer Information Reservation Management Systems as a strategic tool for the small and medium tourism enterprises. *Tourism Management* 14 (5), 366–378.

Buhalis, D. (1998) Strategic use of information technologies in the tourism industry. *Tourism Management* 19 (5), 409–421.

Buhalis, D. (2000) Marketing the competitive destination of the future. *Tourism Management* 21 (1), 97–116.

Buhalis, D. (2003) *eTourism: Information Technology for Strategic Tourism Management*. Upper Saddle River, NJ: Prentice-Hall.

Buhalis, D. (2008) *E-Tourism and Destination Management Organisations. Tourism Insights [online]*, accessed 15 May 2009. Available from http://www.insights.org.uk.libezproxy.bournemouth.ac.uk/articleitem.aspx?title=e-Tourism+and+Destination+Management+Organisations

Buhalis, D. and Law, R. (2008) Progress in information technology and tourism management: 20 years on and 10 years after the Internet – the state of eTourism research. *Tourism Management* 2 (9), 609–623.

Chung, J. and Buhalis, D. (2008) Information needs in online social networks. *Information Technology & Tourism* 10 (4), 267–281.

Daniele, R., Frew, J.W., Varini, K. and Magakian, A. (2009) Affiliate marketing in travel and tourism. In W. Hopken, U. Gretzel and R. Law (eds) *Information and Communication Technologies in Tourism 2009: Proceedings of the International Conference in Amsterdam*. Amsterdam: Springerlink.

Duffy, D.L. (2005) Affiliate marketing and its impact on e-commerce. *Journal of Consumer Marketing* 22 (3), 161–163.

Fesenmaier, D., Gretzel, U., Hwang, Y.H. and Wang, Y. (2003) The future of destination marketing: e-Commerce in travel and tourism. *International Journal of Tourism Science* 32, 191–200.

Fesenmaier, D.R., Wöber, K. and Werthner, H. (2006) Introduction: Recommendation systems in tourism. In D.R. Fesenmaier, K. Wöber and H. Werthner (eds) *Destination Recommendation Systems: Behavioural Foundations and Applications*. Wallingford: CABI.

Fodness, D. and Murray, B. (1997) Tourist information search. *Annals of Tourism Research* 37 (2), 108–119.

Gretzel, U., Yuan, Y.L. and Fesenmaier, D.R. (2000) Preparing for the new economy: Advertising strategies and change in destination marketing organizations. *Journal of Travel Research* 39, 146–156.

Hwang, Y-H., Gretzel, U., Xiang, Z. and Fesenmaier, D.R. (2006) Information search for travel decisions. In D.R. Fesenmaier (ed.) *Destination Recommendation Systems: Behavioural Foundations and Applications* (pp. 3–16). Wallingford: CABI.

Jeng, J. and Fesenmaier, D.R. (2002) Conceptualizing the travel decision making hierarchy: A review of recent developments. *Tourism Analysis* 7, 15–32.

King, J. (2002) Destination marketing organizations: Connecting the experience rather than promoting the place. *Journal of Vacation Marketing* 8 (2), 105–108.

Law, R. (2000) Internet in travel and tourism – part I. *Journal of Travel & Tourism Marketing* 9 (3), 65–71.

Lew, A. (2008) Long tail tourism: New geographies for marketing niche tourism products. *Journal of Travel & Tourism Marketing* 25 (3/4), 409–419.

Litvin, S.W., Goldsmith, R.E. and Pan, B. (2008) Electronic word-of-mouth in hospitality and tourism management. *Tourism Management* 2 (9), 458–468.

Murphy, L., Moscardo, G. and Benckendorff, P. (2007) Exploring word-of-mouth influences on travel decisions: Friends and relatives vs. other travellers. *International Journal of Consumer Studies* 31 (5), 517–527.

Niininen, O., Buhalis, D. and March, R. (2007) Customer empowerment in tourism through consumer centric marketing (CCM). *Qualitative Market Research: An International Journal* 10 (3), 265–281.

Pan, B. and Fesenmaier, D.R. (2006) Online information search: Vacation planning process. *Annals of Tourism Research* 33 (3), 809–832.

Poon, A. (1993) *Tourism, Technology and Competitive Strategies*. Wallingford: CABI.

Rita, P. (2000) *Web Marketing Tourism Destinations. Proceedings of the 8th European Conference on Information Systems*, Vienna, Austria.

Sheldon, P.J. (1997) *Tourism Information Technology.* Wallingford: CABI.

UNWTO (1999) *Marketing Tourism Destinations Online.* Madrid, Spain: WTO, accessed 15 May 2009. http://www.e-unwto.org.libezproxy.bournemouth.ac.uk/content/j41p11/¿p=03a3d22e8dac48ed8af034c3e65811e9&pi=4.

UNWTO (2008) *Handbook on e-Marketing for Tourism Destinations.* Madrid, Spain: WTO, accessed 15 May 2009. http://www.e-unwto.org.libezproxy.bournemouth.ac.uk/content/¿Subject=Marketing&sortorder=asc&o=10.

Wang, Y. and Fesenmaier, D.R. (2006) Identifying the success factors of web-based marketing strategy: An investigation of convention and visitors bureaus in the United States. *Journal of Travel Research* 44 (3), 239–249.

Wang, Y., Yu, Q. and Fesenmaier, D.R. (2002) Defining virtual tourist community: Implications for tourism marketing. *Tourism Management* 23 (4), 407–417.

Werthner, H. and Klein, S. (1999) *Information Technology and Tourism – A Challenging Relationship.* Vienna: Springer.

Wöber, K. (2006) Domain specific search engines. In D.R. Fesenmaier, K. Wöber and H. Werthner (eds) *Destination Recommendation Systems: Behavioral Foundations and Applications.* Wallingford: CABI.

Xiang, Z. and Fesenmaier, D.R. (2006) Assessing the initial step in the persuasion process: Meta tags on destination marketing websites. *Information Technology & Tourism* 8 (2), 91–104.

Xiang, Z., Gretzel, U. and Fesenmaier, D.R. (2009) Semantic representation of the online tourism domain. *Journal of Travel Research* 47 (4), 440–453.

Yoo, H. and Gretzel, U. (2008) What motivates consumers to write online travel reviews? *Information Technology & Tourism* 10 (4), 283–295.

Zhang, L., Pan, B., Smith, W.W. and Li, X. (2009) An exploratory study of travelers' use of online reviews and recommendations: A qualitative approach. *Journal of Information Technology and Tourism* 11 (2), 157–167.

25 Mobility, Migration and Tourism

Esmat Zaidan and Geoffrey Wall

Introduction

A new emphasis in the social sciences that focuses on mobility has far-reaching implications for tourism research. The approach recognises that, in today's world, people are more mobile than they have ever been. Of course, not all people are free to travel, and there may be differential physical, economic, political and other constraints that enable some to be more mobile than others. Furthermore, it is not only people that are on the move. There are movements of goods, money, information and ideas, and their changing distribution, both directly and indirectly, are influenced by the uneven distribution of both traditional (e.g. highways) and new (e.g. the internet) distribution channels. These movements are not discrete phenomena but are closely intertwined, movements of people, money and ideas being interconnected. Furthermore, these movements occur at a variety of overlapping and linked scales. Some observers emphasise globalisation, including the breakdown of international borders, and argue for the declining importance of the nation-state. Conversely, others point out that the world is not flat, that global trends are modified by local circumstances, and that movements occurring at one scale are not interdependent from those taking place at other scales. Thus, interest in mobilities has arisen in recognition of the need to understand and address movements of a multiplicity of phenomena that occur at a variety of spatial scales and are interconnected.

In this broad context, the present chapter examines some of the links between tourism and migration. While these two phenomena have much in common, they have seldom been addressed together and they are usually examined by different researchers, who are largely unaware of each other's research because it is published in different locations. However, this situation is beginning to change. The objective of the chapter is to argue for the utility of a 'mobilities' approach and, for example, to suggest that origins can become destinations and vice versa, and that individuals can have multiple homes with implications for their identities. If these things are true, then there may be far-reaching implications for public policy in a variety of domains including tourism, migration and citizenship, which will influence how both societies and individuals interact both at home and elsewhere. These things are likely to increase in importance if mobility, whether chosen or forced, continues to increase, and more and more people of differing cultures come into contact for varying durations.

In order to address these topics, this chapter starts with a discussion of the definitions of migration and tourism, and their relationships. The important work of Williams and Hall is reviewed, which is initiated by a consideration of consumptive-led migration, and complemented by a brief discussion of a production-led migration process. This leads to a consideration of a particular form of ethnic tourism, sometimes called ethnic reunion, as revealed in VFR travel. In doing so, the validity is questioned of many of the dualities that have underpinned much tourism research.

Definitions of Migration and Tourism

Although much migration and tourism is domestic, this chapter will adopt an international perspective. Many of the points apply to multiple scales, although the crossing of international borders has special attributes and is important for both phenomena. Globalisation entails the rapidly increasing mobility of people across national borders, and is associated with large-scale movements of all kinds – temporary and permanent. Mobility takes two forms: long-term migration and short-term tourism (Bell & Ward, 2000; Castles & Miller, 1998; Williams & Hall, 2000a). Temporary mobility is simply defined as 'the complement of permanent migration: that is, as any form of territorial movement which does not represent a permanent, or lasting, change of usual residence' (Bell & Ward, 2000: 88). Tourism is one form of temporary population movement. Temporary movements as tourism and permanent movements as migration form part of 'the same continuum of population mobility in time and space' (Bell & Ward, 2000: 88).

Definitions of migration

Migration entails the movement of people between two places for a specific period of time. However, it is difficult to determine a precise description for migration. The problem is in defining the distance a person needs to move and the time a person needs to stay away from the original destination. In terms of time: 'there will be some permanence to a move described as a migration' (Boyle et al., 1998: 35). However, according to Williams and Hall (2000b), this criterion is problematic, as no theoretically grounded definition of 'permanence' exists. Therefore, the migration literature includes such terms as temporary migrants, seasonal workers, and travellers for specific forms of non-permanent migration. Spatially, migration is defined as 'movement across the boundary of an areal unit' (Boyle *et al.*, 1998: 34). This criterion is also problematic because areas vary significantly in size. Accordingly, fairly long distance movement of people will *not* be included as a form of migration because people do not cross boundaries, whereas shorter movements *will* be considered as migration when they involve a border crossing. Furthermore, the definition of the areal unit is often crucial, as population movement and distribution between units usually have policy consequences (Boyle *et al.*, 1998). One could move on to specify different types of migration, although that will not be done here.

Definitions of tourism

The definition of tourism is no less problematic than that of migration. Generally speaking, there are two major approaches to defining tourism: technical and conceptual definitions.

A technical approach is usually used by statutory bodies such as tourist boards and national and international organisations (e.g. World Tourism Organization) that measure and record special features of tourism (tourist arrivals, departures and length of stay). The technical definitions focus on defining tourism for the purposes of measuring trips and collecting tourism data (Boyne, 2002: 244). Examples of technical definitions are provided in Table 25.1.

The distance covered in a tourism trip is seldom an issue for it has different meanings in different societies and time periods, is based on transport technology, depends on transport capacity/congestion, and reflects cultural norms in defining 'place of residence' (Boyne, 2002: 245). Scholars often define tourism conceptually to avoid the difficulties associated with the technical definitions. Conceptual definitions aim at providing a comprehensive framework that highlights differences between tourism and other similar activities. Tourism, like migration, also entails travel to surmount the friction of distance between origin and destination areas. Thus, tourism is an 'inherently spatial concept with many overlapping scales' (Wall, 2003: 6). The definitions usually emphasise the intent of returning home and not considering permanent residence or employment, in addition to stressing two main characteristics of tourism. First, tourism takes place outside the usual place of residence and, second, it is temporary. However, according to Williams and Hall (2000a: 5–6), this debate still highlights problems of 'arbitrary time limits', as well as of defining 'permanence' and they argued that it is difficult to determine the 'normal place of residence' for those who lead traveling lifestyles, such as the retired migrant who moves back and forth seasonally between homes in different regions with 'contrasting climatic regimes'.

Table 25.1 Technical definitions of tourism

	Definition
World Tourism Organization (1991)	All travel away from home that involves a stay at the destination for more than one night but less than one year.
United Nations (1994)	Temporary travelling and visiting for at least 24 hours for the purpose of leisure (recreation, holidays, health, study, religion and sport), business, family, mission and meeting.
UK	Same definitions as WTO but with no specific time on stay but with certain activities excluded, such as boarding education or semi-permanent employment (Boyne, 2002).
US Travel Data Center	Travel of at least 160 km in one direction away from home (Boyne, 2002).
Australian Bureau of Tourism Research (BTR)	Travel of at least 40 km in one direction away from home (Boyne, 2002).
Mathieson and Wall (1982: 1)	'temporary movement of people to destinations outside their normal places of work and residence, the activities undertaken during their stay in their destinations and the facilities created to cater to their needs'.

Tourism–Migration Relationships

Migration and tourism are processes that greatly influence each other. For example, the two concepts converge in multi-purpose trips where individuals undertake holiday travel for the purpose of learning about the prospect for migration in the future. Likewise, migration can be a lifestyle choice and be used to expand leisure opportunities. Williams and Hall (2000a, 2000b) further argued that changes in production and consumption in recent decades have resulted in changes in tourism and migration, and in the relationships between these activities. They highlighted the manner in which linkages between migration and tourism systems need to be set within the context of both shifts in capital accumulation and the cultural construction of leisure time and spaces. They identified that the rapid expansion of tourism has two significant implications for immigration. First, the high and rapid growth in destination areas has implications for the requirement for labour migration. Secondly, it has expanded the search spaces of mass tourists of different generations as they go through several phases of their lives.

Furthermore, tourism may generate migration flows. Williams and Hall (2002) developed an idealised four-phase model for conceptualising how tourism and migration are related through a series of economic and cultural mechanisms, which impact search spaces, demand and investment. These four phases are summarised from Williams and Hall (2002) as follows:

Phase 1. Tourists flowing into an area which creates a tourism industry that initially recruits local labour. Areas with limited tourism attractions may not develop and, thus, do not go beyond this stage while areas with substantial tourism attractions develop and move to *Phase 2*.

Phase 2. This stage applies particularly to destinations that attract mass tourism. The growth of tourism increases the demand for labour, especially skilled labourers to provide the services required by tourists. This labour demand cannot be met locally and, therefore, stimulates labour migration from national and international sources, which may be differentiated by nationality, gender, ethnicity and skills. At this stage, the labour migration is most likely to be seasonal. Additionally, immigrants are uncertain about the possibility of permanent migration in a destination that is, to this point, not familiar.

Phase 3. At this phase, the interplay between tourism and migration becomes more complicated. The earlier tourists have generated migration flows from the places of origin which take two main forms. First, consumption-led migration, including retirement migration, takes place mainly because the tourism experience has expanded the search for places in which to retire. These migrants may be permanent or seasonal (temporary mobility). Second, labour migration from tourism origins to tourism destinations may also take place (production-led migration) and seasonal labour migration will be complemented with permanent labour migration. As a consequence, this growth in permanent migrant communities will generate VFR tourism as will the consumption-led migrants from the tourists' origins or from other places. Migrants may return to visit their relatives and friends in the places of origin or they may also invite friends and relatives to visit them. Thus, migration generates flows of tourists in two directions. But it is expected that in the case of consumption-led migrants, the visits will be more frequent because they have more free time and higher incomes.

Phase 4. The main characteristic of the fourth phase is two additional forms of mobility. The first is the permanent migrants (consumption or production led) who may decide to return to their countries of origin or immigrate to other places. Also, the labour migrants who are motivated by failure, homesickness or even by meeting their economic goals may return to retire among their relatives and friends in their places of origin. The second type of flow is where the earlier VFR tourists who visited the immigrants in tourism destinations decide to become migrants. These new migrants have expanded their search spaces by visiting early immigrants and also they are attracted to move to an area where they already have ready-made social networks who may replace those left behind.

Thus not only does tourism lead to migration, but migration also generates tourism flows, particularly by the geographic extension of kinship, ethnic and friendship networks. Immigrants themselves can become poles of attraction for VFR tourist flows, while they become tourists sometimes when they return to visit their friends and relatives in the country of origin.

The sequence of events that has been described is initiated by consumption-led movements to attractive locations. Thus, Williams *et al.* (2000) studied retirement migrants as a focus of VFR tourism and their outcomes, such as property ownership, second-homes, seasonal migration, lifestyle migration and the development of retirement settlements. Their study highlights the significance of such tourism even to mass tourist resorts. For example, they estimated that British migrants to Costa del Sol receive in excess of 300,000 VFR tourist visits each year. These tourists may also become future migrants to this area.

While undoubtedly applicable to many locations, the model may also be regarded as a special case that is applicable to situations that initially experience consumptive-led movements. However, much international migration is production led as people leave peripheral areas to seek their fortunes in the big cities. The removal of the Berlin Wall and its political repercussions, leading to the creation of the EU, have facilitated movements of many kinds, including labour migration. Many migrants, lacking social capital in their new place of residence, end up taking jobs in the tourism industry.

Within the context of tourism–migration relationships, many researchers have examined the significance of different ethnic groups in generating tourism markets to and from their countries of origin (for example, King & Gamage, 1994; Ostrowski, 1991; Rossiter & Chan, 1998). It is important to consider the motivations for travelling as well as the travel experiences of specific minority ethnic groups because the Western (tourist-generating) societies are becoming more cosmopolitan. Although the term 'ethnic tourism' has a variety of meanings (Stephenson, 2002), ethnic reunion involves visiting friends and relatives (VFR travel) (King, 1994) and is often a frequent activity for many ethnic communities living in Western societies (Stephenson, 2002).

Accordingly, ethnic ties are being recognised increasingly as an influential reason for back-and forth visits to family, relatives and friends in the country of origin. Earlier studies have investigated VFR travel as one form of ethnic tourism. Examples of these studies are: Khan (1977) who investigated the Pakistani community in Britain; Western (1992) who investigated Barbadians; Thanopoulos and Walle (1988) who investigated the Greek community; Liu *et al.* (1984) who investigated the Turkish community; Stephenson (2002) who examined the UK Caribbean community; and Hughes and Allen (2010) who examined the Irish diaspora in Manchester. Some of these studies focused on the economic impact of the VFR market on the destination. For example, Liu *et al.* (1984) concluded that ethnic reunion travellers do benefit the destination even if they are not utilising commercial accommodation. Thanopoulos and Walle (1988) concluded that incomes are important in determining the frequency of visits to the country of origin. Jackson (1990) suggested that VFR visits are often underestimated by many National Tourism Organisations (NTOs) because such travellers do not use official tourist facilities. Such studies have undermined the commonly held view that VFR travellers are not a valuable market.

Conclusions

Globalisation is creating new forms of mobility. Researchers in migration, tourism and transport studies are increasingly engaged in thinking about mobility, and its opposite, immobility, at a variety of scales, and incorporating this perspective into their research. Human mobility in terms of people crossing national borders has increased in association with globalisation, which leads to large-scale movements of all kinds: temporary and permanent movement of labour; refugees; individuals and families; highly skilled specialists; and manual workers, and so on. However, attempts to generate definitions of temporary, as well as permanent human mobility based on motivation are no longer successful. Both forms of mobility, short and the long-term, are characterised by mixed motivations: mobility can be undertaken for consumption or production purposes, or for a combination of both.

Neither tourism nor migration studies have adequately explored how migration and tourism interrelate, particularly among ethnic groups with new overseas travel patterns. A survey conducted by Kang and Page (2000: 61) signified that the links between immigration and ethnic reunion have been subject to time–space convergence in immigrants' travel patterns. That is, low levels of ethnic reunion characterised the post-war patterns of immigration due to the relatively higher costs of international travel. Nevertheless, with cheaper and faster travel in the post-1990s, time–space convergence in tourist travel is occurring and new migration–tourism relationships are evolving. This fact highlights that establishing the new overseas travel patterns of immigrants is certainly an area that deserves more academic attention. Notably, modern technological advances in transport and communication have provided more opportunities for ethnic groups in cosmopolitan societies to travel to their places of ethnic importance, thus enabling diasporic minority groups to reinforce their ties with their countries of origin (Stephenson, 2002).

The complex relationships between tourism and migration are likely to become even more obscure in the future as new and modern forms of dwelling, leisure, work and extended social networks emerge Such trends are undermining the utility, if they were ever fully satisfactory, of dichotomies such as tourist and migrant, permanent and temporary, origin and destination, first home and second home, home and away. Along with the growing interest in mobility of all types is an emerging interest in such topics as identity and transnationalism (understood simply as the ability to function across international borders) and their implications for such issues as citizenship and even human rights. Of course, these are not solely the remit of tourism scholars, but tourism can provide an appropriate point of entry for their exploration.

References

Bell, G. and Ward, M. (2000) Comparing temporary mobility with permanent migration. *Tourism Geographies* 2 (1), 87–107.

Boyne, S., Carswell, F. and Hall, D. (2002) Reconceptualising VFR tourism: Friends, relatives and migration in a domestic context. In C.M. Hall and A.M. Williams (eds) *Tourism and Migration: New Relationships between Production and Consumption* (pp. 1–52). Dordrecht: Kluwer Academic Publishers.

Boyle, P.J., Halfacree, K.H. and Robinson, V. (1998) *Exploring Contemporary Migration*. Harlow: Addison Wesley Longman.

Castles, S. and Miller, D. (1998) *The Age of Migration: International Population Movements in the Modern World*. New York and London: Guildford Press.

Hughes, H. and Allen, D (2010) Holidays of the Irish diaspora: The pull of the 'homeland'? *Current Issues in Tourism* 13 (1), 1–19.

Jackson, R. (1990) VFR tourism: Is it underestimated? *Journal of Tourism Studies* 1 (2), 10–18.

Kang, S. and Page, S.J. (2000) Tourism, migration and emigration: Travel patterns of Korean-New Zealanders in the 1990s. *Tourism Geographies* 2 (1), 50–65.

Khan, V.S. (1977) The Pakistanis: Mirpuri villagers at home and in Bradford. In J.L. Watson (ed.) *Between Two Cultures: Migrants and Minorities in Britain* (pp. 57–89). Oxford: Blackwell.

King, B. (1994) What is ethnic tourism? An Australian perspective. *Tourism Management* 15 (3), 173–176.

King, B. and Gamage, M.A. (1994) Measuring the value of the ethnic connection: Expatriate travellers from Australia to Sri Lanka. *Journal of Travel Research* 33 (2), 46–50.

Liu, J., Var, T. and Timur, A. (1984) Tourism income multipliers for Turkey. *Tourism Management* 5 (4), 280–287.

Mathieson, A. and Wall, G. (1982) *Tourism: Economic, Physical and Social Impacts*. New York: Longman.

Ostrowski, S. (1991) Ethnic tourism: Focus on Poland. *Tourism Management* 12 (2), 125–131.

Rossiter, J. and Chan, A. (1998) Ethnicity in business and consumer behaviour. *Journal of Business Research* 42 (2), 127–134.

Stephenson, M. (2002) Travelling to the ancestral homelands: The aspirations and experiences of a UK Caribbean community. *Current Issues in Tourism* 5 (5), 378–425.

Thanopoulos, J. and Walle, A. (1988) Ethnicity and its reference to marketing: The case of tourism. *Journal of Travel Research* 26 (3), 11–14.

UN (1994) *Recommendations on Tourism Statistics*. New York: United Nations Publications.

Wall, G. (2003) The nature of tourism. In G. Wall (ed.) *Tourism: People, Places and Products* (pp. 1–8). Occasional Paper No. 19. Department of Geography, University of Waterloo.

Western, J. (1992) *A Passage to England: Barbadian Londoners Speak of Home*. Minneapolis, MN: University of Minnesota Press.

Williams, A.M. and Hall, C.M. (2000a) Guest editorial: Tourism and migration. *Tourism Geographies: International Journal of Place, Space and the Environment* 2 (1), 2–4.

Williams, A.M. and Hall, C.M. (2000b) Tourism and migration: New relationships between production and consumption. *Tourism Geographies: International Journal of Place, Space and the Environment* 2 (1), 5–27.

Williams, A.M. and Hall, C.M. (2002) Tourism, migration, circulation and mobility: The contingencies of time and place. In C.M. Hall and A.M. Williams (eds) *Tourism and Migration: New Relationships Between Production and Consumption* (pp. 1–52). Dordrecht: Kluwer Academic Publishers.

Williams, A.M., King, R., Warnes, A.M. and Patterson, G. (2000) Tourism and retirement migration: New forms of an old relationship in Southern Europe. *Tourism Geographies: International Journal of Place, Space and the Environment* 2 (1), 28–49.

WTO (1991) *Resolutions of International Conference on Travel and Tourism, Ottawa, Canada.* Madrid: World Tourism Organization.

26 Towards a New Vision for European Tourism Policy: Conclusions

Carlos Costa, Emese Panyik and Dimitrios Buhalis

In this book we aimed to identify the key emerging trends of European tourism planning and organisation by presenting how globalisation has progressively permeated tourism planning in the overture of the new millennium. One of the central arguments offered by the book is that planning and organisation systems form through links between territory and actors on the interface of the physical and the social dimensions of the global world economy (Figure 1.2). Thus, they are constantly exposed to, and shaped by, competing trends of globalisation.

As the world is moving ever further into the 21st century, it has become evident that the greatest challenge faced by the tourism industry in this dynamic environment is to achieve sustainable competitiveness. Worldwide, tourism has proven to be a resilient sector that is able to reinvigorate under the most challenging conditions. However, the reconciliation of the notions of sustainability and competitiveness rests in the ability of tourism planning systems to synchronise their procedural and structural components, notably, the development base and the governance base of planning (Figure 1.1).

On the crossroads of these principal lines of thought, a systematic analysis of tourism planning and organisation systems has been designed and applied in the European context. It is demonstrated that globalisation has impacted on all components and compelled structural and procedural adaptation on the supply side of tourism. The book guides the readers through this spatial and social transformation and presents the way in which the key elements of planning have confronted change. The distinctive context allows for an explicit focus on the practices and strategies used by the European tourism industry to meet the challenges and opportunities emanating from this process. The collection of analyses offered by the book introduces tourism students, academics and practitioners to current issues and trends of

European tourism planning and policy and helps tourism planners formulate strategic agendas guided by the notion of sustainable competitiveness.

The factors of change have been identified at the most fundamental level of the physical and social dimensions. Taking the spatial transformations induced by leisure, recreation and tourism in European urban and cultural landscapes, it is shown in Chapter 2 that industrialisation and urbanisation have been the first agents of global landscape mutation from the late 19th century onwards. These were then followed by increasing population growth, density and mobilisation, particularly after World War II. By now, the quest for attractive leisure environments and the striving to furnish personalised leisure experiences have shortened the life cycle of European leisure and tourism maps, which in turn became ever more dynamic and fragmented.

In the competitive tourist spaces, new values are constantly explored and discovered. Accordingly, destinations are being revalorised and redesigned in order to gain comparative advantages. This, as is argued in Chapter 3, represents a new paradigm of production, where resources are no longer factors to be exploited but rather to be valorised. The 'terroir factor' provides a holistic perspective of locality, which incorporates the distinctive features of the local community, its culture and traditions, as well as the local landscape, its endowments and natural resources. It is increasingly considered a market value and as such it has implications for different tourist spaces across Europe.

On this basis, integrated conservation strategies can be formulated for the development of protected and cultural landscapes. While these landscapes share common grounds, they have been generally approached differently by public authorities. The European centralised landscape policy created a standardised system for quality protection and protected areas and national parks have become the most clearly defined landscape categories. The assertion put forward in Chapter 2 that the comparative advantages of a tourism landscape are directly linked with the presence of cultural resources envisages the convergence of policies regarding different types of landscapes in the near future.

In rural territories, the *terroir* factor represents a vital link between agriculture and tourism. In Chapter 3, it is discussed how the *terroir* contributes to the enhancement of authentic experience and the diversification of the destination product by incorporating wine and food tourism segments. The rural habitat in this interpretation becomes multifunctional which, in addition to its formerly dominant role as a place of production, becomes a place of consumption of new embedded goods and services and an area of protection of endogenous values.

In mature coastal destinations, which also represent a distinct European landscape, the development of Special Interest Products (SIP) may offer a viable solution for the chronic problem of overreliance on the sun-and-sea product and seasonality. As is explained in Chapter 4, the primary driver of these products is the activity offered, whereas the time and the place take a secondary role. By selecting the right product mix that reflects the uniqueness of the destination and matching it with the proper market, SIP can be a crucial factor for stimulating the sustainability and competitiveness of the European tourism sector.

The amalgamation of natural and cultural resources is particularly important in the case of a great number of European destinations that transcend political borders. In this regard, the EU's potential as a supranational entity is perhaps indisputable. In Chapter 5, European cross-border areas are classified according to the scales of trans-boundary networks and exemplified by European initiatives. This analysis highlights that all territorial scales have remarkable implications for tourism. However, endeavours are often hindered by the lack of harmonisation of regulatory frameworks between member states despite standard funding mechanisms. The absence of an integrated European policy framework is also identified in the context of the accommodation sector (Chapter 13), revealing that inadequate policy coordination is a recurrent issue across a range of tourism-related policies.

Conflicting decisions arise from the isolated action of different Commission divisions regarding the same objective, due to the diversity of areas related to tourism. Yet the Directorate-Generals have a significant impact on the future of tourism in the EU. As is seen in Chapter 17, the Directorate-General for Energy and Transport determines the price and capacity of transport systems, which in turn influences the size of the tourism market and patterns of tourism demand. In order to create synergies between transport and tourism sectors, the *Concertour* project is one notable EU-sponsored initiative aiming at fostering competitiveness through closer cooperation between sectors.

In Chapter 15, it is shown how the problem of inconsistent action in tourism-related issues at the EU level is reflected in the context of destination governance. In retrospect, the EU has generally assumed a coordinative role in synchronising actions, resources and stakeholders between different levels of intervention. Recent initiatives such as EDEN or Calypso reinforce the EU's intention to remain in this position. This chapter, however, goes further and stresses the role of the EU and regional decision makers in clearly determining the competences and responsibilities among different stakeholders.

Concerning local service providers, the EU assumes the enabler's role in its approach towards small and medium-sized enterprises (SMEs). Rather than seeking to disseminate funds for small business growth, the Small Business Act adopted in 2008 promotes best practice-led development. It takes measures towards facilitating the operation of SMEs by the establishment of prosperous business conditions and the improvement of the operational environment. In Chapter 7, it is shown that despite the EU's aim to target small business gaps, these principles have scarcely been translated into concrete funding programmes on the national level, again highlighting the policy gap between the European and the national level.

Nevertheless, the complexity of the tourism development process requires regular consultation between various levels, which may lead to better co-ordination in the long term. Considering the principal role played by main-stream funds in the development of European tourism, Chapter 10 argues that tourism will be likely to gain more importance in the EU by making further adjustments to the development priorities of the Structural and the Cohesion Funds and the Central Agricultural Policy.

In response to the dearth of harmonisation of policies and respective national laws in the physical dimension of tourism planning systems, the connectedness perspective prevails in the social dimension of actors and structures in relation to all key stages of planning. It is discussed in Chapter 14 that stakeholder participation has been one of the main themes in European tourism policy during the past decade. In Chapter 8 attention is drawn to the fact that the strengthening of partnerships at all levels of policy making is a central component of the renewed EU tourism policy issued in 2006. Due to the fragmented nature of the European tourism industry and the complexity of tourism offer in tourist destinations, partnerships allow for capacity building by bringing together a diversity of stakeholders. For this reason, a number of key features of sustainable tourism partnerships are identified in Chapter 8. These include: a comprehensive mission statement, which represents the destination rather than any single set of identifiable interests of a sector or a stakeholder group; trust relationships; a powerful representative of the group; and achievements based on a timely and action-able programme.

Undoubtedly, this may convey a strong leverage for destination manage-ment organisations (DMOs) which form the kernel of tourism development. DMOs are responsible for destination strategy implementation by assuming the leadership and coordination of all the stakeholders involved in shaping the destination's future. But beyond that, today's compelling competitive environment demands their effective performance in multiple tactical roles. Considering the existing variances in the organisational structure and func-tions of DMOs, Chapter 6 stresses the importance of extending the DMOs' responsibilities from conventional marketing functions to strategic manage-ment roles. What emerges from this argument is that organisational diversity is a premise of structural flexibility and functional versatility both in terms of composition and functions, which are the key features of sustainable operation.

Considering stakeholder diversity in particular, Chapter 11 delineates a new conceptualisation of public–private partnerships in tourism. Drawing on the economic theory of clubs, the partnerships envisaged here reckon with the strong dependence of the tourism industry on externalities such as natural endowments or historic heritage. Based on the common use of assets which have strong externality effects, these partnerships transform the public goods into club goods. This would entail that public assets and services related to tourism are financed and maintained collectively, and the share of costs is inflicted through negotiations and competition among players. This conceptualisation offers an alternative solution for the state versus market dichotomy in dealing with externalities.

The implications of the network approach are examined in the industry context (Chapter 12) and in the destination context (Chapter 20). As can be seen, formal and informal networking is a principal method for market penetration used by companies to expand their distribution systems. In fact, Chapter 13 shows that the prevalent trend in the EU accommodation sector is concentration, through the outsourcing and franchising of large hotel chains on the one hand and the clustering and networking of SMEs on the other. The market structure is dispersed in the summer holiday tourist destinations but larger units tend to be concentrated in large urban centres. Particularly in the case of start-up ventures or small, resource-constrained businesses, networking offers a way to overcome contingencies in the external and internal organisational environment. Furthermore, since the network perspective provides information on the characteristics of the relational structure of destinations, it helps to locate where the information flow has the most impact on business activity.

A key to tourism development is to acquire a comprehensive understanding of the destination. In order to be able to formulate a strategic vision in an era of increasing competition, a range of tools and techniques has been put forward and explored throughout the book. For more than two decades, tourism satellite accounts (TSAs) have been the focus of tourism statistics. In Chapter 19, the evolution, definition and structure of TSAs are discussed, alongside a critical evaluation of their benefits, limitations and future development. It was argued that TSAs are dynamic, constantly evolving structures that are capable of revolutionising the perception not only of the magnitude but also of the very nature of tourism. Current trends of development suggest that the future generations of TSAs will be capable of extending their territorial focus from the national to subnational levels and expanding their basic coverage to other related policy domains. As such, it is forecast that they will provide a basis for the development of a TSA-related system of indicators.

The analysis of supply and market trends of destination positioning in Chapter 18 reveals that destinations promote their distinctive features by emphasising their emotional appeal, the diversity of offer, accessibility, environmental protection, and cooperative marketing and branding activity. However, as mentioned earlier, the uniqueness of any given destination must be matched with the proper market segments. In the context of forecasting tourism demand, Chapter 21 compares the forecasting performance of economic models using quarterly data on tourist expenditure by inbound international visitors in various destinations. The empirical results provide new evidence of the time-varying parameter model's superior performance in short-term seasonal tourism demand forecasting.

Increasingly, destination planners consider not only the motivational factors of tourists' decision making, but also the influence of a combination of social, economic and political relationships that shape a destination's demand and supply structure. Recent trends in tourism network research identified in Chapter 20 highlight the significant benefits of analysing and modelling the network system of destinations. One far-reaching implication is that network simulation and scenario planning allow for predictions on the impacts of different network configurations on the behaviour of the overall destination system. The formulation of scenarios offers insights into possible future developments and events before they occur. Futurecast, as can be seen in Chapter 22, allows not only the anticipation of such occurrences but also influencing them.

Hence the vision on the future of tourism is constructed, through a synthesis of all the components of planning and organisation systems, yet mindful of possible alternative scenarios. How the new, emerging tourism would look may be extrapolated from the current megatrends in the tourism arena. As demonstrated in Chapter 22, the dramatic changes in consumer behaviour are increasingly giving impetus to the rise of a 'new tourist', shaped by distinct demographic, social, cultural and technological trends. These tourists are characterised by cosmopolitan attitudes and personalised demands in pursuit of experiential, adventurous and self-improving travels. Often developing multiple identities, they exhibit travel patterns that generate new migration flows, transforming origins to destinations and destinations to origins. This new 'mobilities' approach is the focus of analysis in Chapter 25.

Certainly, information and communication technologies (ICT) are the main triggering factors of recent shifts not only in consumer behaviour but also in destination marketing. Increasingly, people in the world are struck by the overwhelming power of the internet, through which global movements, protests and even revolutions are organised, politically separated countries are connected and a sweeping moral force of public opinion is represented which politicians can no longer afford to neglect. Evidently, the internet has not only penetrated virtually all aspects of our everyday life but smoothly changed many of our habits. While the virtual social landscape has become ever more diversified and thematised, social networks such as Facebook, Twitter or Pinterest exert now as much influence on our travel decisions as the travel-specific portals TripAdvisor or Couchsurfing.

Understanding the critical stage of online searching for travel information in the customers' travel planning process is therefore crucial for designing successful online marketing strategies. To this end, a range of online marketing solutions available for destinations is presented and discussed in Chapter 24. Eventually, all these solutions boil down to the superior value of customisation strategies and the authentic, real-life experience of flesh and blood travellers conveyed by user-generated contents across the social media.

The rapid development of ICT raises the standards of human resource skill requirements in the tourism sector, which has already been known for mostly employing a low-skilled workforce. This is one of the main contemporary issues of European tourism human resources (HR) identified in Chapter 9 and an acute problem of SMEs in particular. The shift from the information society towards a knowledge society associated with the pervasiveness of the internet implies that knowledge, rather than merely information, has become a predominant factor of economic growth and that it is more readily applicable to economic activity through ICT.

The need to expand the knowledge base of tourism through education and training is emphasised across the chapters, not only in the context of business environment and accommodation policies, but also in destination management. However, it is argued both in Chapters 16 and 23 that tourism lags behind other economic sectors in embracing knowledge management (KM) and innovation. On this fairly new path of research, Chapter 16 proposes a conceptual framework for the analysis of knowledge processes in public policy. In order to analyse innovative activity, three key aspects have been systematically applied and compared in five European destinations: the strategic change sought by public policy, the instruments used, and the knowledge implications of public intervention. The results confirm the assumption that current European tourism policies are knowledge intensive and largely reliant on qualified knowledge input.

Indeed, it is pointed in Chapter 23 that knowledge creation and transfer, coupled with human qualification, lie at the heart of successful innovation strategies. In this chapter a KM framework for European tourism is introduced. This framework highlights that ICT serves as a tool for knowledge management whereby a learning area for tourism transfer is created. Through this platform of information exchange and partnership building, the social and technological dimensions of KM are linked in the process of knowledge creation.

One of the major conclusions offered by this book is that the absence of policy coordination and a coherent framework affect strategic areas of European tourism, notably conservation and accommodation policies, cross-border cooperation and knowledge management. Ample evidence has shown that mitigating the fragmentation of tourism and non-tourism policies, harmonising the policy frameworks and developing small business act measures in the member states serve as prior conditions towards the formulation of a sustainable and competitive vision of development in European tourism planning and organisation systems.

The book adopts a supply-side focus on planning and organisation in the EU. However, the significance of distribution channels and particularly main tour operators that play an important role primarily in the Mediterranean countries requires extensive and specific research which will be addressed in the near future. Tour operating based on back-to-back charter flights, dominated by vertically integrated organisations such as TUI and Thomas Cook, have a major influence on Mediterranean destinations as they control airlift particularly for insular and peripheral regions. Central and northern European countries are influenced mostly by aviation and transportation routes as well as distribution channels in terms of reservations and representation to markets. This area requires further attention in academic research, where the influence of these organisations on planning and development needs to be examined in detail. The impact of ICT and the interactivity the social media introduce are also areas for further investigation as they will affect the competitiveness of regions and their ability to achieve their strategic objectives.